Coursebook to accompany

ECONOMICS
PRIVATE AND PUBLIC CHOICE

FOURTH EDITION

Coursebook to accompany
ECONOMICS
PRIVATE AND PUBLIC CHOICE

FOURTH EDITION

A. H. Studenmund
Occidental College

Richard L. Stroup
Montana State University

James D. Gwartney
Florida State University

Harcourt Brace Jovanovich, Publishers
and its subsidiary, Academic Press

San Diego   New York   Chicago   Austin   Washington, D.C.

London   Sydney   Tokyo   Toronto

ISBN: 0-15-518883-6

Library of Congress Catalog Card Number: 86-70601

Printed in the United States of America

Preface

In writing this *Coursebook,* we have attempted to strike a balance between economic reasoning and mechanics. Often, a supplementary workbook is little more than a set of mechanical exercises. Such exercises lack substance and meaning for the student who has not yet acquired a firm foundation in the economic way of thinking. Our teaching experience has shown that stressing real-world situations, presenting actual data, providing selected short readings, and explaining why particular answers are correct—as we have done in the *Coursebook*—illuminate the power and utility of economic reasoning.

The *Coursebook* has been structured to maximize the student's comprehension of the concepts presented in each chapter of *Economics: Private and Public Choice,* Fourth Edition. Like the main text, the *Coursebook* contains 33 chapters; each chapter is divided into several sections that combine the instruction of economic principles, as covered in the text, with mechanical exercises.

The first section of each chapter is composed of approximately 13 true–false questions. Although this section has a realistic flavor, mechanics are emphasized. "Problems and Projects," the second section, stresses both mechanics and economic reasoning. This section contains some case-study-type problems as well as some questions that ask students to prepare reports or assemble economic data as meaningful tests of an economic hypothesis. The third section, "Learning the Mechanics—Multiple Choice," contains multiple-choice questions of the type familiar to most students. Many questions are sufficiently difficult to challenge even knowledgeable students. Questions posed in the fourth section, "The Economic Way of Thinking—Multiple Choice," often utilize actual data to emphasize economic reasoning. Some items test the student's ability to distinguish between sound logic and economic nonsense; others ask the student to devise the proper policy for reaching a given set of economic goals. To answer these "complex application"-type questions, the student must be able to apply principles to realistic situations. For students unaccustomed to critical thinking, these questions will be difficult; yet they present a challenge far more stimulating than exercises that test rote learning. One thing is certain: after giving an exam that requires students to apply economic reasoning in this fashion, instructors will hear few complaints of the irrelevance of economics. Finally, each chapter contains discussion questions that are intended to provoke further speculation on economic issues.

More than merely a workbook, the *Coursebook* serves as a reader, presenting a "Perspectives in Economics" in almost every chapter. These selected articles, which we find readable and engaging, will reinforce the classroom presentation of economic lessons and expand upon an important concept discussed in the text. Some articles offer an historical perspective, clearly elucidating the views of renowned economists such as Frédéric Bastiat and Joseph Schumpeter. Others give students the opportunity to read first-hand the ideas of such current economic leaders as Paul Samuelson and Herb Stein. Following each selection are questions asking the student to evaluate the position of the author. Is the reasoning sound? Is it opinionated? Does empirical evidence support the author's contention? This feature of the *Coursebook* again highlights the saliency of economics in our everyday lives.

Answers to virtually every question are provided in the "Answer Key" at the back of the *Coursebook*. The "Answer Key" also contains two new features that will make the questions significantly more useful for student learning. First, all the multiple-choice answers are followed by an explanation of why that particular answer is correct. In addition, we refer the student to the page(s) where the subject of the question is discussed in *Economics: Private and Public Choice*. In this way, a student who does not get the correct answer the first time can get an explanation of that answer. If that explanation is not sufficient, then the student is referred to the corresponding page in the textbook. Students who take the time to master these questions—and who understand the rationale behind each answer—should do very well in introductory economics.

The Fourth Edition of the *Coursebook* has been blessed to an unusual degree with contributions from individuals who were not previously involved with the project. In particular we want to thank Professor Jim Halstead (Occidental College) and Cynthia Schroeder and Gordon Hanson (former Occidental students who will be entering graduate programs in economics at the University of California at San Diego and Massachusetts Institute of Technology). Without the dedicated help of these good friends, most of the innovations of this edition would not have been finished until the *fifth* edition went to press! We also appreciate the assistance of Marguerite L. Egan and Parma Yarkin at Harcourt Brace Jovanovich, and the folks at Jim's and Rax.

A. H. Studenmund
Richard L. Stroup
James D. Gwartney

Contents

I

The Economic Approach

TRUE OR FALSE

T F

☐ ☐   1. Economics postulates that when there is an increase in the benefit derived from an activity, individuals are more likely to choose it.

☐ ☐   2. Leisure is not an economic good.

☐ ☐   3. If human action were not influenced by changes in cost and benefits, economics would not have any predictive value.

☐ ☐   4. Only the actions of selfish men are influenced by economic incentives.

☐ ☐   5. Economic activity often has secondary effects that are not initially observable.

☐ ☐   6. Economic theory cannot be tested because it involves human decision-makers.

☐ ☐   7. One's use of time involves economic choice.

☐ ☐   8. Economists utilize empirical evidence from the real world in order to test the validity of economic theory.

☐ ☐   9. Positive economic statements involve value judgments about how the world ''should be.''

☐ ☐ 10. Scientific methodology can be used to test normative economic statements.

☐ ☐ 11. The following is a positive economic statement: ''An increase in the price of butter will lead to a reduction in the quantity of butter purchased by consumers.''

☐ ☐ 12. If public education is freely provided to the consumer, it will not qualify as a scarce or economic good.

☐ ☐ 13. Economics is based on the principle that changes in economic incentives cause human decision-makers to alter their courses of action.

☐ ☐ 14. Economic analysis applies only to those choices that relate to the production or consumption of physical goods.

☐ ☐ 15. Man's happiness is dependent only on his consumption of material goods.

PROBLEMS AND PROJECTS

1. List eight guidelines that are important to the economic way of thinking. Explain in your own words the meaning of each guideline, giving examples when they are appropriate.

2. Exhibit 1 shows the relationship between gas consumption of a new Chevrolet and the number of miles traveled.

Exhibit I

Total distance traveled (miles)	Amount of gasoline consumed (gallons)
0	0
75	5
150	10
225	15
300	20
375	25
450	30

a. Graph the relationship between miles traveled and gas consumption in the space provided. Measure miles traveled on the horizontal axis (x axis) and gasoline consumption on the vertical axis (y axis). Label the graph clearly.
b. Is gasoline consumption related positively or negatively to distance traveled?
c. How many miles can be traveled on a gallon of gas? What is the slope of the distance traveled–gasoline consumption line ("curve")?

3. Height and weight are usually related. Exhibit 2 presents data for a sample of persons. The average weight for persons of different heights is shown.

Exhibit 2

Number of persons in class	Height of individual (inches)	Mean weight (pounds)
20	70	160
23	71	168
17	72	176
18	73	182
14	74	186

a. Graph the height–weight relationship, plotting height on the horizontal axis and weight on the vertical axis.
b. What is the slope of the line ("curve") between 70 and 71 inches? Between 73 and 74 inches?

(graph for question 2)

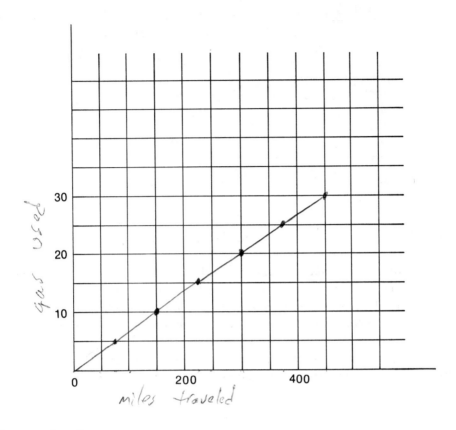

(graph for question 3)

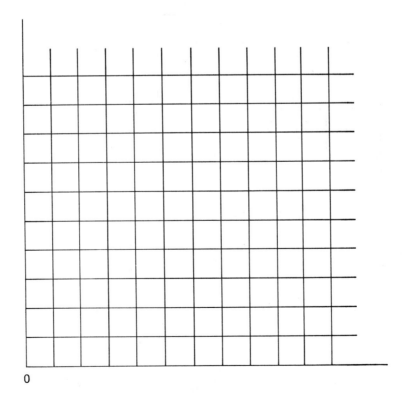

4. Exhibit 3 presents data on national income and consumer spending for the period 1975 to 1981.

Exhibit 3

Year	National income (in billions)	Personal consumption spending (in billions)
1975	$1239	$ 976
1976	1379	1084
1977	1547	1208
1978	1745	1349
1979	1963	1511
1980	2121	1673
1981	2344	1858

Source: *Economic Report of the President 1982,* pp. 233 and 255.

a. Graph the relationship in the space provided. Plot national income on the horizontal axis and personal consumption on the vertical axis.
b. Is the relationship between national income and consumption positive or negative?
c. In 1976–1977, national income increased from $1379 billion to $1547 billion—a gain of $168 billion. How large was the increase in consumption associated with this $168 billion change in income? What is the slope of the consumption–income relationship over this range?
d. Calculate the slope of the consumption–income relationship between 1980 and 1981. Is the slope of the consumption–income relationship constant for each year?

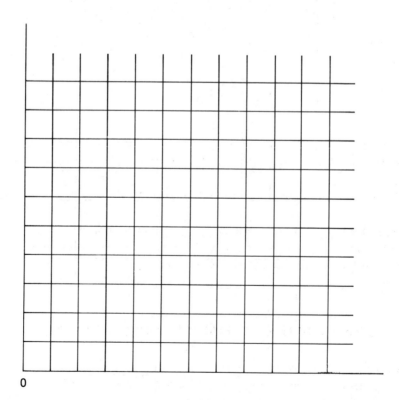

0

5. Each of the following statements ignores or violates one of the eight guideposts to economic thinking discussed in the text. In each case, identify the guidepost and explain how it has been violated.

 a. Before voting in an important election, each voter should learn as much as possible about the issues involved.

 b. Reducing the prices of necessities would clearly benefit the poor. Therefore, government should pass laws (price controls) requiring producers of necessities to sell at low prices.

 c. One way to lower the costs associated with the armed services would be to have a military draft with low pay for those who are required to serve.

 d. Since I get the same satisfaction from reading a book, seeing a movie, or hearing a concert, it makes no difference to me which one I do.

 e. Since criminal activity is associated more with the poor than with the rich, the poor must have lower moral standards than the rich.

 g. I recently heard that some people are hiring others to do their shopping for them. It sure is silly to hire someone to do something you can clearly do for yourself.

 h. If hamburgers and pizza-by-the-slice cost the same and you like pizza more than you like hamburgers, you would always rather have another slice of pizza than another hamburger.

6. Exhibit 4 shows how the quantity of watermelons bought by consumers depends on the price of watermelons and on average consumer income.

Exhibit 4

Price (cents per pound)	Quantity bought (thousands of tons per year) for average income of	
	$10,000/year	$15,000/year
1.5	1500	1690
1.6	1420	1600
1.7	1350	1510
1.8	1280	1430
1.9	1210	1370
2.0	1170	1310

 a. On a piece of graph paper (if you do not have a piece of graph paper, draw your own) graph the relationship between price and quantity bought if income is $10,000. Label this curve D_1.

 b. Graph the relationship between price and quantity bought if income is $15,000. Label this curve D_2.

 c. Are price and quantity bought positively or negatively related?

 d. If price is fixed at 1.7 cents per pound and consumer income rises from $10,000 to $15,000 per year, how much will quantity bought change?

LEARNING THE MECHANICS—MULTIPLE CHOICE

1. Which of the following is a normative economic statement?

 a. An increase in taxes will take some purchasing power away from the consumers.

 b. Unemployment will decline if taxes are reduced.

 c. Higher butter prices will cause consumers to purchase more butter.

 d. Taxes should be raised because the federal budget needs to be balanced.

2. "A nation as wealthy as the United States need not concern itself with further increases in wealth. Government policy must concentrate now on a more equitable distribution of income." This statement is
   a. definitely true.
   b. an objective statement about economic policy.
   c. a normative statement about economic policy.
   d. a testable hypothesis.

3. When an economist states that a good is scarce, she means that
   a. production cannot expand the availability of the good.
   b. there is a shortage or insufficient amount of the good at the existing price.
   c. desire for the good exceeds the amount that is freely available from nature.
   d. people would want to purchase more of the good at any price.

4. Which of the following is a positive economic statement?
   a. The price of gasoline is too high.
   b. The sales tax on food should be repealed.
   c. An increase in the corporate income tax will lead to a higher rate of unemployment.
   d. The present tax structure is not fair to the poor.

5. "The national debt is too large. The government must stop spending so much and start thinking about the resources they are depleting." This statement is
   a. a normative statement about economic policy.
   b. an objective statement about economic policy.
   c. a testable hypothesis.
   d. a conclusion supported by economic theory.

6. Which of the following is *not* a guidepost to clear economic thinking?
   a. The value of a good is subjective.
   b. Scarce goods have a cost.
   c. Incentives matter.
   d. Goods are scarce for the poor but not for the rich.

7. Which of the following is the best example of a positive economic statement?
   a. U.S. energy consumption must be reduced this year.
   b. The government should redistribute income in favor of the middle-income recipients.
   c. The market demand for gasoline increases as consumer income expands.
   d. Automobile firms should lower the price of cars.

8. The economic way of thinking focuses on **(I)** how economic incentives influence human choice, and **(II)** the secondary, as well as the direct, reaction that can be expected from economic activity.
   a. I is true, II is false.
   b. II is true, I is false.
   c. Both I and II are false.
   d. Both I and II are true.

9. A good economist will
   a. think much like an ecologist, recognizing the secondary effects of an action as well as the direct effects.
   b. ignore secondary effects, since in an economy such effects seldom matter.
   c. recognize that, almost always, secondary effects just reinforce the direct effects of a policy action.
   d. analyze the secondary effects of an action, so long as they occur at about the same time as the direct effects.

10. Which of the following is *not* an example of an economic resource?
   a.   Human skills
   b.   A water buffalo
   c.   An atomic reactor
   d.   All of the above *are* (or can be) economic resources.

11. "If I grow more oranges, I will make more money; similarly, if the aggregate output of oranges increases, the earnings of orange growers will expand." This statement is a clear example of
   a.   a normative viewpoint.
   b.   the role of incentives and the economic way of thinking.
   c.   the fallacy of composition.
   d.   economizing behavior by decision-makers.

12. Within the context of economics, the statement "There are no free lunches" refers to which of the following?
   a.   Individuals must always pay for the lunch that they consume.
   b.   Production of a good requires the use of scarce resources regardless of whether it is supplied free to the consumers.
   c.   Restaurant owners act in their own interest.
   d.   Economic man is selfish; therefore, he will not provide anything free for others.

THE ECONOMIC WAY OF THINKING—MULTIPLE CHOICE

1. The basic difference between macroeconomics and microeconomics is that
   a.   macroeconomics looks at how people make choices, and microeconomics looks at why they make those choices.
   b.   macroeconomics is concerned with economic policy, and microeconomics is concerned with economic theory.
   c.   macroeconomics looks at the aggregate economy, whereas microeconomics looks at single components of that economy.
   d.   macroeconomics is associated with the fallacy of composition, whereas microeconomics has little to do with the fallacy of composition.

2. Which of the following is the best example of "economizing behavior" on the part of a student whose only objective in economics is to get an A in the course?
   a.   taking the optional final exam to improve his grade even though an A in economics is already a certainty
   b.   spending the economics lecture hour studying for an exam in another class because he is already assured of an A in economics
   c.   doing outside readings in economics which will not be beneficial for the examination
   d.   spending time reading the text and attending classes even though the teacher informed the student that his present grade, a B, could not possibly change

3. Which of the following actions is consistent with the basic economic postulate (the guidepost that incentives matter)?
   a.   Consumers buy fewer potatoes because the price of potatoes declines.
   b.   A politician votes against a proposal because most of his constituents are in favor of it.
   c.   Fewer students attend lectures in the introductory economics courses because class participation counts 40 percent of their grade.
   d.   Farmers produce less barley because barley prices have declined.

4. Whenever the word "should" is included in an economist's analysis, we know that
   a. the economist is more likely to be engaged in positive economic reasoning than in normative.
   b. the economist knows what is best for us.
   c. the economist is more likely to be engaged in normative economics than in positive.
   d. the economist knows more about economics and is in a position to tell us what to do.

5. Positive economics differs from normative economics in that
   a. positive economics deals with how people react to changes in benefits, whereas normative economics deals with how people react to changes in costs.
   b. positive economic statements are, in principle, empirically testable; normative statements are not.
   c. positive economic statements tell us what we should be doing; normative economics tells us what we should have done.
   d. normative economic statements are theoretical, whereas positive statements focus on the application of the theory.

6. The basic economic postulate concerns human decisions about the allocation of
   a. leisure and work.
   b. food and clothing.
   c. studying and dating time.
   d. all of the above.

7. The basic economic postulate implies that, other things constant, the amount of cheating on an economics exam would
   a. decline as the probability of getting caught increased.
   b. not be influenced by economic incentives if students were basically honest.
   c. increase if the penalty for cheating were made more severe.
   d. not be influenced by economic incentives, since human actions involving morality and fairness cannot be altered.

8. "The price of food usually rises when there is an increase in the general level of prices. High food prices cause inflation." This statement best illustrates fallacious reasoning stemming from
   a. the fallacy of composition.
   b. failure to recognize that association is not causation.
   c. failure to consider the secondary effects of an action.
   d. wishful thinking on the part of the spokesperson.

9. **(I)** A luxury automobile is a scarce good. **(II)** Elementary public schooling in the United States is a scarce good.
   a. I is true, II is false.
   b. I is false, II is true.
   c. Both I and II are false.
   d. Both I and II are true.

10. The best test of an economic theory is
    a. the congruence of its assumptions with reality.
    b. its ability to yield predictions that are consistent with real-world events.
    c. its possibility of being subjected to controlled experiments.
    d. the agreement by a majority of economists that the theory is correct.

11. Economics assumes that decision-makers
    a. always act rationally and act only when they have full information.
    b. base their evaluations on psychic factors, leaving out the utility derived from economic goods.
    c. maximize their utility, insofar as utility indicates the pleasure derived from material goods.
    d. seek to choose those options that will best advance their objectives.

12. The central message of Adam Smith was that the production and wealth of a nation would be magnified if
    a. individuals were left free to act in their own interest.
    b. a central planning agency were established to ensure that labor and capital were allocated efficiently.
    c. the central government provided free education and training to workers.
    d. employers were more humanitarian toward workers and employees more concerned about the importance of efficiency in production.

THE ECONOMIC WAY OF THINKING—DISCUSSION QUESTIONS

1. What is scientific methodology? Can it be applied to economics? How is a theory confirmed?

2. Make a list of several things that are not scarce. Why is it hard to think of goods that are not scarce?

3. "Economics is of limited relevance. Most people will not be directly involved in management or the production of material goods. Neither will they put much money in the stock market. Understanding the economic approach will be of limited value to the typical student." Do you agree or disagree with this view? Be honest. Explain your reasoning.

4. "A tax increase is necessary if we want inflation to subside. Higher taxes will reduce the amount of money available to the consumer, causing his spending to decline. A tax increase is the most reasonable policy alternative at this time." Indicate the positive and normative aspects of these three statements.

5. "Under our plan, health care in the United States will now be free. No citizen will be denied medical care because of inability to pay. The program will be funded by increasing the employer's tax on the wages of his employees."
    a. Use the guidelines for the economic way of thinking to analyze this view.
    b. Will health care be free? For whom?
    c. What are the direct effects of the action? What are the secondary effects?
    d. How are economic incentives changed?
    e. Will the complete impact of the program be felt immediately or only with the passage of time? Explain.

PERSPECTIVES IN ECONOMICS

On Economic Ignorance
By Irving Kristol

[Reprinted with permission from *NYU Business,* Spring 1986.]

As one looks back at the history of the human race, one is appalled at the human misery that can be attributed to sheer economic ignorance. It would be no exaggeration to say that, if it could be given a quantitative measure, this misery might outrank that caused by warfare. Whole populations have been devastated by the economic ignorance of their rulers; whole civilizations have deteriorated and crumbled. To take an easy and relatively modern example: Spain in the 16th century was one of the richest and most powerful nations in Europe. For the next three centuries, it slid ineluctably downhill, becoming one of Europe's most impoverished countries. The only reason for its decline was that Spain's ruling elites were possessed of an invincible ignorance of elementary economics.

Today, whole continents—Africa and Latin America, most notably—are being pushed to ruination by that same seemingly invincible ignorance. There is no reason why the people of Argentina should not be as affluent as the people of Canada—the two countries are almost twins from an economic standpoint. Nor is there a reason why the people who live in Nigeria should be so much poorer than the people (white *and* black) who live in South Africa.

There is a puzzle here. Economic activity has been around almost as long as the human race itself, and one would have thought ruling elites would have benefitted from accumulated experience and wisdom. Moreover, while these elites, being human, are likely to make occasional egregious errors in policy, they are rarely self-destructive in the sense of wishing to persist over long periods in policies that are clearly counterproductive. Except in economics, that is, where such persistence is quite common.

The puzzle is especially exasperating at this time. After all, Adam Smith's *Wealth of Nations,* which distills the economic experience of mankind into plain, readable English, was published over two centuries ago. A 20-page précis of the book would suffice for anyone interested in grasping the fundamentals of an economic policy that leads to growth. Watching the downright economic silliness that prevails in so many countries, one finds oneself wondering: Since we really do know better, why does such silliness persist?

The answer, I suggest, is in two parts. First, it turns out to be less easy to grasp the fundamentals of elementary economics than one might think. Second, while no government likes the idea of presiding over a declining economy, there are many governments that have other priorities. And these two issues are closely related.

Anyone who has tried to teach elementary economics knows that students are quick to grasp the principles—and almost as quick to forget them. This is because those principles, though clear and simple, are often counterintuitive.

It's like trying to understand Einstein's Special Theory of Relativity. It's not hard—I myself have learned to understand it at least a dozen times. The trouble is that, having learned it, I then forget it.

Any economics teacher who touches on the topic of rent control or wage and price controls can attest that something of the same sort happens. Students promptly perceive that the adverse, unanticipated consequences—unanticipated by the economically ignorant, that is—of such controls soon overwhelm the immediate benefits. But for them to remember the essence of what they have learned, they have to have developed the intellectual habit of looking for second-order and third-order consequences. And such a habit is not easily acquired. It involves intellectual formation—a cast of mind—not just learning a few principles by rote. One has to learn to "think economically."

To think economically with any degree of consistency, one has to be motivated. There is rarely an immediate "payoff" to an individual in thinking economically about a matter of public policy—indeed, the benefits to an individual may be most tangible when that policy makes no economic sense. (Just think of all the people who do benefit from rent control!) In short, the habit of thinking economically must be an integral part of the national culture, the sort of thing one does almost instinctively.

In most Western democracies, this process of integration has occurred, at least to some extent. No democratic government can proceed with a policy of economic nonsense without also provoking controversy—and that's about as much as one can reasonably hope for. But in large areas of the world, the national cultures have little but contempt for the "economic way of thinking" even while the people are promised the fruits (affluence, mobility and modern conveniences) that only respect for such an intellectual formation can, in fact, deliver.

In a way, this is easily explained. Historically, most national cultures have regarded money-making, the pursuit of wealth, and the market arrangements that make both possible, as necessary evils at best. They distract from the "higher things" in life—religious piety, military valor, ideological rectitude, imperial aspirations. Any civilized person would have to agree that there is indeed something "higher" (most of the time, anyhow) than the pursuit of wealth. Still, most people, practically everywhere and at every time, do wish to participate in economic growth. Their problem is that they don't know how to think and act to achieve it and their governments either share their ignorance or are willing to impose their own priorities.

To put it another way: for any national culture to be economically rational, it must have a large "bourgeois" component, i.e., it must be sympathetic (or at least not antipathetic) to the mundane aspirations of ordinary men and women, as distinct from "higher" aspirations. Unfortunately, such a culture then incites hostility among its intellectual elites. But that is another story.

Discussion

1. What is Kristol's main point? Do you agree with him? Why or why not?

2. Do you really believe that to "think economically" is different from any other kind of thinking? Why or why not? In particular, how would you characterize the economic way of thinking? [*Hint:* refer to the eight guideposts to economic thinking.]

3. Kristol suggests it is "less easy to grasp the fundamentals of elementary economics than one might think." Such an opinion is similar to a common complaint from beginning students that runs something like "Economics seems so logical when I read it in the book, but when it comes time to apply it myself, I have more trouble." What reasons can you give for economics seeming easier to learn than it actually is? What can *you* do in your studies of economics to make sure that you *do* learn the material?

2

Some Tools of the Economist

TRUE OR FALSE

T F

☐ ☐ 1. The opportunity cost of washing your car is the discomfort and drudgery associated with the task.

☐ ☐ 2. Time is not a component of opportunity cost.

☐ ☐ 3. If you are an avid football fan, the opportunity cost of going for a drive while the Super Bowl game is on television would probably be high.

☐ ☐ 4. The law of comparative advantage helps explain why fathers often have their 12-year-old sons mow the lawn even though the fathers could do it more rapidly.

☐ ☐ 5. It would usually be economical for a lawyer to do his own typing if he could type better than his secretary.

☐ ☐ 6. The economic way of thinking suggests that an individual should consider only monetary cost when making consumption decisions.

☐ ☐ 7. A rainy day often reduces the opportunity cost of a farmer's going to town.

☐ ☐ 8. A country such as the United States, which has an abundance of fertile grain-growing land but little land suitable for raising sugarcane, can gain by exporting wheat to other countries and buying sugar from them.

☐ ☐ 9. The principle of comparative advantage causes both individuals and nations to specialize in the production of those things for which they have the greatest relative advantage.

☐ ☐ 10. According to the principle of comparative advantage, it would never make economic sense for a young doctor to play professional baseball.

☐ ☐ 11. All economies must make decisions about what to produce, how to produce it, and to whom to distribute the goods produced.

PROBLEMS AND PROJECTS

1. Sam and Larry jointly operate a shop. They specialize in the production of tables and chairs. Their respective production possibilities schedules are presented in Exhibit 1.

Exhibit 1

Sam's weekly production possibilities		Larry's weekly production possibilities	
Tables	Chairs	Tables	Chairs
5	0	4	0
4	2	3	1
3	4	2	2
2	6	1	3
1	8	0	4
0	10		

a. In terms of chairs, what is Sam's opportunity cost of producing a table? What is Larry's?

b. On average, they sell three times as many chairs as tables. Thus, Sam currently produces two tables and six chairs, while Larry produces one table and three chairs. Total production is three tables and nine chairs. Is this the maximum joint output that Sam and Larry could produce? If not, how could total output be expanded?

2. Exhibit 2 presents the annual production possibilities schedules for two typical farmers—one in California, the other in Kansas. Currently, the California farmer is producing 200 bushels of oranges and 600 bushels of wheat. The Kansas farmer is producing 100 and 400 bushels of oranges and wheat, respectively. Thus, the total output of the two farmers is 300 bushels of oranges and 1000 bushels of wheat.

Exhibit 2

California farmer		Kansas farmer	
Oranges (bushels)	Wheat (bushels)	Oranges (bushels)	Wheat (bushels)
0	1000	0	800
100	800	50	600
200	600	100	400
300	400	150	200
400	200	200	0
500	0		

a. The California farmer is able to produce more oranges and wheat than his Kansas counterpart. He has an absolute advantage in the production of both goods. Would gains from trade be possible? (Ignore transportation costs.)

b. Suppose both want to consume their initial amounts of wheat—600 for the Californian and 400 for the Kansan. The Kansan decides to specialize in wheat production (800 bushels). Setting aside 400 bushels of wheat for himself, he offers to trade 400 bushels of wheat to the Californian for 150 bushels of oranges. Would the Kansan gain from this transaction? Could the Californian gain if he increased his orange production to 400 and then traded the 150 bushels of oranges to the Kansan for the 400 bushels of wheat? What has happened to total output?

c. Explain why gains from trade are possible, even though the Californian has an absolute advantage in the production of both goods.

3. Given the following constant hours of work required for production, which country would have a comparative advantage in (should specialize in the production of) coffee? (*Hint:* Calculate opportunity costs!)

Exhibit 3

	Hours of work required per ton of	
	Coffee	Tobacco
United States	15	45
Brazil	25	50

4. Exhibit 4 shows the production possibilities curve for growing wheat and corn.

Exhibit 4

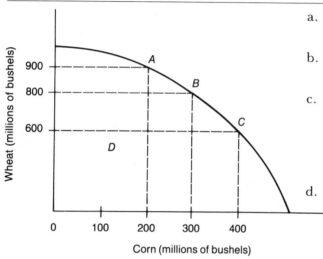

a. Are resources efficiently employed at point *A?* At point *B?* At point *D?*

b. At point *A,* how much wheat is being produced? How much corn?

c. To increase corn production from *A* to *B,* how much wheat must be sacrificed? What is the opportunity cost of one bushel of corn when production moves from point *A* to *B?*

d. What is the opportunity cost of one bushel of corn when production moves from point *B* to *C?*

5. Exhibit 5 presents information regarding expenses for childbirth and the first year of child care for the Whitney family.

Exhibit 5

Medical expenses	$ 2,000
Direct expenses (food and clothing, for example)	
50 percent purchased by family, 50 percent gifts	2,000
Before-tax income of primary-care parent	15,600
After-tax income of primary-care parent	12,000

The primary-care parent quits his/her job for the first year of the child's life. As a fringe benefit, the employer of the spouse of the primary-care parent covers all of the child's medical expenses.

a. What is the cost to the family of the child for the first year?

b. What is the cost to society (which includes the family) of the child for the first year?

c. If this were the case for the typical American family, what do you think would happen to the U.S. birthrate if the cost to the family became equal to society's cost?

LEARNING THE MECHANICS—MULTIPLE CHOICE

1. The opportunity cost to the United States of placing a man on the moon was
    a. the loss of government revenues that were allocated to the moon shot.
    b. the money prices paid to all factors of production involved in the space program.
    c. the loss of utility from the highest valued bundle of products that had to be foregone because of the moon shot.
    d. less than zero, since the long-run benefits of the project will be greater than the cost.

2. When Benjamin Franklin wrote, ''Remember that time is money!'' he understood
    a. the principle of substitution.
    b. the law of comparative advantage.
    c. the concept of opportunity cost.
    d. the Protestant ethic.

3. The opportunity cost of building a new civic auditorium in your town would be
    a. the money cost of the structure.
    b. the necessary increase in tax revenues to finance the building.
    c. the highest valued bundle of other goods and services that must be foregone because of the auditorium construction.
    d. the enjoyment that must be foregone because the capacity of the current structure prevents many people from attending athletic and community events.

4. Which of the following best describes the implications of the law of comparative advantage? If each person sells goods for which he has the greatest comparative advantage in production and buys those for which his comparative advantage is least, then the
    a. total output available to each person can be expanded by specialization and exchange.
    b. total output can be expanded, although some individuals will be net ''losers.''
    c. buyers of goods will gain at the expense of sellers.
    d. total output will increase if, and only if, persons with a comparative advantage also have an absolute advantage, relative to their trading partners.

5. When comparative advantage exists, then
    a. voluntary exchange is likely to occur independent of government action.
    b. economists must inform the public that exchange will improve the general welfare before trade will occur.
    c. trade will occur until the weakest of the parties finds it impossible to continue trading.
    d. exchange can make one trader better off, but only at the expense of the other.

6. Which of the following is *not* one of the basic economic questions that all economies must answer?
    a. What will be produced?
    b. To whom will the goods produced be allocated?
    c. What is the highest opportunity cost method of producing each good?
    d. How will goods be produced?

7. Which of the following is *not* a factor of production?
    a. A human skill
    b. Physical capital
    c. Land
    d. A production possibilities curve

Use the following information to answer questions 8–10. Exhibit 6 outlines the production possibilities of Italia and Slavia for food and clothing.

Exhibit 6

Italia		Slavia	
Food	Clothing	Food	Clothing
0	8	0	32
2	6	2	24
4	4	4	16
6	2	6	8
8	0	8	0

8. What is the opportunity cost of producing one unit of clothing in Slavia?
   a. One unit of food
   b. Two units of food
   c. One-twelfth unit of food
   d. One-fourth unit of food

9. Which of the following is true?
   a. Italia has a comparative advantage in the production of both goods.
   b. Slavia is the high opportunity cost producer of clothing.
   c. Slavia has a comparative advantage in the production of food.
   d. Italia is the low opportunity cost producer of food.

10. The law of comparative advantage suggests that
   a. both countries would gain if Slavia traded food for Italia clothing.
   b. neither country would gain from trade even if the transportation costs for the products were zero.
   c. both countries would gain if Italia traded food for Slavia clothing.
   d. Slavia would not gain from trade because it has an absolute advantage in the production of both goods.

11. When resources are being used wastefully
   a. the production possibilities curve shifts inward.
   b. the production possibilities curve shifts outward.
   c. the economy is operating at a point inside its production possibilities constraint.
   d. the economy is operating at a point outside its production possibilities constraint.

12. The production possibilities curve
   a. assumes that technology is increasing at a constant, long-run rate.
   b. assumes that all individuals have equal incomes.
   c. is normally convex (bowed in) to the origin over its entire range.
   d. assumes that the level of technology is constant.

13. Which of the following is a transaction cost?
   a. The price of a ticket to a concert
   b. The price of food eaten before the concert
   c. Time spent buying the ticket
   d. Time spent driving to the concert

14. Transaction costs
   a. can be reduced by gathering more information about many possible alternative exchanges.
   b. can be reduced by consulting people who specialize in providing information about alternative exchanges.
   c. cannot be reduced by forming consumer cooperatives.
   d. cannot be reduced at all; they are fixed by law.

15. Private property rights exist when property rights are
    a.   exclusively controlled by one owner.
    b.   transferrable to others.
    c.   both a and b.
    d.   neither a nor b.

THE ECONOMIC WAY OF THINKING—MULTIPLE CHOICE

1. Any economy that fails to realize all its potential gains stemming from the domestic division of labor (specialization) is
    a.   operating outside its production possibilities curve.
    b.   operating inside its production possibilities curve.
    c.   operating on its production possibilities curve but in an inefficient manner.
    d.   operating on its production possibilities curve and therefore need not be concerned about comparative advantage.

2. Suppose that the production possibilities of Robinson Crusoe and Friday are as follows:

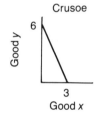 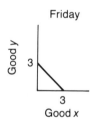

Which of the following would maximize the consumption alternatives available to Crusoe and Friday?
    a.   Crusoe should specialize in the production of good *x* and Friday should specialize in the production of good *y*, but there should be no trade allowed.
    b.   Crusoe should specialize in the production of good *x* and Friday should specialize in the production of good *y* and trade should occur.
    c.   Crusoe should specialize in the production of good *y* and Friday should specialize in the production of good *x* and trade should occur.
    d.   This is a special case. Both individuals should strive for self-sufficiency, since this maximizes output.

3. When an economy is operating efficiently, the production of more of one commodity will result in the production of less of some other commodity because
    a.   all resources are specialized and only imperfectly mobile.
    b.   resources are limited (i.e., scarce) and efficiency implies that all are in use.
    c.   the structure of demand is fixed at any given time.
    d.   material wants are insatiable.

4. ''Since I am going to start school soon, I will have to quit my current job.'' This statement most clearly reflects
    a.   the law of comparative advantage.
    b.   the principle of opportunity cost.
    c.   gains for technology.
    d.   a decision that is inconsistent with economizing behavior.

5. "Now that John washes all the dishes and I mow the lawn, we can finish in two-thirds the time it took when we shared both functions." This statement most clearly reflects
   a. the law of comparative advantage.
   b. gains from capital formation.
   c. gains from technology.
   d. choices that are inconsistent with economizing behavior.

6. "If I didn't have a date tonight, I would save $10 and spend the evening playing tennis." The opportunity cost of the date is
   a. $10.
   b. $10 plus the foregoing of a night of tennis.
   c. dependent upon how pleasant a time one has on the date.
   d. the foregoing of a night of tennis.

7. Use the diagram below to answer the following question.

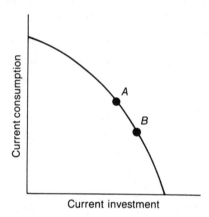

Points *A* and *B* indicate the current levels of consumption and investment for two different economies. Other things constant, which of the two economies is likely to grow more rapidly?
   a. *A*
   b. *B*
   c. They can be expected to grow at the same rate.
   d. Uncertain, since the growth rate is not influenced by the factors indicated in this hypothetical example.

8. Dr. Jones, a dentist, is choosing between driving and flying from Florida to Montana for her vacation. If Jones drove, she would have to close her office three days earlier than if she flew. Her expected income (after taxes) from her practice is $80 per day. Jones's preferences are such that she would rather drive: She would stand to gain $50 worth of nonpecuniary (nonmonetary) benefits if she drove and saw the beautiful countryside. If Jones was a rational decision-maker, she would drive if the price differential (air cost minus driving) was greater than
   a. $50.
   b. $80.
   c. $130.
   d. $190.

9. According to the law of comparative advantage
   a. each producer should strive toward self-sufficiency in order to maximize the total production of the economy.
   b. each product should be produced by the lowest opportunity cost producer in order to maximize output.
   c. one should never compare one's abilities with those of another; in doing so production time is lost.
   d. each product should be produced by the individual who can produce more of that product than any other individual.

 10. "The economic wealth of this country was built primarily by some individuals profiting from a transaction, whereas others were harmed by that transaction." This statement indicates that the spokesman
   a. fails to comprehend the mutual gains resulting from specialization and exchange.
   b. fails to comprehend the fallacy of composition.
   c. fails to understand the significance of the production possibilities constraint.
   d. utilizes the economic way of thinking. The statement is essentially correct.

11. Which of the following people would be most likely to have said, "If Portugal specializes in wine while acquiring cloth from England, the Portuguese will prosper even if both cloth and wine production in Portugal requires less labor than in England"?
   a. Thomas Malthus
   b. John Kenneth Galbraith
   c. David Ricardo
   d. Abraham Lincoln

12. Which of the following is a disadvantage that may arise when individuals specialize in the production of those things for which they are the low opportunity cost producer?
   a. When individuals specialize in production, they have little incentive to trade for other commodities that they may also enjoy.
   b. Specialization does not allow individuals to enjoy the benefits of learning by doing: that is, repetition prevents individuals from developing more efficient methods of production.
   c. A worker may become bored with performing the same monotonous task over a period of time.
   d. Individuals have little incentive to utilize their particular talents.

13. Private property rights give owners a chance to act selfishly, but they also make owners responsible and accountable for their actions. As a result, when deciding on the wisest use of their resources, property owners are likely to
   a. always disregard the wishes of others.
   b. disregard the wishes of others to the extent that accountability for misuse of the property is not enforced.
   c. be concerned about the wishes of others whether or not accountability is enforced.
   d. lose revenue when the wishes of others are taken into consideration.

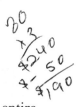

THE ECONOMIC WAY OF THINKING—DISCUSSION QUESTIONS

1. Every individual must answer the same three basic economic questions that face an entire economy. In your own words, describe the basic economic questions from the viewpoint of an individual. Explain how, at the individual level, as well as for the aggregate economy, the answers to the three questions are highly interrelated.

2. "In the progress of the division of labor, the employment of the . . . great body of the people comes to be confined to a few very simple operations, frequently to one or two. . . . The man whose whole life is spent in performing a few simple operations . . . becomes as stupid and ignorant as it is possible for a human creature to become."—Adam Smith, *The Wealth of Nations*.

   a. Smith seems to be saying that specialization carries with it a loss in utility due to monotony and alienation. Do you agree? Why or why not?

   b. If it is true that specialization increases productivity but also increases worker boredom, how do we decide the extent to which we should specialize?

   c. Smith's comments were made in the context of the production specialization as it was known in the 18th century. How applicable is his analysis to today's "high-tech" world? Why?

3. Suppose that your tuition payment for this economics class was $200.

   a. When did you incur this cost?

   b. What is the opportunity cost of *attending* the class lectures?

   c. Should the amount of the tuition payment influence your decision to attend the class lectures? Explain.

4. Explain why it is often efficient for faculty members with training in computer programming to hire student programmers to do their computer work.

5. "It doesn't make sense for me to care for my own lawn when my opportunity cost is $80 per hour." (Quote from a lawyer who knows something about economics.) Do you agree with the lawyer's view? Explain.

PERSPECTIVES IN ECONOMICS

Why Economists Disagree
by Charles Wolf Jr.

[Reprinted with permission of Charles Wolf Jr. from *Newsweek*, November 2, 1981, p. 21.]

Economists and economics have never been as visible, audible and publicized as they are now. Nor have the disagreements and divergent forecasts within the profession ever been as rife.

One consequence of this babble of prophecy is that the repute of economics and its practitioners has fallen to one of the lowest points in the 200 years since publication of "The Wealth of Nations." The reason is simply that the testimony of professional economists is offered on almost any side of each major economic-policy issue.

Is the Reagan tax program inflationary? "Yes," says Walter Heller. "No," says Milton Friedman. "Not necessarily," says Murray Weidenbaum. How do high interest rates relate to inflation? "They contribute to it" (through indexing and cost-of-living adjustments), says economist X. "They're caused by it," says economist Y. "They result from efforts to control it," (through tighter monetary policy), says economist Z.

How will interest rates behave in the next year? Why has the dollar appreciated 30 percent against some European currencies in the past year? Will lower marginal tax rates raise or reduce revenue?

On these and other key issues, the opinions of economists are spread as widely as forecasts of next month's weather.

Suspect: As economists can be found on any side of these questions, the public has come to suspect that they are available as "hired guns"—whoever has a particular interest in espousing some economic policy can find some reputable economist to endorse it. It is one thing for lawyers to have such a reputation. For lawyers are trained to be advocates: experts in organizing the best possible case for either side of an issue.

The analogy is admittedly imperfect. In general, *any* reputable lawyer can be found to defend almost any legally tenable position. The situation for economists is a bit different: it seems there's always *some* economist willing to back any side of most economic-policy issues.

But economists are supposed to be scientists: schooled in seeking, testing and finding "truth," and in acknowledging error when they encounter it. Even if their science is "dismal," it's still supposed to be science. Why then are their disagreements so sharp? There are four reasons:

1. Economists use different benchmarks (often not spelling them out). When Brookings economist George Perry asserts that Ronald Reagan's tax plan is inflationary, he is taking as his benchmark the Reagan expenditure budget already enacted by Congress. (The tax reductions are inflationary *given* that budget.) When Friedman and others rebut Perry, they're comparing Reagan's *package* of lower budget and lower taxes with the higher budget and higher taxes of Jimmy Carter's original program for fiscal year 1982—a different benchmark. (A deficit of specified size will have a smaller inflationary impact at a lower level of total government spending: the Reagan budget for 1982 involves a lower spending level than the Carter budget it replaced.)

2. Economists often make different assumptions about the time period to which their conclusions apply. When Yale economist James Tobin asserts that lower tax rates will increase consumer spending, and macroeconomist Michael Evans contends instead that they will stimulate investment, each has a different period in mind: Tobin's is short-run, Evans's longer-run.

3. Economists are usually reluctant to acknowledge the full extent of their ignorance. One of the great economists of an earlier age, Frank Knight, made a distinction between ''risk'' (knowing the odds), and ''uncertainty'' (not even knowing enough to calculate them). Ignorance is another name for this kind of uncertainty. And the plain fact is that economists share a degree of ignorance whose extent they are understandably loath to admit.

We are on relatively solid ground in the domain of microeconomics—determination of prices in competitive or monopolistic markets, predicting the effects of minimum wages on employment and so on. Our ignorance is formidable in the domain of macroeconomics: the interactions among monetary policy, tax policy, government spending and government regulations in determining aggregate employment, investment and inflation. For all these effects depend on expectations: what is expected to occur will affect what does occur. If prices are expected to rise, consumer spending will tend to aggravate the rise and vice versa.

But the embarrassing truth is that we just don't know how expectations are determined: whether they're ''adaptive,'' based on recent experience; or ''rational,'' based not only on experience but also on estimates of how this experience will be altered as a result of ''expected'' government action or inaction and other ''relevant'' factors.

4. Finally, economists have differing values. Just as there are deep ethical divisions among physicists and engineers over the development of new weapons systems, economists sometimes (often?) disagree on economic policies for reasons of pure (or impure) ideological preference.

When John Kenneth Galbraith decries cuts in minimum social-security benefits or in student loans, he's probably motivated about equally by a distaste for the market's solutions (or a disbelief in their adequacy) and a predilection for government action to remedy them. When Friedman argues in favor of those cuts in government programs, his convictions are no doubt equally strong in the opposite direction: enthusiasm for the market's solutions and a distaste for the failures of meddlesome government.

Moreover, these normative differences are no less real than those that led Edward Teller to argue strongly for ballistic-missile defense and Herbert York to argue with equal vehemence against it.

Recently I had occasion to consult consecutively three orthopedic surgeons about a ligament injury: one recommended immediate surgery; the second suggested a cast for six weeks and then surgery, *maybe;* the third proposed rest and rehabilitation.

Perhaps economics doesn't look so bad if it's compared with medicine. Whether this should be viewed as ground for solace or grief is another question.

Discussion

1. Carefully review Wolf's four main reasons for economists disagreeing. Which one do you think causes most of the disagreement? Why?

2. Wolf correctly points out that some disagreements appear to be normative rather than positive. Have you ever tried discussing an important issue with someone with whom you did not agree on a normative level? What happened?

3. When all is said and done, do you think that economists *should* agree with each other on everything? Why or why not?

3

Supply, Demand, and the Market Process

TRUE OR FALSE

T F

1. Consumers will purchase less beef at higher prices than at lower prices if other factors remain the same.

2. If the price of bananas increased, consumers would substitute oranges, apples, ice cream, and other related commodities for bananas.

3. The law of supply reflects the willingness of producers to expand output in response to an increase in the price of a product.

4. Excess demand in the market will cause the price of a product to decline.

5. An increase in demand for wheat would cause price to rise and producers to expand output.

6. A reduction in the supply of fertilizer relative to its demand would cause the price of fertilizer to decline.

7. Payments to input suppliers provide them with an incentive to acquire skills that are valuable in the production process.

8. The market price is in short-run equilibrium when suppliers are willing to supply only the amount demanded by consumers at the current price.

9. When a market is in long-run equilibrium, the opportunity cost of supplying the product will be equal to the product's market price.

10. When the market price of a product is set below the equilibrium price, shortages will result and sellers will allow the quality of the product to deteriorate.

11. If the government fixed the price of farm products above the competitive equilibrium, consumer demand would increase.

12. An increase in the price of inputs used in the construction industry would cause housing prices to rise and the demand for housing to decline.

PROBLEMS AND PROJECTS

1. Exhibit 1 presents hypothetical supply-and-demand schedules for shoes in a local market area.

Exhibit 1

Price (1)	Initial quantity demanded (2)	Quantity supplied (3)	New quantity demanded (4)
$ 6	270	120	320
9	230	170	280
12	200	200	250
15	170	220	220
18	130	250	180
21	90	300	140

    a.   Graph the initial demand (column 2) and supply (column 3) on the chart below.

    b.   What is the initial equilibrium price?

    c.   The region experiences a boom and consumer income increases, causing an increase in demand. The new demand schedule is indicated in column 4. Graph the new schedule.

    d.   What is the new equilibrium price?

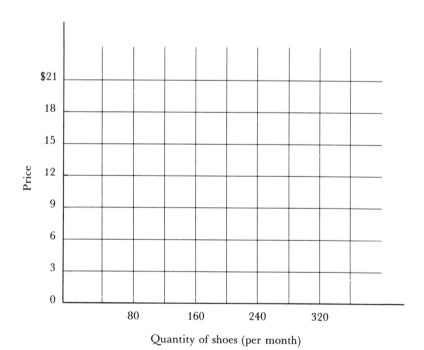

Quantity of shoes (per month)

2. As indicated by Exhibit 2, the initial demand for soybeans was D_1. The supply was S.

    a.   What was the initial market-clearing price? Quantity sold?

    b.   Soybeans have a high protein content and are a substitute for meat. Higher meat prices caused the demand for soybeans to increase to D_2. What is the new equilibrium price? Quantity sold?

    c.   What impact would the change in the price of soybeans have on the demand for wheat and corn, which can often be substituted for soybeans?

3. The pricing system sends out signals that influence the decisions of producers and consumers. Understanding the secondary effects of a change in market conditions is essential if one is to understand how a market system works. For example, what impact did the substantially higher fuel (e.g., gasoline, fuel oil) prices of the mid-1970s have on
   a. the demand for large cars? small cars?
   b. the relative demand for steel and aluminum by the auto industry?
   c. the demand for home swimming pools relative to cross-country driving vacations?
   d. employment conditions in the automobile industry?
   e. the farmer's cost of producing wheat?
   f. the demand for solar heating units and the incentive to produce them?
   g. the demand for home insulation?
   h. the incentive to speed up the development of the Alaskan pipeline during the mid-1970s?
   i. the incentive to undertake research on the development of low-pollution, coal-generated electricity?
   j. the supply of petroleum-derived fertilizers?
   k. the supply of non-petroleum-derived fertilizers?
   l. the short-run price of firewood?

Exhibit 2

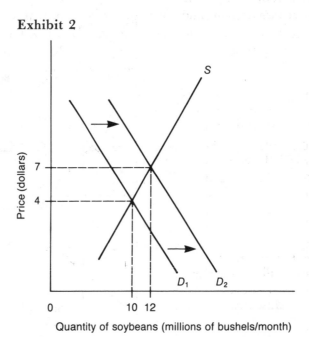

Quantity of soybeans (millions of bushels/month)

4. Use the diagrams below to indicate the changes in demand (D), supply (S), equilibrium price (P) and equilibrium quantity (Q) in response to the events described to the left of the diagrams. First show in the diagrams how supply and/or demand shift in response to the event, and then fill in the table to the right of the diagrams using + to indicate increase, − to indicate decrease and 0 to indicate no change. If an effect cannot be determined show this by using ?. As an example, the first question has been answered.

	Market	Events	Diagrams	D	S	P	Q
a.	Automobiles	Price of gasoline rises; cost of producing autos rises.		—	—	?	—
b.	Oranges	Frost destroys half the Florida orange crop.					
c.	Butter	There is an increase in the supply of margarine.					
d.	Lumber	Lower interest rates cause a construction boom; lumber jacks' wages fall significantly.					
e.	Wine	The cost of growing grapes falls; consumer income decreases.					

5. Exhibit 3 below shows the market for rental housing in Limitville, a small, fictitious town on the California Coast. The curve labelled D is the demand for rental housing, S_{sr} is the *short-run* supply curve and S_{lr} is the *long-run* supply curve.

Exhibit 3

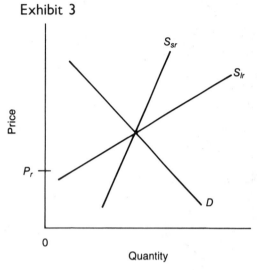

Price

Quantity

a. Indicate in the diagram the equilibrium price and quantity for rental housing in Limitville.
b. If the Limitville Municipal Council decided to limit rentals charged by landlords to P_r, what would happen to the quantity of rental housing demanded?
c. In the short run what is the quantity of rental housing supplied in Limitville at the price P_r? In the diagram, indicate the excess demand ("shortage") of rentals in the short run.

d. Now indicate the excess demand in the long run. Suggest reasons why the reduction in quantity supplied would be greater in the long run than in the short run.
e. At the controlled price of rentals, P_r, is price fully performing its rationing function? What sorts of *non*-price rationing mechanisms might be used to ration rentals?

LEARNING THE MECHANICS—MULTIPLE CHOICE

1. If the price of tickets to the World Series were below the competitive equilibrium price, then
    a. the quantity supplied would be greater than the quantity demanded.
    b. the demand for World Series tickets must be elastic.
    c. there would be no transactions between buyers and sellers of the tickets.
    d. the number of persons seeking to obtain tickets to World Series games would be greater than the number of available tickets.

2. Which of the following would cause the price of wheat to rise?
    a. A decrease in the price of corn, a substitute for wheat
    b. An increase in the price of soybeans, a substitute for wheat
    c. A decrease in the price of fertilizer
    d. A diet craze among Americans that decreases their demand for bread products

3. A demand curve gives the relationship between price and quantity demanded, *other things constant*. These "other things" include all of the following except
    a. consumer preferences.
    b. income.
    c. the price of the commodity.
    d. the price of substitute goods.

4. If cigars and cigarettes are substitute goods, an increase in the price of cigars would result in
    a. an increase in the sales of cigarettes.
    b. a decrease in the price of cigarettes.
    c. a decrease in the sales of cigarettes.
    d. an increase in the sales of cigars.

5. If the price of a bushel of wheat is fixed (say, by government price regulations) *above* its market equilibrium price, the most likely result would be
   a. an increase in the quantity of wheat demanded.
   b. a decrease in the quantity of wheat supplied in the short run.
   c. a decrease in the incentive to expand the future supply of wheat.
   d. a surplus of wheat.

6. Which of the following would be most likely to cause the demand for Miller beer to increase?
   a. An increase in the price of Budweiser beer
   b. A decrease in consumer income
   c. A decrease in the price of the barley used to make Miller beer
   d. An increase in the price of pretzels, eaten with beer

7. The demand curve for a commodity indicates the maximum amount the consumer would be willing to pay for each unit of the good. What will be the effect of an increase in the price the consumer must pay for the product?
   a. There will be a decrease in the quantity demanded.
   b. The entire demand curve will shift to the right.
   c. There will be no effect, since the maximum amount the consumer would be willing to pay stays the same.
   d. The consumer's demand will decrease.

8. All other things constant, a decrease in bus, train, and airplane fares will
   a. shift the demand curve for automobiles to the left.
   b. cause a movement along the demand curve for automobiles.
   c. shift the demand curve for automobiles to the right.
   d. have no impact on the demand curve for automobiles.

9. In the absence of government intervention, the pricing system would ration gasoline to those individuals and firms
   a. who were able and willing to pay the highest price.
   b. who had the highest income.
   c. who lived the farthest from their place of work.
   d. who owned automobiles that used the most gas.

10. If the market price is above the equilibrium price, there will be a tendency for price to fall, causing
   a. quantity demanded to fall and quantity supplied to rise.
   b. quantity demanded to rise and quantity supplied to fall.
   c. both quantity demanded and quantity supplied to fall.
   d. both quantity demanded and quantity supplied to rise.

11. Which of the following is true about Alfred Marshall?
   a. He was the most influential of the Keynesian economists.
   b. More than any other nineteenth-century English economist, he made economics into a science.
   c. He made his living manufacturing scissors, but he is most famous for developing the concept of "marginalism."
   d. He won a Nobel Prize in economics.

12. Alfred Marshall helped develop the concepts of "long run" and "short run." Which of the following is the most accurate description of the distinction between the two?
    a. The short run is a time period of less than three months, whereas the long run covers time periods of more than seven months.
    b. The long run is a time period of sufficient length for decision-makers to make adjustments that are too costly (or impossible) to make in the short run.
    c. The long run is a time period of sufficient length for producers to develop new technologies, whereas in the short run, technology is constant.
    d. The long run is a marathon, whereas the short run is more like the hundred-yard dash.

THE ECONOMIC WAY OF THINKING—MULTIPLE CHOICE

1. The pricing system corrects a shortage by
   a. lowering the price and profits of firms causing the shortage.
   b. raising the product price and producer profits.
   c. lowering product price, but increasing producer profits.
   d. raising product price, but lowering producer profits.

2. "If gasoline were taxed, the price of gasoline would rise. Consequently, the demand for gasoline would fall, causing the price to fall to the original level. Therefore the tax would not be effective." This statement
   a. is essentially correct.
   b. is incorrect—after the demand falls, the price would fall, but to some level higher than the original level.
   c. is incorrect—demand and quantity demanded are confused.
   d. is incorrect—the tax would be effective even if the price fell to the original level, since the demand for gasoline dropped (which was the primary purpose of the tax).

3. Which of the following was a result of the increased prices of gasoline and petroleum-related products in early 1979?
   a. The demand for small cars expanded.
   b. The incentive to use more oil for heating increased.
   c. Tourism in south Florida increased relative to 1977–1978.
   d. The demand for used Cadillacs and Lincoln Continentals increased.

4. About two-thirds of the private rental housing in New York City is subject to rent control. The rent control price is usually set below the market equilibrium price. Economic theory suggests that this rent control price would
   a. increase landlords' profits.
   b. cause many rental units to be abandoned or poorly kept up by landlords.
   c. result in a surplus of rental units in the near future.
   d. reduce housing discrimination against minorities.

5. If the government sets the price of a commodity below the market equilibrium price, then
   a. there will be a surplus of the commodity, which will remain until the controls are removed.
   b. there will be a shortage of the commodity at the below-equilibrium price.
   c. sellers will compete by improving the quality of the product.
   d. the government will have to buy the excess quantity supplied at that price.

6. "The price of wheat rose sharply because (a) the drought reduced the yield per acre, and (b) millers sought to stockpile wheat to protect themselves from future price increases that would occur if the drought were to continue." This quotation suggests that the price rise was caused by
   a. an increase in demand and a movement along the supply curve.
   b. an increase in supply and a movement along the demand curve.
   c. an increase in both demand and supply.
   d. a reduction in supply and a short-run increase in demand.

7. "The winds of the recent hurricanes in Florida are bringing financial gain to California citrus growers. Because of the extensive damage to the Florida citrus crop, California citrus products are commanding their highest prices ever." Which of the following statements best explains the economics of this quotation?
   a. The supply of Florida oranges has decreased, causing their price to increase and the demand for the substitute California oranges also to increase.
   b. The supply of Florida oranges has decreased, causing the supply of California oranges to increase and their prices to rise.
   c. The demand for Florida oranges has been reduced by the hurricane, causing a greater demand for the California oranges and an increase in their price.
   d. The demand for Florida oranges has been reduced, causing their prices to fall and thereby increasing the demand for the substitute California oranges.

8. Which of the following is an example of one of the basic questions being solved with the price mechanism?
   a. What to produce is decided by a central planning board, and the decisions on what prices to charge are passed down to the retailers.
   b. How to produce is decided only after negotiation with union leaders.
   c. What to produce is decided when consumers who want more of a good bid up the price of that good, attracting more production.
   d. For whom to produce is decided by setting up a rationing program and charging a fair price to all consumers.

9. All of the following would affect the supply of automobiles except one. Which would *not* affect the supply of automobiles?
   a. Higher prices for steel and other resources used in the production of automobiles
   b. A successful physical fitness plan encouraging all Americans to walk to their destinations
   c. A technological improvement reducing the production costs of automobiles
   d. Increased wages for the members of the United Auto Workers

10. Per capita expenditures for physicians' services increased from $31.45 in 1960 to $47.70 in 1966, an increase of 35 percent in dollars of constant purchasing power. Most of this change occurred in price, rather than in quantity of services delivered. Economic theory would suggest that the observed data could best be explained as
    a. an increase in supply, but little change in demand.
    b. a decrease in both supply and demand.
    c. an increase in demand, while supply remained relatively constant.
    d. a sharp increase in both supply and demand.

The following quotation relates to questions 11 and 12.

"In 1973, in an effort to halt inflation, the price of beef was fixed. Shortages developed, and in September 1973 the controls were lifted. During the post-control period, prices initially rose but eventually leveled off and declined as beef producers began marketing cattle that they had held off the market while the price controls were in effect."

11. During the control period, the price of beef must have been set
    a. below the short-run equilibrium price.
    b. at the equilibrium price.
    c. above the equilibrium price.
    d. The above quotation does not present any evidence on this issue.

12. Which of the following best explains why beef was held off the market during the control period?
    a. The below-equilibrium current price reduced the incentive for producers to expand the number of cattle sold, and the expectation of higher post-control beef prices increased the incentive to hold cattle off the current market.
    b. The above-equilibrium current price increased the incentive for producers to expand the size of herds, which could be done only by reducing the supply to the current market.
    c. The controlled beef price caused producers to expand the current size of their herds, but reduced their incentive to hold cattle off the market in the future.
    d. The producers did not like the government intervention with the pricing mechanism and deliberately restricted the supply to the current market despite the incentive of higher prices.

THE ECONOMIC WAY OF THINKING—DISCUSSION QUESTIONS

1. Air traffic congestion is a major problem at the municipal airports of many major cities. Some economists have suggested that charging a higher usage price, particularly during peak traffic periods (8–10 A.M. and 5–10 P.M.), would improve the situation. What impact would the higher fees have on the
    a. scheduling of flights?
    b. number of landings and takeoffs during heavy traffic periods?
    c. fuel wastage and other costs of circling the airport?
    d. number of small private planes using major airports?

2. "There should be no charge for campus parking. All spaces should be allocated on a first come, first served basis. Everyone would compete equally for on-campus parking. This is the beauty of the plan. It works because it is used wherever preferential parking has not been implemented. It works because no one can argue that it is unfair." Evaluate this idea. Would you favor this plan for your campus? Why or why not?

3. "The pricing system rations goods to the highest bidders and provides the incentive for businessmen to produce those goods that are most scarce, relative to their cost."
    a. How does the pricing system ration goods?
    b. How does it offer suppliers an incentive to produce goods that are most scarce, relative to their cost?

4. "The higher meat prices caused the demand for meat to decline. Eventually, this decline in demand led to lower prices, easing the family food budget." Analyze the falacies of this quotation.

5. In your own words, explain the interaction of market forces that would cause a temporarily
    a. above-equilibrium price to decline.
    b. below-equilibrium price to rise.

6. Explain the difference between a change in (a) demand and (b) quantity demanded.

7. In an effort to control rising prices during the 1970s, many governments fixed prices (and wages) for extended periods of time. Discuss the economic repercussions of fixed prices.

8. What impact would a rapid increase in population and an accompanying construction boom in Orlando, Florida, have on the price in the Orlando area of each of the following?
    a. Land
    b. Cement
    c. European vacations
    d. Apartment rentals
    e. Services of a local plumber

PERSPECTIVES IN ECONOMICS

Bad Business

Moonshiners in South Find Sales Are Down As Their Costs Go Up

As Number of Illegal Stills Shrinks, Revenue Agents Focus on Guns, Gambling

A Possum for Flavoring

by Jonathan Kwitney
Staff Reporter of THE WALL STREET JOURNAL

[From *The Wall Street Journal,* July 30, 1975. Reprinted with permission from The Wall Street Journal © Dow Jones & Co., Inc. (1975). All rights reserved.]

Habersham County, Ga.

"There probably isn't a family around here that hasn't had at least one member involved with a still," observes Clyde Dixon, executive vice president of the Peoples Bank in Cleveland, Ga. "It hasn't been so long around here since moonshine was the only way to make money. My father made moonshine," Mr. Dixon says.

But two years ago the price of sugar—an essential ingredient in moonshine—tripled, and life in the laurel thickets changed rapidly. It takes at least 10 pounds of sugar to make a gallon of barnyard whiskey. With other inflationary factors added, moonshine that sold a few years ago for $6 a gallon at the still began pushing $15 a gallon.

At that price the moonshine market contracted severely, because for $15 plus retail markup, a customer can buy government whiskey. ("Government whiskey" is the hill country term for legal booze—stuff on which the tax has been paid. Unlike hastily made moonshine, its manufacture relies on slowly drawing natural sugars from the grain being distilled, and therefore its price is unaffected by the sugar market.)

Revenuers Look Elsewhere The price squeeze on moonshine has forced new occupations on a lot of people who were engaged, one way or another, in what may have been, even as late as the 1950s, the largest industry in such counties as Habersham, Dawson and Gilmer. Not all of those people whose employment depended on illegal booze were moonshiners themselves, however.

Billy Corbin is a revenue agent with the Treasury Department's Bureau of Alcohol, Tobacco and Firearms (ATF). He chased moonshiners in North Georgia for 10 years and says his team of five agents used to bust up an average of 10 stills a month. Then, in December, he was transferred to a new office with emphasis on nonwhiskey violations. "When I left (the moonshine post) it was down to no more than one still a month," Mr. Corbin says.

Mr. Corbin's boss, Bill Barbary, agent in charge of ATF's Gainsville, Ga., office, says the 108 revenue agents in Georgia used to spend 75% of their time on liquor offenses, the rest on other crimes, mostly the unlicensed sale of firearms. Now, he says, agents spend only about 25% of their time on moonshine patrol. To help fill the slack, the Treasury Department this year reassigned its gambling tax enforcement to ATF from the Internal Revenue Service.

So, for the government, one beneficial by-product of the sugar inflation and moonshine depression is an increase in arrests for firearms violations and illegal wagering. Some 15 or 20 revenue agents from the countryside were reassigned to Atlanta this spring and broke up a big numbers ring there, federal officials say; they promise to follow up with the indictment of 30 or 40 gambling operators.

The Pot Shuttle On the other hand, with the whiskey business in turmoil, many former moonshine overlords—Mr. Barbary says most of them—have simply reapplied their resourcefulness to trafficking in other illicit goods that are still profitable. They are suspected of being responsible for the recent big increase in the airlifting of drugs, particularly marijuana, from South America to small airstrips in Georgia and neighboring moonshine states.

For example, two long-reputed North Georgia moonshine czars, Garland "Bud" Cochran and Ben Kade "Junior" Tatum, were indicted in federal court in South Carolina last summer for allegedly masterminding a DC-4 pot shuttle from Colombia. Mr. Tatum was convicted and is appealing. Mr. Cochran—who the ATF says was shipping 7,000 gallons of moonshine a month into Atlanta in trailer trucks during the 1960s—has been a fugitive since the smuggling indictment came down. Officials believe he is in South America directing more smuggling operations.

Radical as the change in North Georgia life has been since the price of sugar rose, it actually is the culmination of an evolutionary change that began in the early 1940s.

Revenue agents agree that the old-time, 100% corn liquor made in pure copper stills—the fabled "white lightning"—was as good as or better than bonded whiskey. But when copper became scarce at the start of World War II, moonshiners turned to sheet metal vats, and in more recent times began cooling the liquor in automobile radiators instead of copper coils. The result often is a fatal dose of lead poisoning. In probably the most famous case of this, the late Fats Hardy, a Gainesville moonshine king, was sentenced to life in prison in the late 1950s after many persons died from drinking the moonshine he shipped to Atlanta.

The people who do drink it, authorities say are almost exclusively poor, urban blacks. The biggest retail distribution centers are so-called "shot-houses," operated in private homes or stores in black neighborhoods of Atlanta, Macon and other cities throughout the Southeast. Because the price of a shot has soared to 75 cents, almost the price of safer, stronger legal bar whiskey, the ATF estimates that there are only a few hundred shot-houses in Atlanta now, down from a few thousand before the crunch.

Assistant U.S. Attorney Owen Forrester in Atlanta—who says his grandmother had a still on her land, though she didn't drink—says he doubts that even a new rise in sugar prices could wipe out moonshine entirely. "The revenue agents who work the shot-houses here tell me that there are still a lot of old-timers who like the taste of it," Mr. Forrester says. "There's a certain zang, or sizzle, going down."

How To Make It Hill folks and revenue agents have described the methods moonshiners use to get that "zang" and "sizzle" in there.

First, there's a widespread belief, often put into practice, that horse manure added to the corn mash speeds its fermentation. In addition, sanitary conditions aren't always up to FDA standards. Mr. Dixon, the country banker, says, "I've seen a hog get in (the vat) to drink some of that slop and drown. They just take the hog out and go ahead. They can't afford to lose all that money (by throwing out the contaminated mash). I'll tell you, Jack Daniel's does it a lot cleaner." Mr. Forester, the prosecutor, recalls a moonshiner who "put in dead possums at the end to flavor it."

Later, still other foreign matter is added. Moonshine usually is 110 proof when it's sold at the still to a "tripper," who usually is either an independent truck driver or an employee of an urban distributor. To stretch the product, the distributors usually water it down as much as 50%. Then, to make it look its original strength, they add beading oil, which simulates the swirls that alcohol makes in liquor.

"It's damn hard work to make whiskey," Mr. Dixon says. "They have to hide the stills in laurel thickets on a mountain. You have your barrels and boxes of malt—it's corn meal mostly, some barley malt. They'll carry 200 or 300 pounds of sugar up that mountain at a time on their backs. All the time (the mash) is working it has to be stirred. That corn meal has a tendency to lump up. I've seen them get stark naked and get in there and mash it. If you don't think it's hard work, try it."

Much of the hard work, high price and poor quality is caused by the revenue agents, whose presence puts constant pressure on moonshiners to finish their work fast and get out. Moonshiners need costly sugar because they must dash off each batch of their product in about 72 hours.

Bonded distillers have controlled conditions and plenty of time, so they can apply even heat as required and wait out the two weeks or so it takes to get sugar out of the natural grains.

Byron Davis of Gainesville, who retired in 1968 after 31 years as a revenue agent because "it's a young man's job," says he remembers capturing a lot of moonshiners by cruising the hills looking for smoke. In fact, he attributes the switch in still materials from copper to other metals at least in part to a switch in cooking fuels from wood to butane gas. The butane largely eliminated the telltale smoke trail, he says, but didn't work well with copper equipment.

Keeping tabs on sugar sales also has helped agents to corral a few moonshiners. "One of these little country stores starts selling 500 pounds of sugar a week, you smell a rat," Mr. Corbin says.

Nowadays, however, agents say they make most of their arrests through tips from informants. Moonshiners love to tell on each other, Mr. Corbin says. Certainly the ATF needed informants 18 months ago in order to discover a fabulous 2,000-gallon-a-week underground still, which was entered by opening the trunk of an old Ford sitting in a Habersham County junkyard, and climbing down a ladder. Agents believe that the operator obtained electric power for his still by tapping into nearby underground Tennessee Valley Authority lines.

On the whole, authorities say their problem is less in catching moonshiners than in obtaining justice afterwards.

Judges and juries just "didn't consider whiskey to be a crime," Mr. Forrester recalls of his moonshine trial days. The operator of the underground still beneath the old Ford, for example, pleaded guilty and received a suspended sentence, Mr. Forrester says.

Professional So relaxed is the atmosphere at moonshine trials that one notorious moonshiner from Adairsville, Ga., used to feel comfortable attending them. Mr. Forrester recalls, "Every term he'd come to court with mash all over his pants and listen to testimony in other cases to learn new techniques."

A typical still operation is financed and overseen by a man with substantial income from legitimate business, such as a farm or store. He hires three to six still hands and one or two women who live with them while the still is in operation, to keep house and to make the group appear to be a normal family. While the still hands sometimes wind up serving a year or two in federal prison, the boss, if convicted, usually gets probation, often impressing the judge and jury with letters of commendation from leaders in the community.

Discussion

1. Did the increase in the price of sugar affect the supply of or the demand for moonshine? Use the principles of supply and demand to analyze the moonshine market.

2. Use the principles of supply and demand to analyze the market for federally regulated whiskey.

3. How did the higher sugar prices affect the demand for federal regulatory agents? Why?

4

Supply and Demand for the Public Sector

TRUE OR FALSE

T F

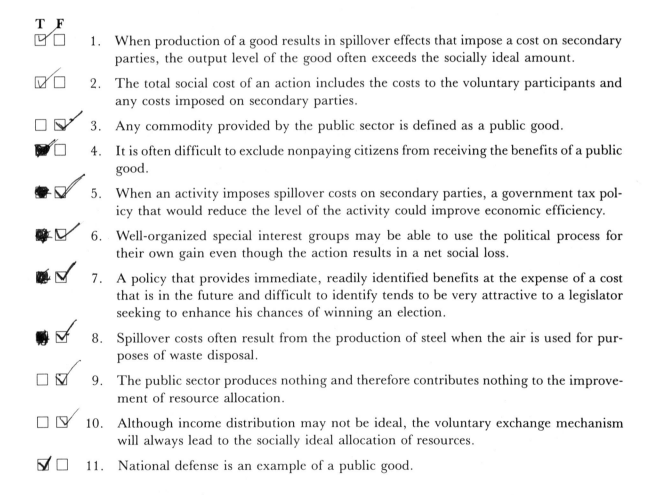

☑ ☐   1.   When production of a good results in spillover effects that impose a cost on secondary parties, the output level of the good often exceeds the socially ideal amount.

☑ ☐   2.   The total social cost of an action includes the costs to the voluntary participants and any costs imposed on secondary parties.

☐ ☑   3.   Any commodity provided by the public sector is defined as a public good.

☑ ☐   4.   It is often difficult to exclude nonpaying citizens from receiving the benefits of a public good.

☐ ☑   5.   When an activity imposes spillover costs on secondary parties, a government tax policy that would reduce the level of the activity could improve economic efficiency.

☐ ☑   6.   Well-organized special interest groups may be able to use the political process for their own gain even though the action results in a net social loss.

☐ ☑   7.   A policy that provides immediate, readily identified benefits at the expense of a cost that is in the future and difficult to identify tends to be very attractive to a legislator seeking to enhance his chances of winning an election.

☐ ☑   8.   Spillover costs often result from the production of steel when the air is used for purposes of waste disposal.

☐ ☑   9.   The public sector produces nothing and therefore contributes nothing to the improvement of resource allocation.

☐ ☑   10.   Although income distribution may not be ideal, the voluntary exchange mechanism will always lead to the socially ideal allocation of resources.

☑ ☐   11.   National defense is an example of a public good.

PROBLEMS AND PROJECTS

1. Indicate which of the following goods is a private good (P), a public good (PG), or has characteristics of both (B). Explain your answer in each case.

    a. A measles shot _____

    _____

    b. A fireworks display _____

    _____

    c. National defense _____

    _____

    d. Neckties _____

    _____

    e. A television program _____

    _____

    f. A filet mignon steak _____

    _____

    g. A taxicab _____

    _____

    h. A rose garden _____

    _____

    i. A flood control project _____

    _____

    j. A poem _____

    _____

2. List as many goods as you can think of that have substantial public good characteristics that are provided by the private sector. Try weather forecasts and television signals for starters.

3. Exhibit 1 illustrates what the world demand for petroleum might look like in the short run. The supply curve (S) represents the world supply of petroleum if petroleum suppliers behave competitively.

Exhibit I

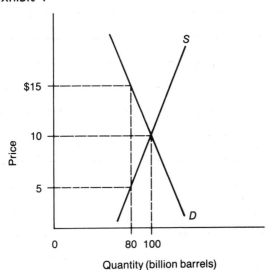

Quantity (billion barrels)

a. What would be the long-run, competitive equilibrium price and quantity of petroleum? Show these in the diagram.

b. At competitive equilibrium, calculate the total revenues earned by petroleum suppliers. (Remember that total revenue is price times quantity sold.)

c. Suppose now that petroleum suppliers agree to restrict the quantity they sell to 80 billion barrels. Draw in the supply curve. What price could they charge? What would total revenue be?

d. If only 80 billion barrels are sold, what is the value (in dollars) of the consumers' valuation of the last barrel produced and sold? Is this consumer valuation of the last unit larger or smaller than the producers' opportunity cost of producing that last unit? Is this an efficient or an inefficient outcome for society?

e. Could government policy have helped avoid this problem? How?

4. Exhibit 2 shows the supply and demand schedules for pulp paper in Academia, a hypothetical country.

Exhibit 2

Price (per ton)	Quantity (tons/year) Demanded	Supplied
$150	1000	7000
140	2000	6000
130	3000	5000
120	4000	4000
110	5000	3000
100	6000	2000

a. On a piece of graph paper, plot the demand and supply curves and show the equilibrium price and quantity for pulp paper in Academia.

b. Suppose that the production of pulp paper results in external pollution costs of $20 per ton produced. In your diagram, show a supply curve that would include these external costs. What are the "ideal" (efficient) price and output for pulp paper? Show these in your diagram.

LEARNING THE MECHANICS—MULTIPLE CHOICE

1. All but one of the following public sector actions will help to provide an economic environment that can facilitate the attainment of gains from market exchange. Which one *reduces* the efficiency of the market process?
   a. promoting competitive markets
   b. protecting persons from fraud
   c. providing a stable monetary framework
   d. protecting consumers by fixing prices below equilibrium

2. Competition among producers is important because it
   a. serves to protect the consumer by providing him with alternatives to the prices offered by any single seller.
   b. serves to protect the producer, assuring her of at least a fair rate of return.
   c. means that the market will always meet the social conditions of ideal economic efficiency.
   d. always leads to prices that reflect the total social cost of producing each good.

3. Ideal public sector action can potentially improve economic efficiency
   a. because political decision-makers are generally concerned with problems associated with income distribution.
   b. if the government sets prices above equilibrium for commodities in a competitive market and below equilibrium for commodities in monopolistic markets.
   c. when spillover or external effects cause market inefficiency.
   d. because of the rational ignorance effect.

4. An action that imposes spillover costs on a secondary party results in
   a. voluntary exchange.
   b. public sector action.
   c. involuntary exchange.
   d. market adjustments that lead to the ideal social outcome.

5. It is difficult for the market process to provide public goods because
   a. they must be produced by government.
   b. it will be difficult to get potential consumers to pay for such goods since there is not a direct link between payment for and receipt of the good.
   c. consumers do not really want public goods, even though such goods are best for them.
   d. individual consumers will fail to gain from the production of goods that benefit the general public.

6. When there is no interference with the market mechanism
   a. the market will under allocate resources to the production of goods with external costs.
   b. the market will over allocate resources to the production of goods with external benefits.
   c. the cost to society from production will be greater than the private cost to producers when external costs are present.
   d. the output of public goods will generally exceed the optimal level of output.

7. Public sector action
   a. promotes economic efficiency except when self-interest leads to political corruption.
   b. sometimes improves efficiency and sometimes generates inefficiency, since proposals that help win elections are not necessarily efficient.
   c. generally leads to economic inefficiency because the public sector is bureaucratic in nature, and bureaucrats are lazy.
   d. promotes economic efficiency when collective decisions are made democratically.

8. All of the following are true about the market and public sectors *except*
   a. competitive behavior is present in both sectors.
   b. the public sector utilizes the price mechanism more than the private sector.
   c. the public sector can break the individual consumption–payment link more easily than can the private sector.
   d. there is more free choice for individual consumers in the private sector than in the public sector.

9. Which of the following is *not* true of the concept of economic efficiency?
   a. Economic efficiency defines the ideal income distribution.
   b. An economically efficient solution occurs when all exchanges that will lead to an improvement in the well-being of individuals have been undertaken.
   c. The largest possible benefit is obtained from a given level of cost.
   d. Each good is produced at the lowest possible cost.

10. Simply stated, the rational ignorance effect explains why
    a. consumers are rational but not very intelligent.
    b. voters are rational but not very intelligent.
    c. voters are intelligent to remain rational.
    d. rational voters remain ignorant.

11. Despite many differences, the market and public sectors are *similar* in which one of the following respects?
    a. In both sectors, income (or power) is distributed on the basis of the same criterion.
    b. Consumers in the market sector and voters in the public sector are equally well informed.
    c. Voluntary exchange, rather than compulsion, is characteristic of both sectors.
    d. It will be costly to use scarce goods, whether through the private or the public sector.

12. Which of the following activities is *least* likely to give rise to external costs or benefits?
    a. Spraying to control mosquitos in your backyard
    b. Driving one's car during rush hour
    c. Inoculating your children during a flu epidemic
    d. Watching fewer movies on television

THE ECONOMIC WAY OF THINKING—MULTIPLE CHOICE

1. Driving your automobile in Los Angeles during the rush hour causes spillover effects because
   a. it adds to congestion and pollution from auto exhaust, reducing the welfare of others.
   b. gasoline is scarce and you must pay for it.
   c. gasoline is a public good.
   d. your actions will benefit others even though you will be unable to charge them for the service.

2. In the absence of government action, the private market probably would not produce as much national defense as citizens desire because
   a. individual citizens do not receive personal benefits from national defense.
   b. private firms do not like to produce goods with public good characteristics.
   c. it would be difficult for private firms to charge for national defense since it cannot usually be withheld from nonpaying customers.
   d. national defense benefits a country but not its citizens.

3. If economic efficiency is the criterion, which of the following is the most important justification for the government, rather than private enterprise, providing certain economic goods and services?
    a. The government can provide political goods free of charge.
    b. The government can redistribute incomes such that the poverty problem is mitigated.
    c. A private market cannot eliminate the misallocation that results from the rational ignorance of consumers.
    d. A private market does not provide a way to sell certain "public goods" because the benefits derived cannot be limited to those persons who pay for them.

4. Apart from income distribution, criteria of ideal economic efficiency require that (I) all trading in which both buyers and sellers can gain take place, (II) no trading take place for which the social cost (including any cost imposed on nonconsenting parties) exceeds the social benefit derived from the exchange.
    a. Both I and II are true.
    b. Neither I nor II is true.
    c. I is true, II is false.
    d. II is true, I is false.

5. Under a market system, individuals normally pay for a particular good; when goods are allocated through the public sector,
    a. an individual "pays" the approximate value of the government service through taxes.
    b. the individual does not pay—nor does anyone else—since the government simply prints money to finance the service.
    c. although the individual consumer often does not pay, costs are incurred that must be covered by someone (or some group).
    d. payment is avoided since the production of the services is not for profit.

The following quotation relates to questions 6 and 7.

> "The ideal policy, from the viewpoint of the state, is one with identifiable beneficiaries, each of whom is helped appreciably, at the cost of many unidentifiable persons, none of whom is hurt very much"—George Stigler, *A Dialogue on the Proper Economic Role of the State.*

6. This statement is probably
    a. incorrect, because voters are well informed on a wide range of political issues.
    b. incorrect, because the political process dilutes the influence of special interest groups, since like other citizens, their members have only one vote.
    c. correct, because the well-informed voter will favor policies that cater to the views of small groups of people.
    d. correct, because voters who have a strong personal interest in an issue will tend to support candidates who cater to their views, whereas most other voters ignore the issue.

7. Which of the following groups does the above quotation suggest would have the most influence on public sector action?
    a. Taxpayers
    b. Nonunion laborers
    c. Special interest groups
    d. Consumers

8. Which of the following "goods" is the best example of a pure public good?
    a. Interstate highways
    b. Clean air
    c. Cultural centers
    d. Public education

9. An action that improves economic efficiency is one
    a. that does not involve any discrimination.
    b. for which the sum of the net benefits to those who favor the action is less than the sum of the net costs imposed on those who oppose the action.
    c. for which the sum of the net benefits to those who gain from the action is greater than the sum of the net costs to those who lose.
    d. that results in a majority of the people benefiting from the action.

10. If there are no spillover effects, voluntary exchange results in (**I**) an expected net gain for all participants in the transaction, (**II**) a social benefit that exceeds the social cost.
    a. Both I and II are true.
    b. Neither I nor II is true.
    c. I is true, II is false.
    d. II is true, I is false.

11. Special interest issues may lead to economic inefficiency since
    a. special interest groups consist, in general, of individuals who are less worthy than the general populace.
    b. politicians are members of special interest groups.
    c. individual voters are irrational in not obtaining information on special interest issues.
    d. the political process is likely to give undue weight to special interest groups, even though contrary action may be more efficient.

12. Economists use the term *short-sightedness effect* to describe which one of the following phenomena?
    a. Politicians tend to support actions that have immediate and easily recognized current benefits.
    b. Individuals are apt to spend their income on goods that bring immediate personal benefits.
    c. Voters elect politicians on the basis of campaign promises, regardless of what they may do once they are in office.
    d. Politicians support the programs of special interest groups in order to get elected; however, special interest support may be detrimental later, costing politicians popularity after the programs are implemented.

THE ECONOMIC WAY OF THINKING—DISCUSSION QUESTIONS

1. State the two conditions for ideal economic efficiency. Give four reasons why an unregulated market mechanism may fail to attain those conditions of ideal economic efficiency. Give three reasons why government intervention may promote inefficiency.

2. "Public sector competition is quite keen. If you want government to do you a favor, you have to be more persuasive, more persistent, and more willing to assist political figures than the competition. Although the public sector will reward the skilled entrepreneur and the well-organized interest group, success requires that one beat the competition." Do you agree or disagree? Is competition always directed in a manner consistent with efficiency? Explain.

3. What are public goods? Why might the market be unable to produce a sufficient quantity of public goods?

4. Can theories of basic human behavior be used to develop theories of political behavior? Can these theories be tested against reality? Do you think that scientific methodology can be applied to collective decision-making? Why or why not?

5. Why are well-organized special interest groups likely to be politically powerful? Why will vote-seeking political entrepreneurs have an incentive to cater to their views?

PERSPECTIVES IN ECONOMICS

New Buzzword, Old Philosophy
A Mobil advertisement

[From the *Los Angeles Times,* February 18, 1986, p. 4. Reprinted with the permission of the Mobil Corporation.]

The "mixed economy," that marriage of public and private enterprise so widely hailed in the 1960s, has lost some of its pizzazz these days. The buzzword of the '80s is privatization, and it's firing the imagination of countries the world over—capitalist, Socialist and Communist alike.

In Europe, for example, the British government has sold more than a dozen state-owned companies—some of the giants of its aerospace, communications, energy, tourism and trucking industries—and shifted more than 400,000 workers from public to private payrolls. Similar moves are taking place in France, Germany, Italy, Spain and Sweden.

In Asia, Japan is divesting the government railway, airline and telephone systems. South Korea is selling off banks and heavy industry. Less developed nations like Bangladesh and Pakistan are returning nationalized jute, textile, rice and flour mills to their former owners.

The economic momentum has even spread to the Communist world. The Cuban government is selling state-owned houses to tenants. More than 10 million self-employed capitalists operate restaurants, street stalls, repair shops and other small enterprises in China. And in rural areas, farmers are prospering by selling surplus produce in the cities, and keeping the proceeds. Entrepreneurs in Hungary bid for the right to run their own businesses, and the system is catching on in other Eastern European nations.

Why the interest in privatization? Mostly because it works. Especially in the Communist lands, privatization has tended to raise the standard of living.

Not surprisingly, privatization is becoming popular in America, too. Prompted by the need to cut the deficit, the Reagan administration is seeking to cut costs by turning over to private operators such traditional loss leaders as Amtrak and the Federal Housing Administration, which insures private mortgages. Other possible initiatives: selling airport landing slots to individual carriers, for example, or letting private companies sort and deliver first-class mail.

Actually, in this country municipal governments have gotten the jump on the feds—contracting out for everything from hospital care to airport management. The town of La Mirada, California, has been one of the leaders, using the private sector for almost all key services—including police and fire protection, social welfare, and public works. Phoenix, Arizona, has saved millions of dollars by having its municipal agencies bid against outside companies for city contracts. A money-losing teaching hospital that the city of Louisville, Kentucky, turned over to a private company in 1983 is not only making money now but also providing better patient care.

Privatization, in short, has meant more efficiency and lower costs—and, usually, better service. And if it involves the sale of an asset, the government gets a whopping one-time capital gain as well. So why has privatization been so long in coming? Fact is, it's been around for some time. Privatization is just a modern-day buzzword for an old, old philosophy. Adam Smith called it the free market. We call it a pretty good deal all around.

Discussion

1. What exactly *is* privatization? Why should a citizen who is not involved in a given industry care whether or not that industry's product is provided to the government by privately owned or publicly owned producers?

2. This article was published as an advertisement paid for by the Mobil Corporation. How could publishing such an ad possibly help to sell gasoline? Does Mobil's decision to publish the ad mean that they are a special interest group? Explain your answers.

3. The advertisement cites a hospital in Louisville, Kentucky. Why do you think that the private hospital was making money while the public hospital was losing money? What sorts of generalizations can you draw from such an example?

5

Government Spending and Taxation

TRUE OR FALSE

T F

☑ ☐   1.   As one's marginal tax rate increases, the percentage of each additional dollar earned *Marg. Tax rate ⬆,* that the taxpayer is permitted to keep for personal expenditures will decline. *% $ earned for personal exp. ⬇*

☑ ☐   2.   If the supply curve of labor were perfectly vertical, the burden of an earnings (or payroll) tax would fall entirely on the employee in the form of a lower after-tax wage rate.

☑ ☐   3.   A tax that takes more dollars from a low-income recipient than it takes from a high-income recipient must be regressive.

☐ ☑   4.   Total government expenditures amount to approximately 20 percent of GNP in the United States.

☐ ☑   5.   The underground economy's share of GNP can best be measured by calculating the share of income taxes that comes from the underground economy.

☑ ☐   6.   Federal expenditures on cash income maintenance constitute a larger share of the federal budget than do expenditures for national defense.

☐ ☑   7.   A tax that is equitable is sure to be economically inefficient because the concepts of equity and efficiency are inherently opposed.

☐ ☑   8.   If the percentage of income that is taxed away increases as an individual's income increases, the tax must be regressive.

PROBLEMS AND PROJECTS

1.   Has government spending been increasing or decreasing in recent years? How have defense and nondefense government expenditures changed since 1960? In dollar terms, how large are per capita government (local, state, and federal) expenditures in the United States? [The *Statistical Abstract of the United States* (annual) and *Facts and Figures on Government Finance* (New York: Tax Foundation, Inc., biannual) will contain the information necessary to answer these questions.]

2.   Suppose that you were running for Congress:
     a.   Write a short campaign position paper outlining your platform on government spending and taxation policy. If you advocate any new programs, what would you say about their tax cost?
     b.   Do you think your positions will help you raise campaign finances? Will they help you get elected? Why or why not? Address these questions in a letter to your finance chairman.

3. Assume that a massive tax reform bill changes the current federal income tax rate schedule to the following simple tax schedule:

Income (dollars)	Marginal tax rate
Under 20,000	10%
20,000–50,000	20%
Over 50,000	30%

a. If your income is $30,000, what is your total tax? (*Hint:* it is not $6,000; that would be correct if 20% were the average tax rate.)
b. If your income is $60,000, what is your total tax?
c. Is this tax schedule progressive or regressive?
d. Assume that the tax bill included indexed marginal tax rates and that inflation last year was 10%. Calculate what the new (indexed) tax schedule would be.

4. Exhibit 1 summarizes a portion of the U.S. federal income tax schedule for married couples filing jointly in 1983.

Exhibit 1

Bracket number	Taxable income	Total tax
1	$12,000	$ 1,166
2	24,000	3,518
3	36,000	6,904
4	48,000	11,214
5	60,000	16,014
6	72,000	21,294
7	84,000	26,574

a. Calculate the average tax rate for brackets 2 and 6. Is this tax rate structure proportional, regressive, or progressive?
b. Calculate the marginal tax rate for a married couple whose income increases from bracket 1 to bracket 2. From bracket 5 to bracket 6. Are these marginal rates greater or smaller than the corresponding average you calculated in part a?

c. Suppose that the tax structure in 1982 was the same as that in Exhibit 1. Suppose also that you had a money income of $48,000 in 1982 and that your money income rose to $60,000 in 1983. If the rate of inflation between 1982 and 1983 had been 25 percent, would you have had an increase in your *constant purchasing power* (real) income? Would you have been required to pay a higher percentage of your income in income taxes? What phenomenon does this represent?

5. Exhibit 2 shows average income tax rates and the aggregate amount of taxable income that would be generated by economic activity at each rate.

Exhibit 2

Average tax rate (percent)	Aggregate taxable income (billions)	Tax revenue (billions)
20	$600	$120
30	500	—
40	450	—
50	400	—
60	350	—
70	300	—
80	250	—

a. Fill in the remaining entries in the tax revenue column.
b. On a piece of graph paper, plot the relationship between the tax rate (on the vertical axis) and tax revenues (on the horizontal axis). What is this relationship called?

LEARNING THE MECHANICS—MULTIPLE CHOICE

1. In the United States, the total tax revenues of the federal, state, and local governments constitute
   a. approximately one-tenth of the gross national product.
   b. approximately one-fifth of the gross national product.
   c. approximately one-third of the gross national product.
   d. approximately one-half of the gross national product.

2. The size of the public sector relative to total ouput is smaller in one of the following countries than for the United States. Which one?
   a. Japan
   b. France
   c. United Kingdom
   d. Sweden

3. The "incidence" of a tax is the term that indicates
   a. the person who is responsible for paying the tax to the Federal Treasury.
   b. the person who actually bears the burden of the tax.
   c. whether the tax is progressive.
   d. whether the tax results in greater benefits than costs.

4. If we assume that the demand for and supply of Big Jim's Sour Mash Whiskey is described by typically sloped demand and supply curves, which of the following would be the most likely impact of a tax placed on Big Jim's whiskey?
   a. Consumers would pay more, and Big Jim would receive more.
   b. Consumers would pay more, and Big Jim would receive less.
   c. Consumers would pay the same amount, and Big Jim would receive less.
   d. Consumers would pay more, and Big Jim would receive the same amount.

5. A progressive tax
   a. takes a similar percentage from all income brackets.
   b. takes a higher percentage from higher income brackets.
   c. takes a lower percentage from higher income brackets.
   d. is one that does not impede progress.

6. If the tax liability of a couple increases from $1000 to $1200 as their income increases from $10,000 to $11,000, the couple's marginal tax rate is
   a. 10 percent.
   b. 11 percent.
   c. 12 percent.
   d. 20 percent.

7. The underground economy is another name for
   a. the black market.
   b. economic activity in underground shopping malls.
   c. unreported production and exchange (usually in cash).
   d. the oil, natural gas, and mineral industries.

8. The largest single source of revenue for local, state, and federal governments (combined) is
   a. the personal income tax.
   b. the sales tax.
   c. the property tax.
   d. the corporate income tax.

9. Which of the following categories represents the largest percentage of total federal expenditures in the 1980s?
   a. Interest on the national debt
   b. Revenue sharing
   c. National defense expenditures
   d. Cash income maintenance—including such expenditures as social security, Medicare, and veterans' benefits.

10. In general, the relative size of the government sector in the United States
    a. is smaller than in countries that are just beginning to develop.
    b. is less than western European nations (such as France, West Germany, and the United Kingdom).
    c. is of no economic significance.
    d. falls primarily on the upper class.

11. Which of the following is clearly an example of a regressive tax?
    a. One that takes more from the rich than the poor
    b. One that is forward looking and leads to future economic growth
    c. One that takes a larger percentage of income as income rises
    d. One that taxes each individual the same number of dollars no matter what his income

THE ECONOMIC WAY OF THINKING—MULTIPLE CHOICE

1. Assuming that individuals are primarily concerned with their own welfare, which of the following taxes are high-income families *least* likely to prefer?
   a. A progressive tax
   b. A regressive tax
   c. A proportional tax
   d. Any type of sales tax

2. A payroll tax is *not* likely to influence
   a. the quantity of labor supplied.
   b. the quantity of labor demanded.
   c. the price of the final product.
   d. the demand for labor (as a function of *total* labor cost).

3. According to positive economic analysis, the corporate income tax
   a. is bad, compared to other taxes.
   b. is good, compared to other taxes.
   c. is, in the end, paid by individuals, since only individuals can bear the burden of taxes.
   d. is not a burden on consumers.

4. In 1986, Congress approved a new tax bill that decreased marginal tax rates and increased the tax base by eliminating a number of deductions (or tax "loopholes"). Which of the following groups would be most likely to oppose such a tax revision?
   a. Low-income taxpayers with few if any deductions
   b. Middle-income taxpayers with few if any deductions
   c. High-income taxpayers with few if any deductions
   d. Employees of an industry whose product's status as a deduction is in danger of being eliminated

5. A 2-cent-per-gallon increase in the gasoline tax caused the price of gasoline to rise by two cents with no change in quantity. The incidence of the gasoline tax fell on
    a. the producers of gasoline.
    b. gasoline station operators.
    c. gasoline station employees.
    d. the consumers of gasoline.

6. Which of the following is *most likely* to be correct?
    a. An increase in tax rates will lead to a proportional increase in tax revenues.
    b. An increase in tax rates will lead to a more than proportional increase in tax revenues.
    c. An increase in tax rates will lead to a less than proportional increase in tax revenues.
    d. An increase in tax rates will always lead to a decrease in tax revenues.

7. The excess burden of a tax refers to
    a. the loss of private purchasing power due to the revenues transferred to the public sector.
    b. the additional tax that must be levied because some taxpayers engage in tax avoidance activities.
    c. the excess tax levied on high-income taxpayers relative to a taxpayer with an average income.
    d. the additional burden imposed on taxpayers because taxes distort prices and eliminate some mutually advantageous exchanges.

8. Which of the following would occur if a nation's tax structure were fully indexed?
    a. If one's money income rose at the same rate as the nation's inflation rate, one's tax liability would be unchanged.
    b. If one's money income rose more rapidly than the inflation rate, one's average tax rate would be unchanged.
    c. If one's money income rose less rapidly than the inflation rate, one's average tax rate would increase.
    d. If one's money income rose at the same rate as the nation's inflation rate, one's average and marginal tax rates would be unchanged.

9. In order to decide whether it is worthwhile to take a second job, a smart taxpayer would consider the
    a. marginal tax rate.
    b. average tax rate.
    c. before-tax income.
    d. wage rate, independent of taxes.

10. Inflation is sometimes called the legislator's painless tax increase because (unless tax rates are indexed)
    a. inflation forces taxpayers to pay less for goods, thus raising sales tax revenues.
    b. inflation automatically pushes taxpayers into higher income tax brackets.
    c. inflation automatically increases tax rates on constant money incomes.
    d. All of the above are correct.

11. George Washington is said to have cautioned his colleagues, during the American Revolution, not to increase a particular tax rate too much for fear of raising less, and not more, revenues for the war effort. If this statement is true, which of the following does it imply about the Laffer curve?

  a. George Washington knew about the Laffer curve.
  b. Laffer stole the idea of his curve from Washington.
  c. The principle behind the Laffer curve has been understood, at least at some levels, for many years.
  d. Nothing at all; the Laffer curve has nothing to do with the relationship between tax rates and total tax revenues.

THE ECONOMIC WAY OF THINKING—DISCUSSION QUESTIONS

1. What are the major sources of federal tax revenues? State revenues? Local revenues?

2. Who bears the burden of a sales tax? Use supply-and-demand analysis to help explain your answer.

3. What's wrong with this way of thinking? "The taxes on people—particularly middle-income taxpayers—are too high. Businesses should pay higher taxes so that individuals will not have to shoulder such a heavy load. In addition, if the rich—taxpayers whose incomes are in excess of $50,000—paid higher taxes, we would cut the taxes of the average American by between 25 and 30 percent."

4. The marginal income tax rate is larger than the average rate for most individuals. For high-salaried people, the social security payroll tax goes the other way: The average rate generally is higher. Can you explain, using numerical examples?

6

Taking the Nation's Economic Pulse

TRUE OR FALSE

T	**F**		
☑	☐	1.	The gross national product (GNP) is a measure of the market value of all "final product" goods and services that were produced during a period.
☑	☐	2.	Typically, a gallon of whiskey adds several times more to GNP than does a gallon of water.
☐	☑	3.	If you paid $800 for a used motorcycle last year, the sale contributed $800 toward last year's GNP.
☐	☑	4.	GNP minus depreciation is equal to national income.
☑	☐	5.	Disposable income is that portion of GNP that is left for households to spend or save as they choose.
☑	☐	6.	In recent years in the United States, disposable income has constituted approximately 70 percent of GNP.
☐	☑	7.	GNP, net national product (NNP), and national income measure different things; thus, they often move in opposite directions.
☐	☑	8.	Net national product (NNP) is the GNP minus the negative aspects of production, such as pollution and the depletion of national resources.
☐	☑	9.	The discovery of a $100 billion Alaskan oil field in 1969 increased GNP by that amount during that year.
☐	☑	10.	If one wanted to measure the change in the annual output of goods and services between 1970 and 1976, money GNP would be a more reliable indicator than real GNP.
☑	☐	11.	During a period of deflation, an increase in real GNP would be greater than the increase in money GNP.
☐	☑	12.	Real per capita GNP in 1973 was approximately three times the 1930 level. This means that the standard of living in 1973 was three times the 1930 level.

47

PROBLEMS AND PROJECTS

1. Exhibit 1 presents economic data for the United States (in billions of dollars) for 1985.

Exhibit 1

Government purchases	$ 815	Indirect business taxes	$ 339
Net exports	−74	Corporate profits	299
Interest income	288	Rents	14
Total personal consumption	2582	Gross private investment	670
Depreciation	438	Compensation of employees	2373
Proprietors' Income	242	Durable goods compensation	361

   a. Calculate GNP and NNP using the expenditure approach.
   b. Calculate GNP and NNP using the resource cost–income approach.

2. Fill in the missing information in Exhibit 2.

Exhibit 2

	GNP (billions)	GNP Deflator (1972 = 100)	Real GNP (1972 dollars)
1970	$ 973	91.45	—
1980	2626	117.36	—

3. Given the following information, calculate GNP and NNP.

Employee compensation	10
Rents	20
Government expenditures	30
Depreciation	40
Gross private investment	50
Personal income taxes	60
Net exports	70
Personal consumption	80
Interest income	90

4. Below is a list of purchases that will occur this year. In the blank preceding each purchase description, place a + if the purchase should be included as part of this year's GNP, place a 0 if it should not count, and place a − if it should be counted negatively (subtracted).

   _____ a. Jim Halstead purchases a hamburger at Fuddrucker's.

   _____ b. Betty Tracy gets a haircut at the Haircutters.

   _____ c. John Keynes buys a share of I.B.M. stock.

   _____ d. Los Angeles County pays Norm Olson for being a substitute teacher.

   _____ e. Robby Moore buys a tennis racket at Eagle Rock Sports Shop.

   _____ f. The Eagle Rock Sports Shop purchases a tennis racket from France.

   _____ g. Manuel Pastor buys a two-year-old car from Betsy Hamilton.

5. Below is a list of activities that occurred in 1985. In the blank preceding each activity description, place a + if the activity would have a positive impact on 1985's GNP, place a − if it would have a negative effect, and place a 0 if it would have no effect.

_____ a.   Ms. Feldman hires a male housekeeper who previously was unemployed.

_____ b.   Ms. Feldman marries her housekeeper, so he no longer receives a salary.

_____ c.   Eric Newhall, a physician, and Michael McAleenan, a lawyer, decide to stop billing each other and simply trade their services.

_____ d.   You work twice as hard during the current school term and as a result your grade point average doubles.

_____ e.   A window in Norm Cohen's new beach house is blown out by a storm and he has it replaced.

_____ f.   Your parents decide to add mowing the lawn to your list of household duties (rather than continuing to hire a lawn-care service).

LEARNING THE MECHANICS—MULTIPLE CHOICE

1. Real GNP, as contrasted with money GNP, refers to
    a.   money GNP minus gifts to other countries.
    b.   money GNP minus total unemployment compensation.
    c.   money GNP adjusted for price changes.
    d.   money GNP adjusted for unemployment changes.

2. Assume that between 1970 and 1980 money GNP increased from $1000 billion to $2500 billion, and the index of prices increased from 100 to 200. Which of the following expresses GNP for 1980 in terms of 1970 prices?
    a. $1000 billion
    b. $1250 billion
    c. $2500 billion
    d. $5000 billion

3. From the producer's viewpoint, GNP is best thought of as
    a.   an indicator of the good things produced during this period.
    b.   an indicator of the total wealth of a nation.
    c.   an indicator of the costs that were incurred by the producers of goods during the period.
    d.   an indicator of the social welfare of the nation.

4. The GNP deflator is designed to measure the degree to which
    a.   incomes are distributed among the poor and rich over time.
    b.   the cost of purchasing a bundle of consumer goods has changed with time.
    c.   consumption patterns have changed with time because of higher prices.
    d.   consumer prices have risen, relative to wages.

5. In terms of 1970 dollars, the 1980 real GNP is the 1980 money GNP [GD stands for GNP deflator]
    a.   multiplied by (GD_{70}/GD_{80}).
    b.   multiplied by (GD_{80}/GD_{70}).
    c.   divided by the GD in 1970.
    d.   divided by the difference between the 1980 and 1970 GD.

6. Which of the following would *not* be counted as part of this year's GNP?
   a. The increase in the value of an antique automobile that was refurbished during the year
   b. The value of a new automobile
   c. The value of a used car at its sale price
   d. The replacement of a worn-out machine used to clean golf balls

7. The largest component of gross national product is
   a. consumption expenditures.
   b. investment expenditures.
   c. government expenditures.
   d. net exports.

8. GNP may be calculated as the sum of
   a. personal consumption expenditures, net private investment expenditures, government purchases, and net exports.
   b. personal consumption expenditures, gross private investment expenditures, and depreciation.
   c. employee compensation, proprietors' income, rents, interest, corporate profits, and net private investment.
   d. net national product and depreciation.

   Use the following table to answer questions 9–12.

Personal consumption expenditures	900
Depreciation	130
Indirect business taxes and business transfers	150
Social security contributions	100
Corporate profits	100
Government transfer payments, net interest paid, and business transfer payments	180
Personal taxes	180
Government purchases	300
Dividends	40
Employee compensation	900
Interest income	60
Proprietors' income	100
Rents	40

9. What is net national product?
   a. 1200
   b. 1260
   c. 1350
   d. 1480

10. What is personal income?
    a. 1050
    b. 1110
    c. 1220
    d. 1350

11. What is disposable income?
    a. 1000
    b. 1040
    c. 1110
    d. 1350

12. What is gross national product?
    a. 1200
    b. 1260
    c. 1350
    d. 1480

THE ECONOMIC WAY OF THINKING—MULTIPLE CHOICE

1. The way in which water or air pollution currently affects the measurement of GNP is that the cost of
    a. pollution is completely ignored because it does not affect economic well-being.
    b. any cleaning up of pollution is added to GNP as part of output.
    c. any clean-up campaigns are subtracted from GNP.
    d. pollution damage is subtracted from GNP.

2. Which of the following constitutes a major shortcoming of GNP?
    a. Goods produced but not exchanged during that period are excluded.
    b. It tends to understate the growth of economic welfare.
    c. The value of production that does not involve a monetary exchange is often excluded.
    d. The inclusion of profit is inappropriate, since it does not measure the well-being of the consumers.

3. If you were asked to study the production of the economy during the last three years, you would use the real GNP series rather than the nominal (or money) series because
    a. the nominal series is more complete than the real series, since it includes the production of the government.
    b. the nominal series is less precise, since it does not take into account the externalities from production; the real series does.
    c. the nominal series does not adjust for underemployment of the workers; the real series does.
    d. the nominal series reflects changes in both output and prices; the real series is designed to reflect changes in output only.

4. If the market values of all the goods and services produced during a given year were summed, which of the following would be true with respect to the total for that year?
    a. It would be equal to GNP.
    b. It would be greater than GNP.
    c. It would be less than GNP.
    d. It would ignore the consumer's valuation of the goods and services produced.

5. The GNP deflator
    a. measures the average level of prices now compared with expected prices in the future.
    b. measures the relative dollar value of a given "bundle" of goods and/or services at different points in time.
    c. pertains to all goods and services rather than an array of goods and/or services.
    d. represents a weighted average of price increases adjusted for quality changes.

6. Suppose that the dollar value of GNP increased by approximately 3 percent between January and May of some year, but the real GNP decreased by 2 percent during that period. Which of the following best explains the phenomenon?
   a. Prices rose by approximately 3 percent.
   b. Prices fell by approximately 2 percent.
   c. The real capacity of the economy was increasing more quickly than money output.
   d. Prices increased by approximately 5 percent.

7. Some economists prefer the concept of NNP over GNP because
   a. it is more easily calculated.
   b. depreciation is difficult to estimate.
   c. it counts net additions, not gross additions, to the capital stock.
   d. NNP is larger.

8. Real GNP differs from money GNP in that
   a. real GNP measures the value of only tangible products, omitting the value of services.
   b. real GNP is corrected for changes in the price level and is therefore not upwardly biased during inflationary periods.
   c. real GNP corrects for depreciation.
   d. real GNP is more easily calculated than money GNP in that prices need not be known.

9. Real GNP may give a misleading measure of change in national output between two periods because
   a. the price level may change.
   b. the share of production being carried out in the nonmarket sector may change between the two periods.
   c. new goods may be produced in the latter period that cannot be easily compared to earlier goods.
   d. Both b and c are correct.

10. The concept of MEW—measure of economic welfare—modifies traditional GNP data in what way?
   a. The estimated cost of economic "bads" such as pollution are subtracted from GNP, whereas the estimated value of nonmarket goods such as leisure are added to GNP.
   b. The impact of inflation is subtracted from GNP.
   c. Expenditures on necessities such as national defense are added to GNP.
   d. The estimated value of depreciation is subtracted from GNP.

THE ECONOMIC WAY OF THINKING—DISCUSSION QUESTIONS

1. Indicate two alternative methods of deriving GNP. Explain why the two yield the same answer.

2. Explain the difference between the money GNP and real GNP. Does it make any difference which of the two is used to gauge economic activity? Explain.

3. Why do government agencies collect data on GNP? Why are private citizens interested in this information? Is GNP data more useful than past data on climatic conditions (for example, monthly rainfall, average temperature, and average days of sunshine)? Explain.

4. What are some of the deficiencies of GNP as a measure of aggregate output? Why do national income accountants not correct these shortcomings?

5. If one seeks to measure output during a period, why should only production of final goods and services be counted?

6. How does MEW differ from GNP? Is it an improvement? Why?

7. Is a higher GNP always better than a lower GNP? Why or why not? What about consumption; is more consumption always a good thing? Why or why not?

PERSPECTIVES IN ECONOMICS

GNP: Pluses and Minuses
Morgan Guaranty Trust Company

[From *Morgan Guaranty Survey*, June 1970, pp. 9–13. Reprinted with the permission of the Morgan Guaranty Trust Company.]

The gross national product in recent years has basked in the warm glow of nearly universal praise. Economists, quite naturally, have been freest with the encomiums. Where else but the GNP could they get in one tidy number a measure of the growth in the mammoth U.S. economy? Businessmen, though not entirely persuaded of the value of statistics, especially esoteric statistics, nevertheless have been known to quote the GNP—possibly because of its powers to impress audiences with the speaker's grasp of the "big picture." Politicians, too, have been extravagant in their admiration of GNP, most especially when it was rising at a brisk pace. Even the ubiquitous cocktail party has paid homage to the GNP as assorted junior executives, research assistants, housewives, and dancing instructors have pronounced on the latest GNP numbers with a solemn and knowing air.

Now all that seems to be changing. GNP increasingly is coming under attack. Dr. Arthur F. Burns, Chairman of the Federal Reserve Board, told Congress recently: "The gross national product—which has been deceiving us all along—is a good deal lower than we think it is." Richard A. Falk, a professor of international law at Princeton told a Congressional committee not long ago: If the U.S. were to double its GNP, I would think it would be a much less livable society than it is today." And Representative Henry S. Reuss of Wisconsin warned earlier this year that "as our GNP grows, national pollution also grows every year."

Such comments suggest a need to take a new hard look at GNP, at what it is and—equally significant—what it is not.

Amoral GNP At the outset, it is important to realize that GNP is an estimate of the *market value* of goods and services produced. The unit of account is always dollars. What is equally important to remember is the GNP measures only those goods and services which are exchanged for money in the market place. In other words, what people, or business, or government are willing to *pay for* gets into the national income and product accounts. Few distinctions are made among the types of expenditures. Thus, the dollars spent in dedicated pursuit of a cancer cure carry the same weight in the GNP as the wages of a lackadaisical ecdysiast. Official compilers of the GNP routinely calculate money spent for medical care, new homes, whiskey, tobacco, and plastic objets d'art. To those who object on aesthetic or even moral grounds, the standard reply is that GNP measures what people actually buy, not what they *ought* to buy. The latter is thought by economists to be more the province of a higher occupational order, such as saints. It should be noted, however, that the accounting rules are not entirely indifferent to moral considerations. Hence, GNP does not include economic activity that stems from illegal operations—such as a bookie parlor, an illicit still, or a doxy's den.

Janus-Faced GNP Thus it is clear that estimating the value of the nation's total spending depends on application of some fairly rigid—some would say arbitrary—rules of inclusion and exclusion. Economic scholars over the years have discussed ways to improve the GNP. Their suggestions can be conveniently split into two groups, the "pluses" and the "minuses." The former school argues that more items should be added to the accounts when striking a total. This school thinks that the GNP, by excluding nonpaid items such as work done by housewives, significantly *understates* the nation's output. Those in the "minuses" group, while not necessarily unreceptive to the other group's proposals, nevertheless see a different set of deficiencies. They charge that GNP is *overstating* national income and progress because it does not, for example, take account of the deterioration of the environment.

At present, the "minuses" school seems to be dominating the headlines. Dr. Burns, for example, while strongly backing maximum production, is suggesting that the nation develop and stress a more meaningful *net* national product, or NNP. This is GNP after deducting the value of capital goods used up in the production process. Such depreciation or capital consumption currently is running about $80 billion a year. From this NNP (published quarterly along with GNP data), Dr. Burns would additionally deduct some unspecified amount that would represent depreciation in the environment.

To illustrate the point, assume that a manufacturer flushes waste products into a river. If $1,000 were spent to remove the sludge from the waterway, such spending would increase the GNP by a like amount. If no effort is made to deal with the pollution there is no effect on GNP. Economists argue that this is improper since, in fact, the situation is analogous to the depreciation of capital assets. In the waterway case, however, the fixed asset is the environment and its depreciation is called pollution. What is wrong with present accounting procedures, according to these analyses, is that pollution has not been removed from GNP in the calculations of the NNP.

Admittedly, adjusting GNP accounting rules to embrace allowances for social values presents some abstruse conceptual problems. Until fairly recently, such social costs were not overwhelmingly important. The elements of the environment were so vast that they appeared to be inexhaustible. Air, for example, was considered to be a "free good." Although air is necessary to life, it was so abundantly available that no one could sell it at a positive price. As a consequence, the destruction of the usefulness of such a prevalent commodity imposed no costs on society.

Now, of course, things are different. There is much concern about the air these days as more and more people in urban areas have come to realize that they cannot breathe deeply without some risk to lung tissue. Air no longer is "free": there is some "cost" to the user.

But how much do you deduct from GNP for dirty air? Or for streams that no longer support fish or waterfowl? Or for a scenic view bulldozed out of existence? For such as these (the list could easily be expanded), any reasonable person would agree that some deduction should be made. But how much? Calculated in what way?

Goodies And Baddies The only practical method so far discovered is to follow the simple test of marketability—can it be sold for a price? Presumably, if people want breathable air, drinkable water, and the noise levels of a sternly supervised library then they will spend the money needed to pay for it all. Such spending is included in the GNP. But the offsetting "depreciation" that makes these expenditures necessary is not now deducted from GNP in arriving at NNP. This is not to say, of course, that the market value approach to calculating environmental depreciation would be easy to apply or entirely satisfactory. But inspired intellectual effort surely could produce a method to account for what one observer has called "man-made bads" to offset the "man-made goods" that go into the GNP.

It is undoubtedly true, as Dr. Burns states, that a GNP which does not take account of environmental pollution overstates growth and progress of the nation. The affluent society, measured by an expanding GNP, is not so affluent as the official numbers indicate.

Or is it? There are, after all, a number of sizable "pluses" not in the GNP which could be added. If this were done, the "minus" of environmental pollution might very well be more than offset.

The single largest item not counted in GNP is the value of work done in the home by housewives. However much this may appear as an antifeminist manifestation, suitable for protestations by women's liberation groups, the plain fact is that placing a value on home-tending presents some very tricky problems in estimation. Besides, unpaid productive work done by husbands in the home, too, does not get into the GNP. An example of such work would be the turning of a basement into a finished playroom. Only the purchased materials would swell GNP; the husband's work would add nothing to GNP even though his house would increase in value as a consequence of the added playroom. However, if the housewife or the husband hired someone to clean the house or finish off the basement, such spending would find its way into GNP.

Other examples of "pluses" that are left out: no allowance is made in GNP for volunteer work, and it is only the out-of-pocket cost, rather than the time spent or the wisdom acquired, that measures the contribution of education. Similarly, no estimates are made of the "income" received by people from services in the public sector—such as use of a park, highway, or library. People receive benefits from such facilities year after year, and yet GNP records only the initial cost when the facility is built and its subsequent maintenance. Here again there are immense problems of estimation. Not all people have access to public facilities, the quality of which, in any case, varies widely all across the nation.

Finally, GNP treats the value of spending on consumer durable goods in different ways depending on their ownership. For instance, money spent by an auto rental agency for its fleet of automobiles is included in the GNP. So is the money spent by people and business to rent the autos year after year. On the other hand, money spent by an individual purchasing a car for himself gets into the GNP only once—as a personal consumption expenditure at time of purchase, even though the buyer will get a stream of services, no different from those he would get from a rental auto, for several years. In other words the "service income" to the owner of any consumer durable good—auto, refrigerator, washing machine, TV—is left out of the GNP.

An exception is made in the case of an owner-occupied house. Since the rent on rented dwellings goes into GNP, the comparable service enjoyed by homeowners from their own dwellings is also included so that the total is not subject to variation resulting merely from changes in the proportion of home ownership. Homeowners simply are regarded as landlords who rent to themselves at going local rates. If all consumer durable goods were to be treated the same way as housing, the result, of course, would be a larger GNP.

Policies that would produce no growth in GNP undoubtedly would hold down pollution. But "costs" to society would be heavy. For one thing, antipollution efforts themselves cost money. Only increased production can provide the resources to tackle pollution—and to reduce poverty, keep up the nation's defenses, meet housing needs, and a thousand other things. Suggestions that consumption of goods be restricted to lessen pollution have a surface kind of logic. But, in practice, what goods would be restricted? From the hands of what groups of people? Would this require the setting up of a new agency: The Department of Consumer Privation? The nation's poor do not have the feeling that they are consuming to an excessive degree. Nor do the millions in the middle class who, after paying taxes and making the mortgage payment, are barely able to keep their heads above water. They would find little comfort if the quagmire that engulfed them when GNP stopped growing were a little purer.

Those who are asking whether the nation can survive with pollution are asking the wrong question. It is unfortunate but true that the nation cannot survive without pollution. The answer is not to jettison growth and push for an anemic GNP, but rather to channel economic growth in new directions. More resources and more talent can be applied to reducing pollution to tolerable levels. In the case of automobiles, for example, increased inputs of capital and labor to produce autos that do not emit noxious fumes would be more sensible than closing down assembly lines to produce fewer automobiles. In short, there need not be a basic contradiction between growth and a livable environment. It is not necessary or even possible to choose one and abandon the other.

Discussion

1. Has the article outlined all the possible errors of commission or omission in the calculation of GNP? If not, what other errors are possible?

2. Should reading this book count toward our nation's GNP? Why or why not?

3. If GNP has so many faults as a measure of macroeconomic activity, what value could it possibly have in today's world?

7

Economic Fluctuations, Unemployment, and Inflation

TRUE OR FALSE

T F

☐ ☐ 1. A business cycle is a series of fluctuations in an aggregate measure of current economic production.

☐ ☐ 2. Frictional unemployment implies a lack of jobs available.

☐ ☐ 3. Faster adoption of technological changes would probably increase structural unemployment, since some jobs would disappear more quickly than they would otherwise.

☐ ☐ 4. Unanticipated inflation changes the terms of exchange for long-term contracts.

☐ ☐ 5. World War II was characterized by high rates of unemployment.

☐ ☐ 6. The consumer price index is to consumption as the GNP deflator is to money income.

☐ ☐ 7. Insufficient aggregate demand is the root cause of structural, but not frictional, unemployment.

☐ ☐ 8. If a corn blight destroyed half of next year's corn crop and drove corn prices up, the result would properly be called inflation.

☐ ☐ 9. Since the turn of the century, the United States has not experienced deflation.

☐ ☐ 10. Only since 1950 has increased inflation accompanied U.S. participation in wars.

PROBLEMS AND PROJECTS

1. Write a short essay outlining the usefulness of the rates of both employment and unemployment as indicators of how well the potential labor force has been utilized from 1971 to the present. Use data from Exhibit 6 in Chapter 7 of the text and update it with more recent figures from the *Monthly Labor Review* (available in your library). Explain how it is possible that the two rates can sometimes move in the same direction.

2. Classify the following unemployed workers as either (a) frictional, (b) structural, or (c) cyclical.

_____ (1) John Smith, a college student, has spent two weeks trying unsuccessfully to find a summer job so he can return to college in the fall.

_____ (2) Carol Jones has not been able to find a job after completing high school and initially entering the labor force.

_____ (3) A sharp cutback in the space program has cost Harold Robinson his $40,000-a-year job as an aerospace engineer. Prospects for employment as an engineer are exceedingly dim. Harold has not been able to find a satisfactory job in other lines of work since his termination six weeks ago.

_____ (4) Sue Blair is re-entering the labor force after having a baby, but has not yet found work.

_____ (5) Fred Mack is one of 10,000 auto workers laid off because of a sharp decline in GNP during the last six months.

_____ (6) Hal Freer, a coal miner, can no longer find work as a miner because automation has reduced the demand for mining labor.

_____ (7) Pat Colson is one of 70 United Airlines pilots laid off after an economic slowdown caused a sharp reduction in the demand for air transportation.

3. a. Because of the time it takes to publish and distribute a book, the inflation and unemployment figures in the text are recent, but not current. Update your knowledge by investigating (in the library) and discovering the current figures (one source is the *Monthly Labor Review*).

   b. Use the above information to decide exactly where the economy is (boom, recession, etc.) with respect to the business cycle.

4. Exhibit 1 presents information from the *Economic Report of the President* regarding population and employment for selected years. Use the data given to calculate the unemployment and labor force participation rates in the last four columns. (*Hint:* Sufficient data are present to make these calculations.)

Exhibit 1

Year	Civilian noninstitutional population	Resident armed forces	Labor force (including armed forces)	Employment (including armed forces)	Unemployment rate (percent)		Labor force participation rate (percent)	
			(Millions of persons 16 years and up)		Total	Civilian	Total	Civilian
1954	108.3	2.1	65.8	62.3	5.3	5.5	59.6	58.8
1964	124.5	2.0	75.1	71.3	—	—	—	—
1974	150.1	1.7	93.7	88.5	—	—	—	—
1984	176.4	1.7	115.2	106.7	—	—	—	—

5. Official definitions of employment status lead to ambiguities and often strange results. The following list represents a variety of job situations for the individuals involved. In the blank preceding each situation, place *U* to designate when the situation means officially unemployed, *E* to designate officially employed, and *N* to mean not officially in the labor force.

    _____   a. Ralph Amey has stopped looking for a job because he believes that employment prospects in his line of work are so poor that it is unlikely he will find work.

    _____   b. Rick Gilman is actively looking for work as a college administrator but meanwhile has worked one hour each weekday as a substitute teacher.

    _____   c. Don Goldland could not find work as a mathematician and decided to re-enroll in school for a refresher course in advanced topology.

    _____   d. Rex Nelson will start his job at JPL in six weeks.

    _____   e. Cindy Schroeder has decided not to accept a $6.00/hour job offer she received last week because she prefers to go to the beach.

LEARNING THE MECHANICS—MULTIPLE CHOICE

1. Frictional unemployment results from
    a. not enough jobs in the economy.
    b. not enough employers.
    c. not enough employees.
    d. scarce information about job opportunities and the time it takes to acquire that information.

2. The definition of the unemployment rate is
    a. the number of persons in the country who are not employed.
    b. the number of persons in the civilian labor force who are not employed.
    c. the percentage of persons in the country who are not employed.
    d. the percentage of persons in the civilian labor force who are not employed.

3. When an economist states the economy is at "full employment," he/she usually means that
    a. there are no unemployed workers.
    b. all those willing to work have jobs, but those not desiring work are unemployed.
    c. about 95 percent of the labor force is employed.
    d. 100 percent of the people are working or looking for a job.

4. Inflation is *best* described as
    a. high prices.
    b. an increase in the level of prices as indicated by a price index.
    c. an increase in the purchasing power of money.
    d. an increase in the price of a particular good or service that is necessary for all consumers.

5. Inflation in the United States
    a. was positive during the Great Depression.
    b. has averaged about 5 percent during the last 40 years.
    c. was higher during war than during peacetime (until 1974).
    d. has been quite constant since World War II.

6. If the Consumer Price Index in 1981 was 300 and the CPI in 1982 was 315, the rate of inflation was
    a. 5 percent.
    b. 10 percent.
    c. 15 percent.
    d. 315 percent.

7. The rate of labor force participation is
    a. the number of persons employed divided by the number of persons unemployed.
    b. the number of persons 16 years of age and older who are either employed or actively seeking work divided by the total noninstitutional population 16 years of age and older.
    c. the number of persons employed divided by the number of persons 16 years of age and older.
    d. the number of persons who are actively seeking work divided by the number of persons who are employed.

8. Debtors gain at the expense of creditors when
    a. prices rise.
    b. prices fall.
    c. prices rise unexpectedly.
    d. prices fall unexpectedly.

9. Which of the following is the best example of inflation?
    a. An increase in the price of food
    b. An increase in the general price level but *not* in every product
    c. An increase in the price of almost every product but (because of some large price decreases) not in the general price level
    d. A decrease in the price of food

10. Structural unemployment means that
    a. employment in the building trades is insufficient.
    b. there are simply not enough jobs to go around.
    c. worker qualifications do not match available jobs.
    d. jobs are plentiful, but workers are scarce.

11. Historical data for the period 1930 to 1980 indicate that
    a. regular business cycles have occurred in the United States approximately every three years.
    b. unemployment has stayed within a rather narrow range, between 1 and 3 percent.
    c. when all the booms and contractions are averaged out, the economy has grown at an average annual rate of approximately 3 to 4 percent.
    d. unemployment has averaged about 6 percent during the 45-year period.

12. Potential GNP
    a. is always less than actual GNP, except during recessions.
    b. minus actual GNP is a measure of production lost due to a business slowdown.
    c. is a measure of the minimum that an economy could be reasonably expected to continue producing at any time.
    d. is 95 to 96 percent of actual GNP, during periods of full employment.

THE ECONOMIC WAY OF THINKING—MULTIPLE CHOICE

1. Even in a truly "efficient" economy, one would expect *some* unemployment because
   a. as an individual, if you wait for a better job offer, you may be better off in the longer run.
   b. wages will increase even when prices are constant.
   c. some persons' expectations are always correct.
   d. unemployment provides the best incentive for stimulating persons to search more diligently for a job.

2. The work force over the last 50 years has changed so that there now is a higher percentage of women in the work force who also have husbands present in the work force. This change quite possibly means that a 10 percent unemployment rate *now* would be
   a. perhaps a bit less catastrophic to families than a 10 percent unemployment rate 50 years ago.
   b. perhaps a bit more catastrophic to families than a 10 percent unemployment rate 50 years ago.
   c. just as catastrophic to families as a 10 percent unemployment rate 50 years ago.
   d. impossible to compare to a 10 percent unemployment rate 50 years ago.

3. Frictional unemployment
   a. would decrease if unemployment compensation payments rose.
   b. would increase if improved methods of disseminating job information among unemployed workers were developed.
   c. would decrease if every individual in the economy had perfect information.
   d. is caused primarily by improper management of government expenditures.

4. As an economy begins to climb out of a long recession, the price index will initially be most likely to
   a. change very little because of an abundance of idle plants, machinery, and manpower.
   b. fall until the deferred consumption demand can be made effective through higher levels of real income.
   c. rise substantially because the expected future increase in prices will stimulate current consumption and investment purchases, thereby giving rise to a situation of excess demand.
   d. rise rapidly because aggregate demand exceeds aggregate supply, thereby forcing inventory levels to fall.

5. In the economy of Myopia, the expected rate of inflation is always zero, and inflation comes as a complete surprise to the Myopians. Their neighbors to the north in Pessimismia, however, always expect 100% inflation and are shocked when the price level rises by less than that (which it always does). Which of the following would you rather be?
   a. A lender in Myopia
   b. A borrower in Pessimismia
   c. A lender in Pessimismia
   d. This question is impossible to answer without knowing more.

6. To most economists, economic growth is
   a. one goal, among others.
   b. not possible without deflation.
   c. clearly undesirable, in view of environmental concerns.
   d. impossible without the decline in demand for labor that generally accompanies high rates of unemployment.

7. The ability to make more accurate forecasts of changes in the aggregate economic conditions would
   a. enable us to adopt policies that would eliminate frictional unemployment.
   b. greatly facilitate our ability to adopt public policy that would reduce cyclical unemployment.
   c. allow us to reduce structural, but not cyclical, unemployment.
   d. make it possible for wise macroeconomic policy to eliminate all unemployment.

8. Unanticipated inflation
   a. will normally hurt creditors, but help borrowers.
   b. has never been a problem for modern economies.
   c. increases the purchasing power of those on fixed incomes.
   d. does not have any noticeable effects.

9. An appropriate description of stagflation is a period when
   a. the male deer gains weight.
   b. an economy is experiencing both substantial inflation and a slow growth in real output.
   c. the rate of employment is rising more slowly than the rate of unemployment.
   d. an economy is experiencing both inflation and unemployment.

10. Which of the following courses of action does *not* make sense if you anticipate an increase in inflation next year?
    a. Attempt to obtain an increased salary to offset the oncoming inflation.
    b. Lend money at an interest rate that is less than the rate of inflation you expect.
    c. Borrow money at an interest rate that is less than the rate of inflation you expect.
    d. Purchase an asset whose value is likely to increase faster than the expected future rate of inflation.

11. Use I and II to choose the correct answer. (**I**) The natural rate of unemployment is increased by public policy, which reduces the worker's opportunity cost of rejecting job offers while he or she continues to search for a more attractive job. (**II**) The natural rate of unemployment rose during the 1970s as the proportion of the labor force made up of youthful workers increased.
    a. I is true, II is false.
    b. I is false, II is true.
    c. Both I and II are true.
    d. Both I and II are false.

12. In a properly operating, dynamic economy
    a. the unemployment rate should remain near zero.
    b. we would expect to have some unemployment, since some labor force participants would temporarily be out of work while changing jobs.
    c. the rate of unemployment will show a slight upward trend as prices rise.
    d. the rate of unemployment will show a slight downward trend as prices fall.

THE ECONOMIC WAY OF THINKING—DISCUSSION QUESTIONS

1. What is inflation? If the price of swimming pools rose during an extremely hot summer, would this be inflationary? How does one measure inflation?

2. Are there some "unemployed" rental apartments in the town (city) where you live? Why? If the occupancy rate were 100 percent, do you think this would be a sign of economic efficiency? Explain.

3. "The burden of inflation falls heavily on savers and creditors, for example, upon wealthy bondholders"—Campbell McConnell, *Economics,* 6th ed. (New York: McGraw-Hill, 1975), p. 380. Is this view correct? Explain.

4. "As long as people are free either to accept or reject a job, some unemployment will be present." Do you agree or disagree? Why?

5. When is an economy at full employment? How are the concepts of frictional and structural unemployment related to the definition of full employment?

6. Much of the analysis in this chapter seems to be about unemployment and inflation, but in reality it is about people. Carefully discuss who is hurt by unemployment and inflation and characterize their situations.

7. Although stagflation raises the possibility that we might be incapable of doing anything at all about inflation or unemployment, it still is important to think through which of the two problems you feel is a more difficult social illness. If you could solve one but not the other, which would you solve? Why?

PERSPECTIVES IN ECONOMICS

The Awful Year Inflation Ran Wild
by Alfred L. Malabre, Jr.

[From *The Wall Street Journal,* August 21, 1973. Reprinted with permission from The Wall Street Journal ©Dow Jones & Co., Inc. All rights reserved.]

Much has been written about the economic and social distress that can occur during a deep recession in business activity. But very little has been said about an economic experience that may today be a more appropriate matter for concern—the distress that can occur in a time of spiraling inflation.

The paucity is perhaps understandable. America's brushes with inflation have been less wrenching than its slumps. But major countries have suffered disastrous inflation in modern times, and detailed, intelligent analyses of these unhappy experiences can be found.

Two of the best involve the horrendous German inflation of the early 1920's. They are "The Economics of Inflation" by Constantino Bresciani-Turroni, an Italian economist, published in 1931, and "Exchange, Prices and Production in Hyper-Inflation: Germany, 1920–1923" by Frank D. Graham, an American economist, published in 1930.

The report that follows draws heavily from these two books, both long out of print. Some disquieting parallels with developments today may be noted, but there has been no deliberate attempt to select such material. Also, it should be stressed that Germany in that period was a defeated country, saddled with war "reparation" debts that unquestionably exacerbated the inflation problem. Inflation-torn countries today, including the U.S., are under no such burden.

Even in today's economic environment, the raw statistics of Germany's inflation make awesome reading. In August 1922, the country's money supply totaled 252 bil-

lion marks. In January 1923, it was 2 trillion. In September 1923, it stood at 28 quadrillion. And in November 1923, it reached 497 quintillion—that is, 497 followed by 18 zeros.

This runaway inflation of the money supply stopped, finally, when the currency became virtually worthless, its stated value worth literally less than the cost of the paper it was printed on. The old mark was replaced in 1924 by a new "reichsmark" whose value was set at 1 billion old marks. The old marks were withdrawn from circulation and ceased to be legal tender.

Hourly Price Changes In late 1923, near the final collapse of the currency, some companies took to reimbursing their employees with special scrip that could be used to acquire company products. Borrowing became well-nigh impossible. All sorts of goods were scarce. Food riots erupted in cities. Prices changed by the hour.

Obviously, there could be no precise record kept of the price spiral in those desperate months. But Mr. Graham's book does trace the country's wholesale price index through December 1922. At the start of the year, the index stood at 4,626 times the 1913 average. By December 1922, it reached 374,563,426,600 times the 1913 average.

Statistics bearing on other facets of the price spiral are available, however, through the entire period. Employment, perhaps surprisingly, held up quite well until just before the currency collapse. As late as July 1923, only 3.5% of the nation's trade union members were jobless. This actually was lower than the rate of 6% in July 1920, three years earlier, when prices were just beginning to spiral.

As things got out of hand near the end of 1923, however, unemployment soared. The jobless rate went from 3.5% in July to 9.9% in September to a ghastly 28.2% in December.

Mr. Graham discussed why employment as well as economic activity generally, remained at a high level until near the end: "The more rapid the rise in prices, the greater became the intensity of demand. Business boomed, unemployment vanished, sales were all too easy. There was of course an enormous amount of buying which, under other circumstances, would have been quite senseless. People purchased not what they wanted to use but whatever they could get. . . . One could produce anything material and be sure of a market.''

An index measuring the volume of the country's physical output of goods, contained in the Graham book, underscores this rising demand, before the collapse, for ''anything material.'' The index stood at 61% of the 1913 average in 1920, rose to 77% in 1921 and then climbed to 86% in 1922. A year later, however, it was down to 54%. As late as 1927, the index was still at the 1922 level.

The inflation's impact on savings also has been recorded. Depositors who left their funds in savings banks through the period lost everything. In 1913, some 19 billion marks were on deposit in savings banks. In November 1924, that sum had the purchasing power of one-quarter of an American penny. The rush to withdraw savings as inflation worsened forced many thrift institutions to close. In 1913, there were 10,890 savings-bank offices in the country. By 1924, there were only 4,870.

The story was much the same in the insurance business. In 1913, there were some 16 million life insurance policies outstanding. By 1924, the total was barely 3 million. At the worst of the price spiral, the postage stamp on an envelope containing an insurance payment to a beneficiary often cost more than the sum written on the enclosed check.

The period wasn't a happy time for stock-market investors. A share-price index was recorded by Mr. Bresciani-Turroni and has been adjusted to express values in dollar terms. It stood at 49.68 at the start of 1919. By February 1920, it was down to 8.47. Then, as business activity became more frenetic, it began to climb, reaching 26.80 by the end of 1922. The climb continued in much of 1923, but share prices plunged again near the end of the year, when economic chaos set in. A study cited by Mr. Bresciani-Turroni found that an investor who had bought a typical group of stocks in 1914 would, by 1924, have retained only one-quarter of his original investment, expressed in terms of gold. By then, company bankruptcies, which had been rare during the boom years, were widespread.

Another victim of the price spiral was efficiency. As evidence of this the Bresciani-Turroni book said that in a typical large manufacturing firm there were 120 ''unproductive'' employees for every 100 actual production-line workers in 1922. This compared with 66 for every 100 in 1913. One reason was that more office personnel were required to handle rapidly changing price lists, more frequent cost-of-living pay supplements, incessant disputes with labor unions, increasingly complex tax and accounting problems and spreading supply and production bottlenecks.

Economic Phenomena A wide range of other economic phenomena occurred. Exports rose briskly in the early inflation years, as the mark got cheaper on foreign exchange markets. But near the end, export volume sagged as shortages developed. Various export controls were imposed to try to prevent still worse shortages. At the same time, the quality of workmanship deteriorated. An ''index of quality'' for various products, published in the Frankfurter Zeitung, a newspaper, dropped from a level of 1.00 in April 1921 to 0.82 in October 1922 to 0.64 in October 1923. After the currency collapse, it began to move up again, reaching 1.24 in April 1924, a time of depressed business activity.

Other trends included a tendency toward greater economic concentration. Large companies gobbled up smaller companies. Fearing shortages, companies that produced, for example, consumer goods sought mergers with companies that supplied them with raw materials. On an individual level, inflation led to a greater concentration of wealth among the rich. Investors with sufficient financial sophistication to foresee the worsening price spiral were able to hedge much more effectively against it than the middle-class, the poor or older persons on fixed incomes.

Crime rose rapidly during the years of inflation. An index reflecting the total number of crimes committed stood at 136% of the 1882 average in 1921. By 1923, it was 170%. After the price spiral ended, however, it fell sharply, to 150% in 1924 and 122% in 1925. Crimes committed by young men, particularly, paralleled price developments. Such crimes soared to 212% of the 1882 average in 1923 and then fell to 153% in 1924 and 87% in 1925.

Other sociological ramifications of the inflation years are less easily pinpointed. It's widely held, however, that the country's increasing prejudice against Jews and the subsequent rise of Hitler can be traced to that time.

Perhaps the most puzzling aspect of the period was the willingness of German leaders to continue along the inflationary path for so long once the hazards had become clear.

Mr. Bresciani-Turroni concluded that the authorities simply lacked ''the courage to resist the pressures of those who demanded ever greater quantities of paper money, and to face boldly'' the temporary business setback that would no doubt have followed a prompter return to more conservative monetary policies. In the economist's view, this lack of courage to curb a developing boom through stricter policies, rather than the burden of World War I debts, was ''the fundamental cause of the depreciation of the mark.''

Discussion

1. If you had lived in Germany in 1923, how could you have protected yourself against inflation? What could you have done to make its impact on you as small as possible?

2. If you had any control over the economy in Germany in 1923, what would you have done to halt the inflation? (This question will be significantly easier to answer after you have read the next few chapters; when you have done so, come back to this question and try again.)

3. Could an inflation as bad as the one described above ever happen in the United States? Why or why not?

8

An Introduction to Basic Macroeconomic Markets

TRUE OR FALSE

T F

□ □ 1. Another name for the resource market might be "the market for the exchange of productive inputs."

□ □ 2. The loanable funds market is nothing more than the market for money.

□ □ 3. Aggregate demand for goods and services is composed of consumption, investment, and net exports.

□ □ 4. The aggregate demand curve is negatively sloped, as you'd expect, but the aggregate supply curve is also negatively sloped because of the natural rate of unemployment.

□ □ 5. Saving is disposable income that is not spent on consumption.

□ □ 6. Equilibrium in an aggregate market is slightly different from equilibrium in a microeconomic market, but it still allows for the simultaneous fulfillment of the plans of both buyers and sellers.

□ □ 7. The money (or nominal) interest rate equals the real interest rate plus an inflationary premium.

□ □ 8. The real interest rate is usually set equal to the expected rate of inflation.

□ □ 9. The real balance effect is the increase in wealth that comes about when aggregate prices fall while the money supply remains constant.

□ □ 10. A bond is nothing more than an IOU; if you own a bond, the issuer of that bond owes you the face amount plus whatever interest is specified (compounded until the bond's date of maturity).

□ □ 11. In the loanable funds market, the "price" of money is actually the interest rate, since the money is only loaned, not purchased permanently.

□ □ 12. When an economy is in macroeconomic equilibrium, each of the three basic macro markets (loanable funds, resources, and goods and services) must be in equilibrium.

PROBLEMS AND PROJECTS

1. Consider the data in Exhibit 1.

Exhibit 1

Year	Actual output (of goods and services)	Sustainable potential output	Unemployment rate (percent)
	(billions of 1972 dollars)		
1933	221.2	335.6	24.9
1969	1087.9	1048.4	3.5
1979	1479.4	1479.4	5.8

a. For each of these three years, draw an aggregate demand/aggregate supply diagram in which you show a short-run aggregate supply curve, a long-run aggregate supply curve, an aggregate demand curve, and the appropriate values for total output. (*Hint:* Assume that the actual output in each year occurs at the intersection between AD and SRAS.)

b. In which of these cases is the unemployment rate greater than the natural rate of unemployment? Explain briefly.

c. In which is the unemployment rate less than the natural rate? Explain briefly.

d. In which are they equal? Again, explain briefly.

2. Exhibit 2 shows the loanable funds market in which the vertical axis measures the money interest rate instead of the real interest rate. *S* and *D* are the supply and demand for loanable funds when lenders and borrowers expect zero inflation.

a. If the actual rate of inflation is zero, what will be the real rate of interest? Explain.

b. If the rate of inflation rises unexpectedly to 6 percent per year, how will the real rate of interest be affected in the short run? Explain.

c. If the inflation rate continues at 6 percent and lenders and borrowers come to expect that inflation rate, how will supply and demand (*S* and *D*) adjust to reflect these expectations? Illustrate these adjustments in the diagram. Under these circumstances, what will be the real rate of interest? Explain.

Exhibit 2

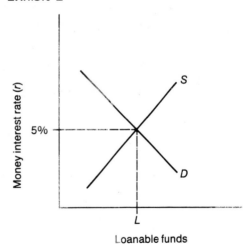

3. Consider the information in Exhibit 3:

Exhibit 3

	1979	1982	1985
Prime interest rate	12.7%	14.9%	9.5%
Inflation rate	11.3%	6.1%	3.9%
Real interest rate	_____	_____	_____

a. Fill in the blanks by calculating the real interest rate for each of the years listed. Was the real interest rate constant, rising, or falling between the three years in question? (*Hint:* The prime interest rate is a well-publicized rate that banks charge some of their better customers and is a good measure of the money rate of interest. Also, since we don't know what rates of inflation were expected, assume that the actual inflation rates are good guesses for the inflationary premiums in those years.)

b. Briefly explain how you think changes in the various interest rates influenced decisions in the loanable funds market between 1979 and 1982 and between 1982 and 1985. When would you have been increasing your willingness to loan money? When would you have been increasing your willingness to borrow? Why?

LEARNING THE MECHANICS—MULTIPLE CHOICE

1. Within the aggregate demand/aggregate supply framework, the quantity variable in the aggregate goods and services market represents
    a. the total amount of government spending.
    b. the total real output of the economy.
    c. the total unemployment of the economy.
    d. the price level of the economy.

2. Which of the following is a reason for a lower price level being associated with a larger aggregate quantity demanded for goods and services?
    a. a reduction in net exports due to the lower price level reducing the price of domestic goods compared to the price of foreign goods.
    b. an increase in interest rates which increases expenditures.
    c. a real balance effect causing purchasers to buy more.
    d. none of the above.

3. In the loanable funds market, the true burden of borrowers and the true yield to lenders derived from a loan is
    a. the real (inflation adjusted) interest rate.
    b. the nominal (money) interest rate.
    c. the inflation rate.
    d. the inflation premium rate (in money terms).

4. The natural rate of unemployment
    a. is the same as the average unemployment rate of the previous three years.
    b. is equal to zero at full employment but is usually more than zero.
    c. occurs when the economy is operating at its long-run supply capacity.
    d. occurs mainly because a certain element of our society doesn't even bother looking for a job.

5. Where the short-run aggregate supply curve intersects the long-run aggregate supply curve
    a. we are at long-run macroeconomic equilibrium.
    b. we are at the natural rate of unemployment.
    c. both a and b.
    d. neither a nor b.

6. The axes in a diagram of the resource market are the quantity of productive resources exchanged and the price of those resources. An example of a resource price is
    a. the price of a truckload of lumber.
    b. the wage of a carpenter.
    c. the price of a house built by the carpenter with the lumber.
    d. a and b but not c.

7. In the U.S. resource market, the percentage of payments that goes to labor is approximately
    a. 80%
    b. 60%
    c. 50%
    d. 40%

8. If the money interest rate is 10% and the inflationary premium is 6%, then the real interest rate is
    a. 16%
    b. 10%
    c. 6%
    d. 4%

9. If the expected rate of inflation is zero, then
    a. the real interest rate also equals zero.
    b. the money (nominal) interest rate also equals zero.
    c. the real interest rate equals the money interest rate.
    d. the economy is in long-run macroeconomic equilibrium.

10. Which of the following will increase the current demand for goods and services?
    a. An increase in the real interest rate
    b. An increase in the cost of resources
    c. An increase in the money interest rate
    d. An increase in the expected rate of inflation

11. Which of the following is the primary factor that coordinates the actions of borrowers and lenders in the loanable funds market?
    a. Inflation rate
    b. Discount rate
    c. Open market operations
    d. Interest rate

THE ECONOMIC WAY OF THINKING—MULTIPLE CHOICE

1. Aggregate demand for goods and services will be inversely related to the price level because
    a. a decline in the price level will permit households with fixed nominal money balances to purchase more goods and services.
    b. a decline in the price level will increase real aggregate supply.
    c. an increase in the price level will induce individuals to substitute for goods and services and hold less money.
    d. an increase in the price level will increase real income even though nominal income may decline.

2. A reduction in aggregate supply will exert an inflationary impact on the economy unless it is
    a. offset by the discovery of an equal amount of gold.
    b. offset by a reduction in aggregate demand.
    c. offset by an increase in government expenditures.
    d. offset by an increase in the size of the planned budget deficit.

3. Within the aggregate goods and services market, if excess demand is present at the current price level, the level of
    a. the natural rate of employment will tend to rise.
    b. prices will tend to rise.
    c. government expenditure will tend to rise.
    d. sustainable real output will tend to rise.

4. Which of the following accurately indicates the relationship between the short-run and long-run aggregate supply curves?
    a. In the short run, aggregate supply is sloped upward to the right, and in the long run it is vertical.
    b. In the short run, aggregate supply is vertical, and in the long run it is sloped upward to the right.
    c. In the short run, aggregate supply is downward sloping, but in the long run, it is sloped upward to the right.
    5. In the short run, aggregate supply is sloped upward to the right, but in the long run it is downward sloping.

5. As decision-makers adjust and fully expect that a new higher price level will be sustained, then
    a. the aggregate supply curve will become horizontal.
    b. the aggregate supply curve will start to become horizontal, but it will take some time for the complete shift to take place.
    c. the aggregate supply curve will not change.
    d. none of the above.

6. If the current price level in the goods and services market is higher than what was expected, then output will be
    a. at the economy's long-run capacity.
    b. below the economy's long-run capacity.
    c. above the economy's long-run capacity.
    d. any of the above; the two items are not rigidly related, as is implied in these answers.

7. When an economy is in macroeconomic equilibrium,
    a. the goods and services market must be in equilibrium, and the loanable funds market and the resources market must be reasonably near equilibrium.
    b. any of the markets individually can be out of equilibrium, but the sum of all three markets must be in equilibrium.
    c. all three markets must be in equilibrium.
    d. none of the above.

8. What is the relationship between long-run and short-run equilibrium in the goods and services market?
    a. If the goods and services market is in long-run equilibrium, then it must also be in short-run equilibrium.
    b. If the goods and services market is in short-run equilibrium, then it must also be in long-run equilibrium.
    c. Neither a nor b is correct.
    d. Both a and b are correct.

9. In the aggregate demand/aggregate supply model, an economy in which the intersection between AD and SRAS is to the left of LRAS will be likely to encounter
    a. increasing inflation.
    b. rising money interest rates.
    c. falling resource prices.
    d. increasing taxes.

10. (I) If long run equilibrium is present in the goods and services market, the current price level will equal the price level buyers and sellers anticipated when they arrived at contractual agreements. (II) When an economy is in long-run equilibrium, the actual rate of unemployment will equal the natural rate of unemployment.
    a. Both I and II are true.
    b. Both I and II are false.
    c. I is true, II is false.
    d. I is false, II is true.

11. Which of the following best explains why the short-run aggregate supply curve slopes upward to the right?
    a. A higher price level tends to improve profit margins in the short run since important components of producers' cost are temporarily fixed.
    b. A higher price level tends to stimulate technological improvements, which enhances our ability to produce goods and services.
    c. A higher price level tends to increase the money interest rate, which encourages buyers to purchase more goods and services during the current period.
    d. A higher price level leads to an increase in the expected rate of inflation, which encourages producers to supply more output during the current period.

12. Which of the following is most likely to increase aggregate supply in the long run?
    a. The discovery of a new technology that substantially reduces the cost of transforming iron ore into steel
    b. Unfavorable weather conditions in agricultural areas
    c. An increase in the expected rate of inflation
    d. Higher real interest rates due to the federal government's large budget deficits

THE ECONOMIC WAY OF THINKING—DISCUSSION QUESTIONS

1. ''Potential GNP equals the economy's long-run capacity and indicates the total amount of production that can ever be possible; you just can't possibly produce more than that.'' Do you agree or disagree? Why? Back up your answer by drawing a short-run aggregate supply curve and commenting about its relationship to your answer.

2. One of your friends recently complained that interest rates just went up again by saying, ''Every time interest rates go up, all that happens is that the banks get more money; there should be a law against high interest rates.''
   a. Comment on the first part of your friend's statement. In the face of a competitive loanable funds market, could a bank consistently ''make more money''? Why or why not?
   b. Comment on the second half of your friend's statement. What would happen to the loan able funds market if there was a usury law that specified a maximum rate of interest allowable?

3. Of the three basic macromarkets, which one are you the most familiar with? Describe your most recent interaction with each market.

4. What is the natural rate of employment? Do you think that there is such a thing as a ''natural'' rate of unemployment? Why or why not? What kind of evidence is there that a natural rate of unemployment does or does not exist? (*Hint:* be sure to recall that the natural rate of unemployment is a long-run concept.)

5. How can we be so simplistic as to think that there is just one interest rate in the economy when there must be hundreds if not thousands of different rates? Is this a major flaw in our model of the loanable funds market?

6. In order to calculate the real rate of interest we must somehow come up with an inflationary premium which is based on our expectation of inflation in the future. Do you have such an expectation? Do your friends? Would an inflation rate of 20% surprise you? If so, does that imply that you do or do not have some sort of expectation about future rates of inflation?

PERSPECTIVES IN ECONOMICS

Still At Work On Full Employment
by Herbert Stein

[From *The Wall Street Journal,* February 13, 1986. Reprinted with permission from The Wall Street Journal © Dow Jones & Co., Inc. (1986). All rights reserved; abridged and edited.]

According to the newspapers, Speaker O'Neill was quite upset when President Reagan said that a number of the unemployed don't want to work. Perhaps the president's language was too colloquial or crude for the Sage of Cambridge. He might have responded less emotionally if Mr. Reagan had said the nation is now at full employment, or at the natural rate of unemployment, or at the non-accelerating-inflation rate of unemployment. He might then have recognized that the statement was an assertion of fact that might be correct or incorrect, but implied no moral judgment of the unemployed or the president.

Sloth is one of the deadly sins. But the unemployment figures do not measure slothfulness. Many employed people are slothful. And unemployed people who ''don't want to work'' are not necessarily slothful, or any more slothful than the people who are employed. A person who is unemployed and doesn't want to work is one who doesn't want to work under certain conditions.

Lesson Of The 1930s When the present kind of unemployment statistics were begun, back in 1940, Franklin Roosevelt was shocked to learn that the count of the unemployed included a Vassar graduate, the daughter of one of his Hyde Park neighbors, who was seeking a job as editor of Vogue, and that only. His shock was not at the young woman, but at the statistician. But we have presumably gotten over FDR's shock at the fact that the young woman is counted among the unemployed. She wants to work under the conditions that she considers suitable and is not willing to work under other conditions that are available to her. We not only do not consider it wrong for her to behave in this way or wrong to count her as unemployed, we are also willing to pay her unemployment compensation if she has been previously employed and now rejects all jobs other than editing Vogue.

But not all unemployment is the result of workers rejecting jobs that do not meet their conditions as to pay or other features. We learned that in the 1930s—or at least almost everyone learned it by then. We became acutely aware of two kinds of conditions in which people who were willing and eager to work at jobs for which they were suited and at a real wage that did not exceed the real value of their product would be unemployed:

1. The unemployed might have been unable to lower their real wages enough to make their employment profitable because a lowering of their nominal wages—expressed in money—would only have caused an equal decline of demand and prices so that their real wages would not fall.

2. Demand and prices might have fallen so fast that although a decline of nominal wages could in principle have prevented a rise in unemployment, such a decline of nominal wages could not ''reasonably'' have been expected, because it would have required of all parties a degree of information and flexibility that never exists, and some would say with good reason.

Recognition of these conditions led to the definition of ''full employment'' as the level of unemployment that would exist when demand was adequate to keep the inflation rate stable. All unemployment at full employment would be voluntary in the sense that anyone who wanted a job would be able to find one by reducing his nominal wage enough to make employing him profitable to someone.

Partly to get away from the implication that full employment meant zero unemployment, economists adopted the term ''natural rate of unemployment.'' Unemployment of that amount could be explained as due to the fact that people don't want to work, in the specific, non-pejorative sense of not wanting the available conditions of employment. Unemployment above that was due to deficiency of demand, presumably resulting from inadequacy of macroeconomic policy. Unemployment could be below that for a time, while inflation was accelerating at an unexpected rate. But since inflation could not continue accelerating at an unexpected rate for very long, unemployment could not be below the natural rate for very long.

When President Reagan and Speaker O'Neill had their exchange, the unemployment rate was 6.6%, although the latest figure available to them was 6.8%. If the natural rate is above 6.8%, Speaker O'Neill should not have been upset.

Whatever the natural rate is, there is no reason to expect it to be a constant over time. It will change with changes in the age-sex composition of the labor force as well as for other reasons. At the end of World War II we thought it was about 4%. I was here at the time and can testify that the number was drawn out of a hat. In the late 1960s economists raised the number toward 5%, mainly because of the increase of the proportion of women and young people in the labor force. Later, other factors seemed to be working to raise the natural rate, and it was observed that high rates of unemployment persisted in the face of high and rising inflation. Without having taken a census, I would guess that the consensus of economists today would put the natural rate at about 6%. Given the uncertainty of such estimates, that consensus does not exclude the possibility that the natural rate is now 7%.

So, neither the president, nor the speaker, nor I know what the natural rate is. But I do not think that Speaker O'Neill should have been upset with the president. Even if the natural rate is 6% rather than 7%, he should have recognized that the president is 85% correct.

National Policy Needed To say that unemployed people don't want to work, in the sense used here of not being willing to take jobs for which they are qualified at the wages they could earn in them, is not to deny that their unemployment is a problem that should be addressed by national policy. Public policy can affect both the qualifications and the willingness. Education and training can raise qualifications, increase potentail earnings and raise the willingness to be employed. Education may raise foresight and increase appreciation of the lifetime value of taking a job that in itself seems to have no future. Enterprise zones may increase the attractiveness of jobs available in some areas. Elimination of the minimum wage might make available job experiences for young people that would open their opportunity for more attractive jobs later.

Although we cannot, for long, get unemployment down below the natural rate, we may by such measures reduce the natural rate. At various times in the past the country has invested a good deal of money and hope in ''manpower programs'' aimed at reducing unemployment. One can fairly say that the results have been disappointing. But with the natural rate apparently as high as it is, and with a frightening concentration on the young and minorities, certainly the problem deserves more thought and effort.

''They don't want to work,'' even if true, is not the end of the matter.

Discussion

1. Stein seems to support the idea that ''full employment'' takes place when there is a non-zero rate of unemployment (the natural rate of unemployment). Would it really be so bad for the economy if the unemployment rate was zero? Why or why not?

2. If it is true that no one knows for sure what percentage of unemployment should be considered the natural rate of unemployment, then how will we ever know when we've reached our goal of full employment? For example, could an incorrect perception of the natural rate of unemployment lead to an incorrect macroeconomic policy? Explain.

3. Stein states that ''we cannot, for long, get unemployment down below the natural rate.'' Is this correct? Why couldn't we sustain a rate of unemployment below the natural rate of unemployment in the long-run if we were willing to put up with high rates of inflation?

9

Working With Our Basic Aggregate Demand/Aggregate Supply Model

TRUE OR FALSE

T	F		
☐	☐	1.	A shift in aggregate demand cannot be caused by a decrease in real income, only by an increase in real income.
☐	☐	2.	Business pessimism tends to reduce aggregate demand, while business optimism tends to increase aggregate demand (other things being equal).
☐	☐	3.	The nominal rate of interest causes shifts in the aggregate supply curve, while the real rate of interest causes shifts in the aggregate demand curve.
☐	☐	4.	Any factor which has an effect on the long-run aggregate supply curve also must have an effect on the short-run aggregate supply curve.
☐	☐	5.	A decline in productivity will tend to cause the price level to rise and decrease real output (all other things being equal).
☐	☐	6.	Technological advances shift the short-run aggregate supply curve to the left.
☐	☐	7.	The permanent income hypothesis states that some income is never spent and instead remains unspent permanently. Since such permanent income is never spent, aggregate demand is decreased.
☐	☐	8.	The permanent income hypothesis implies that if you find $10 on the street, you will not immediately run out and spend that $10.
☐	☐	9.	The extent to which the economy is self-correcting is a matter of much debate among economists.
☐	☐	10.	Adverse supply shocks include major earthquakes, wars, and bad weather.

PROBLEMS AND PROJECTS

1. Draw aggregate demand/aggregate supply diagrams below to illustrate the changes in aggregate demand (AD), short-run aggregate supply (SRAS), long-run aggregate supply (LRAS), the price level (P) and real gross national product (RGNP) in response to the events described to the left of the diagrams. First show in the diagrams how AD, SRAS and/or LRAS shift and then fill in the table to the right of the diagrams using + to indicate increase, − to indicate decrease, 0 to indicate no change, and ? to indicate that either a decrease or an increase is possible.

Events	Diagrams	AD SRAS LRAS P RGNP

a. The government adopts economic policies which lower interest rates.

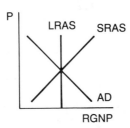

_____ _____ _____ _____ _____

b. A technological break-through in robotics significantly raises labor productivity.

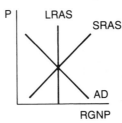

_____ _____ _____ _____ _____

c. Gloomy economic forecasts lead households to save more income for that "rainy day."

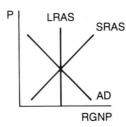

_____ _____ _____ _____ _____

d. An increase in the actual rate of inflation leads to forecasts of higher future inflation.

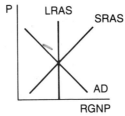

e. The breakup of the OPEC oil cartel leads to significantly lower oil prices and higher oil supplies. (_Hint:_ assume that this country is an oil importer.)

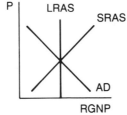

2. Consider once again the data from Exhibit 1 of Chapter 8.
   a. If the economy's self-correcting mechanism operates without impediment, explain how the mechanism leads the economy from its short-run equilibrium in 1969 to a long-run equilibrium. Show the adjustments in aggregate supply and/or demand that would occur in the diagram you constructed for that year.
   b. Do the same for the short-run equilibrium of 1933.
   c. The rate of unemployment in 1933 was 24.9%. Six years later, in 1939, the unemployment rate had fallen only to 17.2%, still far above the natural rate. Why might the self-correcting mechanism have worked so slowly?

3. Using an AD/AS model for the U.S. economy, explain what happens to the price level, the output level, and unemployment in each of the following cases. Assume that the economy is initially in long-run equilibrium and the events initially catch people by surprise.

Event	Prices	Output	Unemployment
a. Immigration from Mexico increases.	____	____	____
b. The President embargoes wheat and computer sales to the USSR.	____	____	____
c. To pay for lobbying expenses, the Teamsters press for higher wages.	____	____	____
d. A Federal tax revision bill is passed giving additional incentives for saving.	____	____	____
e. The U.S.'s trading partners slip into recession, lowering demand for U.S. exports.	____	____	____

LEARNING THE MECHANICS—MULTIPLE CHOICE

1. All of the following will reduce aggregate demand *except*
    a. a decrease in real income.
    b. higher real rates of interest.
    c. increased consumer optimism about the future.
    d. a decline in the expected rate of inflation.

2. An increase in the long-run aggregate supply curve simply means
    a. shifting the curve up.
    b. shifting the curve down.
    c. shifting the curve to the right.
    d. shifting the curve to the left.

3. When people lower their expectations for the future inflation rate, which of the following is most likely to occur?
    a. Short-run aggregate supply will decrease.
    b. Long-run aggregate supply will increase.
    c. Aggregate demand will increase.
    d. Aggregate demand will decrease.

4. With more workers available, we should be able to produce more. This will tend to
    a. shift the SRAS and the LRAS to the right.
    b. shift the SRAS to the right and the LRAS to the left.
    c. shift the SRAS to the left and the LRAS to the right.
    d. shift the SRAS and the LRAS to the left.

5. Productivity refers to
    a. how much we produce in the entire economy.
    b. how much we produce, per hour of employment, in the entire economy.
    c. both a and b.
    d. neither a nor b.

6. An unanticipated increase in the short-run aggregate supply curve will cause
   a. an increase in the price level.
   b. a decrease in the price level.
   c. a decrease in output.
   d. an increase in the real interest rate.

7. In the short-run, equilibrium output in the goods and services market may be either above or below the output at which the long-run aggregate supply curve intersects the X (goods and services) axis, but in the long run
   a. it must be less than that output.
   b. it must be greater than that output.
   c. it must be equal to that output.
   d. it depends on aggregate demand, not just aggregate supply.

8. If unanticipated, which of the following will decrease short-run equilibrium aggregate output in the goods and services market?
   a. A decrease in the real interest rate
   b. A decrease in the cost of resources
   c. A decrease in the money interest rate
   d. A decrease in the expected rate of inflation

9. Which of the following is most likely to result from an unanticipated increase in aggregate supply due to favorable weather conditions in agricultural areas?
   a. An increase in the inflation rate
   b. An increase in the unemployment rate
   c. A decrease in the price level
   d. A decrease in the natural rate of unemployment

10. Which of the following is most likely to accompany an unanticipated reduction in aggregate demand?
    a. An increase in the price level
    b. An increase in employment
    c. An increase in real GNP
    d. An increase in the unemployment rate

11. Which of the following is most likely to accompany an unanticipated reduction in aggregate supply?
    a. An increase in nominal income
    b. A reduction in the real rate of investment
    c. An increase in the price level
    d. A decrease in the unemployment rate

12. In the aggregate demand/aggregate supply model, an economy operating below its long-run potential capacity will experience
    a. falling real wages and resource prices which will stimulate employment and real output.
    b. rising interest rates which will stimulate aggregate demand and restore full employment.
    c. inflation which will stimulate additional spending and thereby restore full employment.
    d. a budget deficit which will cause policy makers to increase taxes, which will help restore full employment.

THE ECONOMIC WAY OF THINKING—MULTIPLE CHOICE

For questions 1–4, assume that the economy is in long-run equilibrium in the aggregate demand/aggregate supply model and that some sort of event takes place. In each case, mark the most likely impact of the event on the aggregate demand/aggregate supply diagram: Feel free to refer to the diagram in Exhibit 1 before answering.

Exhibit I

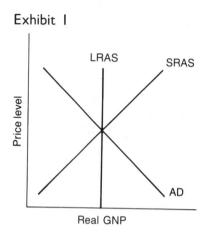

1. Good weather allows crop yields to double in the South.
   a. The aggregate demand curve would shift to the right.
   b. The aggregate demand curve would shift to the left.
   c. The short-run aggregate supply curve would shift to the right.
   d. The short-run aggregate supply curve would shift to the left.

2. The real interest rate suddenly goes up by 2%.
   a. The aggregate demand curve would shift to the right.
   b. The aggregate demand curve would shift to the left.
   c. The short-run aggregate supply curve would shift to the right.
   d. The short-run aggregate supply curve would shift to the left.

3. Consumers and businesses all suddenly decide that the future looks much better than it previously had.
   a. The aggregate demand curve would shift to the right.
   b. The aggregate demand curve would shift to the left.
   c. The short-run aggregate supply curve would shift to the right.
   d. The short-run aggregate supply curve would shift to the left.

4. Legislation is adopted which improves labor productivity.
   a. The aggregate demand curve would shift to the right.
   b. The aggregate demand curve would shift to the left.
   c. The short-run aggregate supply curve would shift to the right.
   d. The short-run aggregate supply curve would shift to the left.

5. What will force an economy that is producing more than its long-run capacity to decrease its output?
    a. Eventually, an adverse supply shock will come along.
    b. Wages and prices will rise until equilibrium is restored at full employment output but a higher price level.
    c. Wages and prices will fall until equilibrium is restored at full employment output and a lower price level.
    d. Nothing; the concept of long-run capacity is only a theoretical one which can be surpassed without difficulty even in the long run.

6. A reduction in aggregate supply that is expected to be temporary will
    a. have no effect on the economy.
    b. cause a higher real interest rate.
    c. eventually cause a lower price level.
    d. cause more spending on capital goods to offset the reduction.

7. The permanent income hypothesis, developed by Milton Friedman, states that
    a. if incomes rise temporarily, consumption spending will increase by a smaller proportion.
    b. if incomes rise permanently, consumption spending will not change at all.
    c. if incomes rise temporarily, consumption spending will also rise by a proportional amount, but only temporarily.
    d. none of the above.

8. If an economy is in equilibrium at a given price level and a given output level, the aggregate demand/aggregate supply (AD/AS) model indicates that an unanticipated decrease in aggregate demand will cause
    a. real output to decline.
    b. the price level to fall, while real output remains unchanged.
    c. nominal output to decline, while real output remains unchanged.
    d. real output to decline, while nominal output remains unchanged.

9. During the mid 1980s, the real price of crude oil declined sharply on the world market. Other things constant, how would such a decrease in oil prices have influenced the price level and output of oil-importing nations?
    a. Both real output and the price level would have fallen.
    b. Both real output and the price level would have risen.
    c. Real output would have fallen, and the price level would have risen.
    d. Real output would have risen, and the price level would have fallen.

10. Which of the following is most likely to accompany an unanticipated reduction in aggregate demand?
    a. An increase in the price level
    b. A decrease in the unemployment rate
    c. A decrease in real GNP
    d. A reduction in the real rate of interest

11. When an economy is temporarily operating at less than capacity, then a market economy will tend to be self-correcting (move towards equilibrium at full employment capacity) since
    a. lower resource prices will increase aggregate supply.
    b. lower retail prices will increase aggregate demand.
    c. both a and b.
    d. neither a nor b.

12. In the aggregate demand/aggregate supply model, what market adjustments cause the economy to return to its long-run capacity when output is temporarily *greater than* the economy's long run potential output?
   a. Lower wage rates and resource prices reduce short-run aggregate supply.
   b. Lower interest rates increase aggregate demand and thereby stimulate output.
   c. Higher wage rates and resource prices reduce short-run aggregate supply.
   d. A decrease in the price level reduces aggregate demand.

THE ECONOMIC WAY OF THINKING—DISCUSSION

1. In 1986, the "group of five" nations, which included the United States, undertook policies to reduce the value of the dollar (i.e., make foreign currencies more expensive for us and the dollar cheaper to them). If this effort was successful and U.S. exports increased while imports fell, what would be the impact on the U.S. economy? Show this outcome with the AD/AS diagram.

2. On the other hand, recent improvements in the quality of Korean goods have made Americans more willing to "buy Korean." Show the impact of this movement on the economy through the AD/AS diagram.

3. Do you really believe that the entire economy can be analyzed in one diagram? What does the AD/AS model leave out? How do you think you might go about attempting to analyze these left-out topics while still using the AD/AS model when it is appropriate?

4. The topic of tax rate changes won't be dealt with specifically until the following chapters, but you won't be surprised to hear that taxes have a profound effect on the economy. Could you analyze the impact of an income tax reduction on the economy with the AD/AS diagram? How?

5. What if everyone started saving quite a bit? What would happen to the economy? What would happen to aggregate demand, output, prices and interest rates? How does this impact fit in with the concept that our economy would be better off with *more* savings? (*Hint:* think about the aggregate supply curve as well.)

10

Keynesian Foundations of Modern Macroeconomics

TRUE OR FALSE

T F

1. Keynes believed that during a time of depression, people could induce more production by saving more.

2. The multiplier concept indicates the amplified effect that a change in income will have on investment.

3. Their views on price and wage flexibility was one important distinction between Keynes and the classicists who came before him.

4. An increase in disposable income, other things being equal, will cause consumption to increase.

5. One, divided by one minus the MPC, yields the multiplier.

6. Investment and saving are quite different; they are done by different people for different reasons.

7. In the Keynesian model, the responsiveness of aggregate demand to changes in supply will be directly related to the availability of unemployed resources.

8. The marginal propensity to consume (MPC) is defined as the total amount of consumption in the economy divided by the change in disposable income.

9. Business pessimism can increase the severity of recessions by reducing investment.

10. In general, the rate of government expenditures is determined by market forces.

11. Since disposable income can only be consumed or saved, the knowledge of an economy's aggregate consumption function will permit one to calculate the economy's aggregate saving function with respect to disposable income.

12. Within the Keynesian model, prices are typically assumed to be constant; if inflation does occur due to an increase in autonomous expenditures, then the multiplier effect of that increase is absent.

13. The idea that the Keynesian model implies an aggregate supply curve that is horizontal below potential output and vertical at potential output is probably a simplification; instead, the SRAS turns from horizontal to vertical more gradually.

PROBLEMS AND PROJECTS

1. Calculate the marginal propensity to consume for the following situations:
   a. Consumption increases by $2,000 when disposable income increases by $3,000.
   b. Consumption increases from $6,000 to $7,000 when disposable income increases from $8,000 to $9,500.
   c. Disposable income decreases from $10,000 to $9,000, causing consumption to do the same.
   d. Disposable income increases by $4,000, causing savings to increase by $1,000. (*Hint:* disposable income must be either spent or saved.)

2. Attempt to estimate your *own* marginal propensity to consume by observing how you change your consumption habits when your disposable income changes.

3. Calculate the value of the multiplier for all four cases in question 1 above.

4. Does the multiplier actually work? To test it, try "spending" an extra dollar in a roomful of friends to see what the total increase in spending will be. (If you prefer, just simulate what your friends would do.)

5. Calculate the equilibrium level of output within the framework of the Keynesian model in each of the following cases (assume net exports are zero throughout):
   a. From a starting equilibrium level of output equal to $600 billion, assume an autonomous increase in gross investment of $50 billion in an economy with a fairly stable MPC of 2/3.
   b. From a starting equilibrium level of output equal to $800 billion, assume an autonomous decrease in gross investment of $100 billion in an economy with a fairly stable MPC of 3/4.
   c. Planned government expenditure is $300 billion (as are expected taxes), planned gross investment is $100 billion, and 3/4 of all disposable income is spent on consumption.
   d. Planned gross investment is $150 billion, government expenditures are $600 billion (while taxes are only $500 billion), and the aggregate consumption function is $C = \$200$ billion $+ 4/5$ (disposable income).

6. Imagine two economies, Savit and Spendit, which are identical in all respects except that Savit has a marginal propensity to consume of 1/2 while Spendit has an MPC of 9/10. Exhibit 1 traces the impact of additional investment spending of $25 million in each economy.

Exhibit 1

Expenditure stage	Savit Additional income	Savit Additional consumption	Spendit Additional income	Spendit Additional consumption
Round 1	25.0	12.5	25.0	22.5
Round 2	_____	_____	_____	_____
Round 3	_____	_____	_____	_____
Round 4	_____	_____	_____	_____
Round 5	_____	_____	_____	_____
All others	_____	_____	_____	_____
Total	_____	_____	_____	_____

a. Fill in the missing entries for the expenditure stages in each of the two countries.

b. In which economy does the increased investment spending have the larger impact? Explain briefly.

c. From the "Total" row, calculate the ratio of total additional consumption to total additional income for each country. Are the magnitudes of these ratios surprising? Explain briefly.

7. Suppose that the current equilibrium level of aggregate income is $500 trillion while the *full employment* level of income is $600 trillion. If the marginal propensity to consume is 4/5, how much would investment spending need to increase for the equilibrium level of income to equal the full employment level? Explain briefly. Attempt to show this situation on both AD/AS and aggregate expenditure diagrams.

LEARNING THE MECHANICS—MULTIPLE CHOICE

1. The multiplier is used to calculate
    a. the change in spending caused by a change in income.
    b. the change in income resulting from a change in saving.
    c. the change in income resulting from an indepenent change in spending.
    d. the change in investment caused by a change in consumption.

2. Which of the following is *not* a major insight of the Keynesian model?
    a. Changes in output, as well as changes in prices, play a role in the macroeconomic adjustment process, particularly in the short run.
    b. A general overproduction of goods relative to total demand is impossible since production stimulates concomitant demand.
    c. The responsiveness of aggregate supply to changes in demand will be directly related to the availability of unemployed resources.
    d. Fluctuations in aggregate demand are an important potential source of business instability.

3. In the Keynesian aggregate expenditure model, which one of the following would be the most likely result of an autonomous $5 billion increase in investment?
    a. An increase in the cost of loans for investment
    b. The expectation of a sharp rise in sales during the next six months
    c. An increase of $5 billion in the national income
    d. A decrease in government expenditures to offset the increase in investment

4. When planned aggregate demands equals total income, which of the following is true?
    a. Saving must equal investment plus government spending.
    b. The undesired change in inventories is just equal to the difference between full employment and present employment.
    c. Full employment is achieved.
    d. There is no automatic tendency toward a change in income.

5. In equation form, Keynesian macroeconomic equilibrium is attained when
    a. total output = real GNP.
    b. real GNP = planned consumption.
    c. planned aggregate expenditures = total output.
    d. $C + I + G + X$ = planned aggregate expenditures.

6. Say's law of the markets holds that supply creates its own demand because
   a. there is a buyer for each new product produced.
   b. the act of producing creates income equal to the value of the goods produced.
   c. prices are stable in the short run; thus, producers know how much to provide.
   d. supply prices are always equal to demand prices.

7. If the MPC is 3/4, the multiplier is
   a. 4
   b. 1-1/3
   c. 1-3/4
   d. undefined until the marginal propensity to save is known.

8. John Maynard Keynes
   a. was an American economist.
   b. did not believe that "supply created its own demand."
   c. was the "father of microeconomics."
   d. did not believe that changes in private investment were an important source of economic instability.

9. The primary determinant of consumer spending is
   a. the interest rate.
   b. disposable income.
   c. expectations of inflation.
   d. the stage of the business cycle.

10. Which of the following is most likely to increase investment?
    a. An increase in the interest rate
    b. An increase in saving
    c. An increase in the expected quantity of future sales
    d. An increase in unemployment

11. The greater the MPC
    a. the greater the multiplier
    b. the larger the change in aggregate expenditure for a given change in spending.
    c. Neither a nor b is correct.
    d. Both a and b are correct.

12. Which of the following best describes a consumption function?
    a. A function that relates consumption to savings
    b. A function that relates investment to the interest rate
    c. A function that relates consumption to disposable income
    d. All of the above are correct; the consumption function includes all three relationships.

13. The idea that the aggregate supply curve implied by the Keynesian model is always horizontal until potential output is reached
    a. makes sense in the real world.
    b. is probably an oversimplification.
    c. is totally false.
    d. means that the economy is automatically self-correcting.

THE ECONOMIC WAY OF THINKING—MULTIPLE CHOICE

1. If consumption equals 800 when disposable income is 1000 and then consumption increases to 1000 when disposable income increases to 1300, the marginal propensity to consume is
    a. 8/10.
    b. 10/13.
    c. 2/3.
    d. 3/4.

2. "If there is unemployment, the average wage rate will decline as the unemployed workers choose lower wages rather than going without a job. The demand curve for labor slopes downward and to the right, so that more workers would be hired at the lower wage rate, restoring full employment." According to the Keynesian view, this quote is
    a. incorrect, because widespread unemployment would cause wages to rise, not decline.
    b. incorrect, because the demand for labor, other things constant, will not be negatively related to wages.
    c. incorrect, because wages and prices tend to be highly inflexible downward.
    d. essentially correct.

3. Which of the following is most likely to lead to an increase in current consumption?
    a. An increase in personal income tax rates
    b. An increase in one's expected future income
    c. A decrease in one's marginal propensity to consume
    d. An increase in the interest rate

4. According to Keynes, Say's Law was incorrect because
    a. the interest rate adjusts so that planned saving and investment are always identical.
    b. saving and investment are done by different individuals and need not be equal.
    c. it assumed that wages are inflexible.
    d. of the permanent income hypothesis.

5. "Independent changes in investment are high-powered because they generate additional income for workers and factory suppliers. In time, this additional income will be spent on consumption, creating an additional stimulus for investment, employment, and income when the economy is at less than full employment." From the Keynesian view, this quote is
    a. incorrect, because changes in investment will have little impact on consumption.
    b. incorrect, because a change in investment cannot lead to an increase in real income.
    c. incorrect, because the higher level of aggregate demand implicit in the statement will merely cause consumption to increase.
    d. essentially correct.

6. The Great Depression provided support for Keynes's declaration that
    a. government action was necessary to ensure that the saving rate remained at the equilibrium level.
    b. falling interest rates would induce consumers to increase their saving.
    c. the average propensity to consume will increase as disposable income rises.
    d. prolonged periods of unemployment were possible.

The following information is relevant to the next two questions.

> Assume that IBM decides, despite an ongoing recession, to build a new branch for computer analysis in Bozeman, Montana. The plant will employ 1500 workers, who will be guaranteed a full-time (40 hours per week) job at $4 per hour for 50 weeks. That is, each worker will have an annual income of $8000.

7. If the marginal propensity to consume in Bozeman was 3/4, what would be the total change in income that would result from the operation of the plant for one year?
   a. $12 million
   b. $48 million
   c. $9 million
   d. $27 million

8. If Bozeman citizens decided to spend more than 3/4 of the additional income
   a. the MPC would decrease.
   b. the multiplier would decrease.
   c. the expansion in income would be larger.
   d. aggregate expenditures would decline.

9. ''Fluctuations in business investment are the major source of economic disturbances. A high level of aggregate demand is essential; otherwise spending may be insufficient to provide the business sector with the incentive to expand, invest, and employ all the workers of the economy.'' According to the Keynesian view, this quote is
   a. incorrect, because investment is not the major source of economic instability.
   b. incorrect, because it ignores the fact that investment is highly responsive to changing interest rates.
   c. incorrect, because a high level of aggregate demand will mean a decline in savings necessary for investment.
   d. essentially correct.

10. As income increases, aggregate
    a. consumption spending falls.
    b. consumption spending rises.
    c. consumption spending rises only if the interest rate also rises.
    d. inflation causes consumption and saving to move in opposite directions.

11. Which of the following is a correct implication of the Keynesian model for the shape of the aggregate supply curve in the goods and services market?
    a. The SRAS is horizontal because prices are assumed to be constant.
    b. The SRAS is vertical because it is impossible to increase real GNP past full employment capacity.
    c. The SRAS is horizontal well below full employment and is vertical at full employment.
    d. The SRAS is vertical well below full employment and is horizontal at full employment.

12. If planned total spending (aggregate expenditures) were $900 billion but GNP were currently $800 billion, Keynesian analysis suggests that
    a. output would fall, incomes would fall, and tax revenues would automatically decrease.
    b. production would be stimulated and output would increase, unless output at full capacity were less than $900 billion.
    c. businesses would accumulate inventories, and output would fall.
    d. businesses would accumulate unplanned inventories, causing output to rise.

13. Which of the following is *not* a reason to prefer the three-market AD/AS macromodel to the aggregate expenditure model of this chapter?
    a. Simultaneous unemployment and inflation are easier to visualize within the AD/AS framework.
    b. The AD/AS model makes it easier to distinguish between long-run and short-run conditions than does the aggregate expenditure model.
    c. The AD/AS model has been at the center of macroeconomics for almost four decades.
    d. Changes in prices and expectations are easier to visualize in the AD/AS model.

THE ECONOMIC WAY OF THINKING—DISCUSSION QUESTIONS

1. What is Say's Law? Explain why classical economists thought that a market economy would always return to a full-employment equilibrium. Why do Keynesians disagree?

2. What is the major determinant of aggregate consumption? How would a tax reduction affect consumption? How would an increase in planned saving influence planned consumption? Explain.

3. If John Maynard Keynes influenced macroeconomic analysis more than any other single economist, how would you characterize that influence? Write a short summary of what you perceive to be the major components of his influence on macroeconomics.

4. How would each of the following influence the equilibrium level of output and employment? Explain your answer.
    a. An increase in planned saving
    b. The expectation of a recession in the near future
    c. The expectation of moderate inflation during the next 12 months
    d. An increase in government spending
    e. A decline in the income tax

5. What is investment? Why do people (firms) invest? Which of the following adds to current aggregate investment?
    a. ABC Shoe Manufacturers purchases a new cutting machine.
    b. A 10 percent expansion in ABC's inventories of shoes is planned to begin this week.
    c. The purchase of 1000 shares of GM stock is made by a consumer.
    d. A new home is built.
    e. Bonds are issued to finance school construction.

6. "Business investment is the major source of economic instability. During good times, business decision-makers expand their plant capacity, add to aggregate demand, and push the economy upward. In contrast, during a business decline, decision-makers cut back on investment. This reduces the level of demand, and causes the economy to plunge downward. A business-directed market economy is inherently unstable." Criticize or support this view. Use empirical evidence to support your position.

PERSPECTIVES IN ECONOMICS

The Impact of Keynes And The General Theory
by Paul A. Samuelson

[From "Lord Keynes and The General Theory." *Econometrica*, July 1946. Reprinted with permission.]

The Impact Of the General Theory . . . I have always considered it a priceless advantage to have been born as an economist prior to 1936 and to have received a thorough grounding in classical economics. It is quite impossible for modern students to realize the full effect of what has been advisably called "The Keynesian Revolution" upon those of us brought up in the orthodox tradition. What beginners today often regard as trite and obvious was to us puzzling, novel, and heretical.

To have been born as an economist before 1936 was a boon—yes. But not to have been born too long before!

Bliss was it in that dawn to be alive,
But to be young was very heaven!

The *General Theory* caught most economists under the age of 35 with the unexpected virulence of a disease first attacking and decimating an isolated tribe of south sea islanders. Economists beyond 50 turned out to be quite immune to the ailment. With time, most economists in-between began to run the fever, often without knowing or admitting their condition.

I must confess that my own first reaction to the *General Theory* was not at all like that of Keats on first looking into Chapman's Homer. No silent watcher, I, upon a peak in

Darien. My rebellion against its pretensions would have been complete, except for an uneasy realization that I did not at all understand what it was about. And I think I am giving away no secrets when I solemnly aver—upon the basis of vivid personal recollection—that no one else in Cambridge, Massachusetts, really knew what it was about for some twelve to eighteen months after its publication. Indeed, until the appearance of the mathematical models of Meade, Lange, Hicks, and Harrod, there is reason to believe that Keynes himself did not truly understand his own analysis.

Fashion always plays an important role in economic science; new concepts become the *mode* and then are *passé.* A cynic might even be tempted to speculate as to whether academic discussion is itself equilibrating: whether assertion, reply, and rejoinder do not represent an oscillating divergent series, in which—to quote Frank Knight's characterization of sociology—"bad talk drives out good."

In this case, gradually and against heavy resistance, the realization grew that the new analysis of *effective demand* associated with the *General Theory* was not to prove such a passing fad, that here indeed was part of "the wave of the future." This impression was confirmed by the rapidity with which English economists, other than those at Cambridge, took up the new Gospel: e.g., Harrod, Meade, and others, at Oxford; and, still more surprisingly, the young blades at the *London School,* like Kaldor, Lerner, and Hicks, who threw off their Hayekian garments and joined in the swim.

In this country it was pretty much the same story. Obviously, exactly the same words cannot be used to describe the analysis of income determination of, say, Lange, Hart, Harris, Ellis, Hansen, Bissell, Haberler, Slichter, J.M. Clark, or myself. And yet the Keynesian taint is unmistakably there upon every one of us.

Instead of burning out like a fad . . . the *General Theory* is still gaining adherents and appears to be in business to stay. Many economists who are most vehement in criticism of the specific Keynesian policies—which must always be carefully distinguished from the scientific analysis associated with his name—will never again be the same after passing through his hands.

It has been wisely said that only in terms of a modern theory of effective demand can one understand and defend the so-called "classical" theory of unemployment. It is perhaps not without additional significance, in appraising the long-run prospects of the Keynesian theories, that no individual, having once embraced the modern analysis, has—as far as I am aware—later returned to the older theories. And in universities, where graduate students are exposed to the old and new income analyses, I am told that it is often only too clear which way the wind blows.

Finally, and perhaps most important from the long-run standpoint, the Keynesian analysis has begun to filter down into the elementary textbooks; and, as everybody knows, once an idea gets into these, however bad it may be, it becomes practically immortal.

The General Theory Thus far, I have been discussing the new doctrines without regard to their content or merits, as if they were a religion and nothing else. True, we find a Gospel, a Scriptures, a Prophet, Disciples, Apostles, Epigoni, and even a Duality; and if there is no Apostolic Succession, there is at least an Apostolic Benediction. But by now the joke has worn thin, and it is in any case irrelevant.

The modern saving-investment theory of income determination did not directly displace the old latent belief in Say's Law of Markets (according to which only "frictions" could give rise to unemployment and over-production). Events of the years following 1929 destroyed the previous economic synthesis. The economists' belief in the orthodox synthesis was not overthrown, but had simply atrophied: it was not as though one's soul had faced a showdown as to the existence of the Deity and that faith was unthroned, or even that one had awakened in the morning to find that belief had flown away in the night; rather it was realized with a sense of belated recognition that one no longer had faith, that one had been living without faith for a long time, and that what, after all, was the difference?

The nature of the world did not suddenly change on a black October day in 1929 so that a new theory became mandatory. Even in their day, the older theories were incomplete and inadequate: in 1815, in 1844, 1893, and 1920. I venture to believe that the eighteenth and nineteenth centuries take on a new aspect when looked back upon from the modern perspective, that a new dimension has been added to the rereading of the Mercantilists, Thornton, Malthus, Ricardo, Tooke, David Wells, Marshall, and Wicksell.

Of course, the great depression of the thirties was not the first to reveal the untenability of the classical synthesis. The classical philosophy always had its ups and downs along with the great swings of business activity. Each time it had come back. But now for the first time, it was confronted by a competing system—a well-reasoned body of thought containing among other things as many equations as unknowns; in short, like itself, a synthesis; and one which could swallow the classical system as a special case.

A new *system,* that is what requires emphasis. Classical economics could withstand isolated criticism. Theorists can always resist facts; for facts are hard to establish and are always changing anyway, and *ceteris paribus* can be made to absorb a good deal of punishment. Inevitably, at the earliest opportunity, the mind slips back into the old grooves of thought, since analysis is utterly impossible without a frame of reference, a way of thinking about things, or, in short, a theory.

Herein lies the secret of the *General Theory.* It is a badly written book, poorly organized; any layman who, beguiled by the author's previous reputation, bought the book was cheated of his five shillings. It is not well suited for classroom use. It is arrogant, bad-tempered, polemical, and not overly generous in its acknowledgments. It abounds in mares' nests or confusions. . . . In it the Keynesian system stands out indistinctly, as if the author were hardly aware of its existence or cognizant of its properties; and certainly he is at his worst when expounding its relations to its predecessors. Flashes of insight and intuition intersperse tedious algebra. An awkward definition suddenly gives way to an unforgettable cadenza. When finally mastered, its analysis is found to be obvious and at the same time new. In short, it is a work of genius.

It is not unlikely that future historians of economic thought will conclude that the very obscurity and polemical character of the *General Theory* ultimately served to maximize its long-run influence. Possibly such an analyst will place it in the first rank of theoretical classics, along with the work of Smith, Cournot, and Walras. Certainly, these four books together encompass most of what is vital in the field of economic theory; and only the first is by any standards easy reading or even accessible to the intelligent layman.

In any case, it bears repeating that the *General Theory* is an obscure book, so that would-be anti-Keynesians must assume their position largely on credit unless they are willing to put in a great deal of work and run the risk of seduction in the process. The *General Theory* seems the random notes over a period of years of a gifted man who in his youth gained the whip hand over his publishers by virtue of the acclaim and fortune resulting from the success of his *Economic Consequences of the Peace*.

Like Joyce's *Finnegan's Wake*, the *General Theory* is much in need of a companion volume providing a "skeleton key" and guide to its contents: warning the young and innocent away from Book I (especially the difficult Chapter 3) and on to Books II, IV, and VI. Certainly in its present state, the book does not get itself read from one year to another even by the sympathetic teacher and scholar.

Too much regret should not be attached to the fact that all hope must now be abandoned of an improved second edition, since it is the first edition which would in any case have assumed the stature of a classic. We may still paste into our copies of the *General Theory* certain subsequent Keynesian additions, most particularly the famous chapter in *How to Pay for the War* which first outlined the modern theory of the inflationary process.

This last item helps to dispose of the fallacious belief that Keynesian economics is good "depression economics" and only that. Actually, the Keynesian system is indispensable to an understanding of conditions of over-effective demand and secular exhilaration; so much so that one anti-Keynesian has argued in print that *only* in times of a great war boom do such concepts as the marginal propensity to consume have validity. Perhaps, therefore, it would be more nearly correct to aver the reverse: that certain economists are Keynesian fellow-travellers only in boom times, falling off the band wagon in depression.

If time permitted, it would be instructive to contrast the analysis of inflation during the Napoleonic and first World War periods with that of the recent War and correlate this with Keynes' influence. Thus, the "inflationary gap" concept, recently so popular, seems to have been first used around the Spring of 1941 in a speech by the British Chancellor of the Exchequer, a speech thought to have been the product of Keynes himself.

No author can complete a survey of Keynesian economics without indulging in that favorite indoor guessing game: wherein lies the essential contribution of the *General Theory* and its distinguishing characteristic from the classical writings? Some consider its novelty to lie in the treatment of the *demand for money*, in its liquidity preference emphasis. Others single out the treatment of *expectations*.

I cannot agree. According to recent trends of thought, the interest rate is less important than Keynes himself believed. . . . As for expectations, the *General Theory* is brilliant in calling attention to their importance and in suggesting many of the central features of uncertainty and speculation. It paves the way for a theory of expectations, but it hardly provides one.

I myself believe the broad significance of the *General Theory* to be in the fact that it provides a relatively realistic, complete system for analyzing the level of effective demand and its fluctuations. More narrowly, I conceive the heart of its contribution to be in that subset of its equations which relate to the propensity to consume and to saving in relation to offsets-to-saving. In addition to linking saving explicitly to income, there is an equally important denial of the implicit "classical" axiom that motivated investment is *indefinitely expansible or contractable*, so that whatever people *try* to save will always be fully invested. It is not important whether we deny this by reason of expectations, interest rate rigidity, investment inelasticity with respect to over-all price changes and the interest rate, capital or investment satiation, secular factors of a technological and political nature or what have you. But it is vital for business-cycle analysis that we do assume definite amounts of investment which are highly variable over time in response to a myriad of exogenous and endogenous factors, *and which are not automatically equilibrated to full-employment saving levels by any internal efficacious economic process*.

With respect to the level of total purchasing power and employment, Keynes denies that there is an *invisible hand* channeling the self-centered action of each individual to the social optimum. This is the sum and substance of his heresy. Again and again through his writings there is to be found the figure of speech that what is needed are certain "rules of the road" and governmental actions, which will benefit everybody, but which nobody by himself is motivated to establish or follow. Left to themselves during depression, people will try to save and only end up lowering society's level of capital formation and saving; during an inflation, apparent self-interest leads everyone to action which only aggravates the malignant upward spiral. . . .

Discussion

1. Samuelson seems to imply that much of the impact of Keynes's thought comes from the enthusiasm and applications of his converts (including, one might add, Samuelson himself). Why do you think this happened? Does it remind you of other great changes in academic thinking?

2. What does Samuelson seem to think is the most important contribution of Keynes? Do you agree? Why or why not?

3. Reread the last paragraph and comment on Keynes's opinion of "the invisible hand." Do you agree with Keynes? Why?

11

Modern Macroeconomics: Fiscal Policy

TRUE OR FALSE

T F

☐ ☐ 1. The crowding-out effect refers to the hypothesis that high marginal tax rates crowd personal consumption out of the market place and therefore reduce the effectiveness of fiscal policy.

☐ ☐ 2. Manipulation of government expenditures is one type of fiscal policy.

☐ ☐ 3. A change in fiscal policy usually changes the full-employment level of output.

☐ ☐ 4. The lowering of income tax rates is a fiscal policy tool.

☐ ☐ 5. A balanced budget is essential if *real* income is to be increased by fiscal policy.

☐ ☐ 6. New classical economists differ from classical economists only in that new classical economists are alive and classical economists are not.

☐ ☐ 7. Unlike increases in investment expenditures, an increase in government spending has no multiplier effect.

☐ ☐ 8. Tax policy can be adjusted in order to encourage or discourage investment.

☐ ☐ 9. Given an economy's resource base and current level of technology, it will be impossible to sustain a real output rate greater than the vertical portion of the economy's long-run supply curve.

☐ ☐ 10. Higher marginal tax rates coupled with an increase in the size of the planned budget deficit (due to a sharp increase in government expenditures) will tend to decrease aggregate supply and increase aggregate demand, causing acceleration in the rate of inflation.

☐ ☐ 11. A budget surplus means that tax revenues exceed government expenditures.

☐ ☐ 12. Economic theory indicates that an increase in marginal tax rates will encourage individuals to substitute work for leisure.

☐ ☐ 13. New classical economists believe that taxes and debt financing as sources of government expenditure are essentially equivalent in their impact on the economy.

☐ ☐ 14. Money income increases faster than real income during a period of inflation.

PROBLEMS AND PROJECTS

1. Suppose that you are the president of a country whose economy is experiencing mild inflation. Assume, too, that political campaign promises restrict you to a balanced government budget. Is there any way in which fiscal policy can solve your problem? If so, what?

2. Indicate which of the following changes will cause a shift in aggregate demand, aggregate supply, or both.
    a. An improvement in technology
    b. An increase in the labor force participation rate of older workers
    c. A change in tax rates
    d. A $100 tax credit (or rebate) for each citizen
    e. A large wheat crop due to excellent weather conditions
    f. An increase in the world price of a country's major export product
    g. An increase in government expenditures
    h. An expansion in the size of the underground economy due to higher marginal tax rates

3. Consider the following two statements made by members of the Reagan administration:

    > (I) According to a news report, "An administration economist calculates that the multiplier effect of an increase in government spending, financed by borrowing, is zero. . . . He estimates that each dollar of such spending crowds out 30 to 70 cents worth of investment. Further, consumption will be reduced" (*The Margin,* October 1985).

    > (II) According to a different news report, "A senior Reagan administration official" called for action soon "to ensure that the deficit cuts required by the new budget law (Gramm-Rudman) don't harm the economy" (*Wall Street Journal,* January 29, 1986).

    a. With respect to I, explain carefully the manner in which the deficit spending described there could "crowd out" private spending. In your explanation, be sure to use both an AD/AS diagram and a loanable funds diagram.
    b. With reference to II, explain carefully the manner in which a reduction in the deficit could "harm the economy." In your explanation, be sure to use an AD/AS diagram.
    c. Could both these quotes have been made by members of the same administration? If the official in I feels that the deficit is bad for the economy, then why is the official in II worried about the side effects of reducing that deficit?

LEARNING THE MECHANICS—MULTIPLE CHOICE

1. Fiscal Policy is defined as
    a. changes in government expenditure to influence equilibrium GNP.
    b. changes in taxation rates to influence equilibrium GNP.
    c. all of the above.
    d. none of the above.

2. Consider an economy whose aggregate demand (AD) is currently $300 billion below the economy's long-run capacity. If the marginal propensity to consume (MPC) is steady at 2/3, by how much would government spending have to rise in order to push AD to capacity?
    a. $100 billion.
    b. $200 billion.
    c. $300 billion.
    d. $900 billion.

3. A balanced budget
    a. means that aggregate consumption is in balance with aggregate saving.
    b. means that government spending is constant from year to year.
    c. means that public spending equals private spending.
    d. means that tax revenues during a period are equal to government expenditures.

4. A decline in marginal tax rates will encourage individuals to
    a. substitute leisure for work.
    b. engage in more barter transactions.
    c. purchase more tax-deductible goods.
    d. allocate more funds into profitable investments expected to yield taxable income.

5. In the simple Keynesian model, inflation
    a. is a problem that cannot arise from fiscal policy.
    b. implies that the full-employment level of income is less than the equilibrium level of income.
    c. automatically leads to unemployment.
    d. is not a problem, since it implies a redistribution of income but has no effect on GNP.

6. The crowding-out effect suggests that
    a. expansionary fiscal policy causes inflation.
    b. restrictive fiscal policy is an effective weapon against inflation.
    c. the reduction in private spending resulting from the higher interest rates caused by a budget deficit will largely offset the expansionary impact of a pure fiscal action.
    d. a budget surplus will cause the private demand for loanable funds, the interest rate, and aggregate demand to fall.

7. Which of the following statements about the national debt is false?
    a. The greatest percentage of the national debt is held by domestic investors.
    b. The fraction of the debt held by foreign investors is about 11 percent.
    c. In recent years, public debt has increased more rapidly than private debt.
    d. Interest payments on the debt increased faster than GNP during the 1970s.

8. The new classical model implies that debt financing
    a. substitutes higher future taxes for lower current taxes.
    b. substitutes higher current taxes for lower future taxes.
    c. affects the magnitude of taxes but not their timing.
    d. increases both the current *and* future tax liability of taxpayers.

9. Which of the following is *not* an example of an automatic stabilizer?
    a. Unemployment payments that rise when unemployment increases
    b. Farm-aid payments that fall when the economy moves toward full employment
    c. An income tax whose revenues fall when income drops below the full-employment level
    d. Investment expenditures that rise as income and expectations rise

10. The new focus that Keynesian analysis gives to changes in taxes is
    a.   to raise revenue for the government.
    b.   to smooth out ups and downs of the business cycle. ✓
    c.   to redistribute tax money to lower income groups.
    d.   to protect governmental budgets from deficits.

11. Crowding out is
    a.   the impact of urbanization on economic activity. As population density increases, productivity tends to fall.
    b.   the impact of budget deficits on private spending. As deficits rise, that borrowing pushes up interest rates, cutting back on private borrowing. ✓
    c.   the impact of the new classical school on fiscal policy effectiveness. As people come to anticipate policy actions, the impact of those actions is reduced or even destroyed.
    d.   none of the above.

12. The new classical model hypothesizes that fiscal policy is an ineffective tool with which to alter aggregate demand because
    a.   the substitution of debt for tax financing causes people to save more in order to pay higher future taxes. ✓
    b.   current macroeconomic policy ignores the supply side and just focuses on the demand side of the economy.
    c.   crowding out causes private spending to be reduced by the amount of the spending increase.
    d.   the long-run aggregate supply curve is vertical, so in the long run, macroeconomic policy makes no difference.

THE ECONOMIC WAY OF THINKING—MULTIPLE CHOICE

1. Although the economy was entering the depression, the Hoover administration followed a policy leading to a balanced budget (as opposed to a deficit). According to Keynesian theory, balanced-budget fiscal policy (instead of that leading to a deficit) is inappropriate in periods of depression because
    a.   it increases economic activity, but not significantly.
    b.   it causes further decreases in economic activity, thus further increasing unemployment. ✓
    c.   it leads to a significant increase in the national debt, thus increasing the level of unemployment.
    d.   it leads to an increase in spending on automatic stabilizers.

2. The national debt does not have to be repaid (reduced to zero) at some date in the future because
    a.   the debt can be refinanced indefinitely.
    b.   it is owed to domestic citizens who do not have a legal right to sue if the federal government defaults. ✓
    c.   repudiation of the debt would exert little impact on the economy.
    d.   the debt is insured by the Federal Deposit Insurance Corporation which would pay bondholders if the U.S. Treasury does not.

3. A $5 billion tax cut was accompanied by an $8 billion increase in consumer spending during a single year. From a Keynesian viewpoint, the most probable reason why consumer spending increased more than taxes decreased is that
   a. additional spending by those with increased disposable incomes led to increased incomes and additional spending by others.
   b. lower taxes led to a reduction in government spending, which induced additional consumer spending. ✓
   c. the tax reduction caused interest rates to decline, inducing additional consumer spending.
   d. the lower taxes increased investment by the same amount.

4. Which of the following would be most likely to cause inflation?
   a. A reduction in investment at a time when businesses are operating at 50 percent of their capacity
   b. An increase in government spending without an increase in taxes during a period of full employment ✓
   c. An increase in government spending and an increase in taxes during a period of slow economic activity
   d. A budget surplus during a period of full employment

5. Suppose that government policy-makers decide that, because of increased investment, the growth rate of GNP will be higher than they had originally planned. What is needed, they feel, is a reallocation of resources away from the production of investment goods and toward the production of consumption goods. Which of the following policy alternatives would be most likely to accomplish this objective?
   a. Adoption of a national sales tax
   b. A higher tax credit allowance for business investment in capital equipment
   c. An increase in the excise tax on gasoline
   d. A reduction in personal income taxes ✓

6. (I) Prior to Keynes, when economists focused on aggregate markets, most of their analysis was on the supply side of those markets. (II) The Great Depression and other economic downturns provide strong evidence that aggregate demand is an important determinant of real output.
   a. Both I and II are true.
   b. Both I and II are false.
   c. I is true, II is false.
   d. I is false, II is true. ✓

7. (I) An increase in marginal tax rates will encourage individuals to substitute tax-deductible expenditures for non-tax deductible expenditures. (II) An increase in marginal tax rates will increase the incentive of investors to undertake investment projects expected to yield taxable income.
   a. I is true, II is false. ✓
   b. I is false, II is true.
   c. Both I and II are true.
   d. Both I and II are false.

8. Which of the following was most likely to have retarded the growth rate of aggregate supply in the United States during the 1970s?
   a. Several tax reductions that were instituted during the decade
   b. The sharply higher price of imported oil ✓
   c. A decline in government expenditures as a share of GNP
   d. The increase in the nominal size of the national debt

9. In the real world, it appears that fiscal policy
    a. has never been a stabilizing influence.
    b. has almost always been a stabilizing influence.
    c. has, at times, been destabilizing.
    d. has had no noticeable impact on the economy.

10. Countercyclical budget policy suggests that
    a. the budget always be balanced.
    b. a deficit is needed if an inflationary gap is present.
    c. a surplus is necessary if full-employment income is less than the present equilibrium level of income.
    d. none of the above

11. ''Expansionary fiscal policy in an economy with some excess capacity will tend to increase current real output.'' Which of the following models would tend to support such a statement?
    a. The Keynesian model and the new classical model, but not the crowding-out model
    b. The Keynesian model and the crowding-out model, but not the new classical model
    c. The Keynesian model, but not the crowding-out and new classical models
    d. All three models

12. Which of the following is *not* a part of the current modern synthesis which most macroeconomists would accept:
    a. During a depression or severe recession, expansionary fiscal policy can stimulate real output and stabilize the economy.
    b. During normal times, the ability of fiscal policy to stimulate real output and stabilize the economy is far more limited than the basic Keynesian model implies.
    c. During inflationary times, fiscal policy is once again capable of having an impact on real output and stabilizing the economy.
    d. Given the potential of ill-timed policy changes, fiscal policy should respond only to major economic disturbances.

13. Which of the following is a possible impact of deficits on capital formation?
    a. If deficits hide the true cost of government, then voter-consumers may not support enough government expenditure.
    b. As government's interest obligations increase relative to its potential, the risk of lending to the government increases and lenders may charge a higher interest rate to all borrowers.
    c. Deficit financing imposes severe supply-side disincentives for capital formation.
    d. Deficit financing has *no* effect on capital formation.

14. The idea that proper timing of fiscal policy is both highly difficult and of crucial importance is
    a. agreed to by most macroeconomists.
    b. of no importance to most macroeconomists because the modern consensus is that fiscal policy does not matter.
    c. supported by new classical economists but not by very many other macroeconomists.
    d. only true if we are operating during a depression or a severe recession.

THE ECONOMIC WAY OF THINKING—DISCUSSION QUESTIONS

1. "A reduction in tax rates will lead to a decline in tax revenues and an increase in the size of the budget deficit. The deficit spending will be inflationary. Thus, there is little reason to believe that a tax cut will be able to alter the real output rate of an economy." Evaluate each of these three sentences.

2. Do you think we should increase or decrease taxes at this time? Defend the appropriateness of your policy suggestion. Might the timing of your policy prescription be important? Why?

3. Despite the presence of a large budget deficit in 1981–1982, the Reagan administration moved to reduce tax rates. Was it irresponsible to lower tax rates while the budget deficit was so large? Why or why not?

4. What is the tax shelter industry? Do you think it is wrong for taxpayers to utilize legal methods to shelter their income from the taxing authorities? Why or why not?

5. What is the full-employment budget? Why is it a better indicator than the actual budget of the expansionary or restrictive impact of fiscal policy?

6. Do you think the size of the national debt is a serious economic problem? Why or why not?

7. Has real-world fiscal policy had a stabilizing effect on the U.S. economy? Cite historical data to support your answer. How do political incentives enter the picture?

8. What's wrong with this economic thinking? "Our biggest problem is the national debt. With a debt of $1.15 trillion and a population of only 230 million, it is clear that every man, woman and child in the United States is roughly $5000 in debt. We're living on borrowed time!"

PERSPECTIVES IN ECONOMICS

To Balance Or Not To Balance
by Herbert Stein

[Reprinted with permission of Herbert Stein, from *The Wall Street Journal*, March 12, 1979.]

The unpoetic but Hamlet-like title of this essay reflects my true uncertainty. Whether to bear the ills of the deficits we have or fly to the balanced budgets whose consequences we know not—or have forgotten?

The problem is not that there are strong arguments on each side of this question. The problem rather is that the arguments on both sides are so weak.

I will offer, dogmatically, a summary of reasons for not being dogmatic about either side of the argument.

Why Balance The Budget? 1. *The people want the budget balanced.* Polls show that a large majority of the American people "favor" a balanced budget. But this has been continuously true for the past forty-five years. During this period the budget has been balanced only eight times. The people have not elected government officials who would balance the budget, or turned out of office those who ran deficits. If the people "favor" balancing the budget, they apparently don't care very much.

2. *Deficits cause inflation.* But deficits don't cause inflation all the time. We have had deficits almost all the time since 1929, and haven't had inflation all that time. Whether deficits are inflationary or not depends on their size, their timing, their rate of change and how they are financed. The currently fashionable view of the connection between deficits and inflation is that deficits cause monetary expansion which is inflationary. However, it is not clear that deficits have been a major cause of excessive monetary expansion in the past, or that deficits need to have this effect in the future. And if this is the problem, the appropriate remedy may lie in the monetary system rather than in the budgetary system.

3. *Deficits cause, or permit, excessive government spending.* The argument is that government will tend to spend too much if it does not have to count the costs of its expenditures fully, and that it would have to count the costs if it had to raise all of its funds by taxation. There are several problems with this. One is that the "discipline" argument assumes that there is a correspondence between a Congressman's perception of his constituents' aversion to higher taxes and the real costs that government spending imposes on the society. This correspondence is loose, at most.

But even at its best this is not an argument for equality of total spending and total taxes. It is an argument for balancing taxes and expenditures at the margin—where decisions are made. For example, we may take it as given that federal expenditures will never again be under $400 billion. Then the discipline requirement would be met by saying that we should collect one dollar of taxes for every dollar by which expenditures exceed $400 billion.

4. *Deficits absorb private saving that would otherwise flow*

into investment, and deficits therefore reduce the rate of economic growth. This argument assumes, in the first place, that private saving is given, or at least that a deficit does not generate an equal amount of private saving. This assumption has been contested by some economists. Moreover, there is no law of nature or economics which tells us that the right amount of private investment is the amount of private saving. In an economy that is rapidly becoming richer for a variety of reasons, one could argue that it is as reasonable for the government to draw funds out of the private saving-investment stream through borrowing as to draw funds out of the private consumption stream through taxing.

Also, it should be noted that if the government makes expenditures which raise the growth rate this argument would not bar financing such expenditures by deficits.

Why Not Balance The Budget? While the arguments for balancing the budget leave many uncertainties, this is also true of the arguments against balance.

1. *Full employment cannot be achieved without a deficit.* This persistent notion is without empirical foundation, and once it is accepted that the money supply matters at all it is without theoretical foundation, since there is always some money supply that will generate full employment, even if the budget is in balance or in large surplus.

2. *The ability to run a deficit of the proper size on the proper occasions increases the government's ability to stabilize the economy.* This proposition is being more and more questioned for several reasons. There is doubt whether variations in the size of the deficit or surplus affect aggregate demand, and also whether the effects on aggregate demand influence the real variables, output and employment, or only the rate of inflation. At a more pragmatic level, there is great skepticism about the ability of the government to manage its deficits and surpluses in a way that contributes to stability rather than to instability.

3. *Unavoidable fluctuations in economic activity affect revenues and expenditures in such a way that even if the government plans to balance the budget a deficit may result.* Of course, if the government made its tax and expenditure decisions so that there would be a large surplus under the forecast economic conditions, there would be a cushion to avoid a deficit even if the economy fell moderately below the forecast path. However, there are probably more realistic solutions to this problem.

One would be to state the budget-balancing requirement in terms of the budget plan, rather than in terms of the budget outcome. Also, the problem is less acute if the requirement is not that the budget be balanced each year but that it be balanced over several years.

4. *Balancing the budget will require that we spend less and/or tax more than we would otherwise have done.* This is obvious, but it is an objection only if it is true that a) there are some expenditures worth borrowing for but not worth taxing for, or b) that some taxes are "worse" than deficits. Many people take one or both of these positions. Undoubtedly there is some truth in both of them. The real question is whether the political process can be trusted to live with this proposition and not make it an excuse for irresponsible behavior.

5. *A requirement that the budget be balanced would be easily and widely evaded.* Government receipts and expenditures as those terms are now defined in the budget are only two of the many ways in which the government can influence the allocation of resources in the economy. "Off-budget" transactions are the most obvious among the other ways available. Probably much more important are regulations which require private parties to make expenditures of kinds specified by the government, as for environmental purposes, or requiring employers to provide certain pension or health benefits to workers, and so on. One can argue that limiting the ability of the government to exert its influence overtly through the budget will force the government's influence into less visible and less efficient forms, which would be a loss.

On the other hand, limitation of the government's options would probably reduce the total scale of its activities, and the options outside the budget are probably less inflationary than financing through the conventional deficit.

One cannot draw strong conclusions from the weak arguments I have briefly covered. Probably the strongest conclusion one can find is to make no irrevocable commitments. This is, in my opinion, an argument against enacting a constitutional amendment in an area about which we still know so little.

Another conclusion is that one cannot hope to achieve all desirable goals for the federal budget by operating on whether the budget is balanced or not. Even if the budget were continuously in balance, we would have to attack the problems of the expenditure level and the taxation level, and there is much room for improving policy and procedures in that regard.

However, the general negativism of the preceding argument does not mean that we are unable to find some rules for deficits or surpluses which are superior to the mixture of political expedience and economic fine-tuning by which we have been living. The combination of inflation, low capital investment and high government expenditures yielding doubtful benefits, from which we are suffering, indicates that the need for better rules of fiscal policy is urgent. And these same conditions suggest that appropriate rules would include elements of the budget-balancing idea in some form.

These rules would not be simple—as "balance the budget" only seems to be—but neither would they be incomprehensible. I believe that they might include a variant of the idea of balancing the budget at high employment, advanced by the Committee for Economic Development in 1947, and modernized primarily to take account of the fact of inflation.

However, it is not my point here to advance a specific proposal in this regard. It is only to suggest that we need to get beyond the shouting-match between the fundamentalists who keep repeating "balance the budget" and the economist-politicians who say, "Leave it to us and we will take care of the budget." If the current furor over budget-balancing should settle down to a constructive search for a synthesis of what is valid in both viewpoints, it will have been most valuable.

Discussion

1. Review Stein's four arguments in favor of balancing the budget and his five arguments against it. Which side do you find most convincing?

2. Senator Proxmire said (about the time this article came out):

    "If a student in Economics I were given this scenario in fiscal policy, that is, there is . . . 8 percent inflation and rapidly expanding employment . . . and asked 'should, under those circumstances, the federal government balance its budget?' [as opposed to running a deficit], there is no way he could get a passing grade if he said no."

    Do you agree with Senator Proxmire? Why or why not? Do you expect to pass this course?

3. If the federal budget were *always* balanced, would the problem of economic instability be solved forever? Why or why not?

12

Money and the Banking System

TRUE OR FALSE

T F

☐ ☐ 1. The two major kinds of money in the United States are paper currency and coins.

☐ ☐ 2. Doubling the supply of money would most likely double the value of money to society as a whole.

☐ ☐ 3. Fractional reserve goldsmithing is analogous to our current system of fractional reserve banking in that newly created money (gold) would, after a time, have a multiplied effect on the total money supply.

☐ ☐ 4. A reserve requirement of 25 percent implies a potential deposit expansion multiplier of 25.

☐ ☐ 5. The Federal Reserve System (Fed) has mainly commercial banks and manufacturing corporations as customers.

☐ ☐ 6. The Fed helps commercial banks with check clearing.

☐ ☐ 7. Paper currency accounts for about half of the total money supply.

☐ ☐ 8. Raising the reserve requirement is one way in which the Fed can reduce the money supply.

☐ ☐ 9. Raising the discount rate encourages consumers to deposit more cash in banks and thereby expand the supply of money.

☐ ☐ 10. The U.S. Treasury is the money-creating branch of the Fed.

☐ ☐ 11. The Fed often purchases bonds issued by the U.S. Treasury.

☐ ☐ 12. During the last decade, the Fed has been consistently able to expand the money supply within the range of the money-growth targets it announced at the beginning of the each year.

PROBLEMS AND PROJECTS

1. If banks lend 75 percent of their total deposits, explain how the deposit expansion multiplier would be determined. What is its numerical value?

2. Suppose that the money supply is $600 billion and the reserve requirement is 20 percent. An Arab nation suddenly withdraws $5 billion from its bank account in New York and fails to

deposit the money elsewhere. To what level could the money supply change? (Assume that the level of excess reserves is the same both before and after the withdrawal.)

3. In question 2, if the Fed wanted to respond to the drop in the money supply with open market operations, should it purchase or sell bonds? How many dollars worth of bonds should be involved? (*Hint:* Assume that all transactions are with corporations that adjust their demand deposits to compensate for the transactions.)

4. Anne Howells recently broke open a Mickey Mouse bank into which she had been putting her spare change at the end of each day. Somewhat to her surprise, she discovered a total of $2,000, which she quickly deposited in her commercial bank. Exhibit 1 is designed to follow the course of *potential* demand deposit expansion generated by this new currency deposit assuming that no bank at any stage in the process holds idle excess reserves and there are no currency leakages.

Exhibit 1

	Cash deposits	Required reserves	Excess reserves	Loans	Demand deposits
Initial deposit	$2,000	$ 500	$1,500	_____	_____
Second stage	_____	_____	_____	_____	_____
Third stage	_____	_____	_____	_____	_____
Fourth stage	_____	_____	_____	_____	_____
Fifth stage	_____	_____	_____	_____	_____
All others	_____	_____	_____	_____	
Total	_____	_____	_____	_____	_____

a. What is the value of the required reserve ratio implied by the first two entries under "Initial deposit" in Exhibit 1?

b. Use the reserve ratio you determined in part *a* to fill in the remaining entries in Exhibit 1.

c. If at each stage of the process (including the initial one) individuals decided to keep 15 percent of new cash rather than deposit it in banks, how would this affect the *total* amount of new loans the banking system could extend?

LEARNING THE MECHANICS—MULTIPLE CHOICE

1. An important aspect of a decrease in the discount rate is that
   a. it increases the Federal Reserve System's earnings.
   b. it increases the interest yield of new issues of U.S. securities.
   c. it automatically results in a decrease in the interest rate that commercial banks charge to customers.
   d. it increases the willingness of banks to go into debt, acting as a financial intermediary for the sectors of the economy requesting the funds.

2. Money does *not* serve as
   a. a method of holding wealth.
   b. a medium of exchange.
   c. a common denominator in evaluating bundles of goods.
   d. an end in itself, most of the time.

3. Money is valuable *to society as a whole*
   a. in proportion to the amount of gold backing the dollars in circulation.
   b. in proportion to the amount in circulation.
   c. in a manner that is largely independent of the total amount in circulation, so long as that total is limited.
   d. only if the supply of money is not limited by the central bank.

4. A tool that is *not* used by the Fed to alter the supply of money is
   a. open market operations.
   b. the discount rate.
   c. taxes.
   d. buying and selling of U.S. securities.

   Suppose that the Fed sells $5 million of U.S. securities to the public. Assume a reserve requirement of 10 percent and that all banks initially have zero excess reserves. (Use in answering questions 5 and 6.)

5. The *direct* result of this action on the money supply is
   a. an increase of $4.5 million.
   b. a decrease of $4.5 million.
   c. an increase of $5 million.
   d. a decrease of $5 million.

6. The *total* impact of this action on the money supply (assuming no leakages in the system and no excess reserves) several weeks later is
   a. an increase of $50 million.
   b. a decrease of $50 million.
   c. an increase of $4.5 million.
   d. an increase of $5 million.

7. Monetary expansion and contraction
   a. are the major concern of the Federal Reserve System.
   b. are the concern of the president, under expert advisement from the Federal Reserve System.
   c. are the concern of the Treasury.
   d. are the concern of Congress.

8. A reserve requirement of 10 percent
   a. implies a potential money deposit multiplier of 1.
   b. implies that the discount rate must be less than 10 percent.
   c. implies a potential money deposit multiplier of 10.
   d. implies a smaller multiplier than would be present if the reserve requirement were 25 percent.

9. Suppose that a bank with no initial excess reserves received a demand deposit of $5000 that created excess reserves in the amount of $4000. What was the legal reserve requirement?
   a. 20 percent
   b. 10 percent
   c. 15 percent
   d. 25 percent

10. Fiat money is defined as
    a. deposits denominated in U.S. dollars at banks and other financial institutions outside the United States.
    b. money used to buy small Italian sports cars.
    c. money that has little intrinsic value; it is neither backed by nor convertible to a commodity of value. ✓
    d. vault cash plus deposits with Federal Reserve Banks.

11. The Federal Reserve monetary growth targets are
    a. ranges of the rate of growth of the money supply that the Fed announces as goals for particular years. ✓
    b. difficult to achieve because the Treasury usually prints too much money, causing excessive monetary growth.
    c. difficult to achieve because of the changing nature of money; a substantial component of the money supply is now used primarily to conduct transactions rather than for savings.
    d. impossible to ever achieve.

12. The primary weapon used by the Fed to control the money supply in recent years has been
    a. NOW accounts.
    b. open market operations. ✓
    c. changes in the discount rate.
    d. changes in reserve requirements.

13. The monetary control act of 1980 restructured the banking industry by eliminating most of the distinctions between
    a. commercial banks and savings and loan associations. ✓
    b. M-1 and M-2.
    c. the theoretical deposit expansion multiplier and the actual deposit expansion multiplier.
    d. open market operations and changes in the discount rate.

THE ECONOMIC WAY OF THINKING—MULTIPLE CHOICE

1. If the government wanted to follow an antirecessionary *fiscal* policy, it would plan
    a. a decrease in the money supply.
    b. a government budget deficit.
    c. a government budget surplus.
    d. an increase in the money supply.

2. If the Federal Reserve wanted to expand the supply of money as part of an antirecessionary *monetary* policy, it might
    a. decrease the reserve requirements.
    b. urge the Treasury to buy more U.S. securities.
    c. sell U.S. securities in the open market.
    d. increase the discount rate.

3. The Federal Reserve System, the central bank of the United States, regulates the money supply largely by
    a. regulating the volume of Federal Reserve notes issued, since these notes constitute the major part of the U.S. money stock.
    b. regulating the extent to which the Treasury coins money.
    c. affecting the volume of bank reserves, primarily by its open market policy.
    d. using its power to set the reserve requirements, thereby influencing the ability of banks to issue currency.

4. Our current monetary system resembles early goldsmithing in that
   a. our money is backed mainly by the gold in Fort Knox.
   b. neither goldsmiths nor current banks would have enough gold (money) on hand to pay all depositors simultaneously.
   c. in both cases the required reserves were approximately 20 percent.
   d. excess reserves are not allowed by law.

5. Which of the following is correct?
   a. Federal Reserve purchases of securities put upward pressure on the discount rate.
   b. The Federal Reserve notes in your wallet are an asset of the Federal Reserve System.
   c. Federal Reserve sales of securities reduce the reserves of banks.
   d. The Federal Reserve System controls the currency/demand deposit ratio.

6. The larger the reserve requirement
   a. the larger the potential deposit multiplier.
   b. the smaller the potential deposit multiplier.
   c. the more profitable the banks will be.
   d. the larger the proportion of an additional deposit that is available to the bank for the extension of additional loans.

7. As a result of banking deregulation during the early 1980s
   a. banks can no longer pay interest on checking account deposits.
   b. the Fed's ability to buy and sell U.S. securities was limited.
   c. the Secretary of Treasury was removed from the Board of Governors of the Fed.
   d. The Fed now applies similar regulatory requirements to all depository institutions.

8. Which of the following was *not* an institutional change mandated by the Deregulation and Monetary Control Act of 1980?
   a. All depository institutions were permitted to offer interest-earning checking accounts.
   b. The Fed was prohibited from establishing reserve requirements for depository institutions other than member commercial banks.
   c. The interest rate ceilings on time and savings accounts at depository institutions were scheduled to be phased out.
   d. All depository institutions were placed under the jurisdiction of the Fed.

9. The amount of the actual deposit expansion may fall short of the product of the amount of new reserves times the inverse of the required reserve ratio because
   a. banks may choose to hold some excess reserves rather than lending all excess reserves.
   b. some individuals prefer to hold demand deposits rather than holding currency.
   c. instead of a monopoly banking system, there are many banks.
   d. the discount rate may be too low.

10. Which of the following is *not* a method used by the Fed to control the money supply?
    a. An increase in the reserve requirement when restrictive monetary policy is desirable
    b. An increase in the discount rate when restrictive monetary policy is desirable
    c. An open market sale when a restrictive monetary policy is desirable
    d. An increase in government expenditures when expansionary monetary policy is desired

11. Open market policy concerning purchases and sales of government bonds by the Federal Reserve System is set by
    a. The Treasury Department.
    b. the president in consultation with Congress.
    c. the Federal Reserve Open Market Committee.
    d. the individual commercial banks, which vote according to their share of ownership in the Federal Reserve.

12. A recent development in banking, NOW accounts, allows banks, in effect, to pay interest on checking accounts. This should
   a. cause customers to switch funds from savings accounts to checking accounts.
   b. cause customers to switch funds from cash to checking accounts.
   c. cause customers to switch funds from bonds to checking accounts.
   d. All of the above are correct.

13. The nature of the narrowly defined money supply, M-1, is different today than it was prior to the financial deregulation of the early 1980s because
   a. money market deposit accounts, which are part of M-1, have increased rapidly.
   b. interest-earning other-checkable deposits, which are part of M-1, have increased rapidly.
   c. the definition of M-1 has been changed to no longer include deposits at savings and loan associations.
   d. the definition of M-1 has been changed to now include credit card purchases.

THE ECONOMIC WAY OF THINKING—DISCUSSION QUESTIONS

1. If an *individual* suddenly found an amount of money equal to his existing cash balance, would he be better off? What if *every* individual simultaneously found such an amount of cash (equal to their current money holdings)—would they all be better off? Why or why not?

2. "Our currency can no longer be exchanged for gold. It is useless pieces of paper. It is only a matter of time until people realize that a dollar bill is worthless. Exchanging pieces of paper that are not backed by valuable minerals cannot go on forever." Do you agree or disagree? Explain.

3. "If the U.S. Treasury sold government securities to private individuals, it would fail to change the supply of money. If the Federal Reserve sold government securities to these same individuals, the supply of money would decline by some multiple of the amount of securities sold." Can this view be correct? Explain.

4. What is the difference between the U.S. Treasury and the Federal Reserve banking system? Who controls the money supply, the Treasury or the Fed? Explain.

5. What impact will the following actions have on the money supply?
   a. The Fed buys $2 billion of U.S. securities from the public.
   b. The Fed raises the discount rate from 10 percent to 11 percent.
   c. The Treasury increases the national debt by selling $2 billion of U.S. securities to the public.
   d. The Treasury sells $2 billion of securities directly to the Fed.
   e. The Fed reduces the reserve requirements on transaction accounts from 6 percent to 5 percent.

6. Would it be a good thing if everyone had twice the amount of their current clothes, housing, and food supplies? Would it be a good thing if everyone had twice as much money? How does money differ from other goods?

7. Why can banks continue to hold reserves that are only a fraction of the demand deposits of their customers? Is your money safe in a bank? Why or why not?

8. Carefully define M-1 and M-2. How are they different? Which seems to be a more realistic way of accounting for the role of money in influencing economic activity?

PERSPECTIVES IN ECONOMICS

How The Federal Reserve Decides How Much Money To Put Into The Economy
by Edwin L. Dale Jr.
Special to The New York Times

WASHINGTON, May 4—Only one thing is entirely agreed, accepted and understood about the somewhat mysterious and often controversial subject of the Government's monetary policy, which is conducted by the semi-independent Federal Reserve Board.

This is that the Fed, as it is commonly known, can create money out of thin air by writing a check on itself without any deposits to back that check. It can do so in unlimited amounts. And only it can do so—the Treasury cannot.

Yesterday, Arthur F. Burns, chairman of the Federal Reserve Board, disclosed to Congress the Fed's intentions and targets for creation of money in the year ahead. But he gave his targets in the form of range, not a precise number, and he is the first to admit that he and his colleagues are not at all certain what exactly is the ''right'' amount of money to create for the good of the nation's economy.

The Government's ''printing press'' is literally in the Bureau of Engraving and Printing, which turns out currency notes in amounts that depend on the public's demand for them. But the true printing press is a little known man named Alan R. Holmes who sits in an office in the Federal Reserve Bank of New York and decides every day, under instructions and guidelines from a powerful body of the Federal Reserve known as the Open Market Committee, how much money to create.

Orders Securities Mr. Holmes creates money by placing an order in the money market for Treasury bills or other Government securities. He pays for them by writing a check on the Federal Reserve Bank of New York. If the order is for $100 million, an additional $100 million in cash suddenly flows into the economy, possessed originally by the people who sold the Government securities to the Fed.

Mr. Holmes can ''extinguish'' money, too. If he places

How the Federal Reserve Board Can Create Money

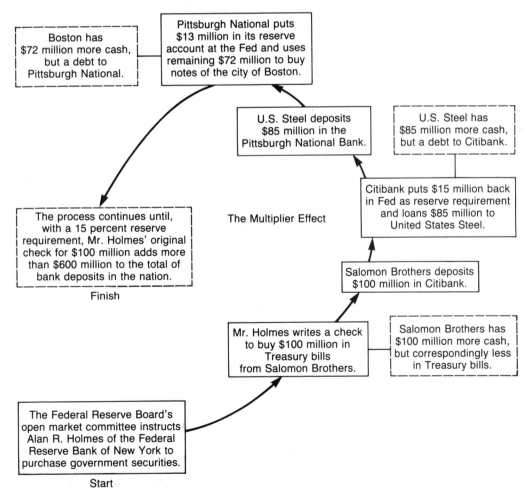

a sell order in the market, the Fed sells securities to a money market dealer or bank and gets a check in payment. The amount of money in that check essentially vanishes. The buyer of the securities from the Fed has less cash but the Fed, in effect, tears up the check.

How much money Mr. Holmes creates makes a good deal of difference to the performance of the economy—the rate of inflation, the expansion of production and jobs, interest rates and indeed general well-being—because the amount of money affects how rapidly the wheels of the economy turn.

But what Mr. Holmes does is cause of controversy because the creation of additional money is also linked by economists to inflation. Friedrich Hayek, the Pulitizer Prize-winning Austrian economist, asserts unequivocally that "inflation is an all monetary phenomenon." Mr. Hayek has innumerable followers. While other economists think his view is a little oversimplified, nearly all of them agree that "money matters."

What is more, the check that Mr. Holmes writes is only the beginning of the process of creating money. That initial $100 million starts a process by which the nation's money supply—currency plus deposits in banks—will grow not by $100 million but by some multiple of that amount.

It is at this point that things begin to get a little more complicated. In brief, the "multiplier" effect arises from the way the nation's—any advanced nation's—banking system works. It is called a "fractional reserve" system and it works this way:

Suppose that Salomon Brothers receives Mr. Holmes's check on the Federal Reserve Bank of New York and deposits it in Citibank, where deposits are now higher by $100 million.

Under the Fed's "reserve requirement" regulations, which are crucial to the multiplier process, Citibank must deposit about $15 million of this in its "reserve" account at the Fed. But then it can, and does, lend the remaining $85 million to, say, the United States Steel Corporation, which needs money to pay wages while it waits for its inventories of steel to be bought.

U.S. Steel gets the money from Citibank and deposits it at the Pittsburgh National Bank, and the multiplying process goes on. Pittsburgh National puts about $13 million in its reserve account at the Fed and uses the remaining $72 million to buy notes of the city of Boston, which deposits this income in the First National Bank of Boston.

At this point Mr. Holmes's original $100 million has already become $257 million, as follows:
- Salomon Brothers has $100 million more cash (but correspondingly less in Treasury bills).
- U.S. Steel has $85 million more cash (but a debt to Citibank).
- Boston has $72 million more cash (but a debt to Pittsburgh National).

The process continues until, with a 15 percent reserve requirement, Mr. Holmes's original check for $100 million eventually adds more than $600 million to the total of bank deposits in the nation, the nation's money supply. And that money, obviously, can be and is spent. Sometimes more spending is desirable to bring forth production and add to jobs, but by no means always.

The more money there is in circulation, the easier it is for sellers to raise prices, whether to cover higher wages and other costs or to increase profits, because customers around the nation have more to spend. When prices go up all over, this is inflation. But it is impossible to know precisely just how much money is enough or how much is too much at any given time. But there is obviously a point of "too much," as all of history teaches.

For policy makers, there are the two following questions:
- What targets for Mr. Holmes should the Open Market Committee, which consists of seven members of the Federal Reserve Board and the presidents of five of the twelve regional Federal Reserve banks, establish? The relationship of the money supply to the economy at large, including inflation, is by no means clear, even to the experts.
- Because Mr. Holmes's buying and selling affects short-term interest rates as well as the money supply, which should he concentrate on?

At the bottom, the nation's central bank is controversial, and frequently unpopular, because it is a "nay-sayer." Whenever inflation rears its head, the job of the Fed is to slow the creation of money and, for a while at least, that often means higher interest rates and sometimes a cutback in production and a loss of jobs.

Switching Of Funds The right policy will always be a matter of judgment. But at the moment the problem of setting the target for Mr. Holmes is complicated by what Mr. Burns calls the "new financial technology," such as those little electronic "tellers" that many banks now make available to their depositors. Among other services they permit immediate switching of funds from savings to checking accounts by the push of a button and even payment of some bills, such as utilities bills, directly out of savings.

The "money supply" as long defined meant currency plus checking accounts (known in the jargon as M1). There were fairly well-established relationships between the growth of M1 and the overall courage of the economy, including the rate of inflation, but now that people, and business, too, have learned to use savings accounts as almost the equivalent of checking accounts, those relationships have gone awry.

"Our equations are all fouled up," a high Federal Reserve official concedes.

The report of the Open Market Committee on its meeting of last January disclosed that the panel, puzzled by a slow growth in money but a rapid growth in the economy, threw up its hands and simply gave Mr. Holmes an unusually wide "target range" for money growth in the period immediately ahead. This meant that he was not to take any special action to create or extinguish money as long as M1 growth stayed within a very wide band.

The Fed also keeps track of and sets targets for M2, which includes savings accounts. But Mr. Holmes cannot tell when he writes one of his checks how much of the ultimate deposits will be in checking or savings accounts. Thus his art will always be imprecise and his results subject to criticism. At present, the Fed does not know whether M1 or M2 is the more important measure, though in the end it controls the growth of both.

The interest rate problem is a different one.

When Mr. Holmes intervenes in the market to buy or sell Government securities, he not only changes the amount of money in the economy but, unavoidably, also affects what are called "money market interest rates"—the rates on very short-term instruments such as Treasury bills.

Rate On Bank Loans The impact of his intervention decisions shows up first in the most sensitive and closely watched of all rates, called the "Federal funds" rate, which is the interest rate charged on loans from one bank to another. In daily operations some banks wind up short of their required reserve deposits with the Federal Reserve and some have an excess, and this gives rise to overnight loans from one bank to another.

Eventually, a rising prime rate brings along with it higher interest rates to ordinary consumers and other borrowers.

Sometimes, as occurred last week, Mr. Holmes is instructed to intervene in such a way as to "nudge up" the Federal funds rate himself, as a signal that the Federal Reserve feels the money supply is growing too rapidly. In either case, whether he "lets" the rate go up or pushes it up himself, the result is higher interest rates. And these days that often means a quick drop in the stock market, as happened in the last few days.

Every time Mr. Holmes writes a check he adds to bank reserves and makes the Federal funds interest rates "easier"—that is, lower or less likely to rise.

Discussion

1. Explain how the Federal Reserve System is actually creating money when Alan Holmes places an order in the money market for Treasury bills or other government securities. How will this money-supply change affect employment and output?

2. The article refers to "the multiplier." Is this the same multiplier that we talked about in Chapter 10? If not, what is it?

3. Who actually decides to expand the money supply—the Treasury, Alan Holmes, the Open Market Committee, or the Board of Governors of the Federal Reserve Board?

13

Modern Macroeconomics: Monetary Policy

TRUE OR FALSE

T F

☐ ☐ 1. The interest rate is the opportunity cost of *obtaining* money.

☐ ☐ 2. If the demand for money does not shift, an increase in the money supply would lower the interest rate in the short run.

☐ ☐ 3. If other factors remain unchanged, higher interest rates make fewer investment projects worthwhile.

☐ ☐ 4. Purchases of government bonds by the monetary authority tend indirectly to decrease the amount of investment activity.

☐ ☐ 5. An unanticipated expansionary monetary policy makes less credit available in the economy, causing interest rates to rise.

☐ ☐ 6. The early classical economists did not believe that changes in the supply of money would exert an independent impact on real output and employment.

☐ ☐ 7. For monetarists, government itself is often a villain, insofar as monetary instability has led to general economic instability.

☐ ☐ 8. Anticipated and unanticipated monetary policy have the same aggregate impact; the main difference between the two is the length of time it takes to achieve that impact.

☐ ☐ 9. When aggregate demand expands, the rate of capacity utilization will be approximately equal in all sectors of the economy.

☐ ☐ 10. During the Depression, monetary and fiscal authorities undertook policies that made things worse instead of better.

☐ ☐ 11. The major consequences of long-run rapid monetary growth are inflation and higher nominal interest rates.

☐ ☐ 12. While differences between Keynesians and monetarists still exist, a modern consensus view of monetary policy has emerged.

PROBLEMS AND PROJECTS

1. The modern consensus view of monetary policy depends not on whether your views are monetarist or Keynesian but instead on whether the policies are anticipated and on the length of time between the policy and the impact.

   Attempt to organize each of these views by filling in Exhibit 1, which analyzes the impact of a sudden increase in the money supply caused by open market purchases of bonds by the Federal Reserve System.

Exhibit I

	Short run	*Long run*
Unanticipated increase in money supply	Real interest rates fall Aggregate demand increases Aggregate output increases Unemployment falls	
Anticipated increase in money supply		

2. For the six months immediately preceding the 1980 elections, the money supply grew at an annual rate of 14.7 percent, but then it slowed over the next year to only 3.6 percent growth. Why do you think such a policy was undertaken? Do you think that the elections had any impact on the choice of policies? Consult the *Federal Reserve Bulletin* to see what happened to interest rates, prices, and unemployment following these developments. Were the events in the real world consistent with theory? Now find similar data for the 1984 election. Did the same phenomenon occur?

3. Exhibit 2 below illustrates the macroeconomy initially in equilibrium at the real GNP level of Y_1, price level of P_1, and nominal and real interest rates of i_1 and r_1, respectively.

Exhibit 2

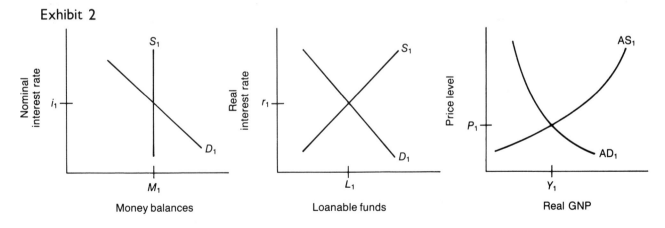

a. Suppose the Fed conducts an open market sale of government securities. Show the short-run impact of this sale in the money balances and loanable funds markets. Briefly explain the changes you make in the diagrams.

b. Now show the short-run impact of these changes in the financial markets on real GNP and the price level. Again, explain briefly the changes you make in the diagram.

4. Exhibit 3 illustrates the macroeconomy in equilibrium initially at real GNP level Y_f (the full-employment level) and price level P_1. There is no long-run growth of real GNP and initially the money supply is constant. Therefore, prices are stable at P_1. Suppose now that, all else equal, the Fed increases the money supply at some constant percent per period.

Exhibit 3

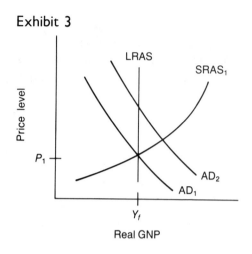

a. If the increase in the money supply raises aggregate demand in the second period to AD_2, what will be the short-run impact on real GNP and the price level? Explain briefly.

b. Will the increase in real GNP you described in part a above be sustainable in the long run? Explain, modifying the diagram as necessary.

c. What will happen in the long run if there is no growth in real GNP and the Fed continues to increase the money supply so that aggregate demand continues to increase? Explain briefly and illustrate the process in your diagram.

5. One day you are riding home on the bus and the man sitting on your left is reading a newspaper with the headline, "Fed announces drastic new program of Open Market bond purchases!" In the informal discussion that this headline causes the various bus riders to immediately develop, the woman to your right casually wonders what an aggregate supply/aggregate demand model of the Fed's actions would look like, and everyone (including the bus driver) looks at *you*! What can you do to get the bus going again? You have to show the impact of the purchases (starting from long-run equilibrium shown in Exhibit 4) on the price level, real GNP, and interest rates. (Assume that the change, or at least the size of the change, is unanticipated.)

Exhibit 4

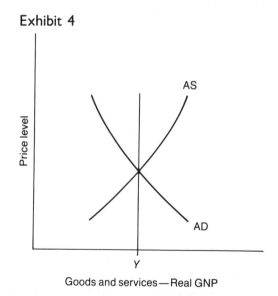

LEARNING THE MECHANICS—MULTIPLE CHOICE

1. Which of the following is *not* a primary determinant of the demand for money balances?
   a. Transactions demand
   b. Nominal demand
   c. Speculative demand
   d. Precautionary demand

2. Which of the following best describes the difference between monetary policy and fiscal policy?
   a. Fiscal policy is used to control the rate of unemployment, whereas monetary policy is used to control the rate of inflation.
   b. Fiscal policy refers to tax changes and monetary policy refers to total payments made by the government.
   c. Fiscal policy determines the volume of government bonds outstanding (national debt), whereas monetary policy determines the interest rate that must be paid on them.
   d. Fiscal policy concerns the tax and expenditure policy of the government, whereas monetary policy concerns interest rate and money supply policy.

3. If the unemployment rate were 8 percent and prices were falling at a rate of 5 percent annually, which of the following would be the most appropriate policy?
   a. An increase in the discount rate
   b. Unanticipated purchases of U.S. securities by the Federal Reserve
   c. An increase in the Fed's reserve requirements
   d. The sale of U.S. securities by the Fed

4. Starting from an initial macroeconomic equilibrium, an increase in the money supply will, in the short run,
   a. lower the demand for money, lower interest rates, and shift the aggregate supply curve to the right.
   b. lower the demand for money, lower interest rates, and shift the aggregate demand curve to the right
   c. leave the demand for money unchanged, lower interest rates, and shift the aggregate supply curve to the right.
   d. leave the demand for money unchanged, lower interest rates, and shift the aggregate demand curve to the right.

5. Suppose the macroeconomy is initially experiencing full employment, stable prices, and zero long-term growth in real GNP. An unanticipated increase in the rate of growth of the money supply will
   a. raise real GNP in the short run, causing temporary inflation in prices and a return to full-employment real GNP.
   b. raise real GNP in the short run, causing permanent inflation at a permanently higher level of real GNP.
   c. raise real GNP in the short run, causing permanent inflation at a level of real GNP close to the full employment level.
   d. leave real GNP unchanged in the short run, causing permanent inflation at the full employment level of real GNP.

6. To the extent that an unanticipated increase in the money supply convinces decision-makers that the Fed will be forced to slow down the rate of growth of the money supply in the future,
   a. monetary policy will become more expansionary.
   b. monetary policy will become less expansionary.
   c. the effectiveness of monetary policy will be unchanged.
   d. decision-makers will be consistently wrong.

7. In the equation of exchange, V stands for
    a. velocity, or the annual rate at which money changes hands in the purchase of final products.
    b. the investment component of aggregate demand.
    c. the amount of money demanded per unit of output.
    d. a constant, 3.1416, discovered by classical economists.

8. The demand curve for money
    a. would shift if the interest rate changed.
    b. shifts with an increase in the reserve requirement.
    c. shows the relationship between the quantity of money demanded and the interest rate.
    d. is a relationship between the quantity of investment demanded and the interest rate.

9. An unanticipated excess supply of money may
    a. cause individuals to increase their demand for a wide range of goods and services as they try to reduce their holdings of money.
    b. cause an increase in real output and/or an increase in the price level.
    c. not have its effect only through a change in the interest rate.
    d. all of the above are correct.

10. Which of the following would be most likely to increase nominal interest rates (according to the consensus view) in the short run?
    a. An unanticipated decrease in the money supply
    b. An unanticipated increase in the money supply
    c. An anticipated decrease in the money supply
    d. An anticipated increase in the money supply

11. According to the consensus view, monetary policy
    a. only works through the interest rate if it is going to be effective.
    b. does not work through the interest rate at all.
    c. can work through the interest rate and also work directly on aggregate demand.
    d. operates by a transmission mechanism involving tax cuts which decrease the interest rate.

12. When we expand the money supply, what actually happens?
    a. The Treasury prints more currency, and then Congress spends it.
    b. The Federal Reserve System prints more currency.
    c. The Treasury prints more money, but it is the Federal Reserve System that actually buys the bonds.
    d. None of the above.

13. Since the introduction of interest-bearing checkable deposits has changed the nature of M-1, individuals are less likely to transfer temporarily idle balances from checking accounts to savings deposits. The impact of this tendency will be to
    a. increase M-2 and decrease M-1.
    b. increase the velocity of money.
    c. both a and b.
    d. neither a nor b.

THE ECONOMIC WAY OF THINKING—MULTIPLE CHOICE

1. In the three-market model, unanticipated expansionary monetary policy
   a. increases aggregate supply in the short run.
   b. increases the supply of loanable funds and aggregate demand in the short run.
   c. decreases aggregate supply but increases aggregate demand in the long run, and also increases the supply of money in the short run.
   d. increases the supply of loanable funds and decreases aggregate demand in the short run, but actually increases aggregate demand in the long run.

2. Professor A. Genius, chief economic adviser to President Ring Leader, informs the president that the present status of the economy is such that the government should adopt a "neutral" macropolicy (that is, a government spending, tax, and monetary policy that is neither significantly expansionary nor restrictive). President Leader has already decided to increase government expenditures on his favorite projects, including an expanded welfare program and the development of a new weapons system. Since President Leader is increasing planned government expenditures, what other actions will Professor Genius most likely suggest?
   a. A tax reduction and/or expansionary monetary policy
   b. A tax increase and/or expansionary monetary policy
   c. A tax reduction and/or restrictive monetary policy
   d. A tax increase and/or restrictive monetary policy

3. Use statements I and II to answer this question. (**I**) According to the quantity theory of money, the velocity of money and aggregate output are largely determined by factors outside the control of macropolicy-makers. (**II**) Classical economists, who adhered to the quantity theory of money, believed that an increase in the money supply would cause the general level of prices to increase proportionally.
   a. Both I and II are true.
   b. Both I and II are false.
   c. I is true, II is false.
   d. I is false, II is true.

4. A steady (and expected) growth in the money supply would
   a. cause even wider swings in the business cycle.
   b. cause the interest rate to remain unchanged, since inflation would be of less importance.
   c. reduce an important element of uncertainty and make monetary arrangements involving future payments more efficient.
   d. remove any time lag between the point when a policy change is needed and when the impact of fiscal policy is felt.

5. "Inept government monetary policy is the major source of economic instability. Monetary expansion has been the source of every major inflation. Every major recession was perpetuated by monetary contraction. We would have less instability if we simply required the monetary authorities to stabilize the growth rate of the money supply. If the government would fulfill the function of providing a stable monetary environment, only minor disturbances would result." This quote is indicative of the views of
   a. the classical economists.
   b. both the Keynesians and monetarists.
   c. the monetarists.
   d. the Keynesians.

6. Which of the following may be a reason for opposing the use of restrictive monetary policy as an anti-inflationary tool?
   a. Restrictive monetary policy has no effect, since it may unbalance the budget.
   b. Restrictive monetary policy has uneven effects; the restrictive effects are more severe in interest sensitive sectors.
   c. Restrictive monetary policy cannot have any effect on inflation independent of fiscal policy.
   d. Restrictive monetary policy always causes inflation to accelerate because of its effect on interest rates.

7. All of the following contributed to the severity of the Great Depression except one. Which one was *not* a major cause of the Great Depression?
   a. A sharp reduction in the supply of money in the early 1930s
   b. Tax increases (to balance the budget) in the early 1930s
   c. Tariff increases (to protect domestic industry) in 1930
   d. Farm price supports and increasing farm prices, which made it harder for consumers to be able to afford to eat in the 1930s

8. If the unemployment rate is 8 percent and prices are stable, the *initial* impact of unanticipated expansionary monetary policy would probably be
   a. an increase in prices and a decline in output.
   b. an increase in prices and no change in output.
   c. a small increase in output and a sharp increase in prices.
   d. an increase in output with little change in prices.

9. Which of the following is *least* likely to have an expansionary effect on the economy?
   a. An increase in the demand for money
   b. A decrease in the discount rate
   c. A purchase of government bonds by the Fed
   d. A decrease in reserve requirements of banks

10. The amount of money demanded would probably increase if
    a. the rate of interest rose.
    b. the level of income rose.
    c. individuals began using credit cards for purchases instead of currency or demand deposits.
    d. the Fed sold bonds to commercial banks.

11. Suppose that a federal budget deficit was financed by the sale of U.S. securities to the public. As a result of this action, the money supply will
    a. increase, because the demand deposits of the Treasury will increase.
    b. decrease, because the demand deposits of the public will decrease.
    c. decrease, because the money in the hands of the Fed will increase.
    d. remain unchanged as long as the government spends the proceeds that were borrowed.

12. Starting from a position of macroeconomic equilibrium at the full employment level of real GNP, a one-time increase in the money supply will in the short run
    a. if unanticipated, lower real interest rates, raise the price level, and leave real GNP unchanged.
    b. if anticipated, leave real interest rates unchanged, raise the price level, and leave real GNP unchanged.
    c. if unanticipated, lower nominal interest rates, raise the price level, and leave real GNP unchanged.
    d. if anticipated, leave nominal interest rates unchanged, raise the price level, and leave real GNP unchanged.

13. Suppose we begin from equilibrium in the loanable funds market with the actual and expected rates of inflation equal to zero and the nominal and real rates of interest equal to 4 percent. More rapid monetary expansion leading to an actual and expected inflation rate of 6 percent would
    a. raise both the nominal and real rates of interest to 10 percent.
    b. leave both the real and nominal rates of interest unchanged.
    c. leave the real rate of interest unchanged but raise the nominal rate to 10 percent.
    d. leave the nominal rate of interest unchanged but raise the real rate to 10 percent.

THE ECONOMIC WAY OF THINKING—DISCUSSION QUESTIONS

1. "The Great Contraction (1929–1939) is a tragic testimony to the power of money—not as Keynes and so many of his contemporaries believed, evidence of its unimportance"—Milton Friedman.
    a. Explain why you either agree or disagree. Present empirical evidence to support your view.
    b. Do you think the Great Depression is most consistent with the Keynesian or monetarist view of the business cycle? Why?
    c. Do you think there will ever be another Great Depression? Why or why not?

2. Explain the relationship between the national debt, the willingness of the Federal Reserve System to purchase more U.S. bonds in order to finance an expansion in the national debt, and the creation of money. Does debt financing increase the supply of money? Explain.

3. "I've read this chapter three times, and I still can't figure out why monetary policy has an effect on output sometimes and not others, and has an effect on prices sometimes and not others. It seems to me that monetary policy *either* should or should not have an effect on output and/or prices. Why doesn't it?"
    a. How would you respond to this question?
    b. What are the keys to remembering when monetary policy has an effect on output? on prices?

4. As full employment is approached, why might the general level of prices begin to rise? Explain why expansionary macropolicy is likely *initially* to have an effect on output rather than on the price level.

5. "A tax cut and budget deficit will expand consumer income, causing consumer spending to rise. However, unless the deficit is financed by borrowing from the Federal Reserve, it will also increase the demand for loanable funds, causing higher interest rates and a decline in investment spending." Do you agree with this view? Why or why not?

6. Would a government deficit be more expansionary if it were financed by borrowing from the Federal Reserve rather than the general public? Explain.

7. Refer to "Problems and Projects" exercise #5. Now suppose that someone asks if monetary policy works exactly the same way for decreases in the money supply as it does for increases. Would your answers to questions #2 and #4 above be identical (except in the reverse direction) for a decrease? Why? If not, how would they differ?

14

Expectations, Inflation, and Unemployment

TRUE OR FALSE

T F

□ □ 1. As it was developed by economist A. W. Phillips, the Phillips curve analysis indicates that inflation causes the rate of unemployment to rise.

□ □ 2. The economic record of the 1970s strengthened the faith of economists in the Phillips curve analysis.

□ □ 3. The adaptive expectations hypothesis suggests that after a few years of inflation, decision-makers begin to anticipate the current rate of inflation. Once the inflation is fully anticipated, the trade-off between inflation and unemployment will tend to disappear.

□ □ 4. Once decision-makers begin to anticipate a 10 percent rate of inflation, a policy of macrodeceleration designed to retard the rate of inflation will result in above-normal rates of unemployment under the adaptive expectations hypothesis.

□ □ 5. Under rational expectations, the anticipated impact of a macropolicy change is unpredictable.

□ □ 6. Changes in the composition of the U.S. labor force during the 1970s made it easier for macroplanners to achieve lower rates of unemployment.

□ □ 7. To the extent that decision-makers adjust to demand-stimulus policies, persistent expansionary macropolicy will lead to inflation while permanently reducing the unemployment rate below its normal long-run rate.

□ □ 8. The short-run Phillips curve may be downward sloping, but the long-run Phillips curve is horizontal, or nearly horizontal.

□ □ 9. The exemption of youthful workers from minimum wage regulation would most likely cause an increase in the rate of unemployment of teenagers.

□ □ 10. The rational expectations hypothesis implies that decision-makers are less well informed than proponents of the adaptive expectations hypothesis.

□ □ 11. The unemployment compensation system actually helps lower the unemployment rate in most cases.

□ □ 12. Everything else being equal, the natural unemployment rate in the 1990s will be higher than the natural unemployment rate in the early 1980s because of changes in the composition of the labor force.

114

T F

☐ ☐   13. A change in the minimum wage is likely to change the long-run natural rate of unemployment.

PROBLEMS AND PROJECTS

1. In the 1970s, prices in the United States rose by approximately 100 percent. Write a short essay explaining
    a. the major cause of the inflation.
    b. whether public policy could have prevented the inflation.
    c. If so, how? At what cost?
    Use empirical evidence to support the positions that you take.

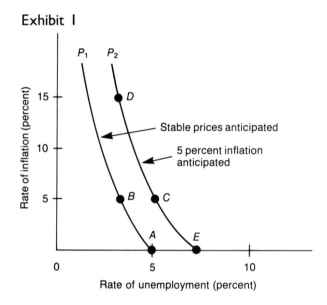

Exhibit 1

2. a. Assume the economy was initially at point A on the Phillips curve P_1 in Exhibit 1. The unemployment rate was 5 percent, and decision-makers expected stable future prices. Political entrepreneurs, planning for the next election, followed an expansionary macropolicy. What would happen to the rates of unemployment and inflation in the short run? In the long run? Explain.
    b. Suppose the economy were at C on the Phillips curve P_2. How could the *short-run* rate of unemployment be reduced to less than 5 percent? What would happen to prices? Could the lower rate be maintained?
    c. When the economy is at point C, what would happen if the macropolicymakers pursued a course that would return the economy to price stability? Would this course be attractive to political entrepreneurs? Explain.
    d. In what way are your answers affected by the manner in which expectations are developed?

3. Tammy is a great believer in adaptive expectations. Last year, when the inflation rate was 10%, she bought a new car (after borrowing her mom's car for months) that carried a nominal interest rate of 13%. Unfortunately, at least for her, this year's inflation rate is only 4%. For Tammy, calculate the following:
    a. The rate of inflation she expected.
    b. The real interest rate she expected to pay.
    c. The real interest rate she actually paid this year.
    d. Has the fall in the inflation rate made her happy or unhappy (at least with respect to the interest rate she is paying on her car)?

4. Exhibit 2 illustrates the macroeconomy of Lookbak where expectations are of the adaptive variety only. Initially Lookbak is in macroequilibrium at P_{100} and Y_f with unemployment at the long-run natural rate of 6 percent and stable prices. Suppose that the monetary authorities introduce some demand stimulus in an attempt to reach real GNP level Y_2 which represents only 3 percent unemployment.

Exhibit 2

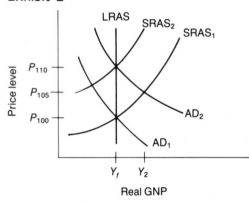
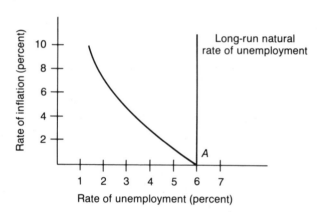

a. If in the short run Lookbak's economy moves to price level P_{105} and real GNP level Y_2, locate the corresponding point in the Phillips curve diagram. (*Hint:* What is the rate of inflation as the price level rises from an index of 100 to 105?) Label this point B. (*Hint:* define the short run as one year.)

b. In the long run (the second year), the SRAS will react to the demand stimulus by shifting to $SRAS_2$. (Be sure you understand why.) Find this point in the Phillips curve diagram and label it C. Illustrate how the Phillips curve will adjust and explain briefly.

c. Now suppose that folks in Lookbak form adaptive expectations regarding the recent inflation they have experienced. Illustrate how the Phillips curve will adjust and explain briefly.

5. Exhibit 3 illustrates the macroeconomy of Lookatall, which is identical to Lookbak except that in Lookatall expectations are of the rational variety. Initially, Lookatall is in macroequilibrium at Y_f and P_{100}, just as for Lookbak in the previous problem, and the monetary authorities raise demand to AD_2.

Exhibit 3

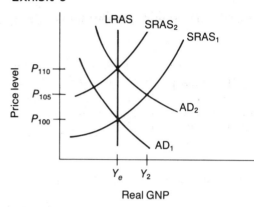 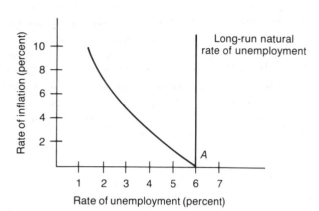

a. Assuming the folks in Lookatall accurately predict the rate of inflation, illustrate how the Phillips curve will adjust and label the new point B in the Phillips curve diagram.
b. Under the assumed conditions, will the monetary authorities of Lookatall be able to lower the actual rate of unemployment below the natural rate of unemployment even temporarily? Explain briefly.

LEARNING THE MECHANICS—MULTIPLE CHOICE

1. Between 1967 and 1973 the annual rate of inflation exceeded 4 percent. The rate of inflation accelerated during the latter part of this period. Given these conditions, we should expect that, in early 1974
    a. the Phillips curve shifted upward (to the northeast) relative to the position that it would have occupied if prices had been stable during the period from 1967 to 1973.
    b. the money interest rate was low, reflecting the monetary expansion that accompanied the inflation of the period.
    c. the money interest rate was low, reflecting the fact that loans could now be paid back with cheaper dollars.
    d. the Phillips curve was in the same position it would have assumed had prices been stable before 1973.

2. If both monetary and fisal policy became much more restrictive, Keynesians and monetarists would agree that
    a. the change in fiscal policy would control primarily the rate of unemployment, whereas the change in monetary policy would affect mainly prices.
    b. unemployment would initially rise if the adaptive expectations hypothesis is valid.
    c. real growth would continue as before, but the rate of inflation would decline.
    d. the Phillips curve would remain unchanged with the passage of time.

3. Empirical evidence suggests that, from 1968 to 1980, the Phillips curve in the United States
   a. shifted downward (to the left).
   b. was nearly vertical.
   c. shifted upward (to the right).
   d. was highly consistent with the theory of the Phillips curve developed by economists during the 1960s.

4. During the late 1980s, the proportion of the population in middle-age groupings (ages 35–54) will rise. This demographic change will
   a. decrease the natural rate of unemployment.
   b. decrease the rate of saving from personal income.
   c. reduce the average skill/experience level of the U.S. workforce.
   d. cause the inflation rate to accelerate.

5. The modern view of the Phillips curve indicates that expansionary macroeconomic policy
   a. will reduce the unemployment rate if policymakers are willing to accept the required rate of inflation.
   b. will reduce the unemployment rate only when people underestimate the inflationary effects of the expansionary policy.
   c. will reduce the unemployment rate only when people overestimate the inflationary effects of the expansionary policy.
   d. will reduce the unemployment rate if people accurately anticipate the inflationary effects of the expansionary policy.

6. According to the rational expectations hypothesis
   a. individuals expect the rate of inflation in the past few years to continue into the future.
   b. individuals expect the rate of inflation to be rational and not random.
   c. individuals expect the rate of inflation to be predictable from the direction of current macropolicy.
   d. individuals will continuously underestimate the rate of inflation because they are constantly surprised that monetary acceleration and inflation are linked.

7. If individuals base their expectations on the immediate past, then
   a. the initial effects of macroacceleration will be on prices rather than output.
   b. the initial effects of macroacceleration will be on output rather than prices.
   c. the initial effects of macroacceleration will be unpredictable.
   d. the initial effects of macroacceleration will be the same as the long-run effects.

8. Use statements I and II to answer this question. (**I**) The short-term link between monetary acceleration and inflation is often a loose one. Initially, monetary acceleration often causes real output to increase while the inflation rate increases only slightly, if at all. (**II**) Persistent, prolonged inflation will not occur without an expansion of the money supply relative to the availability of goods and services.
   a. I is true, but II is false.
   b. II is true, but I is false.
   c. Both I and II are true.
   d. Both I and II are false.

9. According to the adaptive expectations hypothesis
   a. people will adapt to whatever income they are earning.
   b. the more people save, the less total savings will be available to the economy.
   c. the anticipated rate of inflation is based on the actual rates of inflation experienced during the recent past.
   d. the expected rate of inflation is adapted to macropolicy changes.

10. Suppose that Congress cuts taxes and that the monetary authorities accelerate the annual growth rate of the money supply from 5 to 10 percent. If decision-makers *underestimate* the impact of these policy changes on the price level
    a. the unemployment rate will rise.
    b. the unemployment rate will fall.
    c. there will be no effect on the unemployment rate.
    d. the unemployment rate will fall if the change in monetary policy dominates but will increase if the change in fiscal policy dominates.

11. Anticipation of an increase in the rate of inflation will
    a. cause the short-run Phillips curve to shift upward (to the right).
    b. cause an increase in the real rate of interest.
    c. reduce the long-run normal rate of unemployment.
    d. cause the rate of inflation to slow, other things constant.

12. In the early 1980s, unemployed persons under 25 constituted approximately
    a. the same proportion of the total unemployed as their proportion in the total population.
    b. 50 percent of the total unemployed.
    c. 25 percent of the total unemployed.
    d. 10 percent of the total unemployed.

THE ECONOMIC WAY OF THINKING—MULTIPLE CHOICE

Use the Phillips curves diagram in Exhibit 4 to answer questions 1–3.

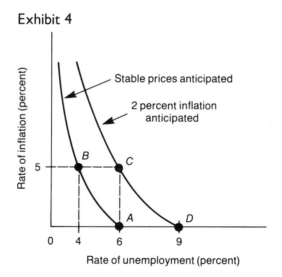

Exhibit 4

1. Suppose that the economy is initially experiencing stable prices and 6 percent unemployment (point *A*). The incumbent president asks his economic advisers to recommend a policy that will reduce the rate of unemployment in the next 12 months. Which of the following is least likely to be recommended?
    a. A reduction in personal income taxes and monetary expansion
    b. An increase in government spending
    c. An increase in corporate taxes
    d. A decrease in the capital gains tax

2. The president follows the advice of his economic advisers, and unemployment falls to 4 percent. However, prices soon begin to rise at an annual rate of 5 percent. This state of affairs continues for two or three years. Eventually, everyone comes to expect a 5 percent rate of inflation. What will happen to unemployment?
   a. It will remain stable at 4 percent.
   b. It will increase to 9 percent if the macroexpansion continues.
   c. It will increase to 6 percent if the macroexpansion is able to maintain a 5 percent rate of inflation.
   d. It will rise to 6 percent only if the Federal Reserve attempts to counteract the government's policies through a tight money policy.

3. After people come to anticipate correctly the 5 percent inflation, what would happen to the unemployment rate if the administration followed a macropolicy sufficient to stabilize prices completely?
   a. It would initially increase to more than 6 percent.
   b. It would eventually decline to 4 percent after the zero rate of inflation comes to be anticipated by everyone.
   c. It would initially decrease to 4 percent unless the inflation persists.
   d. It would fall in the short run, but later it would return to the 6 percent rate after decision-makers adjust to the lower rate of inflation.

4. Suppose that the rate of unemployment is currently 4.5 percent, and prices are increasing at an annual rate of 6 to 8 percent. If we follow a restrictive macropolicy designed to stabilize prices, what would be the most likely result?
   a. An above-normal rate of unemployment, at least until the expectation of inflation has subsided
   b. Lower interest rates in the short run, reducing unemployment
   c. Unemployment would remain at normal levels, but interest rates would decline.
   d. Unemployment would decline, but interest rates would rise.

5. An individual who believed in rational expectations would be most likely to
   a. disregard all current governmental and Fed policies because the impact of macropolicy is unpredictable.
   b. always disagree with the expectations of someone who believed in adaptive expectations.
   c. use all pertinent information when formulating views about the future.
   d. never anticipate stable prices, because the monetary authorities continually expand the supply of money rapidly.

6. The program below that might best be expected to reduce the rate of unemployment without causing the rate of inflation to accelerate is
   a. a reduction in government spending on a product for which demand is currently weak.
   b. a reduction in government spending in an industry in which unemployment has increased recently.
   c. an expansion in government spending in states where the unemployment rate is above the national average.
   d. an expansion in government spending in all sectors of the economy.

7. Unemployment and welfare benefits
   a. may decrease the net cost of being unemployed, but they are also likely to increase the natural rate of unemployment.
   b. are sure to decrease the rate of unemployment because of their effects on workers' incentives.
   c. have no effect on the rate of unemployment in the long run, but may cause more unemployment in the short run.
   d. All of the above are true.

8. Economic analysis suggests that an increase in unemployment benefits (if other factors do not change) increases the average rate of unemployment. This is attributed to the assumption that
   a. higher costs for this program will reduce government expenditures and, thus, aggregate demand.
   b. rational individuals will realize the decreased penalty for failing to accept a job they are not pleased with.
   c. those who are unemployed will discontinue their job search.
   d. unemployed people become lazy when handed money.

9. If policy makers wanted to increase saving they might
   a. make interest (expense) payments a tax credit instead of merely a deduction from taxable income.
   b. make interest income from saving a deduction from taxable income.
   c. decrease government interest payments on government bonds so as to decrease the deficit.
   d. pass laws designed to increase the number of savings and loan institutions in the country.

10. The rapid growth rate in the number of younger people (ages 18–34) and older people (over age 65) during the 1970s probably
    a. reduced the natural rate of unemployment.
    b. reduced the inflation rate.
    c. contributed to the decline in the personal saving rate.
    d. contributed to the increase in the growth rate of real income.

11. Which of the following would be the policy most likely to reduce the rate of unemployment without causing the rate of inflation to accelerate?
    a. An across-the-board increase in government spending
    b. An exemption of youthful workers from minimum wage rates
    c. An increase in unemployment compensation benefits
    d. An increase in the corporate profits tax

12. Which of the following best describes the impact of expectations on the body of economic theory we call macroeconomics?
    a. Expectations help explain stagflation, but they make the task of stabilizing the economy even more difficult.
    b. Expectations make the use of discretionary macropolicy much easier.
    c. Expectations really have no impact on macroeconomics at all; they only allow us to understand the actions of individual consumers better.
    d. Expectations are important, but they do not hinder the ability of policymakers to stabilize the economy.

THE ECONOMIC WAY OF THINKING—DISCUSSION QUESTIONS

1. Why does an increase in the number of youthful and female workers in the labor force exert upward pressure on the natural rate of unemployment?

2. "It is possible to run a capitalist system at high levels of employment—admittedly, paying the price of a considerable degree of inflation"—Robert Heilbroner, *Understanding Macroeconomics*, 4th ed. Englewood Cliffs, NJ: Prentice-Hall, 1972, p. 246.
    a. Do you agree with this view? Why or why not?
    b. Does the experience of the 1970s suggest that inflation reduced unemployment? Use empirical evidence to support your view.

3. "The biggest obstacle to stable prices and a low rate of unemployment in the long run is politics, not a lack of economic knowledge. Since an expansionary policy results in an initial decline in unemployment, followed later by a higher rate of inflation, astute politicians can be expected to favor macroexpansion as an important election approaches—planting the seeds for a higher rate of inflation and more instability after the election. Greedy business entrepreneurs and union leaders can always be blamed for the inflation that is sure to follow." Either criticize or defend this view.

4. "In the long run, macropolicies can do little to change the average rate of unemployment." Either support or criticize this view.

5. "Increasing unemployment compensation payments reduces the incentive of unemployed workers to take available jobs. High unemployment benefits are a source of high rates of unemployment." Does this view make sense? Explain.

6. "Decision-makers will eventually come to anticipate continued inflation. Once inflation is anticipated, it becomes increasingly difficult to stabilize prices without causing a major recession. Inflation as a means of promoting short-run expansion is like committing suicide with pep pills." Evaluate this view.

PERSPECTIVES IN ECONOMICS

A Rational View of Rational Expectations
by Neil G. Berkman

[Reprinted with permission from the January/February 1980 issue of the *New England Economic Review*, pp. 18–29; abridged.]

Economic policy in the postwar period may be broadly characterized as "activist" in the sense that changes in the setting of the instruments of monetary and fiscal policy have frequently been undertaken with the expressed intention of offsetting instability in the private sector. For example, evidence that the economy is in recession has often resulted in such activist policy responses as a tax cut or an increase in government spending. . . .

The government's willingness to pursue activist stabilization policies reflects a long-standing belief in the proposition that monetary and fiscal actions through their influence on aggregate demand and supply have predictable effects on real income and employment, at least in the short run, a proposition that virtually all economists would

have agreed to in principle until recently. The theoretical foundation for activist policy is usually attributed to J.M. Keynes, although monetarists such as Milton Friedman have advanced equally compelling alternative arguments.

Theoretical developments in the past few years have shifted the focus of this debate. Building on earlier models of the economy, economists have shown that under certain assumptions concerning the formation of expectations and the effects of expectations on economic decisions, systematic and predictable changes in monetary and fiscal policy will have no effect whatsoever on the behavior of real income and employment, even in the short run. In this so-called *rational expectations* view, attempts to stabilize the economy through activist policies are doomed to failure; indeed, rather than reducing the magnitude of fluctuations in the system, activist monetary and fiscal policies, in so far as policy adjustments are unsystematic and unpredictable, will actually contribute to economic instability.

The argument that activist policies should be abandoned has achieved widespread acceptance in the popular financial press, although the message appears to have been adopted far too uncritically by many in this group, and to a more limited extent in the economics profession.[1] But professional opinion is far from unanimous on the validity of the "policy impotence" view. Much current macroeconomic research attempts to specify precisely those circumstances in which the traditional conclusions regarding the efficacy of activist policy still hold, and to determine if these circumstances more accurately describe the real world than do those underlying the rational expectations results. The purpose of this paper is to review these important theoretical developments.

Rational Expectations Systematic monetary or fiscal actions will have a predictable impact on real output and employment in the short run only if people follow a certain pattern of behavior in response to the policy maneuver. In particular, people's expectations about the inflationary consequences of a policy change must be systematically incorrect—more specifically, people must systematically *underpredict* the inflation induced by the stimulus for at least a short period of time—if the policy is to produce the intended result. By contrast, the essential argument of the rational expectations school is that people's expectations about the impact on prices and wages of a given change in policy are not systematicaly incorrect *even in the short run*. Because firms' profits and losses, and households' real wages and real consumption depend in part on realized wages and prices, people have a strong incentive to form their expectations as accurately as possible; expectations should depend on all available information, including information about the likely course of monetary and fiscal policy. If expectations are rational in this sense, then systematic, and therefore predictable, activist policies can have no predictable real effects.

An example will help to clarify the reasoning behind this conclusion. Suppose the monetary authority announces its intention to increase the money stock in the months just ahead, that everyone is convinced the authority will actually do so, and that the money stock increases as announced. In a world in which expectations are rational, people will react to this information by increasing their price and wage expectations to match the price increases most likely to result from the monetary stimulus. Employment and production plans will be adjusted as well to reflect the revised inflation outlook. If everyone forecasts correctly the wage and price implications of the policy move—the assumption that expectations are rational requires that this be the case on average—then . . . the increase in the money supply will cause inflation without changing the real wage, the expected real profitability of production, employment or output.

The rational expectations view recognizes that the revision of expectations induced by an anticipated policy change will not be precisely correct in every case. Although on average people will accurately predict the impacts of an expected policy action, sometimes the revision of expectations will be in error. If people should by chance underestimate inflation, then employers may for a time mistak-

enly believe that the increased price of their product reflects not only the anticipated economy-wide inflation but also a relative demand shift in their favor. For similar reasons, workers may mistakenly believe that the observed increase in nominal wages reflects not only the anticipated economy-wide inflation but also an increase in the real wage caused by a relative increase in the demand for their services. As a result, employment and output will tend to rise until the expectational error—the difference between the actual and the expected inflation rate—is recognized and incorporated into everyone's behavior.

The crucial distinction between the traditional activist view and the rational expectations view involves first, the formation of expectations and, second, the speed of adjustment of actual wages and prices to changes in expectations. The traditional view contends that the inflationary effects of a policy are eventually fully and accurately reflected in expectations and in actual wages and prices. It also contends that uncertainty about the exact magnitude of these ultimate price effects and slow adjustment of actual wages and prices create the opportunity for activist policies to have real effects in the short run.

Since expectations play an important role in traditional analysis, the notion that individual behavior depends on anticipated events is not a proprietary contribution of the rational expectations school. Rather, the fundamental insight of this school is that anticipated policy changes (and for that matter any other anticipated event) cause people acting in their own self-interest to alter their behavior in such a way as to render the ultimate aggregate impact of the policies unpredictable.

An excellent example of this process is the cost of living clause in labor contracts. As people come to realize the consequences for prices and wages of stimulative activist policies they protect their real wages by insisting that nominal wages be automatically adjusted when prices rise; thus, activist policies that rely for their effectiveness on slow nominal wage adjustment will be rendered impotent because of this change in the structure of the economy induced by individuals' reaction to policy-makers' own past actions. Attempts to "fine tune" the economy by applying the policy prescriptions suggested by statistical analysis of the *average* historical relationships between policy instruments and ultimate policy objectives are doomed to failure because historical relationships are not stable.

But if this is true—if people always act to offset the destabilizing influence of anticipated events—how can unemployment and production ever depart from their long-run equilibrium levels (as they so manifestly do)? The answer is that although anticipated events have no systematic aggregate impact, *unexpected* events invalidate people's plans and thus set in motion the kinds of adjustments described in the previous section.

What's Wrong With Rational Expectations? Perhaps the most appealing feature of the rational expectations view is that its policy conclusions seem to depend only on the natural and rather flattering assumption that "the people cannot be fooled," at least not very often and certainly not systematically. But a careful analysis of the process through which expectational adjustments offset the aggregate real effects of anticipated events reveals that this assumption is far less innocuous than it may first appear and that several even less appealing assumptions are also crucial for establishing the model's strikingly nontraditional results. To the extent that these assumptions are unpalatable, one is jus-

---

[1]For example, in the article "The People Can't be Fooled" (*Wall Street Journal,* June 25, 1979, p. 20), Charles I. Plosser and Clifford W. Smith, Jr. argue that, "the idea of rational expectations says people watch what policymakers do and attempt to guess what the future course of policy will be . . . a sound economic policy is one that is as stable and predictable as possible."

tified in questioning the validity of the policy impotence view despite the other undeniably endearing characteristics of the rational expectations theory.

One obvious criticism of the rational expectations approach is that it requires people to know more about the operation of the economy and about the data it continuously generates than is realistically possible.

The heterogeneity of products and factor services that characterizes the real world is the source of a second and probably a more damaging criticism of the rational expectations approach. . . .

The discussion in the previous section was intentionally vague about the nature of the adjustments to expected shifts in demands and supplies induced by anticipated events; recall that the argument was simply that the implied changes in relative prices lead people to undertake "appropriate" and "instantaneous" real output and employment adjustments. But unless all factors of production are suitable for producing all goods, unless labor and capital can be shifted from place to place costlessly and immediately, unless information flows between markets are completely unobstructed—that is, unless real adjustment costs are zero—how can this possibly happen?

Consider again the private sector's reaction to an anticipated increase in government spending. People anticipate an increase in the demand for "government goods" and because of the rise in interest rates a corresponding decline in investment goods demand. But if real adjustment costs are not zero, the supply response may take quite some time to materialize. Thus, GNP and employment may for a time rise in response to the activist fiscal policy not because people are fooled or are behaving in any way "irrationally" but because economic and technological considerations dictate that real adjustments simply cannot occur instantaneously.

A related criticism of the rational expectations model is that it apparently ignores the existence of contracts. Like the traditional monetarist school, the rational expectations view holds that relative price adjustments occur quickly in response to disturbances to demand and supply in particular markets. While this may be true in some markets—the securities and commodities markets, for example—it may not be true in those markets where prices are fixed by long-term contractual agreements.[2] Unless these contracts are subject to immediate renegotiations every time a change in the policy environment is imminent, or unless they are written with built-in escalator clauses that permit both upward and downward price changes in response to the *anticipated* price impact of anticipated events (in contrast to escalators based on *realized* price changes), the requisite relative price adjustments induced by expected activist policy can occur only slowly. . . .

Conclusion: The Emerging Synthesis The rational expectations model as widely interpreted implies that systematic and predictable activist stabilization policies have no impact on real output or employment in the short run. This paper explains why this conclusion depends on a set of highly restrictive assumptions that do not describe condi-

tions in the real world. From a practical point of view, then, the rational expectations model does not establish a compelling case against the continued use of activist stabilization policies.

This is not to say that actual historical policies have been ideal or even desirable. In fact, only if the rational expectations view is *false* can one indict activist policy as destabilizing (unless activist policies have increased the magnitude of unanticipated policy shocks). And even if true, the rational expectations model does not imply that *no* policy—including built-in stabilizers such as unemployment insurance and the progressive income tax—affects real output and employment in the short run.[3] Thus, even on its own terms the conclusions of the rational expectations school must be interpreted with caution.

On the other hand, it is incorrect to argue that the rational expectations school has contributed nothing to our understanding of the channels through which policy actions influence the real economy or that the traditional rationales for activist policy have emerged unscathed from the rational expectations onslaught. . . .

Under "ideal" conditions, . . . interdependence between individual behavior and anticipated policy renders policy impotent. Under more realistic assumptions about information flows, real adjustment costs, and wage and price adjustment than are required to produce the strict rational expectations results, the model still implies that the impact of activist policy on real output and employment is substantially smaller than was previously believed to be the case.[4] While the presence of adjustment costs and other impediments to the frictionless flow of information and resources makes it impossible for individuals completely to offset anticipated events, their effort to do so up to the point justified by these costs reduces the impact of policy nonetheless.

What emerges is a synthesis in which activist policies still "work" for the traditional reason—that real adjustments cannot be made instantaneously—but work less powerfully and predictably than was customarily believed for a new reason—that stabilization policy is not a "game" against nature whose reactions do not alter in response to policy stimuli but a game against intelligent agents whose reactions depend on policy moves. This point, long understood instinctively by skilled practical policy-makers, rather than the extreme policy impotence position, is the important contribution to macroeconomic theory made by the rational expectations school.

[2]See Stanley Fisher, "Long-Term Contracts, Rational Expectations, and the Optimal Money Supply Rule," *Journal of Political Economy* 85, February 1977, pp. 191–206.

[3]For a proof that built-in stabilizers are effective even under those conditions where activist policies are not, see B. T. McCallum and J. K. Whitaker, "The Effectiveness of Fiscal Feedback Rules . . . " The importance of tax parameters in influencing real behavior is also discussed in Ray C. Fair, "A Criticism of One Class of Macroeconomic Models with Rational Expectations," *Journal of Money, Credit and Banking* 10, November 1978, pp. 411–17.

[4]Empirical evidence in support of this position is provided in Ray C. Fair, "An Analysis of a Macro-Econometric Model with Rational Expectations in the Bond and Stock Markets," *American Economic Review* 69, September 1979, pp. 539–552. Fair concludes that in his model "anticipated policy actions are about one-fourth as effective (with respect to real output changers) when there are rational expectations in (the bond and stock) markets than when there are not."

Discussion

1. Carefully go through the argument that rational expectations make activist macropolicy unpredictable. Do you understand why the proponents of rational expectations make that claim?

2. Look over Berkman's three major criticisms of rational expectations. Which do you agree with? Why?

3. If Berkman's conclusion is correct, what is the logical impact of the rational expectations debate on macroeconomic policy? How should we change to take rational expectations into account?

15

Stabilization Policy, Output, and Employment

TRUE OR FALSE

T F

☐ ☐   1. Wide fluctuations in the general level of business activity make personal economic planning easier.

☐ ☐   2. A major difference between activists and nonactivists is that activists think that the economy is inherently unstable while nonactivists think that the economy is inherently self-correcting.

☐ ☐   3. Both activists and nonactivists agree that past policy errors have contributed to economic instability.

☐ ☐   4. The index of leading indicators is more useful to nonactivists than to activists.

☐ ☐   5. To date, the record of econometric models in making accurate macroeconomic forecasts is mixed.

☐ ☐   6. Nonactivists admit that recognition lags, administrative lags, and impact lags all make discretionary macroeconomic policy work well, but they still hold to their position that the economy is inherently self-correcting.

☐ ☐   7. Discretionary macroeconomic policy may be used to pursue political objectives as well as stabilization objectives.

☐ ☐   8. The theory of rational expectations indicates that predictable changes in macropolicy will help make the economy more stable.

☐ ☐   9. Monetarists, led by Milton Friedman, favor a policy of constant money supply growth.

☐ ☐   10. Nonactivists can't agree on a reasonable detailed fiscal policy program.

☐ ☐   11. Activists, as well as nonactivists, are aware of the difficulties involved in the proper timing of macropolicy.

126

PROBLEMS AND PROJECTS

1. R. Leader, the head of the House Ways and Means Committee, is convinced that we are heading toward a recession, and he wants to fund a number of public expenditure programs. For each of the possible programs, his staff has estimated (see Exhibit 1) the administrative lag, the impact lag, and the percent of the program expenditures that will go to Congressman Leader's home district.

Exhibit 1

Expenditure program	Administrative lag	Impact lag	District's %
Pork barrel	6 months	8 months	25
Big dam	12 months	6 months	0
Useless highway	10 months	16 months	100
Acid rain remover	9 months	3 months	10
Trash pickup plan	1 month	4 months	15

a. Unfortunately, Congressman Leader's staff is uncertain how long or deep the upcoming recession will be. If the public expenditure programs take effect after the economic upturn, then they will be potentially inflationary, since they will come at a time of macroeconomic expansion rather than contraction. If the maximum time before the upturn is a year, which programs should be enacted?

b. If the maximum time before the upturn is two years, which programs should be enacted?

c. If R. Leader is especially concerned with next year's Congressional elections, which programs will he support in committee? Why? Does your answer depend on the maximum time before the upturn? Is R. Leader being irrational? Why or why not?

2. Would the following economists have agreed or disagreed with this statement (with apologies to novelist Jerzy Kosinski)? "An economy is like a garden; after a period of decline, a time of growth will naturally follow."

a. Milton Friedman
b. Robert J. Gordon
c. John Maynard Keynes
d. Allan Meltzer

Explain your reasoning in each case.

3. Suppose you adopt the monetarist view of the functioning of the macroeconomy. Starting from the initial equilibrium points in the two sets of diagrams below, show both the short-run and long-run impacts on interest rates (r), the quantity of loanable funds (F), real gross national product (Y), and the price level (P) of a discretionary increase in deficit spending by the government if

    a.   the deficit is financed by borrowing from the public, or

    b.   the deficit is "monetized" by the Fed.

    c.   How would your answers to a and b above be affected by the manner in which expectations are formed?

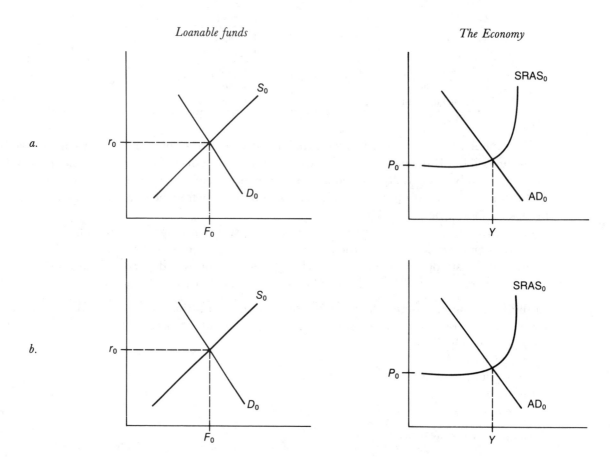

LEARNING THE MECHANICS—MULTIPLE CHOICE

1. The strategy of using discretionary monetary and fiscal policy to moderate economic fluctuations is called

    a.   a nonactivist strategy.

    b.   a monetarist strategy.

    c.   an activist strategy.

    d.   a rational expectations strategy.

2. Nonactivists can best be described as wanting to adopt rules and guidelines that will create macroeconomic policies that are

    a.   independent of current economic conditions.

    b.   dependent only on inflation but not unemployment.

    c.   dependent only on political circumstances.

    d.   none of the above; nonactivists do not believe in macroeconomic policies of any sort.

3. A typical activist policy during a recession would be to
   a. increase the rate of growth of the money supply.
   b. decrease tax rates.
   c. increase government spending.
   d. all of the above.

4. A typical nonactivist policy during a recession would be to
   a. increase the rate of growth of the money supply.
   b. decrease tax rates.
   c. increase government spending.
   d. none of the above.

5. The index of leading indicators is
   a. an alphabetical listing of all the most popular indicators in the economy for a given month.
   b. a composite index of indicators that provides information on the future direction of the economy.
   c. an alphabetical listing of the most important indicators of the current economic well-being of the U. S. economy.
   d. a composite index of the most important indicators of the current economic well-being of the U. S. economy.

6. Well-timed discretionary anti-inflationary policy should be undertaken
   a. when the inflation rate is at its highest.
   b. when the inflation rate begins to increase.
   c. before the inflation rate begins to increase.
   d. none of the above; the timing of anti-inflationary policy isn't important as long as it is eventually undertaken.

7. Which of the following is *not* cited by nonactivists in their criticism of discretionary policy's inability to react to economic problems in time?
   a. Recognition lag
   b. Political objectives lag
   c. Administrative lag
   d. Impact lag

8. The policy ineffectiveness theorem offers
   a. the possibility that policy is ineffective because of lags.
   b. the possibility that policy is ineffective because it is anticipated by decision-makers.
   c. the possibility that policy is ineffective because macroeconomic conditions really don't have much of an effect on the lives of individual decision-makers.
   d. the possibility that policy is ineffective because politicians choose policies that are best for their re-election.

9. Which of the following is considered the leading spokesman for nonactivist stabilization policies?
   a. Edward Tufte
   b. Paul Samuelson
   c. Milton Friedman
   d. Mohatma Gandhi

10. Which of the following is a criticism that many activists have of the practical fiscal policy suggestions proposed by the nonactivists?
    a. The monetary targets announced by the Fed cause increased weight to be given to the path of aggregate monetary supply.
    b. Such policy changes cannot be timed properly, and economic instability results.
    c. As policymakers stay on course, the public will develop confidence in the future stability of the policy.
    d. The nonactivists have yet to agree on a detailed, fiscal policy program.

11. Why do nonactivist macroeconomists oppose the use of discretionary monetary and fiscal policies as a stabilization tool?
    a. Nonactivists do not think monetary and fiscal policies affect the economy.
    b. Nonactivists think the use of discretionary policy creates additional uncertainty and thereby exerts a destabilizing rather than stabilizing effect on the economy.
    c. Nonactivists do not think economic instability is a problem.
    d. Nonactivists think that the response of private decision-makers will offset the effects of the policy.

THE ECONOMIC WAY OF THINKING—MULTIPLE CHOICE

1. Which of the following supports the nonactivist view that the best policy is a steady policy?
    a. Discretionary policy can improve economic stability, but only by a small amount.
    b. Discretionary policy has no effect on the economy.
    c. Discretionary policy can contribute to economic instability.
    d. A market economy is self-correcting if only given enough time.

2. The activist view that the best policy is one of discretionary intervention into the macro-economy is most in keeping with which of the following?
    a. A market economy is inherently self-correcting.
    b. A market economy is inherently unstable because politicians force incorrect policies on the people.
    c. A market economy is inherently unstable because of inevitable economic shocks and investment fluctuations.
    d. A market economy is inherently unstable, but no one really knows why.

3. A good example of an activist stabilization policy at the beginning of a recession is
    a. cutting government expenditures.
    b. the Fed selling bonds on the open market.
    c. lowering tax rates.
    d. all of the above.

4. Most activists believe that the *most* expansionary way to finance a budget deficit is by
    a. selling treasury securities to the public.
    b. selling government bonds to corporations.
    c. borrowing from the Fed.
    d. increasing taxes.

5. If we could forecast the economy better, in what way do you think most nonactivists would change their positions on discretionary macroeconomic policy?
   a. They would still be nonactivists.
   b. They would become activists.
   c. They would be willing to use discretionary policy in situations where the impact lag was less than the length of time before the policy's impact was needed.
   d. They would only use discretionary policies when those policies met their political goals.

6. Which of the following is true about the impact of expectations on the actions of decision-makers?
   a. If expectations are formed adaptively, then decision-makers will adapt to future policies, rendering those policies ineffective.
   b. If expectations are formed rationally, then decision-makers will anticipate future policies, rendering those policies ineffective.
   c. If expectations are formed rationally, then decision-makers will rationally ignore future policies, since they are known to be ineffective.
   d. If expectations are formed adaptively, then decision-makers will be able to perfectly predict future policies, making them ineffective.

7. What's wrong with this statement: "If the nonactivists can't even agree on what the best fiscal policy should be, then the activists must be right."
   a. The activists might be right, but they are not right *because* the nonactivists can't agree with each other.
   b. The activists have more trouble coming to a mutual agreement than do the nonactivists.
   c. The fact that the activists are right does not prove in and of itself that the nonactivists can't agree on what the best fiscal policy is.
   d. The statement is incorrect; the nonactivists *do* agree as to what the best fiscal policy is, and the activists are the ones who can't agree.

8. Which one of the following accurately states the view of *activists* who favor the use of discretionary stabilization policy?
   a. The index of leading indicators and other forecasting tools provides policymakers with valuable information that permits them to institute stabilizing changes in macroeconomic policy.
   b. Since we have only limited ability to forecast the future direction of the economy, the best policy is to do nothing.
   c. Since it takes time for macroeconomic policy to work, policymakers will often make mistakes that destabilize the economy.
   d. In recent years, our ability to forecast the future direction of the economy has improved to the extent that discretionary macroeconomic policy can fine-tune the economy if policymakers follow the advice of leading economists.

9. Which of the following factors substantially reduces the effectiveness of changes in tax rates or government expenditures as a stabilization tool?
   a. Economic research indicates that fiscal policy exerts no effect on aggregate demand.
   b. When fiscal policy is altered, the Fed generally alters monetary policy in an effort to cancel out the impact of the fiscal action.
   c. The political process that is used to institute changes in tax rates and expenditures operates slowly and is subject to conflicting pressures.
   d. Changes in government expenditures and taxes are always offset by equal changes in private spending.

10. The capacity utilization rate measures
    a. the extent to which an economy's industrial facilities are operating at their potential.
    b. the extent to which the labor force of the economy is fully utilized.
    c. the rate of increase in the cost of purchasing the typical bundle of goods consumed by an urban family of four.
    d. the capacity of the banking system to utilize reserves supplied by the economy's central bank.

11. Use statements I and II to answer this question. (I) Discretionary macroeconomic policy can effectively combat business instability by injecting demand stimulus during a recession and demand restraint during an inflationary boom. (II) Given our inability to forecast the future accurately and our limited knowledge as to when a policy change will exert its major impact, discretionary policy is often a source of economic instability.
    a. I represents the views of activists, while II represents the views of nonactivists.
    b. I represents the views of nonactivists, while II represents the views of activists.
    c. Both activists and nonactivists would agree with the two statements.
    d. Neither activists nor nonactivists would agree with the two statements.

12. Which of the following is an argument *against* a monetary rule (growth of the money supply at a constant rate such as 4 percent)?
    a. Since the time lag between when a change in monetary policy is instituted and when the change exerts its major effect is unpredictable, changes in monetary policy are difficult to time properly.
    b. Inability to forecast the future direction of the economy makes it difficult to time monetary policy properly.
    c. A monetary rule would prevent the monetary authorities from taking action to offset abrupt changes in the velocity of money.
    d. A monetary rule would reduce the likelihood that monetary planners could stimulate an economic boom just prior to a major election.

THE ECONOMIC WAY OF THINKING—DISCUSSION

1. Some of the debate between activists and nonactivists boils down to whether or not economists can forecast the future. Is it realistic to *ever* expect to be able to forecast totally unexpected events? If not, does this mean that the activist point of view is totally without merit? Explain your answers.

2. It appears that persons marketing economic forecasts have sometimes oversold the ability of economics in this area. Why do you think that competition between forecasters hasn't driven the bad forecasters out of business?

3. There is a distinct psychological side to the argument between activism and nonactivism. In particular, which side seems to be almost ''fatalistic'' in its acceptance of the economic future? Which side wants to intervene and ''do something'' even if that something can potentially make things worse? Do you think it possible that some economists choose sides on this issue because of their personalities rather than on the basis of economic theory?

4. Suppose you were President of the United States and were faced with the activist/nonactivist debate. How would you go about making up your mind? Would the lack of a clear unified message from the economics profession make you more or less likely to make decisions based on political rather than economic grounds? Does this seem to be happening in the real world?

5. Martin Feldstein is justifiably considered by many to be one of the leading economists in the world today, and yet, when he was chairman of President Reagan's Council of Economic Advisors, he was not a major architect of the economic policies of the administration that appointed him. What does this say about the importance of economic analysis in today's economy? Who was being unrealistic, Professor Feldstein or President Reagan?

6. When all is said and done, what do *you* think? Should we attempt to steer the ship of state (to continue Robert Gordon's analogy) away from obstacles that appear to be in our path, or should we steer a steady course in order to avoid mistakes and the possibility of running into something worse? Are you an activist or a nonactivist? Why?

PERSPECTIVES IN ECONOMICS

Fiscal Policy: An Ineffective Stabilizer?
by J. Ernest Tanner

[Reprinted with permission from the *Economic Review of the Federal Reserve Bank of Atlanta*, August 1982, pp. 45-51, abridged.]

Introduction The belief that fiscal policy can be an effective tool in stabilizing the economy has weakened substantially since it peaked in the mid to late 1960s. The present economic structure appears to many to have changed significantly and, therefore, is less responsive to the fiscal policies that worked in earlier periods. Indeed, some argue that present problems stem from a misguided belief in the beneficial effects of stimulatory fiscal policy reflected by government deficits.

It would be wonderful to be able to say that recent research has found a solution to these difficulties. Unfortunately, that isn't the case, and economists, judging from the political rhetoric we hear, are not yet in agreement about the potential role fiscal policy should and could play. However, some recent research does suggest that major portions of the Reagan economic recovery program are consistent with the best advice academic economists have to offer. This article will analyze the current discussion of the use of fiscal policy to stabilize the economy.

The New "New Macroeconomics" The new "new macroeconomists" or rational expectations economists support the proposition that the public discounts the taxes implied by government debt.

This implies that the outstanding government debt has no effect on current consumption. Because the private stock of capital increases consumption from a wealth effect—for a given level of income, the more wealth a consumer has, the more he will consume—the absence of any effect of the outstanding stock of government debt on consumption means it is not treated as wealth by all consumers.

However, government bonds have value to their holders because they expect to receive interest payments. But where can the government obtain the funds to pay the bonds? Only from the taxpayers. If the same discount rate is used by the bond holder and the taxpayer, the discounted capital value of the tax liabilities to the taxpayer is equal to the capital value to the bond holder. In such a case, variations in the value of the government debt will have no real wealth effect. Government debt is simultaneously both a liability and an asset.

Because governments can pay for expenditures in only two ways, by taxing or by borrowing, the above result says they are equivalent if consumers look at "permanent" income informing their consumption decisions. The issue of a bond to finance current expenditures leads to future interest payments and possible ultimate repayment of principal. It implies future taxes that would not be necessary if the expenditures were financed by taxes.[18]

Others have argued that this theory can not be right because consumers have finite lives while the government is infinitely lived. For the consumer, the relevant horizon for future taxes is much less than for interest payments and repayment of principal. As a result, the value of government debt to the bond holder must exceed the perceived liability to the taxpayer.[19]

In the model of overlapping generations used by many macro theorists in recent years, this argument is moot. This framework basically says that people worry about their children and take care of them by inheritance. As a consequence, current taxpayers will not consume at the expense of their heir but rather will increase their personal savings so that their bequests, net of the government debt, would be the same as if the government deficit had not occurred. "This extra private savings to increase the bequest just offsets the reduced public savings associated with a government deficit."[20]

---

[18]For arguments along these lines, see Martin Bailey, "The Optimal Full-Employment Surplus," *Journal of Political Economy*, July 1972, pp. 649-661, Levis Kochin, "Are Future Taxes Anticipated by Consumers?" *Journal of Money, Credit, and Banking*, August 1974, pp. 385-394, Merton Miller and Charles Upton, *Macroeconomics: A Neoclassical Introduction*, Homewood, Illinois, 1974, and Ernest Tanner, "Empirical Evidence on the Short Run Real Balance Effect in Canada," *Journal of Money, Credit and Banking*, November 1970, pp. 473-485.

[19]This argument is made most forcefully by Earl Thompson in "Debt Instruments in Both Macroeconomic Theory and Capital Theory," *American Economic Review*, December 1976, pp. 1196-1210.

[20]Ernest Tanner, "Fiscal Policy and Consumer Behavior," *Review of Economics and Statistics*, May 1979, p. 317. For a comprehensive theoretical treatment of this model, see Robert Barro, "Are Government Bonds Net Wealth?" *Journal of Political Economy*, December 1974, pp. 1095-1118.

Empirical evaluation of this theory using U.S. data is not inconsistent with it. Not only is the bequest motive a strong factor in explaining aggregate savings,[21] but also the evidence suggests that government surpluses reduce private savings while deficits increase private savings.

The implications for contracyclical policy are obvious. The automatic fiscal stabilizers which have been part of the system in the post-World War II period appear to have significantly less effect than commonly thought. Any change in the deficit which occurs as a result of the normal fluctuations in the economy is widely expected and would be offset by changes in savings. As a result, the higher tax rates at cycle peaks do not curb consumption demands nor do the lower tax rates during cycle downturns stimulate consumption demands. Consumption remains more or less constant over the cycle with savings rates climbing in periods of recessions but falling during expansions.

Discretionary fiscal policies may not be any better as stabilizing tools. Because the consumer takes into account known public action in making his consumption decisions, discretionary fiscal actions such as those in 1968 and 1975 would be expected to affect only savings rates, leaving consumption largely unaffected. As a result, neither discretionary fiscal actions nor the automatic stabilizers should be expected to serve our needs for a policy tool contributing to short run economic stability.

The empirical evaluation and testing of this theory is not inconsistent with the hypothesis. Unexpected deficits—largely unexpected government spending changes—lead to increases in aggregate demand above balanced budgets. The evidence for unexpected deficits appears to conform exactly to the Keynesian theory. Not only do unexpected deficits cause aggregate demand to rise, but also they cause interest rates to rise and increase real output.[22] Although the evidence is not crystal clear, it does indicate that un-

expected deficits may have little inflation effect because of the sharp short run rise in output and in interest rates.[23]

Some Concluding Thoughts On Fiscal Policy As a tool for short-term economic stability, fiscal policy has come almost full cycle in the past 50 years. From a position of no status in the classical model that dominated economic thinking until 1935, contracyclical fiscal policy reached its pinnacle in the 1960s—the heyday of Keynesian macroeconomics. It may now be on the wane as the new "new macroeconomics" of rational expectations replaces the Keynesian model.

In the rational expectations framework where bequests are an important motive for savings, perceived deficits are no more expansionary than equal government spending financed by taxes. Because deficits mean higher taxes in the future, the consumer's optimal response is to save the amount of the deficit. If this is done, the implied future tax liabilities do not make the consumer better off than if the government budget were balanced in the present by a higher level of taxes.

The evidence indicates that contracyclical fiscal policies have had little effect on the stability of the U.S. economy in the past 30 years. Only unexpected or "unperceived" fiscal policies work as Keynes suggested. Unfortunately, these unperceived policies cannot work for long or consistently in the desired direction because they rely on misperceptions. And as we all know, you cannot fool all the people all the time. Yet that is what must be done if we attempt to use fiscal policies to solve the business cycle.

---

[21]Kotlikoff and Summers write "The evidence presented indicates that intergenerational transfers account for the vast majority of aggregate U. S. capital formation; only a negligible fraction of actual capital accumulation can be traced to life-cycle or 'lump' savings." Laurence J. Kotlikoff and Lawrence Summers, "The Role of Intergenerational Transfers in Aggregate Capital Accumulation," *Journal of Political Economy*, 1981, p. 706.

[22]This research is not published but is contained in Ernest Tanner, "Will Monetary and Fiscal Stabilization Policies Work?" Working Paper, Tulane University, 1981.

[23]Robert Hall argues that a transitory increase in aggregate demand (if the deficit is unperceived, it must be transitory) will raise the real rate of interest. This increased real rate of interest will be perceived as being temporary and workers will respond by working harder now as the higher real rate of interest makes future goods cheaper in terms of the unchanged price of present goods, if the worker is in equilibrium in his work/leisure trade-off today and decreases it in the future. Robert Barro's test of the proposition involved looking at military and non-military expenditures. He found substantial real output effects of transitory military spending but was unable to precisely measure the output effects of non-defense federal expenditures. See Robert Hall, "Labor Supply and Aggregate Fluctuations," *Carnegie-Rochester Series on Public Policy*, Spring 1980, pp. 7–33 and Robert Barro, "Output Effects of Government Purchases," *Journal of Political Economy*, 1981, pp. 1086–1121.

Discussion

1. For fiscal policy to work, must we "fool all the people all the time," as Tanner states? Why or why not?

2. What does this article have to do with the debate between the activists and the nonactivists with respect to macroeconomic policy? Where do you think Tanner stands on this debate?

3. Tanner argues that automatic stabilizers "appear to have significantly less effect than commonly thought." If he is right, what should we do about this lack of effectiveness? In particular, is there *anything* that could be done to make automatic stabilizers more effective from the point of view of the "new macroeconomic" theory?

16

Demand and Consumer Choice

TRUE OR FALSE

T	F	
☐	☐	1. The consumer's desire for goods usually exceeds what his income can buy; thus choice is essential.
☐	☐	2. The price of diamonds exceeds that of water; therefore, consumers derive more total utility from diamonds than water, according to the law of diminishing marginal utility.
☐	☐	3. The law of diminishing marginal utility suggests that you would value the third milk shake on a given day higher than the fourth.
☐	☐	4. The market demand curve is a reflection of the law of diminishing marginal utility—thus, one would expect price to be negatively related to amount purchased.
☐	☐	5. In the 1970s, the price of gasoline increased dramatically, causing the demand for gas to fall.
☐	☐	6. A decline in the price of automobiles would almost certainly cause the demand for cars to increase.
☐	☐	7. An increase in the price of wheat would probably cause a decline in the demand for corn, a substitute product.
☐	☐	8. An increase in consumer income would cause the demand for most commodities to increase.
☐	☐	9. If people expected the price of General Electric stock to rise in the near future, the current demand for shares of GE would increase.
☐	☐	10. If consumers expected the price of automobiles to increase by 20 percent next week, the current demand for automobiles would fall.
☐	☐	11. Economists assume that price or money cost is the only factor that influences consumer decisions.
☐	☐	12. The opportunity cost of a bus trip from New York to Los Angeles includes both the money and time cost to the consumer.
☐	☐	13. When demand is elastic, an increase in the price of a good causes total revenue to rise.
☐	☐	14. The demand for hamburger is more elastic than the demand for beef.
☐	☐	15. The short-run demand for gasoline is less elastic than the long-run demand.

PROBLEMS AND PROJECTS

Exhibit 1

| Price of gasoline (per gallon) | Consumption level | | |
	Auto tires (millions)	Yellowstone tourists (millions)	Air travel passenger miles (millions)
$0.30	40	3.5	7.500
0.50	38	3.2	8.000
0.75	36	3.0	9.000
1.00	34	2.6	12.000

1. Exhibit 1 presents data on the effect of a change in the price of gasoline on the amount consumed of automobile tires, tourism in Yellowstone National Park, and air travel. Which of the following goods are substitutes: gas and tires? gas and Yellowstone tourism? gas and air travel? Which are complementary? Explain how you could tell from the data.

Exhibit 2

Price	Quantity (million bushels)	Total revenue	Elasticity of demand
$1	1500	_____	_____
2	700	_____	_____
3	550	_____	_____

2. Exhibit 2 indicates the estimated demand schedule for wheat in the United States.
   a. Fill in the total revenue schedule. Is the demand schedule elastic or inelastic between $1 and $2? Between $2 and $3? How can you tell?
   b. Calculate the price elasticity coefficient over the $1 to $2 range; the $2 to $3 range. Use arc elasticity.

Exhibit 3 Demand and Marginal Utility

| Food | | | Clothing | | | Housing | | |
Quantity	Total utility	Marginal utility	Quantity	Total utility	Marginal utility	Quantity	Total utility	Marginal utility
1	30	_____	1	10	_____	1	35	_____
2	55	_____	2	17	_____	2	65	_____
3	75	_____	3	22	_____	3	85	_____
4	90	_____	4	26	_____	4	100	_____
5	100	_____	5	28	_____	5	110	_____
6	105	_____	6	29	_____	6	118	_____

3. Exhibit 3 provides Sam Smith's hypothetical total utility schedule for three goods—food, clothing, and housing.

a.   Fill in the marginal utility schedule for each of the goods.

b.   Assume that the price of food was $20, clothing $10, and housing $30. What is the marginal utility *per dollar* derived from consumption of the first unit of each of the three commodities? If Smith had only $20 to spend, which good(s) would he buy?

c.   Assume that Smith's income is $130 per week. If he purchased only the three commodities and faced the price structure indicated in b, how many units of each good would he demand per week?

30 + 10 + 30 = 70

7

d.   Assume that Smith's weekly income, the price of clothing, and the price of housing remain constant, but the price of food increases from $20 to $30. How much would he buy? How much food would Smith demand at $15 per unit? Indicate these points on Smith's demand schedule for food, assuming that his weekly income is $130 and the prices of clothing and housing are $10 and $30, respectively.

e.   What would happen to Smith's demand curve for food if his income rose from $130 to $250 per week? (Assume prices indicated in b.)   *48%*

4.   Suppose that in reviewing the material of this chapter you were sitting in your college cafeteria sipping coffee for two or three hours. Exhibit 4 below shows some information about your preferences regarding coffee. The column "Marginal valuation" refers to the maximum amount you would be willing to pay for the particular unit of the good in the first column (e.g., you would be willing to pay a maximum of $0.10 for the 5th cup of coffee).

Exhibit 4

Quantity of cups	Marginal utility	Marginal valuation
1	200	$2.00
2	100	1.00
3	50	.50
4	25	.25
5	10	.10
6	5	.05
7	0	.00

a.   If you behave according to the theory of consumer choice developed in this chapter, how many cups of coffee will you purchase if the price of coffee is $0.25 per cup?

b.   Calculate the value of your consumer surplus at a price of $0.25 per cup.

c.   Suppose (again at a price of $0.25) you bought seven cups of coffee. Calculate the value of your consumer surplus in this case. How does it compare to the value for consumer surplus in part b above?

5.   Fill in the missing entries in Exhibit 5.

Exhibit 5

Price elasticity	Change in price	Change in total revenue
0.2	down	_____
3.5	_____	down
1.0	up	_____
0.9	_____	up
_____	down	none
6.3	down	_____

LEARNING THE MECHANICS—MULTIPLE CHOICE

1. A rise of 15 percent in the price of beef reduces the consumption of beef by 30 percent. As the result of the price increase, households
    a. spend more money on beef.
    b. spend less money on beef.
    c. spend the same amount on beef as before.
    d. spend more on goods that are complementary with beef.

2. Which of the following would *not* cause a shift in the demand curve for green peas?
    a. An increase in the income of consumers
    b. A decrease in the price of potatoes (a complement)
    c. A decrease in the price of green peas
    d. A decrease in the price of beans (a substitute)

3. Which of the following statements most accurately reflects the basic postulate of demand theory?
    a. Individuals act purely out of selfish motives, but they will be less likely to pursue selfish ends as these actions become more costly.
    b. Individuals act primarily out of humanitarian motives; this explains why less of a product is bought at a higher price.
    c. Individuals respond from a variety of motives, including both selfish and humanitarian impulses; however, they are less likely to follow a course of action (for example, purchase a commodity) as the cost of the action increases.
    d. Individuals' behavior has many causes, but their actions are affected by changes in the cost of activities only when they are motivated by self-interest, narrowly defined.

4. Consumer surplus is
    a. the surplus of goods owned by consumers that has not been consumed.
    b. the difference between the amount that consumers would be willing to pay and the amount they actually pay for an item.
    c. the surplus of goods produced for consumption that have not been purchased.
    d. the difference between the amount that consumers would be willing to pay and the producer's cost of an item.

5. An inferior good is distinguished by
    a. a negative price elasticity of demand.
    b. a positive price elasticity of demand.
    c. a positive income elasticity of demand.
    d. a negative income elasticity of demand.

6. If the price of grapefruit rose, the market demand curve for the substitute good (oranges) would
    a. shift to the right.
    b. shift to the left.
    c. remain stationary.
    d. become horizontal.

7. When an economist says that the demand for a product has increased, he means that
    a. the demand curve has shifted to the left.
    b. product price has fallen and, as a result, consumers are buying more of the product.
    c. the product has become particularly scarce for some reason.
    d. consumers are now willing to purchase more of this product at any given price.

8. If the money income of consumers decreased and, as a result, the demand for product A increased, it could be concluded that product A is
    a. an inferior good.
    b. a substitute good.
    c. a complementary good.
    d. a normal good.

9. An increase in the demand for milk can be explained most reasonably by which of the following?
    a. The supply of milk has increased because costs of production have declined.
    b. The price of milk has declined and, as a result, consumers want to purchase more of it.
    c. Consumer preferences have changed in favor of milk so that they now want to buy a larger quantity at the current market price.
    d. The price of milk has increased and, as a result, consumers want to purchase less of it.

10. "After listening to nothing but rock music on my vacation, I was anxious to return home and play something different." This statement most clearly reflects the law of
    a. the budget constraint.
    b. consumer irrationality.
    c. greater demand elasticity with time.
    d. diminishing marginal utility.

11. Which of the following would be most likely to cause the demand for beef to increase?
    a. A decrease in the price of pork
    b. An increase in the price of catsup, a complementary good
    c. An increase in consumer income
    d. A decrease in the price of bean curd, a substitute good

12. Demand theory implies that, for pork chops, price is negatively related to quantity demanded, all other things constant. The "all other things" include each of the following *except*
    a. the price of pork chops.
    b. consumer preferences.
    c. the price of hamburger.
    d. consumer income.

13. If a 50 percent increase in the price of hula hoops led to a 10 percent reduction in the quantity of hula hoops purchased, this would suggest that
    a. an additional 20 percent increase in price would surely cause a sharp reduction in sales.
    b. the demand for hula hoops was elastic over this range.
    c. the income elasticity for hula hoops was low.
    d. households increased their spending on hula hoops.

THE ECONOMIC WAY OF THINKING—MULTIPLE CHOICE

1. "The year 1963 was a year tobacco makers are unlikely to forget. It was a year that regular-size cigarettes received their worst publicity ever. The discussion of a possible link between cigarette smoking and cancer reached alarmist proportions. Increasingly, people were buying aids designed to reduce the smoking habit." This statement indicates that
   a. the supply of cigarettes was reduced because of the possible adverse effects of cigarette smoking.
   b. as income increases, the demand for cigarettes declines because their income elasticity is negative.
   c. the price of cigarettes had finally reached the point at which people began to turn to substitute products.
   d. the demand for cigarettes decreased because of a change in the preferences of consumers.

2. "Because of the unseasonably cold weather, Florida orange growers expect (a) fewer bushels of oranges to be harvested and (b) larger total revenues from this year's crop." Assuming that the demand for Florida oranges is constant, the statement would most likely be correct if
   a. the demand for Florida oranges were elastic.
   b. the supply of Florida oranges were highly inelastic.
   c. the demand for Florida oranges were inelastic.
   d. the supply of Florida oranges were elastic.

Exhibit 6

	Butter		Margarine	
	Unit price (cents)	Per capita consumption (pounds)	Unit price (cents)	Per capita consumption (pounds)
1950	72.9	10.7	30.8	6.1
1960	83.0	5.5	28.4	10.8

3. Exhibit 6 contains the prices and quantities consumed of butter and margarine in 1950 and 1960. Which of the following statements most accurately describes the changes indicated by Exhibit 6?
   a. As consumer income steadily increased during the period, consumption of both butter and margarine increased roughly proportionally.
   b. As the price of margarine fell relative to butter, consumers substituted margarine for butter.
   c. While the demand for both butter and margarine increased during the period, the data do *not* suggest that the two goods are related.
   d. The demand for butter is very inelastic, whereas the demand for margarine is elastic.

4. The law of demand states that less of a commodity or factor of production will be purchased at a higher price. In 1960, the United States consumed 80.6 thousand tons of tin when the price was $1.01 per pound. However, in 1965, after the price of tin had increased to $1.78 per pound, the consumption level also increased to 84.0 thousand tons. Which of the following is the most probable explanation?
   a. Although the law of demand holds for most goods, it is not true for some, tin being an example.
   b. The high price in 1965 resulted from a reduction in supply.
   c. The demand for tin conforms to the law of demand. Demand increased relative to supply between 1960 and 1965.
   d. The demand for tin would have conformed to the law of demand had the prices of close substitutes not decreased during the period.

5. Which of the following will most likely cause a decrease in the *current* demand for fuel oil?
   a. An increase in income
   b. The expectation that the future price of fuel oil will increase
   c. A decline in the price of fuel oil
   d. A decline in the price of electricity, a substitute good

6. As the price of precious gems (diamonds, pearls, etc.) increases, other things constant, the quantity demanded may also increase. Which of the following offers the best explanation of this phenomenon?
   a. The demand for precious gems is like the demand for other goods.
   b. Precious gems are an inferior good.
   c. The demand for precious gems is subject to a ''snob'' effect, in which higher prices increase their marginal utility.
   d. The demand for precious gems is inelastic.

7. ''A number of mass transit systems have been experiencing declining revenues despite fare increases.'' This statement suggests
   a. that the automobile is a poor substitute for mass transit in urban areas.
   b. that the demand for the mass transit service was inelastic.
   c. that the demand for the mass transit service was elastic.
   d. that a profit-maximizing firm would have raised the price charged for mass transit service by a larger amount.

8. Operators of the midway at the Seattle Center reduced the price of admission to their carnival rides after Labor Day even though ''for all practical purposes, once our weekly schedule is announced, all our costs are fixed costs,'' as one manager explained. The change in prices would increase the firm's profits if
   a. marginal costs were now zero.
   b. the elasticity of demand were unitary.
   c. the demand for rides at the Seattle Center were elastic.
   d. the income elasticity for carnival rides were negative.

9. The Radio Corporation of America (RCA) is considering a 10 percent price reduction on its black-and-white television sets, whereas the firm's price for color television sets (a substitute) is held constant. With this information, what can we say about how the price reduction will affect the firm's total revenue?
    a. Revenues from black-and-white sets will fall, whereas revenues derived from color sets may either increase or decrease.
    b. Revenues from black-and-white sets will increase, whereas revenues derived from color sets will fall.
    c. Revenues from color sets will fall, whereas revenues from black-and-white sets could either increase or decrease.
    d. Revenues from color sets will increase, whereas revenues derived from black-and-white sets will fall.

10. (I) The number of fly rods owned by a fly fisherman will probably be limited because income necessitates choice. (II) The number of fly rods owned by a fly fisherman will probably be limited because of the law of diminishing marginal utility.
    a. Both I and II are true.
    b. Both I and II are false.
    c. I is true, but II is false.
    d. II is true, but I is false.

11. Use the diagram below to answer this question.

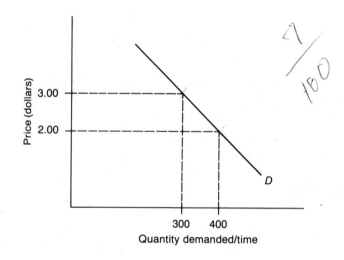

For this demand curve, the price elasticity of demand is
    a. more elastic at $3 than at $2.
    b. more elastic at $2 than at $3.
    c. identical at $2 to that at $3.
    d. equal to 1.0 over the range from $3 to $2.

12. If the owners of Pac-Kong, a video arcade game, increased the price they charged for one play of the game from 25 cents to 50 cents, what can be said about their perception of the elasticity of demand with respect to the price of a game of Pac-Kong?
    a. It is impossible to say anything about the owners' perceptions without interviewing them
    b. The owners expect that the price elasticity of demand for Pac-Kong is elastic.
    c. The owners expect that the price elasticity of demand for Pac-Kong is unitary (equal to one).
    d. The owners expect that the price elasticity of demand for Pac-Kong is inelastic.

Use the following information to answer the next three questions: Mike is a lawyer and a fan of jazz music. He buys several records each year and spends hours each week listening to them. His professional reputation as a lawyer is growing, and his hourly pay rate is increasing. He has more work than he wants.

13. The *substitution effect* in demand theory suggests that Mike will
    a. buy fewer records, because he has become richer.
    b. buy fewer records, because the opportunity cost of listening to records has increased.
    c. buy more records with his extra money.
    d. not change his record-buying habits, since record prices have not changed.

14. In demand theory, the *income effect* suggests that because of his higher earnings, Mike would
    a. buy fewer records, if records were a normal good.
    b. buy fewer records, since listening has become relatively more expensive.
    c. buy more records, if records were a normal good for him.
    d. buy more records, if records were an inferior good for him.

15. If Mike's income has increased as a result of inheriting a modest trust fund but his reputation and hourly rate had stayed the same, we would expect that he would
    a. not experience a substitution effect, since relative prices were unchanged by the inheritance.
    b. buy fewer records because of the substitution effect from the inheritance.
    c. buy more records because of the substitution effect of the inheritance.
    d. not change his record-buying habits at all, since prices had not changed.

THE ECONOMIC WAY OF THINKING—DISCUSSION QUESTIONS

1. Explain the difference between
   a. a change in demand and
   b. a change in quantity demanded.
   What are six major factors influencing consumer decisions that economists hold constant when they construct the demand curve for a product?

2. How will each of the following factors affect the demand for electricity?
   a. An expansion in consumer income
   b. An increase in the price of natural gas, a substitute product
   c. Higher electricity prices
   d. The expectation that electricity prices will rise sharply in the future
   e. Lower prices for air conditioners powered by electricity

3. For each of the following pairs of products, indicate which you think will have the lower price elasticity of demand. Explain your reasoning.
   a. Salt or green peas
   b. Volkswagens or all automobiles
   c. Electricity (short run) or electricity (long run)
   d. Tires (short run) or tires (long run)
   e. Physician services or bus transportation

4. "Affluent consumers spend much of their income on useless items. If consumers limited their purchases to those items they needed, our economic problems would be reduced to manageable proportions."
   a. What items do people spend their money on that are not necessary? Do you buy things you do not need? If so, why?
   b. "If people spent less time working to purchase more things that they do not need, they would have more leisure time." Is leisure a "useless" item that people do not need? Explain.
   c. How can you determine if an item is useful or needed? Are demand and usefulness the same thing?

5. Does advertising create and shape consumer demand? Does advertising have any effect on the types of goods the consumer purchases? Cite evidence to support your answers to these two questions.

6. Explain in your own words why diamonds, which appear to be useless, are more expensive than water, which is life supporting. Which law of economics helps to explain why diamonds are more expensive than water?

7. Goods vary in the amount of time required for consumption. More time is foregone in the consumption of television football games or reading books than for a new suit of clothes, for example. Explain why, as one's wage rate increases, *ceteris paribus,* one will consume relatively less time-intensive consumption items. Do these statements have any implications for the measurement of inequality in the distribution of income? Explain.

8. What's wrong with this way of thinking? "Although economists argue that the amount demanded is negatively related to price, the evidence doesn't always support this view. For example, in 1970 the average price for the installation of a 20 × 40 home swimming pool was $4000. By 1980 the price had soared to more than $8000. Yet Americans bought 50 percent more swimming pools in 1980 than 1970. The higher price did not discourage sales."

PERSPECTIVE IN ECONOMICS

Chicken Price Rises Exceed Expectations As Costlier Beef and Pork Spur Demand
by Robert R. Bogda

[From *The Wall Street Journal,* July 11, 1978, p. 30. Reprinted with permission of the Wall Street Journal © Dow Jones & Co., Inc. All rights reserved.]

With prices of beef and pork heading skyward, consumers are snapping up all the chickens that farmers can produce. Thus, despite a record level of chicken-raising this year, prices of these broilers are climbing faster than many analysts had expected.

Still, chickens remain considerably cheaper than other meats. "Folks still want some elegance in their dinners and they don't particularly enjoy paying $3 to $4 a pound for steak," says Bill Roenigk, research director of the National Broiler council, a chicken-producers' trade group.

The latest figures from the U.S. Bureau of Labor Statistics show the retail price of fresh, whole chickens was 65.6 cents a pound in May, up 8% from a year earlier. The price of hamburger climbed 27% to $1.10 a pound in May while pork roast prices jumped 19% to $1.53 a pound.

But the fact that chicken prices are much higher at all surprises most analysts. Current market conditions "are a lot different than we were expecting late last year," says

William E. Cathcart, an Agriculture Department poultry economist. Prices for other meats, particularly pork, have soared "higher than anyone anticipated," Mr. Cathcart says.

Chicken Output Increases Indeed, while high beef prices have been expected as a result of previous low prices that caused cattlemen to reduce the size of their herds, "the big surprise is that pork supplies have been lagging well behind earlier expectations," observes R. Lee Taylor, vice president of Federal Co., whose Holly Farms Poultry industries is a major chicken producer. As a result, pork prices are running ahead of expectations.

Chicken producers have moved to take advantage of the reduced supplies of other meats. They can adjust to changing meat-market conditions more quickly than producers of hogs or cattle, because it takes less than three months to raise a market-weight chicken from a newly laid egg. By contrast, from conception, it takes 10 months to raise a hog to market weight and 27 months to raise a steer.

Chicken production this year is running as much as 7% ahead of last year's output, but increased consumer demand has pushed average wholesale prices 7% above year-earlier levels, despite the added supplies. The rate of output isn't likely to wane any time soon, either, industry observers say, pointing to expectations of continued low supplies of beef and pork.

Broiler output in the second half could average 10% more than 1977's second half, and prices should climb 15% to 20% from year-earlier levels, says Mr. Cathcart, the Agriculture Department economist.

Poultry In Parts Besides tight supplies of red meat, marketing innovations have boosted demand for chicken, analysts say. Ten years ago, almost the only way to get chicken was to buy the whole bird, but today some companies market more than 30 different combinations of chicken parts, such as breasts, legs and necks, says the broiler council's Mr. Roenigk.

Boneless and skinless chicken breasts have been selling "faster than anything else," because they offer the "elegant" alternative that consumers are looking for, Mr. Roenigk adds. Export markets take up other parts of the bird.

Through May this year, overseas shipments of chicken parts have risen 14% from the first five months of 1977 to 44 million tons. But exports of whole chickens dropped 3% in the period to 21.5 million tons. Japan, the biggest buying nation, shows a marked preference for legs.

The booming broiler market bodes well for U.S. corn and soybean farmers, analysts say. During the current feeding year, which ends in September, broilers will consume 7.8 million tons of corn, or 7.4% of all the corn that will be fed to domestic animals, the Agriculture Department estimates. Also, the nation's broiler flock consistently is the single largest consumer of soybean meal, analysts note.

Options Volume Rises Traders say firm chicken prices have sparked renewed interest in trading of broiler futures on the Chicago Board of Trade, where volume in the first half was up 13% from a year earlier, although it still was only 44.723 contracts. In the corn and soybean futures markets, that many contracts often change hands in a day.

To boost trading in the little-used broiler contract, the exchange earlier this month made several technical changes in its specifications, partly by providing more flexibility to traders who don't want to take delivery of chickens. Traders say it's too early to tell what effect these changes may have on volume.

Yesterday, future prices for iced broiler chickens rose on renewed demand. Some traders said the market had been oversold recently and that wholesale prices have been improving.

Discussion

1. Why should increases in the prices of beef and pork affect the price of chicken? Use a supply-and-demand diagram to show that effect.

2. This result is typical of most substitutes: an increased price in one item increases the demand for, and therefore the price of, its substitutes. What would have happened to the price of chicken if beef and pork were complements? Why?

3. The article states that chicken producers can adjust more quickly than hog or cattle producers. Use this information to describe the long-run and short-run elasticities of supply in the three markets.

ADDENDUM: CONSUMER CHOICE AND INDIFFERENCE CURVES

1. All points on an indifference curve represent
   a. combinations of goods that are equally preferred by a consumer.
   b. combinations of goods that are of equal cost to a consumer.
   c. combinations of goods that are available to consumers.
   d. combinations of goods that are equally preferred by society.

2. Which of the following is *not* a characteristic of indifference curves?
    a. Indifference curves slope downward to the right, reflecting the degree to which goods can be substituted.
    b. Higher indifference curves (those lying farther to the northeast) represent higher levels of consumer satisfaction.
    c. Indifference curves will generally intersect, since the law of diminishing marginal utility applies to consumption.
    d. The indifference curves for two goods will be convex when viewed from the origin.

3. Which of the following relationships is present when a consumer attains his highest possible level of satisfaction at a specified level of income?
    a. $P_a/MU_a = P_b/MU_b$
    b. $P_a/P_b = MU_b/MU_a$
    c. The price of good B must be cheaper than that of good A.
    d. The price of good A must be cheaper than that of good B.

Use the diagram below to answer the next two questions:

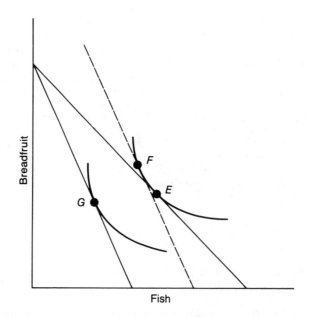

4. Initially, Crusoe's economy was in equilibrium at consumption bundle *E*. The price of fish increased as indicated in the diagram. The "substitution effect" associated with the increase in the price of fish is represented by the move from
    a. *E* to *F.*
    b. *F* to *G.*
    c. *E* to *G.*
    d. *G* to *E.*

5. The "income effect" associated with the increase in the price of fish is represented by the move from
    a. *E* to *F.*
    b. *F* to *G.*
    c. *E* to *G.*
    d. *G* to *E.*

17

Costs and the Supply of Goods

TRUE OR FALSE

T F

☐ ☐ 1. Implicit costs involve the foregoing of opportunities, even though monetary costs are not incurred.

☐ ☐ 2. Rental income foregone because the Widget Manufacturing Company uses its business-owned 200,000-square-foot structure to produce widgets is an example of an implicit cost.

☐ ☐ 3. The economist's concept of costs imputes an implicit market rate of return to capital assets that are owned by a business firm.

☐ ☐ 4. Average fixed costs (AFC) will always decline as output is expanded in the short run.

☐ ☐ 5. Average per unit costs usually increase with the rate of output, but decline with volume of output.

☐ ☐ 6. The law of diminishing returns alone implies that the long-run average total cost (ATC) curve will be U-shaped.

☐ ☐ 7. When a firm's output level is small (relative to plant size), ATC is high because of the high AFC.

☐ ☐ 8. Marginal cost (MC) represents the opportunity cost of producing an additional unit.

☐ ☐ 9. MC is equal to ATC at the point where ATC is a minimum.

☐ ☐ 10. ATC will always decline when MC is less than ATC.

☐ ☐ 11. A profit-maximizing business entrepreneur never sells a good for less than his ATC.

☐ ☐ 12. The owner of a drugstore may fail to make an economic profit even though his total revenues exceed his costs on labor, wholesale products, and equipment.

☐ ☐ 13. A firm can reduce its total fixed cost by reducing output.

☐ ☐ 14. A firm can avoid the opportunity cost of interest by using its own monetary resources in the business.

147

PROBLEMS AND PROJECTS

Exhibit I Income Statement

Revenues		Costs	
Sales	$55,000	Wholesale clothing	$30,000
Inventory adjustment	2,000	Equipment	2,000
		Labor	15,000
		Utilities and insurance	1,000
Total revenues	$57,000	Total costs	$48,000

1. Exhibit 1 represents the annual income statement of Joe's Clothing Store for 1986. Joe worked full time in the store and invested $30,000 to buy the store and stock it with merchandise. He recently turned down an offer of a salaried position paying $10,000 per year to manage another clothing store. He did not pay himself a salary during the year. According to Exhibit 1.
    a. what were Joe's accounting profits?
    b. what major items did he exclude from his costs?
    c. assuming that the market rate of interest was 10 percent recalculate Joe's total costs.
    d. what was the economic profit or loss of Joe's Clothing Store in 1986?

Exhibit 2 Costs and Output

Output (per week)	Total Cost	Total fixed cost	Total variable cost	Average total cost	Average variable cost	Marginal cost
1	$100	$50	_____	_____	_____	_____
2	140	_____	_____	_____	_____	_____
3	177	_____	_____	_____	_____	_____
4	216	_____	_____	_____	_____	_____
5	265	_____	_____	_____	_____	_____
6	324	_____	_____	_____	_____	_____
7	399	_____	_____	_____	_____	_____
8	496	_____	_____	_____	_____	_____

2. Harry owns a small shop and produces dining room sets. Exhibit 2 presents data on his expected total cost per set at various output levels.
    a. Complete Exhibit 2.
    b. At what output level is Harry's average total cost at a minimum?
    c. At what output level are diminishing marginal returns (given the current plant size) confronted?
    d. Graph the firm's average total cost, average variable cost, and marginal cost curves.

3. The data necessary to evaluate the cost of owning and operating two alternative automobiles are in Exhibit 3.

Exhibit 3

	Auto A	Auto B
Purchase price	$5000	$4000
Annual fee for insurance and license	200	100
Operating cost per mile including gas, oil, and maintenance	0.15	0.14
Resale value one year from now	4000	2800

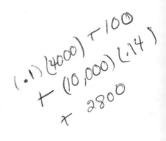

a. Assuming that the market rate of interest is 10 percent, calculate the average cost per mile of owning the automobile one year and driving it 10,000 miles for both auto A and auto B. Which is cheaper?

b. If the automobiles were driven 20,000 miles during the year, their respective resale values would be $3700 for A and $2200 for B. Which would be cheaper to purchase, own, and drive 20,000 miles during the year? Explain.

c. What happens to the average total cost per mile as the miles driven per year increase? Explain.

4. Carl Bergstrom is harvesting some wheat that he planted in the spring. Bergstrom uses a variety of fixed inputs (land, machines, and so on), the fixed costs of which are $100 per day. The only variable input is labor. Exhibit 4 shows the relationship between the quantity of labor Bergstrom can hire at $50 per day and the total output.

Exhibit 4

Daily labor inputs	Total product (bushels/ day)	Marginal product (bushels/ day)	Marginal cost (dollars/ bushel)	Total cost (dollars/day)
1	20			150
		30	1.67	
2	50			200
		___		
3	70			___
		___		
4	85			___
		___		
5	95			___
		___		
6	100			___
		1	50.00	
7	101			

a. Fill in the missing information in the table.

b. On a piece of graph paper plot the marginal product curve and the marginal cost curve. Does marginal cost rise when marginal product falls?

LEARNING THE MECHANICS—MULTIPLE CHOICE

1. Economists argue that the short-run average total cost curve is U-shaped because
   a. initially the law of diminishing marginal returns is operating, but later the law of increasing returns takes effect.
   b. factor prices will be higher for both small and large firms.
   c. the average fixed costs are high when output is low, and marginal costs are high when a plant is used too intensively.
   d. large plants are usually more efficient than small ones, but eventually bureaucratic inefficiency causes costs to rise.

2. The law of diminishing marginal returns indicates why
   a. beyond some point, the extra utility derived from additional units of a product will yield the consumer larger and larger additional amounts of satisfaction.
   b. the demand curve for goods produced by purely competitive industries is downward sloping.
   c. a firm's long-run average total cost curve is U-shaped.
   d. a firm's marginal costs will eventually increase as the firm expands output in the short run.

3. Which of the following is most likely to be an implicit cost?
   a. Rental income foregone on assets owned by the firm
   b. Salaries paid to the firm's board of directors
   c. Transportation cost on raw materials
   d. Interest payments on an outstanding loan of the firm

4. Use statements I and II to answer this question. (I) The demand for a product represents the voice of consumers instructing firms to produce the good. (II) Costs of production represent the desire of consumers for other items that could be produced with the resources.
   a. I is true, II is false.
   b. I is false, II is true.
   c. Both I and II are true.
   d. Both I and II are false.

5. The short run is a time period of insufficient length for the firm to change its
   a. output.
   b. amount of labor utilized.
   c. plant size and heavy equipment.
   d. price.

6. Sunk or "historical" costs are
   a. costs associated with current operational decisions.
   b. costs that have already been incurred as the result of past decisions.
   c. costs that add to the firm's marginal costs.
   d. costs that form the major component of the firm's variable costs.

7. The corporation enables a single business firm to raise large amounts of capital because
   a. stockholders like to participate in the operation of large firms.
   b. the limited liability concept protects the stockholder from potential debts incurred by the corporation.
   c. stockholders usually participate in the daily operations of the firms in which they own shares.
   d. large firms are operated more efficiently than small firms.

8. All but one of the following help to explain why the long-run average total costs are often lower for larger firms than for smaller ones. Which does *not* explain why the long-run average total costs decline, at least initially, as output is expanded?
   a. Learning-by-doing helps workers and management to become more efficient.
   b. Large-scale production permits more specialization.
   c. The average wage rate of workers is generally lower for large firms than for smaller ones.
   d. Large firms have an opportunity to adopt mass-production techniques that may be uneconomical for small firms.

9. Which of the following factors is *not* likely to have shifted the cost curve for Danelski's Demon Rum upward?
   a. The demand for rum has increased, pushing up its price.
   b. The price of glass for bottling the rum has increased.
   c. The excise tax on alcoholic beverages has increased.
   d. A new law requiring the purchase of an extra rum filtration machine was enacted by the Federal Demon Rum Administration.

10. The firm's average total costs will be a minimum at the output level where
    a. the firm just begins to confront diminishing returns to the variable factors.
    b. the marginal costs are a minimum.
    c. the firm's profits would always be a maximum.
    d. the marginal cost curve crosses the firm's average total cost curve.

11. Economic profit is frequently
    a. greater than total revenue.
    b. defined as total revenue minus total fixed cost.
    c. irrelevant to the owner of a firm who is concerned instead with accounting profit.
    d. less than accounting profit.

12. The law of diminishing returns states that
    a. as we continually add variable factors to a fixed amount of other resources, output eventually increases at a decreasing rate.
    b. as we increase plant size, costs must diminish.
    c. old industrialists never die, they just get smaller returns on their investment.
    d. as fixed costs increase, profits diminish.

13. The average variable cost curve and average total cost curve tend to converge as output rises because
    a. the marginal cost curve intersects the average total cost curve at its minimum.
    b. average fixed costs are constant as output rises.
    c. the difference between them (average fixed cost) declines.
    d. output is rising more rapidly than inputs are being increased.

THE ECONOMIC WAY OF THINKING—MULTIPLE CHOICE

1. "During the past five years, the prices of raw materials in our industry have increased, and the costs of both labor and machinery are up. Yet we have held our product price constant, and our profits have actually increased." Which of the following statements offers the best explanation for this phenomenon?
    a. Technology and/or economic efficiency has improved in the industry, making it possible to produce at low per unit cost, in spite of the increase in input prices.
    b. Economically speaking, the statement is a logical impossibility.
    c. The number of firms in this competitive industry has decreased so that the law of diminishing marginal returns decreased fixed costs.
    d. The demand for the product has increased enough to offset the higher per unit costs of output.

2. Which of the following represents a long-run adjustment?
    a. A steel manufacturer cuts back on its purchases of coke and iron ore.
    b. A farmer uses an extra dose of herbicide on his zucchini crop.
    c. The owner of a hamburger stand hires an additional carhop.
    d. A publisher builds a new plant to produce paperbook books.

3. The fact that the physical constraints (size of buildings, number of operational machines, etc.) of a plant are more binding over a month's time than over a six-month period explains why
    a. it is less costly to increase output rapidly than slowly.
    b. the long-run average cost curve is ∪-shaped.
    c. it is less costly to produce output in the present, rather than in the future.
    d. the quantity supplied is more flexible in the long run than in the short run.

4. "Actually, big businesses are generally no more and no less efficient than medium-sized businesses even when the gains wrung by monopoly power are included in efficiency. This is the one general finding in comparative cost studies and comparative profitability studies." This quotation from Professor George Stigler would most accurately reflect that
    a. the minimum long-run per unit costs of medium-size and large-size firms are similar.
    b. the short-run average costs fail to increase as medium-size firms produce larger outputs.
    c. the long-run average total cost curve is ∪-shaped.
    d. the law of diminishing marginal returns is the major explanation of why long-run marginal cost increases.

Exhibit 5

Purchase price	$1000
Gas and oil (7¢ per mile—5000 miles)	350
Depreciation	300
Insurance	100
Maintenance	75
License tag	30
Total	$1855

5. A political science major has calculated the cost of *owning* and *operating* a used car for one year. He included the items in Exhibit 5. Which of the following constitutes the best appraisal of his calculations?
    a. They are correct.
    b. There is only one error—depreciation should not be included.
    c. They contain only one error—omission of the interest earnings.
    d. There are two errors—the purchase price should not be included, but the interest earnings foregone because of buying the car should be.

6. A homeowner will be away from his house for six months. The monthly mortgage payment on the house is $300. The local services, *to be paid by the owner,* cost $100 per month if the house is occupied; otherwise zero. If the owner wishes to minimize his losses from the house, he should rent the house for as much as the market will bear, as long as monthly rent is greater than which of the following? (Assume wear and tear to be zero regardless of whether the house is occupied.) *Hint:* Remember the concept of opportunity cost.
    a. $0
    b. $100 $ 400
    c. $200
    d. $400

7. The best way to think about marginal product is as
    a. the profit margin due to production.
    b. total product divided by average product.
    c. the change in total output associated with each additional unit of an input (like labor).
    d. total output divided by the total number of units of an input (like labor).

8. Craig inherited a pizza store and enough money to pay the inheritance tax. The store did not cost him a cent. If Craig operated it, paying himself the full opportunity cost of his time, plus interest on the money he used to buy supplies and the like, his accounting profits would apparently be
    a. equal to his economic profit.
    b. less than his economic profit by the amount of salary he could earn elsewhere.
    c. greater than his economic profit by the value of the store's rental value.
    d. greater than his economic profit by the amount of salary he could earn elsewhere.

9. Which of the following constitutes a good reason for selling a product for less than it cost to produce?
    a. The product is about to spoil and will become worthless.
    b. Market conditions have changed, and the equilibrium price is now well below what it was expected to be.
    c. Both of the above.
    d. Neither of the above; it never pays to sell a product for less than its production costs!

10. Mark owns a firm that makes waterbeds. Last year his average total cost per bed was $210 while his selling price was $195. He tells his banker that if the bank would lend him more money, he could keep his price the same, and make a profit by selling more beds. The banker knows that rent, labor, materials, and other resource costs will not decline. Mark says he is losing money on each unit, but plans to make it up by selling more and more units. Mark is
    a. clearly a con artist—he is not telling the truth.
    b. correct, if fixed costs were a small enough part of last year's costs.
    c. correct, if fixed costs were a large enough part of total costs.
    d. correct, if the law of diminishing marginal returns had already begun to affect his firm.

11. If consumers suddenly increased their demand for oranges, the average total cost curve would probably shift upward for growers of
    a. bananas, if bananas were frequently consumed with oranges.
    b. apples, which consumers often substitute for oranges.
    c. exotic hogs, which often eat discarded orange peels.
    d. grapefruit, since grapefruit growers use the same land and labor pool as orange growers.

12. Which of the following factors is most likely to shift the cost curves of an Iowa corn farmer downward?
    a. An increase in the price of fertilizer
    b. An increase in the tax on diesel fuel, which is used by the farmer
    c. The development of a new, more efficient corn harvester
    d. An increase in the demand for land such as his by soybean farmers

THE ECONOMIC WAY OF THINKING—DISCUSSION QUESTIONS

1. Is accounting profit the same as economic profit? If a firm's accounting statement revealed that it was making profits, would the firm always want to continue in business? Explain.

2. What is marginal cost? Explain why marginal cost will increase with time as the firm expands its output in the short run. Explain why the firm's average total cost curve in the short run is typically ∪-shaped.

3. Indicate the major reasons why the per unit costs of production are often lower for large firms that produce large outputs (both rate and volume) than for their smaller counterparts.

4. How would each of the following influence the cost of producing new housing?
    a. An increase in the price of lumber
    b. The development of a new lighter brick that reduced labor requirements without increasing the costs of material
    c. A reduction in the price of cement
    d. A new "occupational safety" regulation that required all construction workers to wear safety glasses, aluminum hats, and steel-toed shoes
    e. Passage of state legislation requiring all contractors to pay a $10,000 licensing fee

5. "A profit-maximizing firm should supply additional units *in the short run* as long as it can cover its marginal cost. However, *in the long run,* the good should be supplied only if the firm can cover its average total cost." True, false, or uncertain? Explain.

6. Indicate the characteristics of the corporate legal structure that make it attractive to owners.

7. Indicate why you either agree or disagree with the following statements:
    a. "I have to keep driving my old car in order to make up for the loss that I took when the transmission went out." (*Hint:* Remember the relevance of sunk costs.)
    b. "It does not make sense to keep operating an old machine when new machines can produce more efficiently."
    c. "Accounting costs yield valuable information, but they are not the relevant cost consideration when making business decisions."
    d. "A profit-maximizing firm will never sell a product for less than it costs to produce."

8. In 1911, Thomas Edison wrote in the *Wall Street Journal:*

    > Thirty years ago my balance sheet showed me that I was not making much money. My manufacturing plant was not running to its full capacity. I couldn't

find a market for my products. Then I suggested that we undertake to run our plant on full capacity and sell the surplus products in foreign markets at less than the cost of production. Every one of my associates opposed me. I had my experts figure out how much it would add to the cost of operating the plant if we increased this production 25 percent. The figures showed that we could increase the production 25 percent at an increased cost of only about 2 percent. On this basis I sent a man to Europe who sold lamps there at a price less than the cost of production in Europe.

a. When Edison suggested that he would sell in foreign markets "at less than the cost of production," of what cost was he speaking?
b. What was happening to Edison's marginal cost as he expanded output by 25 percent?
c. Edison's pricing idea was opposed by his associates. Assuming that he was motivated by profit, who was right—Edison or his associates? Explain.

PERSPECTIVES IN ECONOMICS

Marginal-Cost Policy Making and the Guy Next Door
by Thomas L. Wyrick

[From *The Wall Street Journal,* April 12, 1984, abridged. Reprinted with permission of the Wall Street Journal © Dow Jones & Co., Inc. (1984). All rights reserved.]

Imagine yourself in a supermarket when the manager announces that for the next five minutes bottles of your favorite soft drink will be sold two for $1 rather than the regular price of $1 each. "Buy one, get one free."

Back at home a half-hour later, a neighbor with unexpected company calls to ask if you would sell him a bottle of the same soda. You agree, but before he gets there you must decide how much to charge him. Three possibilities come to mind—$1, 50 cents or nothing—but there doesn't seem to be any way of knowing which is appropriate.

It doesn't take long to narrow your choices to two. Only the most altruistic would figure that the neighbor was getting the free bottle anyway, and shouldn't have to pay for it.

If you concentrate on the average price per bottle, then 50 cents will seem correct. After all, it is impossible to say which bottle was purchased and which one was "free," so it may appear reasonable to split the difference and charge your neighbor 50 cents.

But before the neighbor arrives, you have two bottles of soda. Once he leaves you will have one bottle and 50 cents, if you charge according to average cost. Since the two-for-one sale was a one-time thing only, it will be necessary to spend an additional 50 cents of your own money to replace the bottle once it is gone.

So averaging costs to set a price reduces your wealth by the difference between replacement cost for the soda and its average cost to you.

Now, you may charge the neighbor 50 cents just to prevent hard feelings in case he later learns about the two-for-one special. But that is the consequence of placing friendship above economic considerations. If the deal is purely an economic one, then it is proper to charge the neighbor $1. This represents the soda's replacement cost, or the marginal cost incurred by you when selling the soda.

Sound simple? That's because it is. Unfortunately, however, government officials often have difficulty translating such ideas into policy.

Our nation's energy policies have usually been based on the naive view that firms set prices according to their average costs of doing business. Instead, profit-seeking firms use marginal-cost pricing. Thus policies can (and often do) have consequences opposite to those intended.

Recall the experience with oil price controls in the 1970s. The price of domestic crude oil was held down to artificially low levels to try to lower the costs of producing gasoline. As everyone knows, though, gasoline prices have declined (rather than increased) since President Reagan abolished controls in early 1981. This is contrary to what price controllers had expected, so they generally explain the (three-year) decline as temporary.

But a different explanation emerges from the marginal-cost pricing perspective. Oil refiners produce gasoline (and other products) from crude oil purchased from both domestic and foreign sources. Controls held the price of U.S. oil to $2 or $3 a barrel while foreign suppliers charged $36 or more in 1979. Refiners rationally bought all of the U.S. crude available, and turned to OPEC members only as a last resort.

Like a person selling soda to his neighbor, however, refiners charge customers a price based on their marginal costs of selling oil. That is, because Exxon or Texaco had only a limited amount of $2 oil available, a sale of that oil meant they had to rely on OPEC sources to replenish their inventories. Since that meant an additional (marginal) outlay of $36 a barrel, then the price of gasoline had to be high enough to reflect this cost rather than the lower controlled price.

So price controls on oil allowed refiners to pay less than a market price on some of their inputs, while they charged a market price on all of their output. Thanks to Congress, refiners' profits were at an all-time high during the price-control years. Of course, U.S. landowners and others who sold crude to refiners were harmed in proportion to the latter's gain.

The 1981 removal of price controls gave domestic owners of oil reserves more incentive to find and sell crude, and they responded in kind. As new domestic supplies came into competition with foreign oil, OPEC and others were forced to lower their prices to the current range of $28 to $29. This lowered refiners' marginal costs of doing business, and allowed them to lower the price of gasoline.

Meanwhile, because of the average cost–marginal cost confusion, Congress remains unwilling to remove price controls from certain categories of natural gas. Doing so, it is thought, would result in price increases for consumers—perhaps by 50% or more within a few months.

In reality, however, controls cause owners of artificially low-priced gas to hold down production, so pipeline companies must turn to more expensive (uncontrolled) sources to satisfy customer demands. That drives up the latter's price, increases marginal costs for pipelines and utility companies, and pushes up prices to consumers.

Decontrol would allow all natural gas to sell for the same price. The owners of decontrolled gas would increase production to profit from higher prices, and the now familiar dynamic would be seen again. Lessened demand for higher-priced gas on the margin would bring down the market price of gas. And lower marginal costs for pipelines would ultimately help reduce the heating bills of consumers.

The lesson to be learned is that market participants respond to marginal costs, not average costs. If a firm's costs rise by X dollars when it produces and sells one more unit of output, then price will tend toward X dollars regardless of the firm's costs averaged over all units of output.

Policy makers intent on helping consumers, borrowers and others would do well to stop trying to control the various components of production costs. Such efforts usually end up reducing the total supply of the good or service in question, and customers pay higher retail prices as a result. Public officials should spend more effort understanding how the private economy works; then they wouldn't waste so much energy trying to fix it.

Discussion

1. How much would *you* have charged your neighbor for the bottle of soda? Why?

2. Wyrick seems to be arguing that getting rid of price controls on crude oil actually helped *reduce* the retail price of gasoline. How is this possible? Why is the role of marginal cost crucial in all of this?

3. Do you agree with Wyrick's prediction that removing price controls from natural gas would decrease natural gas prices rather than increase them (even though an increase is what most people seem to expect)? Why or why not?

18

The Firm Under Pure Competition

TRUE OR FALSE

T F

☑ ☐ 1. The model of pure competition assumes that a large number of independent firms produce a homogeneous product.

☐ ☑ 2. Competitive firms will never be able to earn economic profit.

☑ ☐ 3. A firm under pure competition faces a perfectly elastic demand curve for the product it sells.

☑ ☐ 4. A profit-maximizing competitive firm will expand output as long as the market price exceeds marginal cost.

☑ ☐ 5. An increase in market demand would cause price to rise, profit to increase, and competitive firms to expand their short-run output level.

☑ ☐ 6. Economic profits provide an incentive for competitive firms to allocate resources toward the production of goods for which the consumers' valuation exceeds the opportunity cost of production.

☐ ☑ 7. Competitive firms always produce at the level of output at which average total costs are a minimum.

☐ ☑ 8. In the competitive model, the firm's average total cost curve is also its short-run supply curve.

☐ ☐ 9. Economic losses cause firms to exit from an industry in the long run, and the market supply declines.

☐ ☐ 10. The firm's marginal cost curve indicates the opportunity cost of producing additional units of the product in the short run.

☐ ☐ 11. The minimum point of the firm's long-run average total cost curve represents the opportunity cost of producing the good in the long run.

☐ ☐ 12. In a constant cost industry, an increase in demand will cause price to rise in the long run.

☐ ☐ 13. The market supply curve usually becomes more inelastic with time.

☐ ☐ 14. The competitive model suggests that an increase in the demand for wheat would cause prices to rise, profits to increase, and consumers to buy less.

PROBLEMS AND PROJECTS

Exhibit 1

Monthly output	Total cost	Average total cost	Average fixed cost	Average variable cost	Marginal cost
1	$ 25	___	0	___	___
2	50	___	___	___	___
3	69	___	___	___	___
4	84	___	___	___	___
5	100	___	___	___	___
6	119	___	___	___	___
7	140	___	___	___	___
8	168	___	___	___	___

1. The student government of a major university arranges a monthly campuswide "flea market" sale where talented students can sell products they produce in their leisure time. Harold brings his handmade wallets to sell at the flea market. Since there are several other suppliers, Harold has no control over the market price. Harold's estimated cost and output data are presented in Exhibit 1.
   a. Fill in the missing cost information.
   b. If Harold was a profit maximizer, how many wallets would he produce monthly if the market price was $20? Indicate his economic profit (or loss).
   c. Indicate what Harold's monthly output and maximum profit would be if the price rose to $25.

Exhibit 2

Housing units per month	Total cost per month	Fixed cost (FC)	Variable cost (VC)	Average total cost (ATC)	Average fixed cost (AFC)	Average variable cost (AVC)	Marginal cost (MC)
0	$ 40,000	___	___	___	___	___	___
1	60,000	___	___	___	___	___	___
2	80,000	___	___	___	___	___	___
3	100,000	___	___	___	___	___	___
4	120,000	___	___	___	___	___	___
5	142,000	___	___	___	___	___	___
6	168,000	___	___	___	___	___	___
7	198,000	___	___	___	___	___	___
8	232,000	___	___	___	___	___	___
9	270,000	___	___	___	___	___	___
10	315,000	___	___	___	___	___	___

2. Joe Green operates a construction firm, Joe's Construction Company, Inc., that specializes in the production of small frame houses. Joe's expected cost schedule is presented in Exhibit 2.
   a. Complete the chart indicating Joe's FC, VC, ATC, AFC, AVC, and MC.
   b. The current market price for houses of the quality produced by Joe's Construction is $29,500. Assume Joe wants to maximize profits. How many houses should he produce per month? What is his profit (or loss)?
   c. Suppose that there is population growth in the area, causing the demand for housing to expand. The market price of the houses increases to $32,000. Indicate Joe's new profit-maximizing monthly output and profit (or loss).
   d. Indicate Joe's output and maximum profit (or minimum loss) if the market price were to fall to $25,000; to $21,000. Should Joe continue in business at the latter price? Explain.

Exhibit 3

Price	Quantity demanded (new housing)	Quantity supplied (new housing)
$21,000	850	400
25,000	700	500
29,000	600	600
31,000	500	700
35,000	450	900

3. Market conditions stabilize in the market area served by Joe's construction firm. The market demand schedule for housing of the quality produced by Joe is presented in Exhibit 3.

   a. Suppose that there are 100 competitive firms—including Joe's Construction—that supply the market area. Each firm has the cost conditions indicated in Exhibit 2. What is the market supply schedule?

   b. What is the short-run market-clearing price?

   c. What is the profit or loss of the firms? Is there any incentive for new firms to enter the market?

   d. Given competitive conditions, what will happen to the market price with time? Explain.

4. Exhibit 4 presents selected monthly information relating to a single firm in a purely competitive market.

Exhibit 4

Price	$ 8
Total Revenue......................................	8000
Total Variable Cost	7000
Output	———
Average Total Cost	8
Total Cost..	———
Marginal Revenue.................................	———
Marginal Cost	8
Total Profit......................................	———

   a. Fill in the missing information in the exhibit.

   b. Is this firm in *long-run* equilibrium?

Suppose the government decides that firms in this market must be licensed to operate and establishes a licensing fee of $6000 payable by each firm yearly regardless of the economic circumstances of the firm.

   c. In the *short-run,* how will the firm adjust its output in response to the licensing fee?

   d. If the firm expects market conditions to remain the same in the long run, how will it adjust its output?

5. Exhibit 5 shows a situation of long-run equilibrium for both the market and a typical firm in the cheese industry. Suppose that government decides (perhaps to raise incomes for dairy "farmers") to place a price support on dairy products at the level P_s and enforces this price by agreeing to purchase any quantity of dairy products produced but not sold to the private sector.

Exhibit 5

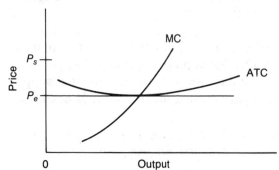 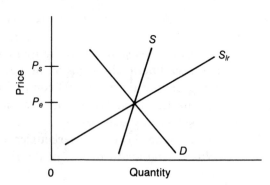

a. For the short run, indicate in the diagrams how the market and the typical firm will adjust to this price support policy. (Indicate the new quantity demanded in the market and the new quantity supplied both in the market and by the typical firm.) How much cheese will the government need to buy in the short run in order to maintain the price, P_s?

b. Now indicate how the market and the typical firm will adjust to the price support policy in the long run. (Remember that an upward-sloping long-run supply curve indicates that the industry is an increasing-cost industry.) Will the government be required to purchase more cheese per period in the long run than in the short run?

c. Is this policy consistent with the achievement of *productive efficiency* in the dairy products industry? Is it consistent with the achievement of *allocative efficiency*? Explain. (*Hint:* Be sure to decide how long the "long" run is.)

LEARNING THE MECHANICS—MULTIPLE CHOICE

1. The reason we do not refer to long-run variable cost as distinguished from long-run cost is that
    a. all costs are fixed in the long run.
    b. all costs are constant in the long run.
    c. all costs are variable in the long run. ✓
    d. all costs decline in the long run.

2. A decrease in demand that results in economic losses in industry A will
    a. induce new, more efficient firms to enter the industry.
    b. cause the existing firms in industry A to expand the scale of their operation.
    c. induce both new and existing firms in industry A to bid more resources away from other industries.
    d. encourage owners of resources to move their resources from industry A to other industries. ✓

3. If the firms in a competitive industry were incurring costs that were less than the prices they were charging, the firms
    a. would enjoy short-run economic profits that would be offset by long-run economic losses.
    b. would face new competition, which would drive price down to the cost of production in the long run.
    c. would enjoy long-run economic profit.
    d. must be colluding or otherwise "rigging the market."

4. Which of the following statements is correct?
    a. In order to maximize profits in the short run, a purely competitive firm should produce at the output level where marginal cost is equal to price.
    b. In long-run equilibrium, a purely competitive firm will produce at the level of minimum average variable cost.
    c. A purely competitive firm will produce in the short run, so long as total receipts are sufficient to cover total fixed costs.
    d. A purely competitive firm will always close down in the short run, whenever price is less than average total cost.

5. Which of the following would be most likely to lead to a reduction in the price of a competitively produced product X?
    a. An increase in the price of Y, a substitute
    b. A decrease in the price of Z, a complementary product
    c. A decrease in the price of K, a factor of production that is utilized to produce X
    d. A decrease in the price of L, a factor of production utilized to produce Z, the complementary product

6. In an industry with low barriers to entry, when positive economic profits are present and expected
    a. firms will exit from the industry.
    b. the marginal cost curve will shift down.
    c. the average fixed cost curve will shift up.
    d. firms will enter the industry, forcing the price down such that only zero economic profits will be possible.

7. The long-run supply curve is more elastic than the short-run supply curve because, given sufficient time
    a. production techniques become more expensive.
    b. new firms can enter the industry and old firms can increase their plant size.
    c. producers become less competitive.
    d. consumers become more demanding.

8. In the short run, the basic relationship between an individual firm's supply curve under perfect competition and the market supply curve under perfect competition is
    a. the individual firm's supply curve is horizontal, but the market supply curve is upward sloping.
    b. the individual firm's supply curve is vertical, but the market supply curve is upward sloping.
    c. the market supply curve is the summation of all the individual firms' supply curves.
    d. the market supply curve is equal to the average of all the individual firms' supply curves.

9. The actions of a firm in a purely competitive industry have no effect on market price; therefore, the demand curve faced by the firm is
    a. unknown.
    b. a downward-sloping curve.
    c. a horizontal line at the level of market place. ✓
    d. the firm's total revenue curve.

10. A study of the dairy industry indicates that the long-run elasticity of supply of milk with respect to its price is
    a. much more elastic than would have been expected. ✓
    b. much more inelastic than would have been expected.
    c. dependent on the demand for milk.
    d. none of the above.

11. The difference between the short-run and the long-run supply curves for a product is that the short-run supply curve is usually
    a. horizontal.
    b. more inelastic than the long-run curve.
    c. more elastic than the long-run curve. ✓
    d. of unitary elasticity.

THE ECONOMIC WAY OF THINKING—MULTIPLE CHOICE

1. If firms in a competitive industry were forced to install antipollution devices that increased their production costs, we should expect
    a. the demand for their product to decline.
    b. the market price of their product to increase in the short run, but not in the long run.
    c. that the firms in the industry would be saddled with long-run economic losses.
    d. that the firms in the industry would make normal economic profits in the long run, as the higher production costs were passed along to consumers. ✓

    Use the following table in answering the next two questions:

	Price, July 1972 (bushel)	Price, August 1973 (bushel)
Wheat	$1.70	$ 4.90
Oats	0.80	2.06
Rye	1.01	3.86
Soybeans	3.50	12.00

2. In July 1972, the Nixon administration announced it had concluded the largest agricultural commodity sale in history—selling 25 percent of the American wheat crop to the Soviet Union. Which of the following best explains the impact of this transaction?
    a. The demand for American wheat increased sharply, the short-run supply was highly inelastic, and price rose sharply. ✓
    b. The domestic production of wheat declined, and price rose sharply in spite of the highly elastic demand.
    c. The demand for American wheat increased, but the price change suggests that the short-run supply was highly elastic.
    d. The supply of American wheat fell sharply, but the price change suggests that the current demand was elastic.

3. Which of the following would *not* result from the Russian wheat deal?
    a.   The income and profits of American farmers would increase.
    b.   The price of agricultural land—particularly land suitable for growing grain products—would rise.
    c.   The price of wheat would rise more in the short run than over a longer period of time that would allow for a supply response.
    d.   The price of breakfast foods, bread, and beef to the American consumer would be unaffected by the wheat deal.   ✓

4. The agricultural sector is often said to approximate closely the competitive market structure because of the large number of firms and the low barriers to entry. Assume that the government fixes the price of wheat above the market equilibrium price and pledges to purchase quantities of wheat that cannot be sold to private purchasers. Wheat farmers will
    a.   expand the output of wheat and bid up the prices of factors used in the production of wheat.
    b.   expand the output of wheat and continue to make long-run economic profits.
    c.   increase their sales of wheat to private consumers because of the higher price.✓
    d.   produce less wheat because of higher factor prices and therefore increased cost.

5. If the demand for food increased drastically over the next ten years in the United States, and farmers became much more productive during the same period, then
    a.   the price of food would definitely fall over the next ten years.
    b.   the price of food would definitely rise over the next ten years.
    c.   it is possible that the price of food would not increase over the next ten years, relative to its current level.   ✓
    d.   the supply curve for food would shift to the left because of increased farm productivity and the increased demand for food.

6. The competitive market tends toward a state of long-run normal rate of return (zero economic profits) because
    a.   firms will moderate their price demands under fear of government legislation.
    b.   with firms able to enter and leave the industry freely, competition between rivals will drive prices down to the level of production costs.   ✓
    c.   cutthroat competition will cause some firms to incur losses, but barriers to entry will result in profits for others.
    d.   barriers to entry will prevent firms from earning excess profits.

7. Suppose that there is a sharp increase in the demand for small cars as drivers seek to conserve fuel during the energy crisis. The most likely long-run market adjustment would be
    a.   lower short-run small car prices because of greater sales volume, but higher prices as the long-run stock of small cars is depleted.
    b.   higher short-run prices, leading to an increase in long-run quantity supplied which would moderate the long-run price increase.   ✓
    c.   moderate increases in short-run prices, followed by larger long-run price increases as the stock of small cars is depleted.
    d.   higher short-run prices because of greater sales volume and still higher prices later, as plant sizes are adjusted.

8. During peak periods, like the middle of the day during a summer hot spell, power companies often experience brownouts because the quantity of electricity demanded exceeds the capacity of the power company. These brownouts are costly, since they reduce available electricity without regard to the need for that electricity, and they may damage sensitive machinery. These costs could be reduced if
   a. the barriers to entry in the utility industry were reduced.
   b. the long-run demand for electricity was perfectly elastic.
   c. the long-run supply of electricity was perfectly elastic.
   d. the power company had the right to charge a higher price for electricity consumed during peak periods.

9. Which portion of the marginal cost curve is used to create a firm's short-run supply curve?
   a. the entire marginal cost curve
   b. the marginal cost curve above its intersection with the average variable cost curve
   c. the marginal cost curve above its intersection with the marginal revenue (demand) curve
   d. the marginal cost curve above its intersection with the average total cost curve

10. "My fixed costs are killing me. I am only covering my variable costs plus a third of those fixed costs. I see no change coming in either my costs of production or in product prices." Economic analysis indicates that this producer will minimize his losses by
   a. shutting down and selling out immediately.
   b. shutting down only when variable costs cannot be covered.
   c. continuing to produce, recognizing that true economic profits do not include fixed costs.
   d. continuing to produce as long as marginal costs are covered.

11. "I have been making furniture for 27 years. I have never heard of either marginal costs or Adam Smith. Fancy economic theories mean nothing to me. I just know how to do well in this business. Common sense and watching the market are good enough for me." For producers like this, the competitive model
   a. will not usually predict their behavior accurately.
   b. indicates nothing about the behavior of such producers.
   c. will probably predict their actions fairly accurately.
   d. does not apply, because the producers do not understand the terminology.

12. "Our marginal cost exceeds our marginal revenue at current factor prices." In plain English, this means that
   a. profit would increase if one more unit were produced.
   b. producing one more unit right now would either reduce the profit or enlarge the loss of the firm.
   c. management must be operating correctly right now.
   d. the firm should shut down and cease production even in the short run.

THE ECONOMIC WAY OF THINKING—DISCUSSION QUESTIONS

1. Explain when and why the firm's marginal cost curve (above its average variable cost) is its supply curve in the short run. Indicate the relationship between the firm's supply curve and the market supply curve in the short run.

2. Use the competitive model to indicate how each of the following would affect the market price of green vegetables:
    a. Higher fertilizer prices
    b. Development of a hybrid bean seed that triples output per acre
    c. An increase in meat prices
    d. Higher wages for farm laborers because of unionization
    e. Passage of a general sales tax on agricultural products, including vegetables

3. Does intense rivalry exist among firms in the competitive model? Would a firm gain significantly if misfortune befell two or three of its competitors? Clearly indicate the distinction between
    a. a competition in the rivalry sense, and
    b. pure competition.

4. A winter freeze destroys 50 percent of the orange trees in Florida. What impact would the freeze have on
    a. the current supply of oranges?
    b. the price of grapefruit?
    c. the incomes of California orange growers?
    d. the incomes of Florida orange growers?

5. Use the competitive model to explain fully how a reduction in demand for shrimp would affect (a) the economic profit or loss of shrimp producers and (b) the market price and output in both the short and long run. Use diagrams relating the adjustments of the producers (firms) to the market in explaining your answer.

6. "In competitive industries, profits and losses are merely signals providing producers with the incentive to produce what consumers want." Evaluate.

7. Think about the human side of pure competition. Who gets hurt when a firm is forced to go out of business?

8. Is our economy better off or worse off when a firm leaves one industry and enters another? Why? Would you need any additional information to be sure of your answer? What information would you need, and how would your answer depend on that information?

PERSPECTIVE IN ECONOMICS

The Economic Organization Of A Prison Camp
by Richard A. Radford

[Abridged from "The Economic Organization of a Prison Camp," *Economica*, November 1945, pp. 189–201. Reprinted with permission.]

After allowance has been made for abnormal circumstances, the social institutions, ideas and habits of groups in the outside world are to be found reflected in a Prisoner of War Camp. One aspect of social organization is to be found in economic activity, and this is to be found in any P.O.W. camp. True, a prisoner is not dependent on his exertions for the provision of the necessaries, or even the luxuries of life, but through his economic activity, the exchange of goods and services, his standard of material comfort is considerably enhanced.

Everyone receives a roughly equal share of essentials: it is by trade that individual preferences are given expression and comfort increased. All at some time, and most people regularly, make exchanges of one sort or another. Our essential interest lies in the universality and the spontaneity of this economic life: it came into existence not only by conscious imitation but as a response to the immediate needs and circumstances. Any similarity between prison organization and outside organization arises from similar stimuli evoking similar responses.

The Development And Organization Of The Market We reached a transit camp in Italy and received one-quarter of a Red Cross food parcel each a week later. At once exchanges, already established, multiplied in volume. Starting with simple direct barter, such as a non-smoker giving a smoker friend a cigarette issue in exchange for a chocolate ration, more complex exchanges soon became an accepted custom. Stories circulated of a padre who started off round the camp with a tin of cheese and five cigarettes and returned to his bed with a complete parcel in addition to his original cheese and cigarettes: the market was not yet perfect. Within a week or two, as the volume of trade grew, rough scales of exchange values came into existence. Sikhs, who had at first exchanged tinned beef for practically any other foodstuff, began to insist on jam and margarine. It was realized that a tin of jam was worth one-half pound of margarine plus something else; that a cigarette issue was worth several chocolate issues, and a tin of diced carrots was worth practically nothing.

By the end of a month, when we reached our permanent camp, there was a lively trade in all commodities and their relative values were well known, and expressed not in terms of one another, but in terms of cigarettes. The cigarette became the standard of value. In the permanent camp people started by wandering through the bungalows calling their offers—"cheese for seven" (cigarettes)—and the hours after parcel issue were bedlam. The inconvenience of this system soon led to its replacement by an Exchange and Mart notice board in every bungalow, where sales and wants were advertised. When a deal went through, it was crossed off the board. The public and semi-permanent records of transactions led to cigarette prices being well known and thus tending to equality throughout the camp, although there were always opportunities for an astute trader to make a profit from arbitrage. With this development everyone, including nonsmokers, was willing to sell for cigarettes, using them to buy at another time and place. Cigarettes became the normal currency, though, of course, barter was never extinguished.

The unity of the market and the prevalence of a single price varied directly with the general level of organization and comfort in the camp. A transit camp was always chaotic. Organization was too slender to include an Exchange and Mart board, and private advertisements were the most that appeared. Consequently a transit camp was not one market but many. The price of a tin of salmon is known to have varied by two cigarettes in 20 between one end of a hut and the other. Despite a high level of organization in Italy, the market was morcellated in this manner at the first transit camp we reached after our removal to Germany. In this camp there were up to 50,000 prisoners of all nationalities. French, Russian, Italian and Jugo-Slavs were free to move about within the camp: British and Americans were confined to their compounds, although a few cigarettes given to a sentry would always procure permission for one or two men to visit other compounds. The people who first visited the highly organized French trading center, with its stalls and known prices, found coffee extract—relatively cheap among the tea-drinking English—commanding a fancy price in biscuits or cigarettes, and some enterprising people made small fortunes that way.

The permanent camps in Germany saw the highest level of commercial organization. In addition to the Exchange and Mart notice boards, a shop was organized as a public utility, controlled by representatives of the Senior British Officer, on a no-profit basis. People left their surplus clothing, toilet requisites and food there until they were sold at a fixed price in cigarettes. Only sales in cigarettes were accepted and there was no higgling. The capital was provided by a loan from the bulk store of Red Cross cigarettes and repaid by a small commission taken on the first transaction. Thus the cigarette attained its fullest currency status, and the market was almost completely unified.

There was an embryo labor market. Even when cig-

arettes were not scarce, there was usually some unlucky person willing to perform services for them. Laundry advertised at two cigarettes a garment. A good pastel portrait cost thirty. Odd tailoring and other jobs similarly had their prices.

There were also entrepreneurial services. There was a coffee stall owner who sold tea, coffee or cocoa at two cigarettes a cup, buying his raw materials at market prices and hiring labor to gather fuel and to stoke: he actually enjoyed the services of a chartered accountant at one stage. After a period of great prosperity he overreached himself and failed disastrously for several hundred cigarettes. Such large-scale private enterprise was rare but several middlemen or professional traders existed. One man capitalized his knowledge of Urdu by buying meat from the Sikhs and selling butter and jam in return: as his operations became better known more and more people entered this trade, prices in the Indian Wing approximated more nearly to those elsewhere, though to the end a "contact" among the Indians was valuable, as linguistic difficulties prevented the trade from being quite free. Some were specialists in the Indian trade, the food, or even the watch trade. Middlemen traded on their own account or on commission. Price rings and agreements were suspected and the traders certainly cooperated. Nor did they welcome newcomers. Unfortunately the writer knows little of the workings of these people: public opinion was hostile and the professionals were usually of a retiring disposition.

One trader in food and cigarettes, operating in a period of dearth, enjoyed a high reputation. His capital was originally about 50 cigarettes, with which he bought rations on issue days and held them until the price rose just before the next issue. He also picked up a little by arbitrage; several times a day he visited every Exchange or Mart notice board and took advantage of every discrepancy between prices of goods offered and wanted. His knowledge of prices, markets and names of those who had received cigarette parcels was phenomenal. By these means he kept himself smoking steadily—his profits—while his capital remained intact.

Credit entered into many transactions. Naturally prices varied according to the terms of sale. A treacle ration might be advertised for four cigarettes now or five next week. And in the future market "bread now" was a vastly different thing from "bread Thursday." Bread was issued on Thursday and Monday, and by Wednesday and Sunday night it had risen at least one cigarette per ration. One man always saved a ration to sell then at the peak price: his offer of "bread now" stood out on the board among a number of "bread Monday's" fetching one or two less, or not selling at all—and he always smoked on Sunday night.

The Cigarette Currency   Although cigarettes as currency had certain peculiarities, they performed all the functions of a metallic currency as a unit of account, as a measure of value and as a store of value, and shared most of its characteristics.

Cigarettes were also subject to the working of Gresham's Law. Certain brands were more popular than others as smokes, but for currency purposes a cigarette was a cigarette. Consequently buyers used the poorer qualities and the Shop rarely saw the more popular brands: cigarettes such as Churchman's No. 1 were rarely used for trading. At one time cigarettes hand-rolled from pipe tobacco began to circulate. Pipe tobacco was issued in lieu of cigarettes by the Red Cross at a rate of 25 cigarettes to the ounce and this rate was standard in exchanges, but an ounce would produce 30 home-made cigarettes. Naturally people with machine-made cigarettes broke them down and re-rolled the tobacco, and the real cigarette virtually disappeared from the market. For a time we suffered all the inconveniences of a debased currency.

While the Red Cross issue of 50 or 25 cigarettes per man per week came in regularly, and while there were fair stocks held, the cigarette currency suited its purpose admirably. But when the issue was interrupted, stocks soon ran out, prices fell, trading declined in volume and became increasingly a matter of barter. This deflationary tendency was periodically offset by the sudden injection of new currency. Private cigarette parcels arrived in a trickle throughout the year, but the big numbers came in quarterly when the Red Cross received its allocation of transport. Several hundred thousand cigarettes might arrive in the space of a fortnight. Prices soared, and then began to fall, slowly at first but with increasing rapidity as stocks ran out, until the next big delivery. Most of our economic troubles could be attributed to this fundamental instability.

Price Movements The general price level was affected by other factors. An influx of new prisoners, proverbially hungry, raised it. Heavy air raids in the vicinity of the camp probably increased the non-monetary demand for cigarettes and accentuated deflation. Good and bad war news certainly had its effect, and the general waves of optimism and pessimism which swept the camp were reflected in prices. Before breakfast one morning a rumour of the arrival of parcels and cigarettes was circulated. Within ten minutes I sold a treacle ration for four cigarettes (hitherto offered in vain for three). By 10 o'clock the rumour was denied, and treacle that day found no more buyers even at two cigarettes.

Changes in the supply of a commodity, in the ration scale or in the make-up of Red Cross parcels, would raise the price of one commodity relative to others. Tins of oatmeal, once a rare and much sought after luxury in the parcels, became a commonplace in 1943, and the price fell. In hot weather the demand for cocoa fell, and that for soap rose. A new recipe would be reflected in the price level: the discovery that raisins and sugar could be turned into an alcohol liquor of remarkable potency reacted permanently on the dried fruit market. The invention of electric immersion heaters run off the power points made tea, a drug on the market in Italy, a certain seller in Germany. Any change in conditions affected both the general price level and the price structure.

Public Opinion Public opinion on the subject of trading was vocal if confused and changeable. Certain forms of trading were more generally condemned; trade with the Germans was criticized by many. At one time, when there had been several cases of malnutrition reported among the more devoted smokers, no trade in German rations was permitted, as the victims became an additional burden on the depleted food reserves of the Hospital. But while certain activities were condemned as antisocial, trade itself was practised, and its utility appreciated, by almost everyone in the camp.

Taken as a whole, opinion was hostile to the middleman. His function, and his hard work in bringing buyer and seller together, were ignored; profits were not regarded as a reward for labour, but as a result of sharp practice. Despite the fact that his very existence was proof to the contrary, the middleman was held to be redundant in view of the existence of an Official Shop and the Exchange and Mart. Appreciation only came his way when he was willing to advance the price of a sugar ration, or to buy goods spot and carry them against a future sale. In these cases the element of risk was obvious to all, and the convenience of the service was felt to merit some reward. Particularly unpopular was the middleman with an element of monopoly, the man who contacted the ration wagon driver, or the man who utilized his knowledge of Urdu.

There was a strong feeling that everything had its "just price" in cigarettes. While the assessment of the just price, which incidentally varied between camps, was impossible of explanation, this price was nevertheless pretty closely known. It can best be defined as the price usually fetched by an article in good times when cigarettes were plentiful. The "just price" changed slowly; it was unaffected by short-term variations in supply, and while opinion might be resigned to departures from the "just price," a strong feeling of resentment persisted.

Conclusion The economic organization described was both elaborate and smooth-working in the summer of 1944. Then came the August cuts and deflation. Prices fell, rallied with deliveries of cigarette parcels in September and December, and fell again. In January 1945, supplies of Red Cross cigarettes ran out; and prices slumped still further; in February the supplies of food parcels were exhausted and the depression became a blizzard. Food, itself scarce, was almost given away in order to meet the non-monetary demand for cigarettes. Laundries ceased to operate, or worked for £'s or Reichmarks: food and cigarettes sold for fancy prices in £'s, hitherto unheard of. The Shop was empty and the Exchange Mart notices were full of unaccepted offers for cigarettes. Barter increased in volume, becoming a large portion of a smaller value of trade.

By April, 1945, chaos had replaced order in the economic sphere: sales were difficult, prices lacked stability. Economics has been defined as the science of distributing limited means among unlimited and competing ends. On 12 April with the arrival of elements of the 30th U.S. Infantry Division, the ushering in of an age of plenty demonstrated the hypothesis that with infinite means economic organization and activity would be redundant, as every want could be satisfied without effort.

Discussion

1. The prisoners used cigarettes as their medium of exchange. Was this a good choice? What else could they have used?

2. Were the prisoners' exchanges *really* similar to what would take place under perfect competition? Could you diagram these exchanges on supply and demand graphs? Try it!

3. How moral is it to use the price mechanism to allocate food when life and death may be at stake? Can you think of a better method than the one that was used?

19

Monopoly and High Barriers to Entry

TRUE OR FALSE

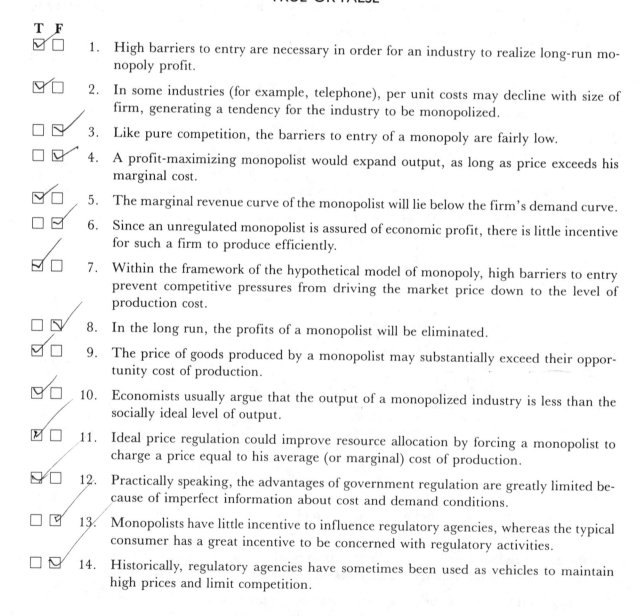

T F

1. High barriers to entry are necessary in order for an industry to realize long-run monopoly profit.

2. In some industries (for example, telephone), per unit costs may decline with size of firm, generating a tendency for the industry to be monopolized.

3. Like pure competition, the barriers to entry of a monopoly are fairly low.

4. A profit-maximizing monopolist would expand output, as long as price exceeds his marginal cost.

5. The marginal revenue curve of the monopolist will lie below the firm's demand curve.

6. Since an unregulated monopolist is assured of economic profit, there is little incentive for such a firm to produce efficiently.

7. Within the framework of the hypothetical model of monopoly, high barriers to entry prevent competitive pressures from driving the market price down to the level of production cost.

8. In the long run, the profits of a monopolist will be eliminated.

9. The price of goods produced by a monopolist may substantially exceed their opportunity cost of production.

10. Economists usually argue that the output of a monopolized industry is less than the socially ideal level of output.

11. Ideal price regulation could improve resource allocation by forcing a monopolist to charge a price equal to his average (or marginal) cost of production.

12. Practically speaking, the advantages of government regulation are greatly limited because of imperfect information about cost and demand conditions.

13. Monopolists have little incentive to influence regulatory agencies, whereas the typical consumer has a great incentive to be concerned with regulatory activities.

14. Historically, regulatory agencies have sometimes been used as vehicles to maintain high prices and limit competition.

PROBLEMS AND PROJECTS

Exhibit 1

Price	Quantity demanded (per week)	Marginal cost	Total revenue	Marginal revenue	Fixed cost	Total cost
$60	1	$50	_____	_____	$40	_____
55	2	20	_____	_____	_____	_____
50	3	26	_____	_____	_____	_____
45	4	30	_____	_____	_____	_____
40	5	40	_____	_____	_____	_____
35	6	50	_____	_____	_____	_____

1. Suppose that you produce and sell dining tables in a localized market. Past experience permits you to estimate your demand and marginal cost schedules. This information is presented in Exhibit 1.
   a. Fill in the missing revenue and cost schedules.
   b. If you were currently charging $55 per dining table set, what should you do if you wanted to maximize profits?
   c. Given your demand and cost estimates, what would be the maximum weekly profit you could earn?

2. Exhibit 2 indicates the demand and long-run cost conditions in an industry.
   a. Explain why the industry is likely to be monopolized.
   b. Indicate the price that a profit-maximizing monopolist would charge and label it P.
   c. Indicate the monopolist's output level and label it Q.
   d. Indicate the maximum profits of the monopolist.
   e. Will the profits attract competitors to the industry? Why or why not? Explain.

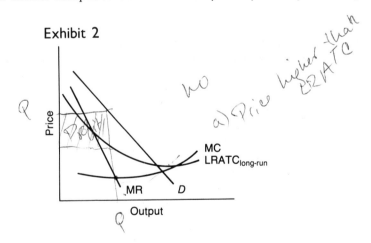

Exhibit 2

3. The food service at many university campuses is operated by a single firm. Suppose that Exhibit 3 indicates the monthly demand for meals and total operating cost for the food service firm of your campus.

Exhibit 3

Sales (in 1000s)	Price (per meal)	TR	MR (per 1000)	Total cost	MC (per 1000)
4	$1.60	————	————	$ 6000	————
5	1.40	————	————	6400	————
6	1.30	————	————	6800	————
7	1.20	————	————	7300	————
8	1.10	————	————	8000	————
9	1.00	————	————	9000	————
10	0.90	————	————	10200	————

a. Fill in the firm's TR, MR, and MC schedules.
b. What price (of those shown) would a profit-maximizing monopolist choose?
c. Is the monopolist making economic profits? If so, how large per month?
d. Students often complain about the price and quality of food. Suppose that a group of economics majors was asked to regulate the monopolists by setting a price for meals that would maximize consumer welfare. What price would they choose? (Total costs must be covered or service will cease.)
e. In the absence of student regulation, suppose that the university competitively auctioned the food service rights to the highest bidder. How much would a firm pay for this property right for one year? Who would reap the monopoly profits under this arrangement?

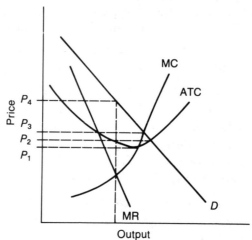

Exhibit 4

4. Exhibit 4 indicates the demand, marginal revenue, marginal cost, and average cost curves for a monopolist.
a. What price would an unregulated private monopolist set?
b. Suppose that a regulatory agency wanted to reduce the price to consumers and force a "normal rate of return" on the monopolists. What price would the regulating agency attempt to set?
c. What price would be most efficient from the viewpoint of allocative efficiency, assuming there was no change in demand and cost conditions? (Assume that any profit or loss is absorbed by the government.)
d. Indicate factors that complicate the ability of a "real-world" regulatory agency to set the ideal price.

5. When a seller can effectively separate his or her total market into two segments, the theory of price discrimination indicates that a higher product price will be charged in the market segment with the lower elasticity of demand. For each of the markets below, indicate in the blank which segment, (1) or (2), you think will be charged the higher price and be ready to explain why you think that segment has a lower elasticity of demand.

_____ a. Sales of movie tickets to (1) adults (2) children

_____ b. Sales of airline tickets to (1) business travelers (2) spouses traveling with them

_____ c. Sales of new cars to (1) those who presently own a car (2) those who do not

_____ d. Sales of cosmetic surgery to (1) the poor (2) the rich

LEARNING THE MECHANICS—MULTIPLE CHOICE

1. Which of the following best defines a monopoly?
   a. A firm that is the sole producer of a product for which there are no good substitutes ✓
   b. A firm that produces a differentiated product
   c. A firm that is licensed by the government
   d. A firm that has made profits over a long-run time period

2. Which of the following is a major economic criticism of monopoly as a source of economic inefficiency?
   a. Monopolists fail to expand output to the level where the consumer's valuation of the additional unit is just equal to its opportunity cost.
   b. Monopolists have no incentive to produce efficiently, because even the inefficient monopolists can be assured of high economic profits.
   c. Monopolists will always make profits, and profits are an indication that prices are too high.
   d. Monopolists have an unfair advantage since they can purchase inputs, including labor, at a lower price than competitive firms in other industries.

3. If economies of scale could not be realized in an industry, imposition of the monopoly industrial structure on an otherwise purely competitive industry would result in
   a. higher prices and a smaller industry output.
   b. higher prices and a larger industry output.
   c. lower prices and a larger industry output.
   d. lower prices and a smaller industry output.

4. Use statements I and II to answer this question. (I) If a monopolist's marginal revenue exceeded marginal cost at the current price and output level, the monopolist should reduce price and expand output in order to maximize its profits. (II) A monopolist will maximize its profits by charging a price that maximizes the difference between its sale price and its average total cost.
   a. I is true, II is false.
   b. I is false, II is true.
   c. Both I and II are true.
   d. Both I and II are false.

5. When economies of scale are important, and therefore when an industry tends toward natural monopoly, breaking the industries into several firms of small size would
    a. lead to lower short-run prices.
    b. lead to higher prices or at least to a higher per unit cost for the smaller firms.
    c. cause prices to rise if demand were inelastic, but fall if it were elastic.
    d. cause prices to fall because of the decline in producer profits.

6. Which of the following best describes the supply policy of a monopolist? The monopolist will expand supply until
    a. total revenues equal total cost.
    b. per unit profits are at a maximum.
    c. average total costs are at a minimum.
    d. marginal costs equal marginal revenues.

7. All of the following except one are sometimes a source of monopoly. Which one is not a source of monopoly?
    a. Substantial economies of scale
    b. Government licensing of producers
    c. Control over an essential resource
    d. Inefficiency because of bureaucratic decision-making procedures

    Use the following quotation in answering questions 8 and 9.

    > "It is commonly argued that, for criteria of ideal economic efficiency to be met, production of a good should be expanded as long as consumers are willing to pay a price that is greater than the cost of producing one more unit."

8. How will the actions of an unregulated, profit-maximizing, *competitive* firm compare with this standard of efficiency?
    a. Output will be too small, and price will be too low.
    b. Output will be too small, and price will be too high.
    c. Output will be too large, and price will be too high.
    d. Output and price will be consistent with the ideal standard.

9. How will the actions of an unregulated, profit-mazimizing *monopolist* compare with this standard?
    a. Output will be too small, and price will be too low.
    b. Output will be too small, and price will be too high.
    c. Output will be too large, and price will be too high.
    d. Output and price will be consistent with the ideal standard.

10. Which of the following factors limits the monopoly power of a firm?
    a. Competition from producers of substitute products
    b. Potential competition from entrepreneurs who may develop substitute products
    c. Competition from all other producers seeking the dollar votes of consumers
    d. All of the above

11. The oldest and most effective way to protect a business from competition is through
    a. legal barriers.
    b. economies of scale.
    c. natural monopoly.
    d. understocking the market.

12. Use statements I and II to answer this question. (**I**) Since patent rights give firms a monopoly on the production and marketing of a product, the patent system is a potential source of static economic inefficiency. (**II**) Since a patent system enables owners to enforce their property rights over a new product and technique, it encourages the development of new lower-cost products, essential to dynamic economic efficiency.
    a. I is true, II is false.
    b. I is false, II is true.
    c. Both I and II are true.
    d. Both I and II are false.

THE ECONOMIC WAY OF THINKING—MULTIPLE CHOICE

1. A major problem with regulatory agencies is that they
    a. have no real legal power over the industries they are supposed to regulate.
    b. tend to be too tough on the firms they are regulating.
    c. often underestimate the firm's cost of production, and consequently force regulated firms into a loss position.
    d. often become a vehicle to be used by the existing producers to limit the competition of potential rivals.

2. Government policy is sometimes proposed to reduce monopoly's inefficiency. In positive economic terms, which of the following options will be the most effective toward that end?
    a. Government production, because the government is able to sell its output below cost
    b. Government regulation to eliminate the product scarcity contrived by the producer
    c. Legislation that would place a ceiling on all profits greater than a normal return
    d. Economic theory does not yield a general answer to the question.

3. Suppose that all wholesale liquor distributorships in your state were brought under the control of a single firm and that government licensing was used to eliminate the potential competition of rivals. Relative to a competitive situation, economic theory suggests that the monopoly firm would
    a. charge higher prices and restrict output.
    b. charge lower prices and restrict output.
    c. charge higher prices and expand output.
    d. charge lower prices and expand output.

4. (**I**) "Economic theory suggests that regulatory policy, if properly utilized, could promote lower prices and larger outputs in industries characterized by monopoly and economies of scale." (**II**) "Economic theory suggests that regulatory power, developed via the political process, will act in the best interest of consumers and at the expense of monopoly business and labor interests."
    a. I is true, but II is false.
    b. I is false, but II is true.
    c. Both I and II are true.
    d. Both I and II are false.

5. For which of the following reasons do regulatory agencies sometimes fail to bring the price and output of a natural monopoly to the ideal level?
    a. The regulatory agency does not have all the information concerning opportunity costs.
    b. Monopolists may conceal profits by inflating the costs of items that are in accord with their personal objectives.
    c. Regulatory agencies often come to reflect the views of the industries they are supposed to regulate.
    d. All of the above.

6. Economic theory suggests that government-operated monopolies will
    a. be highly efficient and follow policies that are in the consumers' interest.
    b. be dominated by persons who, while seeking to serve the public interest, are not hard nosed enough to run a business efficiently.
    c. be inefficient, because no small group of persons is in a position to capture the benefits from operational efficiency.
    d. favor the consumer at the expense of special interest groups in and out of government.

7. Which of the following firms best fits the description of a monopolist?
    a. General Motors
    b. Columbia Broadcasting System
    c. Your local power company
    d. Exxon Corporation

8. Economic theory implies that the incentive for a manager of a publicly operated firm (for example, state universities, post office) to promote business efficiency would be
    a. strong, because inefficiency is easily detected and leads to the loss of voter support.
    b. strong, because public officials are unconcerned about personal gain.
    c. weak, because it is difficult for voters to detect inefficiency and for public officials to gain from improving efficiency.
    d. weak, because government employees are less competent than those who work in the private sector.

9. In a famous antitrust case, the government charged the DuPont Company with attempting to monopolize the cellophane industry. The company argued that, while it was the major producer of cellophane, it was competing in the broader market of "flexible packaging," a very competitive industry. Waxed paper, glassine, and aluminum foil all had sizable shares of the flexible packaging market. To determine whether DuPont was, in fact, competing in the flexible wrap industry, one would be interested in determining
    a. evidence of collusion between flexible wrap producers.
    b. the per unit cost as a function of output for cellophane.
    c. the income elasticity of demand for cellophane, relative to the other flexible wraps.
    d. whether other potential flexible wraps were actually good substitutes for cellophane.

10. "I heard an economist claim that when the trucking industry was completely deregulated, more freight would be hauled by trucks now making empty return runs. This is ridiculous. Even if a trucker lowered his price on the return run, only so much freight can be hauled on that return run." Economic theory indicates that this statement about the impact of the high regulated price on the total amount of freight shipped is
   a. essentially correct.
   b. incorrect, because at some lower price for the return trip, more freight almost surely would be hauled.
   c. incorrect, because regulators always set the monopoly price, so that output is always restricted.
   d. incorrect, because we know that truckers already turn down return loads at the existing low regulated rates. If barriers to entry were not high, competition would keep prices about the same but force truckers always to haul full loads.

11. "A firm with a secure monopoly in its market and with no fear of regulation or new entrants will never want to operate at a price at which its demand curve is inelastic." Economic theory suggests that this statement is
   a. correct.
   b. correct only if the firm's costs are constant.
   c. correct only if the firm's costs are rising.
   d. correct only if the firm's costs are decreasing.

THE ECONOMIC WAY OF THINKING—DISCUSSION QUESTIONS

1. Economists have historically had a very negative view of monopoly. Indicate the major criticisms of monopoly.

2. "The Houston Astros are the only major league baseball team in Houston. They have a monopoly on the product they sell." Do you think the Astros are a strong monopoly? Why or why not?

3. "In some industries, pure competition would result in higher prices and a greater waste of resources than monopoly." Do you agree? Can you think of any such industries? Discuss.

4. Outline the major problems involved in regulating the activities of a monopolist. Why is the regulatory function likely to become a source of economic inefficiency with time? Explain.

5. What are the major sources of monopoly? Can a monopolized industry sometimes be transformed into a competitive industry? Why may it sometimes be costly to break up a monopoly into several smaller independent firms? Explain.

6. Use economic analysis to evaluate the government-operated firm as an alternative to monopoly. What factors will influence the price, output, and operational efficiency of the public sector firm? Explain.

7. Regulatory agencies primarily use profits as the basis for their price-regulating activities.
   a. Why are profits used rather than cost and demand curves?
   b. Why would a regulatory agency be interested in profits when making price regulation decisions?
   c. Would conditions of ideal economic efficiency have been attained if a monopolist were making zero economic profit? Why or why not? Explain by using Exhibit 4, page 170.

8. It is frequently suggested, a casual reflection seems to confirm, that the opportunities for price discrimination are greater on the whole in the sale of *services* than they are in the sale of *commodities*. What is it about the nature of services as compared to commodities that would account for this? Can you think of some examples of this?

PERSPECTIVES IN ECONOMICS

The Parable Of The Parking Lots
by Henry G. Manne

[From *Public Interest*, No. 23 (Spring 1971), pp. 10–15, copyright © by National Affairs Inc., 1971. Reprinted by permission.]

In a city not far away there was a large football stadium. It was used from time to time for various events, but the principal use was for football games played Saturday afternoons by the local college team. The games were tremendously popular and people drove hundreds of miles to watch them. Parking was done in the usual way. People who arrived early were able to park free on the streets, and latecomers had to pay to park in regular and improvised lots.

There were, at distances ranging from 5 to 12 blocks from the stadium, approximately 25 commercial parking lots all of which received some business from Saturday afternoon football games. The lots closer to the stadium naturally received more football business than those further away, and some of the very close lots actually raised their price on Saturday afternoons. But they did not raise the price much, and most did not change prices at all. The reason was not hard to find.

For something else happened on football afternoons. A lot of people who during the week were students, lawyers, school teachers, plumbers, factory workers, and even stock brokers went into the parking lot business. It was not a difficult thing to do. Typically a young boy would put up a crude, homemade sign saying "Parking $3." He would direct a couple of cars into his parents' driveway, tell the driver to take the key, and collect the three dollars. If the driveway was larger or there was yard space to park in, an older brother, an uncle, or the head of the household would direct the operation, sometimes asking drivers to leave their keys so that shifts could be made if necessary.

Some part-time parking lot operators who lived very close to the stadium charged as much as $5.00 to park in their driveways. But as the residences-turned-parking-lots were located further from the stadium (and incidentally closer to the commercial parking lots), the price charged at game time declined. In fact houses at some distance from the stadium charged less than the adjacent commercial lots. The whole system seemed to work fairly smoothly, and though traffic just after a big game was terrible, there were no significant delays parking cars or retrieving parked cars.

But one day the owner of a chain of parking lots called a meeting of all the commercial parking lot owners in the general vicinity of the stadium. They formed an organization known as the Association of Professional Parking Lot Employers, or APPLE. And they were very concerned about the Saturday parking business. One man who owned four parking lots pointed out that honest parking lot owners had heavy capital investments in their businesses, that they paid taxes, and that they employed individuals who supported families. There was no reason, he alleged, why these lots should not handle all the cars coming into the area for special events like football games. "It is unethical," he said, "to engage in cutthroat competition with irresponsible fender benders. After all, parking cars is a profession, not a business." This last remark drew loud applause.

Thus emboldened he continued, stating that commercial parking lot owners recognize their responsibility to serve the public's needs. Ethical car parkers, he said, understand their obligations not to dent fenders, to employ only trustworthy car parkers, to pay decent wages, and generally to care for the customers' automobiles as they would the corpus of a trust. His statement was hailed by others attending the meeting as being very statesmanlike.

Others at the meeting related various tales of horror about nonprofessional car parkers. One homeowner, it was said, actually allowed his fifteen-year-old son to move other peoples' cars around. Another said that he had seen an $8,000 Cadillac parked on a dirt lawn where it would have become mired in mud had it rained that day. Still another pointed out that a great deal of the problem came on the side of the stadium with the lower-priced houses, where there were more driveways per block than on the wealthier side of the stadium. He pointed out that these poor people would rarely be able to afford to pay for damage to other peoples' automobiles or to pay insurance premiums to cover such losses. He felt that a professional group such as APPLE had a duty to protect the public from their folly in using those parking spaces.

Finally another speaker reminded the audience that these "marginal, fly-by-night" parking lot operators generally parked a string of cars in the driveways so that a driver had to wait until all cars behind his had been removed before he could get his out. This, he pointed out, was quite unlike the situation in commercial lots where, during a normal business day, people had to be assured of ready access to their automobiles at any time. The commercial parking lots either had to hire more attendants to shift cars around, or they had to park them so that any car was always accessible, even though this meant that fewer cars could park than the total space would actually hold. "Clearly," he said, "driveway parking constitutes unfair competition."

Emotions ran high at this meeting, and every member of APPLE pledged $1 per parking space for something mysteriously called a "slush fund." It was never made clear exactly whose slush would be bought with these funds, but several months later a resolution was adopted by the city council requiring licensing for anyone in the parking lot business.

The preamble to the new ordinance read like the speeches at the earlier meeting. It said that this measure was designed to protect the public against unscrupulous, unprofessional and undercapitalized parking lot operators. It required, *inter alia,* that anyone parking cars for a fee must have a minimum capital devoted to the parking lot business of $25,000, liability insurance in an amount not less than $500,000, bonding for each car parker, and a special driving test for these parkers (which incidentally would be designed and administered by APPLE). The ordinance also required, again in the public's interest, that every lot charge a single posted price for parking and that any change in the posted price be approved in advance by the city council. Incidentally, most members were able to raise their fees by about 20 percent before the first posting.

Then a funny thing happened to drivers on their way to the stadium for the next big game. They discovered city police in unusually large numbers informing them that it was illegal to pay a non-licensed parking lot operator for the right to park a car. These policemen also reminded parents that if their children were found in violation of this ordinance it could result in a misdemeanor charge being brought against the parents and possible juvenile court proceedings for the children. There were no driveway parking lots that day.

Back at the commercial parking lots, another funny thing occurred. Proceeding from the entrance of each of these parking lots within twelve blocks of the stadium were long lines of cars waiting to park. The line got larger as the lot was closer to the stadium. Many drivers had to wait so long or walk so far that they missed the entire first quarter of the big game.

At the end of the game it was even worse. The confusion was massive. The lot attendants could not cope with the jam up, and some cars were actually not retrieved until the next day. It was even rumored about town that some automobiles had been lost forever and that considerable liabilities might result for some operators. Industry spokesmen denied this, however.

Naturally there was a lot of grumbling, but there was no agreement on what had caused the difficulty. At first everyone said there were merely some "bugs" in the new system that would have to be ironed out. But the only "bug" ironed out was a Volkswagen which was flattened by a careless lot attendant in a Cadillac Eldorado.

The situation did not improve at subsequent games. The members of APPLE did not hire additional employees to park cars, and operators near the stadium were not careful to follow their previous practice of parking cars in such a way as to have them immediately accessible. Employees seemed to become more surly, and the number of dented-fender claims mounted rapidly.

Little by little, too, cars began appearing in residential driveways again. For instance, one enterprising youth regularly went into the car wash business on football afternoons, promising that his wash job would take at least two hours. He charged five dollars, and got it—even on rainy days—in fact, especially on rainy days. Another homeowner offered to take cars on consignment for three hours to sell them at prices fixed by the owner. He charged $4.00 for this "service," but his subterfuge was quickly squelched by the authorities. The parking situation remained "critical."

Political pressures on the city council began to mount to "do something" about the inordinate delays in parking and retrieving cars on football afternoons. The city council sent a stern note of warning to APPLE, and APPLE appointed a special study group recruited from the local uni-

versity's computer science department to look into the matter. This group reported that the managerial and administrative machinery in the parking lot business was archaic. What was needed, the study group said, was less goose quills and stand-up desks and more computers and conveyor belts. It was also suggested that all members of APPLE be hooked into one computer so that cars could be really shifted to the most accessible spaces.

Spokesmen for the industry took up the cry of administrative modernization. Subtle warnings appeared in the local papers suggesting that if the industry did not get its own house in order, heavy-handed regulation could be anticipated. The city council asked for reports on failures to deliver cars and decreed that this would include any failure to put a driver in his car within five minutes of demand without a new dent.

Some of the professional operators actually installed computer equipment to handle their ticketing and parking logistics problems. And some added second stories to their parking lots. Others bought up additional space, thereby raising the value of vacant lots in the area. But many simply added a few additional car parkers and hoped that the problem would go away without a substantial investment of capital.

The commercial operators also began arguing that they needed higher parking fees because of their higher operating costs. Everyone agreed that costs for operating a parking lot were certainly higher than before the licensing ordinance. So the city council granted a request for an across-the-board ten percent hike in fees. The local newspaper editorially hoped that this would ease the problem without still higher fees being necessary. In a way, it did. A lot of people stopped driving. They began using city buses, or they chartered private buses for the game. Some stayed home and watched the game on TV. A new study group on fees was appointed.

Just about then several other blows fell on the parking lot business. Bus transportation to the area near the stadium was improved with a federal subsidy to the municipal bus company. And several new suburban shopping centers caused a loss of automobile traffic in the older areas of town. But most dramatic of all, the local university, under severe pressure from its students and faculty, dropped intercollegiate football altogether and converted the stadium into a park for underprivileged children.

The impact of these events on the commercial parking lots was swift. Income declined drastically. The companies that had borrowed money to finance the expansion everyone wanted earlier were hardest hit. Two declared bankruptcy, and many had to be absorbed by financially stronger companies. Layoffs among car parkers were enormous, and APPLE actually petitioned the city council to guarantee the premiums on their liability insurance policies so that people would not be afraid to park commercially. This idea was suggested to APPLE by recent congressional legislation creating an insurance program for stock brokers.

A spokesman for APPLE made the following public statement: "New organizations or arrangements may be necessary to straighten out this problem. There has been a failure in both the structure of the industry and the regulatory scheme. New and better regulation is clearly demanded. A sound parking lot business is necessary for a healthy urban economy." The statement was hailed by the industry as being very statesmanlike, though everyone speculated about what he really meant.

Others in the industry demanded that the city bus service be curtailed during the emergency. The city council granted every rate increase the lots requested. There were no requests for rate decreases, but the weaker lots began offering prizes and other subtle or covert rebates to private bus companies who would park with them. In fact, this problem became so serious and uncontrollable that one owner of a large chain proclaimed that old-fashioned price competition for this business would be desirable. This again was hailed as statesmanlike, but everyone assumed that he really meant something else. No one proposed repeal of the licensing ordinance.

One other thing happened. Under pressure from APPLE, the city council decreed that henceforth no parking would be allowed on any streets in the downtown area of town. The local merchants were extremely unhappy about this, however, and the council rescinded the ordinance at the next meeting, citing a computer error as the basis for the earlier restriction.

The ultimate resolution of the "new" parking problem is not in sight. The parking lot industry in this town not very far from here is now said to be a depressed business, even a sick one. Everyone looks to the city council for a solution, but things will probably limp along as they are for quite a while, picking up with an occasional professional football game and dropping low with bad weather.

MORAL: If you risk your lot under an apple tree, you may get hit in the head.

Discussion

1. In this fable, who was protected by the regulations? From what? At what cost?

2. Do you see similar situations in regulated businesses in your own area? In state or federally regulated industries? How are they similar? How do they differ? Who gains, and at what cost?

20

The Intermediate Cases: Monopolistic Competition and Oligopoly

TRUE OR FALSE

T F

☐ ☐ 1. Oligopolistic industries will be dominated by a small number of firms.

☐ ☐ 2. Economies of scale are an important reason for oligopoly in the automobile, typewriter, and steel industries.

☐ ☐ 3. There are no legal restraints on collusive behavior by oligopolistic firms.

☐ ☐ 4. Firms in oligopolistic industries make profits because they are free from competitive pressures.

☐ ☐ 5. Collusion would be easier (less costly) if the barriers to entry were higher and the number of producers in the industry were smaller.

☐ ☐ 6. Inability to police the nonprice characteristics of a product offered by a competitive firm reduces the likelihood of successful collusion among oligopolists.

☐ ☐ 7. The kinked demand curve analysis is based on the assumption that competitors will usually match a price increase, but not a price reduction.

☐ ☐ 8. A monopolistically competitive firm maximizes profits by producing at the level of output at which price is equal to short-run marginal cost.

☐ ☐ 9. In recent years, concentration has increased in almost all manufacturing industries.

☐ ☐ 10. Monopolistically competitive firms often emphasize quality, location, and advertising as competitive weapons (in addition to price competition).

☐ ☐ 11. The smart investor will purchase the stock of firms in oligopolistic industries since the high average rate of profit in these industries will mean a greater return on the investor's dollar.

☐ ☐ 12. The larger the number of competitors and the more similar the products offered by the firms of a monopolistically competitive industry, the greater will be the elasticity of the individual seller's demand curve.

☐ ☐ 13. The monopolistic competitor who is better able to correctly anticipate changes in consumer demand and adjust to those changes is, *ceteris paribus,* more likely to make economic profits.

PROBLEMS AND PROJECTS

Exhibit I

Output (market)	Price	Total revenue (market)	Total revenue (each firm)	Average total cost (firm)
1,000	$750	——————	——————	$200
2,000	500	——————	——————	170
3,000	450	——————	——————	150
4,000	400	——————	——————	150
8,000	300	——————	——————	150
12,000	250	——————	——————	150
16,000	200	——————	——————	150
20,000	175	——————	——————	150
24,000	150	——————	——————	150
28,000	125	——————	——————	150
32,000	100	——————	——————	150

1. Currently there are four rival firms in the typewriter industry. Assume that the four firms are of identical size, produce similar products (consumers think they are homogeneous), and have identical cost schedules. The cost schedule for a *firm* along with the market demand schedule is presented in Exhibit 1.
   a. Fill in the missing information.
   b. What price would prevail if there were no collusion and each firm sought to offer the consumer a better deal than that available from rivals (as long as the firm's opportunity cost of production was covered)? How many units would be sold in the market? How many would each firm sell?
   c. If each firm produced one-fourth of the total market, what market price would prevail when *each firm* supplied 1000 units? 2000 units? 3000 units?
   d. Which of the listed prices would prevail if the firms acted cooperatively (so as to maximize their joint profit)?
   e. Given the demand and cost conditions in this oligopolistic industry, what outcome would be most likely to prevail in the real world? Explain.

2. Johnson Tricycle Manufacturers currently sells 20,000 tricycles per month at a price of $10 each. The firm's fixed costs are currently 60 percent of sales revenues. At the current level of production, the firm's average variable cost per tricycle is $4. The firm is just covering its total cost. The sales manager argues that a reduction in the price of tricycles to $9 would enable the firm to earn a monthly profit of $5000 as the results of increased sales. Since the firm has ample capacity, the necessary expansion in output could be accomplished without any increase in the average variable cost of tricycles.
   a. Does the sales manager's argument make sense? Explain.
   b. How much would sales have to increase in order for the firm to earn a monthly profit of $5000? (*Hint:* Remember that fixed costs will not vary with output.)
   c. What price elasticity of demand is necessary for the sales manager's prediction to be realized?

3. Sociable Corporation (SC) produces and sells gizmos in an oligopolistic market comprised of only a very few firms. Exhibit 2 presents two different demand schedules for SC. The first one shows how SC's quantity demanded varies when the industry price varies, and the second one shows how SC's quantity demanded varies when only SC's price varies. Assume throughout that SC's marginal cost is constant at $10 per gizmo and that fixed costs are zero.

Exhibit 2

	Demand when industry price varies				Demand when SC's price varies		
Quantity	Price	Total revenue	Marginal revenue	Quantity	Price	Total revenue	Marginal revenue
1	$130	$130	$130	1	$100	$100	$100
2	110	220	90	2	90	180	80
3	90	____	____	3	80	____	____
4	70	____	____	4	70	____	____
5	50	____	____	5	60	____	____
6	30	____	____	6	50	____	____
7	10	____	____	7	40	____	____
8	0	____	____	8	30	____	____
9	0	____	____	9	20	____	____
10	0	0	0	10	10	____	____

a. Fill in the missing information.

b. Suppose the industry could engage in successful collusion. What price would SC want the industry to set? Calculate SC's profits at this price.

c. Suppose the industry has established the collusively determined price of part b above and that SC believes it could "cheat" on the agreement and not be detected. Assuming that sales of gizmos must be in whole units, what quantity would SC decide to sell? What price would it charge? Compare SC's new profit level to the level it achieved in part b.

d. If each firm in the industry believes what SC believes, could each firm increase its profits the way SC believes it can? Explain.

4. International Oil, Incorporated (IOI) has come under public criticism for earning excessive profits. In its defense, IOI releases information indicating that profit constitutes only $0.01 of the firm's price of $1.00 per gallon of gasoline. Is this information useful in resolving the issue? If not, what type of profit information would you want in order to attempt a resolution?

5. Write a research paper on competition. What is meant by competition? How does the element of monopoly in monopolistic competition affect the process of competition? Why is competition important if markets are to work efficiently? Can competition protect the consumer from the market power of sellers? Is competition sometimes destructive or counterproductive? Defend or criticize competition as a method of allocating goods and resources. Be specific. Feel free to suggest and defend alternatives that you think are superior to the competitive market process.

LEARNING THE MECHANICS—MULTIPLE CHOICE

1. Long-run economic profit requires
   a. barriers to market entry that limit potential competitors.
   b. an inelastic market demand for the product.
   c. free entry, but a small number of competitors.
   d. a differentiated product.

2. Which of the following factors will weaken the ability of an oligopolist to charge a price in excess of production cost?
   a. The existence of a small number of competitors
   b. An inelastic demand for one's product
   c. Quality competition from one's rivals
   d. Licensing procedures and other factors that limit entry into the industry

3. For the monopolistic competitor
   a. price will exceed the firm's short-run marginal cost at the profit-maximizing output level; in the long run, however, economic profit will be eliminated.
   b. price will equal marginal cost at the profit-maximizing output level; long-run profits will be positive.
   c. price will always equal average total cost in the short run; in the long run either profits or losses may result.
   d. marginal revenue will equal average total cost in the short run; long-run economic profits will be zero.

4. Which of the following factors will make it more difficult for oligopolistic firms to collude on prices?
   a. A reduction in the number of firms
   b. A homogeneous product
   c. High barriers to entry
   d. Instability and uncertainty concerning the demand and cost conditions in the industry

5. Economic theory suggests that prices in oligopolistic industries will
   a. be above the cost of production, but less than what a monopolist would charge.
   b. be below the firms' marginal costs, but higher than their average total costs.
   c. be equal to the firms' per unit costs.
   d. rise as the number of rival firms in the industry increases.

6. The kinked demand curve analysis helps to explain price inflexibility because it implies that an oligopolist would
   a. gain few additional customers from a price reduction, since the firm's competitors would also reduce price.
   b. lose many of its customers if it raised its prices, since rivals would not follow suit.
   c. often find that $MR = MC$ at the same output level even after costs had increased.
   d. All of the above are correct.

7. Using industrial concentration ratios as the measure of competitiveness, one finds that during the last three decades, the U.S. economy has
   a. become more competitive.
   b. become less competitive.
   c. on balance, changed little in competitiveness.
   d. become fully dominated by highly concentrated, oligopolistic industries.

8. Amy is widely known among restauranteurs in Seattle as the best fast-food restaurant manager in town. Since the restaurant business is monopolistically competitive, Amy
   a. would make more money if she could establish her own restaurant.
   b. would make just as much money working for one of the many firms bidding for her services as she would with her own firm.
   c. can never be paid what she is really worth in such an industry.
   d. could make long-run economic profit if she established her own restaurant.

9. It would be difficult for a group of oligopolists to follow a price and output policy similar to that of a monopolist if
   a. there were many producers.
   b. firms could not compete on the basis of quality (of the product).
   c. supply of substitute products were highly inelastic.
   d. prices charged in some states were higher because of higher sales taxes.

10. The concentration ratio of an industry provides
    a. an excellent measure of competitiveness in the industry.
    b. an indication, albeit an imperfect one, of competitiveness in the industry.
    c. a measure of the availability for the products of the industry.
    d. no indication at all of competitiveness in the industry.

11. Which of the following is the most accurate description of the conditions that exist under the monopolistically competitive market structure?
    a. Barriers to entry are low; firms will consistently incur economic losses in the short run.
    b. Barriers to entry are low; firms will realize normal profits in the short run, but losses in the long run.
    c. Barriers to entry are low; firms may realize either profits or losses in the short run, but they will tend to realize a normal profit in the long run.
    d. Barriers to entry are high; firms will consistently realize economic profits in the short run.

12. If economic profits were present in a monopolistically competitive industry
    a. production inefficiency would develop, causing costs to increase until the profits had been eliminated.
    b. firms would operate in the short run, but they would be forced out of business in the long run as competition eliminated the economic profit.
    c. competition from new entrants would expand supply and depress prices until the economic profits had been eliminated.
    d. the firms would lower their prices, since profits would attract government regulation.

THE ECONOMIC WAY OF THINKING—MULTIPLE CHOICE

1. If large automobile manufacturers were to collude secretly on prices, as has often been charged, what short-run factor might tend to undermine the effectiveness of their agreements?
    a. The economies of scale in the industry
    b. The size of the firms in the industry
    c. The ease with which a new competitor could enter the industry if profitability increased
    d. The difficulty of policing style and quality competition among firms

2. Economists have often pointed out that the American Medical Association, because of its indirect power to license physicians, has control over the supply of doctors practicing in the United States. If this were true, which of the following policies would be most likely to (a) increase the quality of service provided by physicians, and (b) lower the *market* price of this service?
    a. Revision of tax laws to provide for a 50 percent tax rebate for medical expenses incurred during the year
    b. Federal grants to medical schools and students, and a lowering of state medical licensing standards
    c. An expanded medical insurance program that covered all citizens
    d. Larger income tax deductions for medical expenses

3. If you were going to invest in the stock market, you would be
    a. wise to purchase the stock of an oligopolist so that you could share in the oligopoly profits.
    b. unwise to purchase only the stock of an oligopolist, because the inefficiency of oligopoly often leads to losses.
    c. wise to purchase the stock of an oligopolist if the firm had made economic profit in the long run.
    d. unwise to purchase only the stock of an oligopolist, because the expectation of future profits has already increased the current market value of the stock.

4. Neither pure nor monopolistic competitors will be able to earn long-run economic profit because
    a. with free entry and exit, competition between rivals will drive prices down to the level of production costs.
    b. high barriers to entry will prevent the firms from earning excess profits.
    c. government legislation will cause firms to moderate their price demands.
    d. cutthroat competition will cause some firms to incur losses, but barriers to entry will result in profits for others.

5. Comparative profitability studies between oligopolistic and competitive industries suggest that
    a. dynamic competitive forces are one important determinant of profitability in oligopolistic as well as competitive industries.
    b. collusion and monopoly profit are prevalent in almost all oligopolistic sectors.
    c. competition has little effect on the profitability of firms.
    d. large firms almost always earn a higher rate of return than their smaller counterparts.

6. The local plumbing contractors have called a meeting to discuss ways to improve their long-run profitability. Of the four plans being discussed seriously, which would most likely increase their long-run profits?
    a. A "gentlemen's agreement" that each contractor would increase his prices by an average of 7 percent
    b. Passage of legislation requiring the local government to share the cost of installing all private sewage systems
    c. Passage of legislation requiring *new* contractors to pass a stiff licensing exam and to pay a $5000 fee to obtain a contractor's license
    d. Repeal of the current tax on installations of plumbing units

7. "If a few firms colluded successfully and looked forward to long-run economic profits, they would lose all monetary incentive to innovate. Successful collusion eliminates any contribution to profit that innovation would otherwise make." This statement is
    a. essentially correct.
    b. correct, if quality competition had been eliminated.
    c. correct, if there were few substitutes for the product produced by the colluding firms.
    d. incorrect, because lower costs for producing the same good *or* a better product for the same cost would benefit even a group of colluding oligopolists.

8. Suppose that recent fuel shortages and rising fuel prices haver raised the delivery costs for diaper services in Los Angeles. If that industry were characterized by monopolistic compe-titon, we could expect that
    a. competition would keep the price of diaper service the same as before, until eventually some firms were forced out of business by rising costs.
    b. diaper service prices would rise quickly (by the full amount of the cost increase multiplied by the market rate of interest).
    c. diaper service prices would rise, and in the long run the full amount of increase in cost would be passed along to consumers.
    d. if the diaper service industry were in long-run equilibrium before the cost increase, its economic profits would absorb the cost increase; there would be no change in price.

9. Introducing a new process that produces widgets at half the current cost with identical product quality would be most valuable in the long run to a firm in
    a. a purely competitive industry.
    b. a monopolistically competitive industry.
    c. an oligopolistic industry with little hope of successful collusion.
    d. an oligopolistic industry with successful collusion and little fear of new entrants in the future.

10. An oligopolist's incentive to ''cheat'' on a secret collusive agreement increases when
    a. quality competition is more easily detected.
    b. the demand for his product at the current price is shrinking.
    c. the demand for his product at the current price is expanding.
    d. his marginal cost is closer to the oligopoly price.

11. Which of the following would be the most likely to happen if the firms in a monopolistically competitive industry were suffering economic losses?
    a. The firms would eliminate production inefficiencies, which must be the source of the losses.
    b. Some firms would leave the industry, and the market price would rise.
    c. Some firms would operate in the short run, but all firms would go out of business in the long run.
    d. All firms in the industry would continue producing at their current output levels, but they would charge a higher price.

12. A profit-maximizing oligopolist who has invested heavily in brand-name advertising does not want adverse publicity. The owner of such a firm would pay more to avoid shoddy output and to keep its good (brand) name if
    a. it were part of an oligopolistic group of firms that looked forward to high economic prof-its.
    b. government price regulation were about to be imposed, ensuring low future profits.
    c. it were part of an oligopolistic group of firms in which secret competition was hindering collusion.
    d. it dealt with buyers who shopped only for the lowest available price.

13. One large motel chain uses the slogan ''the best surprise is no surprise'' to advertise that its motels are always about the same. Critics charge that this approach fails to take advantage of local architecture, local customs, and—in general—is just too ''drab'' and ''plastic.'' The motel's profits have been high enough to attract many competitors. Since the motel industry is monopolistically competitive, our economic model
    a. is contradicted, since this firm does *not* offer much variety.
    b. is contradicted, since *economic* profits do not fit into the model.
    c. is contradicted by the fact that the firm advertises.
    d. indicates that some travelers appreciate predictability at the expense of other values.

THE ECONOMIC WAY OF THINKING—DISCUSSION QUESTIONS

1. Do firms in oligopolistic industries have an incentive to collude? What factors will reduce the likelihood of successful collusion (from the viewpoint of the firms)? Will the threat of potential new rivals in an oligopolistic industry influence the price and output policies of the existing firms in the industry? Explain.

2. Will oligopolistic firms be able to charge prices that are higher than average cost? What factors may limit their ability to do so? Will firms in an oligopolistic industry make high profits? Why or why not?

3. How does monopolistic competition differ from pure competition? In what ways are they similar? Compare the price and output policies of a monopolistic firm with those of a pure competitor.

4. Does the town where you live have too many gas stations or quick-stop minifood stores? Is this duplication and competitiveness wasteful? Does it result in higher prices than those that would prevail under alternative arrangements? Explain why you think that monopolistic competition is either
   a. wasteful and inefficient, or
   b. consistent with efficiency and a consumer-directed economy.

5. Explain why economic theory predicts that collusion to rig the market against consumers will be far more prevalent under oligopoly than under monopolistic competition.

6. What are the major factors that influence the profitability of an oligopolistic firm? Does an oligopolist have an incentive to produce efficiently, that is, to be "cost conscious"? Why or why not?

7. Assume that the Barbers Association for Short Hair (BASH) successfully convinced the state of Florida to pass legislation increasing the price of haircuts to $6. Suppose that there are no barriers to entry into the barbering profession, but that everyone who charges a price for cutting hair must comply with this legislation (i.e., charge $6). What would you expect to happen to the
   a. sales revenues of Florida barbers?
   b. profits of Florida barbers in the short run? Long run?
   c. waiting time to get a haircut?
   d. quality of a haircut and the auxiliary services provided with it?
   e. number of black market haircuts?

PERSPECTIVES IN ECONOMICS

Capitalism, Big Business, And The Process of Creative Destruction
by Joseph A. Schumpeter

[From *Capitalism, Socialism, and Democracy*, 3rd edition, by Joseph A. Schumpeter, pp. 81–86. Copyright, 1950 by Harper & Brothers. Reprinted by permission of Harper & Row, Publishers.]

The theories of monopolistic and oligopolistic competition and their popular variants may in two ways be made to serve the view that capitalist reality is unfavorable to maximum performance in production. One may hold that it always has been so and that all along output has been expanding in spite of the secular sabotage perpetrated by the managing bourgeoisie. Advocates of this proposition would have to produce evidence to the effect that the observed rate of increase can be accounted for by a sequence of favorable circumstances unconnected with the mechanism of private enterprise and strong enough to overcome the latter's resistance. However, those who espouse this variant at least avoid the trouble about historical fact that the advocates of the alternative proposition have to face. This avers that capitalist reality once tended to favor maximum productive performance, or at all events productive performance so considerable as to constitute a major element in any serious appraisal of the system; but that the later spread of monopolist structures, killing competition, has by now reversed that tendency.

Capitalist Reality First, this involves the creation of an entirely imaginary golden age of perfect competition that at some time somehow metamorphosed itself into the monopolistic age, whereas it is quite clear that perfect competition has at no time been more of a reality than it is at present. Secondly, it is necessary to point out that the rate of increase in output did not decrease from the nineties from which, I suppose, the prevalence of the largest-size concerns, at least in manufacturing industry, would have to be dated; that there is nothing in the behavior of the time series of total output to suggest a "break in trend"; and, most important of all, that the modern standard of life of the masses evolved during the period of relatively unfettered "big business." If we list the items that enter the modern workman's budget and from 1899 on observe the course of their prices not in terms of money but in terms of the hours of labor that will buy them—i.e., each year's money prices divided by each year's hourly wage rates— we cannot fail to be struck by the rate of advance which, considering the spectacular improvement in qualities, seems to have been greater and not smaller than it ever was before. If we economists were given less to wishful thinking and more to the observation of facts, doubts would immediately arise as to the realistic virtues of a theory that would have led us to expect a very different result. Nor is this all. As soon as we go into details and inquire into the individual items in which progress was most conspicuous, the trail leads not to the doors of those firms that work under conditions of comparatively free competition but precisely to the doors of the large concerns—which, as in the case of agricultural machinery, also account for much of the progress in the competitive sector—and a shocking suspicion dawns upon us that big business may have had more to do with creating that standard of life than with keeping it down.

Process Of Creative Destruction The essential point to grasp is that in dealing with capitalism we are dealing with an evolutionary process. It may seem strange that anyone can fail to see so obvious a fact which moreover was long ago emphasized by Karl Marx. Yet that fragmentary analysis which yields the bulk of our propositions about the functioning of modern capitalism persistently neglects it. Let us restate the point and see how it bears upon our problem.

Capitalism, then, is by nature a form or method of economic change and not only never is but never can be stationary. And this evolutionary character of the capitalist process is not merely due to the fact that economic life goes on in a social and natural environment which changes and by its change alters the data of economic action; this fact is important and these changes (wars, revolutions and so on) often condition industrial change, but they are not its prime movers. Nor is this evolutionary character due to a quasi-automatic increase in population and capital or to the vagaries of monetary systems of which exactly the same thing holds true. The fundamental impulse that sets and keeps the capitalist engine in motion comes from the new consumers' goods, the new methods of production or transportation, the new markets, the new forms of industrial organization that capitalist enterprise creates.

The contents of the laborer's budget, say from 1760 to 1940, did not simply grow on unchanging lines but they underwent a process of qualitative change. Similarly, the history of the productive apparatus of a typical farm, from

the beginnings of the rationalization of crop rotation, plowing and fattening to the mechanized thing of today—linking up with elevators and railroads—is a history of revolutions. So is the history of the productive apparatus of the iron and steel industry from the charcoal furnace to our own type of furnace, or the history of the apparatus of power production from the overshot water wheel to the modern power plant, or the history of transportation from the mailcoach to the airplane. The opening up of new markets, foreign or domestic, and the organizational development from the craft shop and factory to such concerns as U.S. Steel illustrate the same process of industrial mutation—if I may use that biological term—that incessantly revolutionizes the economic structure *from within,* incessantly destroying the old one, incessantly creating a new one, this process of Creative Destruction is the essential fact about capitalism. It is what capitalism consists in and what every capitalist concern has got to live in. This fact bears upon our problem in two ways.

Statics Versus Dynamics First, since we are dealing with a process whose every element takes considerable time in revealing its true features and ultimate effects, there is no point in appraising the performance of that process *ex visu* of a given point of time; we must judge its performance over time, as it unfolds through decades or centuries. A system—any system, economic or other—that at *every* point of time fully utilizes its possibilities to the best advantage may yet in the long run be inferior to a system that does so at *no* given point of time, because the latter's failure to do so may be a condition for the level or speed of long-run performance.

Second, since we are dealing with an organic process, analysis of what happens in any particular part of it—say, in an individual concern or industry—may indeed clarify details of mechanism but is inconclusive beyond that. Every piece of business strategy acquires its true significance only against the background of that process and within the situation created by it. It must be seen in its role in the perennial gale of creative destruction; it cannot be understood irrespective of it or, in fact, on the hypothesis that there is a perennial lull.

But economists who, *ex visu* of a point of time, look for example at the behavior of an oligopolist industry—an industry which consists of a few big firms—and observe the well-known moves and countermoves within it that seem to aim at nothing but high prices and restrictions of output are making precisely that hypothesis. They accept the data of the momentary situation as if there were no past or future to it and think that they have understood what there is to understand if they interpret the behavior of those firms by means of the principle of maximizing profits with reference to those data. The usual theorist's paper and the usual government commission's report practically never try to see that behavior, on the one hand, as a result of a piece of past history and, on the other hand, as an attempt to deal with a situation that is sure to change presently—as an attempt by those firms to keep on their feet, on ground that is slipping away from under them. In other words, the problem that is usually being visualized is how capitalism administers existing structures, whereas the relevant problem is how it creates and destroys them. As long as this is not recognized, the investigator does a meaningless job. As soon as it is recognized, his outlook on capitalist practice and its social results changes considerably.

Progress And Competition The first thing to go is the traditional conception of the *modus operandi* of competition. Economists are at long last emerging from the stage at which price competition was all they saw. As soon as quality competition and sales effort are admitted into the sacred precincts of theory, the price variable is ousted from its dominant position. However, it is still competition within a rigid pattern of invariant conditions, methods of production and forms of industrial organization in particular, that practically monopolizes attention. But in capitalist reality as distinguished from its textbook picture, it is not that kind of competition which counts but the competition from the new commodity, the new technology, the new source of supply, the new type of organization (the largest-scale unit of control for instance)—competition which commands a decisive cost or quality advantage and which strikes not at the margins of the profits and the outputs of the existing firms but at their foundations and their very lives. This kind of competition is as much more effective than the other as a bombardment is in comparison with forcing a door, and so much more important that it becomes a matter of comparative indifference whether competition in the ordinary sense functions more or less promptly; the powerful lever that in the long run expands output and brings down prices is in any case made of other stuff.

It is hardly necessary to point out that competition of the kind we now have in mind acts not only when in being but also when it is merely an ever-present threat. It disciplines before it attacks. The businessman feels himself to be in a competitive situation even if he is alone in his field or if, though not alone, he holds a position such that investigating government experts fail to see any effective competition between him and any other firms in the same or a neighboring field and in consequence conclude that his talk, under examination, about his competitive sorrows is all make-believe. In many cases, though not in all, this will in the long run enforce behavior very similar to the perfectly competitive pattern.

Faulty Illustrations Many theorists take the opposite view which is best conveyed by an example. Let us assume that there is a certain number of retailers in a neighborhood who try to improve their relative position by service and "atmosphere" but avoid price competition and stick to methods as to the local tradition—a picture of stagnating routine. As others drift into the trade that quasi-equilibrium is indeed upset, but in a manner that does not benefit their customers. The economic space around each of the shops has been narrowed, their owners will no longer be able to make a living and they will try to mend the case by raising prices in tacit agreement. This will further reduce their sales and so, by successive pyramiding, a situation will evolve in which increasing potential supply will be attended by increasing instead of decreasing prices and by decreasing instead of increasing sales.

Such cases do occur, and it is right and proper to work them out. But as the practical instances usually given show, they are fringe-end cases to be found mainly in the sectors furthest removed from all that is most characteristic of capitalist activity. Moreover, they are transient by nature. In the case of retail trade the competition that matters arises not from additional shops of the same type, but from the department store, the chain store, the mail-order house and the supermarket which are bound to destroy those pyramids sooner or later. Now a theoretial construction which neglects this essential element of the case neglects all that is most typically capitalist about it; even if correct in logic as well as in fact, it is like *Hamlet* without the Danish prince.

Discussion

1. According to Schumpeter, what is the major source of economic progress?

2. Does Schumpeter view competition as a process? Does he believe that competition is dependent on the number of firms in an industry?

3. What does Schumpeter mean when he states that a system may "at every given point of time fully utilize its possibilities to the best advantage" and still, in the long run, "be inferior to a system that does so at *no* given point of time"?

21

Business Structure, Regulation, and Deregulation

TRUE OR FALSE

T F

☐ ☐ 1. Bigness and lack of competition are not always synonomous.

☐ ☐ 2. Predatory pricing is another term for high, monopolistic pricing.

☐ ☐ 3. An exclusive contract is commonly involved in dealerships.

☐ ☐ 4. One of the shortcomings of regulatory agencies is that with the passage of time they tend to represent broad groups such as consumers at the expense of labor and business interests.

☐ ☐ 5. The effectiveness of the Sherman Act encouraged Congress to pass the Clayton Act.

☐ ☐ 6. Most economists believe that antitrust policy has had a dramatic impact on market structure.

☐ ☐ 7. John McGee and John Kenneth Galbraith agree that antitrust policy can and should be made tougher.

☐ ☐ 8. Social regulation seeks to provide a cleaner, safer, healthier environment for workers and consumers.

☐ ☐ 9. The antitrust position of the Reagan administration might best be characterized as ''bigness necessarily means badness.''

☐ ☐ 10. A recent study by the Federal Trade Commission indicates that the relaxation of entry barriers and rate fixing policies in the trucking industry has had no real impact on that industry.

☐ ☐ 11. There is some indication that the mandatory inspection and maintenance programs for motor vehicles that exist in a majority of the states have little impact on the safety of motor vehicle travel.

☐ ☐ 12. Federal farm programs cost about $2 billion per year in direct costs.

PROBLEMS AND PROJECTS

1. Consider the problem of regulating your local water company. Originally, huge amounts of money had to be spent to install pipe, build water treatment plants, and construct aquaducts between your town and the local sources of water. The costs of building these facilities were met with a bond issue, the annual payments on which are fixed. Given the existence of these facilities, however, the marginal cost of an extra gallon of water is quite low (consisting mainly of the marginal cost of treating the water plus maintenance and billing activities). Suppose that the following chart describes the cost structure of your local water company:

Exhibit 1

Quantity supplied (millions of gallons)	Total fixed cost (millions of dollars)	Average fixed cost (cents per gallon)	Marginal cost (cents per gallon)	Average total cost (cents per gallon)
40	$10	.25	.06	.31
50	10	.20	.06	_____
60	10	_____	.06	_____
70	10	_____	.06	_____

a. Fill in the missing information in Exhibit 1 above.

b. Suppose regulators set price equal to marginal cost (which will make consumers happy and increase the quantity demanded). What is the water company's profit/loss situation at each output level?

c. Suppose regulators set price equal to average total cost (which will make consumers unhappy and decrease the quantity demanded). What is the water company's profit/loss situation at each output level?

d. Is either pricing mechanism a good option in this case? How do you balance the goal of economic efficiency with that of fairness to the owners of the water company? What would you do if you were on the town's water regulation board?

Research and write a short paper on one of the following topics:

2. The size, power, and role of big business in the U.S. economy. [Selected references that might be helpful: Walter Adams, *The Structure of American Industry,* 4th ed. (New York: Macmillan, 1971); William N. Leonard, *Business Size, Market Power, and Public Policy* (New York: Crowell, 1969); M.A. Adelman, "Two Faces of Economic Concentration," *Public Interest,* Fall 1970; Joe Bain, *Barriers to New Competition* (Cambridge, MA: Harvard University Press, 1956); John S. McGee, *In Defense of Industrial Competition* (New York: Praeger, 1971); Yale Brozen, *The Competitive Economy: Selected Readings* (Morristown, NJ: General Learning Press, 1975); and William Shepherd, *The Economics of Industrial Organization* (Englewood Cliffs, NJ: Prentice-Hall, 1979).]

3. The Galbraithian view of our modern industrial economy—its strengths and weaknesses. [Selected references: J.K. Galbraith, *The New Industrial State,* 2nd ed. (Boston: Houghton Mifflin, 1972) and *Economics and the Public Purpose* (Boston: Houghton Mifflin, 1973); Harold Demsetz, "Where Is the New Industrial State?" *Economic Inquiry,* March 1974; F.A. Hayek, "The Non Sequitur of the Dependence Effect," *Southern Economic Journal,* April 1961; Charles Lindblom, *Politics and Markets* (New York: Basic Books, 1977).]

LEARNING THE MECHANICS—MULTIPLE CHOICE

1. According to the empirical evidence, using either value added or share of employment as the measure of size, the largest 200 firms own approximately what percent of the total tangible assets of nonfinancial corporations?
   a. 11–13 percent
   b. 19–22 percent
   c. 33–38 percent
   d. More than 40 percent

2. The concept of economic regulation typically involves
   a. the regulation of product price and production processes in various industries.
   b. the regulation of product price but not production processes or industrial structure in various industries.
   c. the regulation of product price and industrial structure but not production processes in various industries.
   d. the regulation of industrial structure in various industries.

3. (**I**) ''Most economists feel that antitrust legislation has helped to promote the competitiveness of the U.S. economy.'' (**II**) ''Regulatory agencies (for example, ICC and CAB), trade restrictions, and bureaucratic cost imposed on business have often served to reduce the competitiveness of U.S. economy.'' Analysis of the historical record suggests that
   a. I is true, II is false.
   b. II is true, I is false.
   c. Both I and II are true.
   d. Both I and II are false.

4. Data on value added and employment by sector suggest that the private economy in the United States is
   a. dominated by small firms that produce in industries approximating the conditions of pure competition.
   b. dominated by large firms that produce in industries approaching monopoly conditions.
   c. made up of three sizable sectors—a ''competitive'' sector with low barriers to entry, an unregulated oligopolistic sector with high barriers to entry, and a highly regulated sector.
   d. increasingly coming to be dominated by manufacturing—a sector whose revenues are increasing more rapidly than our national income.

5. All but one of the following are clearly illegal under current antitrust laws. Which is usually *not* illegal?
   a. collusion and conspiracies to restrain trade
   b. horizontal mergers that tend to lessen competition
   c. serving on the board of directors of a competing firm with assets of more than $1 million
   d. conglomerate mergers

6. Between 1980 and 1984, the cost of U.S. government dairy programs to consumers and taxpayers was estimated to average $2.22 billion per year (in 1984 dollars). Out of this total, how much was estimated to have been received by farmers?
   a. $2,070 million
   b. $1,270 million
   c. $720 million
   d. $270 million

7. Use statements I and II to answer this question. (**I**) Regulation of business firms and labor interests tends to be inflexible. It often fails to adjust very rapidly to dynamic changes that affect a competitive market. (**II**) The demand for regulation often stems from organized groups seeking to profit from the regulation, rather than from forces seeking an economically efficient solution.
   a. I is true, II is false.
   b. I is false, II is true.
   c. Both I and II are true.
   d. Both I and II are false.

8. Since 1950, which of the following sectors has grown most rapidly in the United States?
   a. Agriculture
   b. Manufacturing
   c. Service and government
   d. Construction

9. Which of the following is not prohibited by current antitrust legislation?
   a. Tying contracts that substantially lessen competition
   b. Collusion to fix prices of products in competitive markets
   c. Quantity discounts that reflect cost savings stemming from a large purchase
   d. Horizontal mergers that serve to lessen competition

10. If one firm produced 60 percent of an industry's output, the industry's four-firm concentration ratio would be
    a. about 15 percent.
    b. about 30 percent.
    c. between 60 and 100 percent.
    d. about 240 percent.

11. Buick and Oldsmobile are divisions of General Motors. If we were to consider the incentives facing the officers of each division, we would expect
    a. complete cooperation and no rivalry between them.
    b. a good deal of rivalry, as well as cooperation, between them.
    c. no cooperation, but simply an intense rivalry between the two.
    d. no interest in what the other is doing.

12. Use statements I and II to answer this question. (**I**) The new social legislation seeks to improve the health, safety, and quality of the environment. (**II**) Whereas the older economic regulation generally increased costs of production, social regulation usually reduces the cost of production and, in turn, the price of products to the consumer.
    a. Both I and II are true.
    b. Both I and II are false.
    c. I is true, II is false.
    d. I is false, II is true.

THE ECONOMIC WAY OF THINKING—MULTIPLE CHOICE

1. When state governments use business licensing to limit the entry of potential competitors into an industry and create a situation whereby the licensed firms can earn *long-run* economic profit, profit-seeking business entrepeneurs
   a. have an incentive to use both economic and political means in attempting to obtain the valuable licenses.
   b. have little incentive to enter the licensed industry.
   c. would enter the industry only if the licenses were free.
   d. would use economic methods, but not political ones, in attempting to obtain the valuable licenses.

2. Which of the following best explains why competitive private firms seek to produce efficiently?
   a. The pressures of competition demand efficient production, which, other things constant, is rewarded with larger profits or smaller losses.
   b. Efficient production results because private decision-making is invariably less bureaucratic.
   c. Employees in the private sector know that they must produce, whereas waste and inefficiency characterize public sector production.
   d. Analysis of incentives does *not* suggest that competitive firms will produce efficiently.

Use the following quotation to answer the next question.

> The world's first plant for the manufacture of gasoline from natural gas will be shut down as uneconomical, it was announced today by the Amoco Chemicals Corporation. J.H. Forrester, president of Amoco, a subsidiary of Standard Oil Company (Indiana), said, "We have determined that the plant cannot make gasoline and chemicals from natural gas at present market prices as cheaply as they can be made by other processes." [*New York Times,* September 14, 1957.]

3. If the facts of this quotation are correct, a decision by the firm to close down the plant
   a. results in economic inefficiency, because of the abandonment of a technically sound project.
   b. is consistent with economic efficiency, because lower-cost alternative production methods were available.
   c. will increase the demand for gasoline because of its lower cost.
   d. is sound from the firm's point of view, but not from the point of view of society.

4. Suppose that the Barbers' Association of Florida (BAF) was designing legislation to increase the average earnings of its members. Which of the following proposals would be most likely to lead to large and permanent net income gains for those already in the barbering profession in Florida?
   a. Legislation fixing the minimum price of haircuts at $6, and instituting the free licensing of any graduate of a U.S. barber college
   b. Establishment of strict licensing requirements that would prevent any new entrants into the barbering business without the approval of BAF
   c. Legislation requiring that all employees in the barbering profession be paid double time for any hours worked beyond the normal 40-hour week
   d. Establishment of a $6-per-hour minimum wage for barbers who are paid hourly wages

5. Which of the following is most descriptive of public policy toward competitive markets?
   a. Public policy has consistently promoted competitive markets.
   b. Public policy has tolerated big business while following a regulatory and taxation policy that favors smaller businesses.
   c. Public policy has sometimes promoted competition, but it also has used regulatory, tariff, and subsidization powers to stifle and weaken competitive markets.
   d. Public policy has attempted to promote competition, although the effort has been negated by the rapid growth of the manufacturing sector, which has been spurred on by modern technology.

6. The governmental guaranteed support price for Grade A milk has encouraged
   a. an excess demand for Grade A milk.
   b. an excess supply of Grade B milk.
   c. more spending on dairy barns, milking equipment, and feed.
   d. less spending on dairy barns, milking equipment, and feed.

7. "Big firms in the United States are growing primarily because the manufacturing sector, which is dominated by big firms, is growing in importance." This statement is
   a. essentially correct.
   b. incorrect, because bigness is declining among U.S. firms.
   c. incorrect, because manufacturing has produced 75–80 percent of the output in the United States for many years.
   d. incorrect, because since 1950 manufacturing has constituted a shrinking percentage of our output.

8. Which of the following would increase an economist's expectations that competitive pressures were present in an industry?
   a. A high concentration ratio
   b. An increase in the availability of close substitutes made by another industry
   c. Few entrants into the industry
   d. A decrease in the availability of foreign products similar to those produced in the industry

9. Regulation that requires the producers of a product to adopt more costly production techniques will
   a. increase supply and lead to a lower market price of the product.
   b. decrease supply and lead to a higher market price of the product.
   c. increase demand and lead to a higher market price of the product.
   d. leave the market price unchanged, since producers are forced to bear the burden of regulatory costs.

10. The experience of very large firms over the last several decades indicates that bigness
   a. is a virtual guarantee of success in the corporate world.
   b. is a guarantee of success, at least in manufacturing.
   c. is a guarantee of success, except in manufacturing.
   d. is no guarantee of success over time, since so many firms come and go from the "top 50" or "top 100" firms over a 20- or 30-year period.

11. Economic studies on the regulatory policies of the Interstate Commerce Commission suggest that
    a. shipping rates are much lower than they would be in the absence of trucking-industry regulation.
    b. regulated carriers coordinate their routes in order to minimize waste.
    c. the ICC sets price equal to marginal cost for all regulated services.
    d. the regulatory powers of the agency have been used to restrict competition, thereby contributing to the higher transportation prices than would have prevailed in the absence of regulation.

12. An example of a government action designed to promote competition among producers is
    a. the institution of higher tariffs (import taxes) on Volkswagens.
    b. an extension of occupational licensing procedures to many additional occupations.
    c. imposition of additional regulations on small businesses.
    d. legislation prohibiting interlocking corporate directorates.

THE ECONOMIC WAY OF THINKING—DISCUSSION QUESTIONS

1. Outline your views of proper public policy that would both promote competitiveness and be consistent with economic efficiency. Explain why your program should be adopted.

2. How competitive is the U.S. economy? Is it less competitive today than three or four decades ago? Has the importance of power of big business grown in recent decades? Explain.

3. In recent years there has been considerable dissatisfaction with regulatory policies in the airline and trucking industries. This has led to significant movements toward deregulation in these industries. How successful has deregulation been? Do you think deregulating these industries is a good idea? Why or why not?

4. Compare and contrast the new social regulation with the older economic regulation. Do you think social regulation will be more or less successful in attaining its stated goals than was economic regulation? Use economic analysis to defend your position.

5. Suppose that the government uses licensing to limit the number of firms in the retail liquor industry. Thus, ignoring the cost of a license, firms in the industry make substantial economic profit.
    a. Analyze the price, costs, and profits of firms when the limited number of licenses (good for five years) are auctioned off to the highest bidders. Assume that ownership of the licenses is widespread, so there is no problem of collusion.
    b. Analyze the price, costs, and profits of firms when the limited number of licenses are granted "free" to persons approved by a committee appointed by the legislature (or governor).
    c. When choosing between these two, state legislatures have almost exclusively chosen alternative b. Can you explain why?

6. Do you think General Motors is too big? Would you vote to have it broken up into several smaller firms? What are the major factors that influence your views on this question? Assume that the head of the Pontiac division of General Motors earns his bonuses and promotions on the basis of how Pontiac division (not GM as a whole) performs. The same applies to the heads of Chevrolet, Buick, and other GM divisions. Can you explain why rivalry and competition among divisions should be expected? Will there also be cooperation? What kinds? Will testing laboratories be shared? Will consumers gain? What might consumers lose if GM is *not* broken up? Write a short essay either defending GM or arguing for its breakup. Address the questions raised here.

PERSPECTIVES IN ECONOMICS

Single-Digit Oil and Auto Mileage Standards Don't Mix
by Robert W. Crandall

[From *The Wall Street Journal,* April 3, 1986, p. 26. Reprinted with permission of the Wall Street Journal © Dow Jones & Co., Inc. (1986). All rights reserved.]

As we watch the demise of the world petroleum cartel, debate continues about whether fuel-economy standards for automobiles prescribed by Congress during the heyday of OPEC should be adjusted slightly. We are even treated to the unsightly spectacle of one Big Three auto company—Chrysler—arguing for the retention of the Corporate Average Fuel Economy program just to hobble the other two companies. Surprisingly, almost no one has suggested the abolition of the entire fuel-economy program—the only sensible decision.

To understand why we have government-mandated fuel-economy standards for cars, one has to return to the 1970s and the unstable oil market of that time. In 1975, most people believed that the real price of fossil fuels would rise ad infinitum. In this environment, Congress enacted the CAFE program for all manufacturers selling new passenger cars in the U.S., requiring that their fleet averages rise from 18 to 27.5 miles per gallon between 1978 and 1985 with subsequent years' standards to be set by the secretary of transportation.

At the time, this policy seemed a not too irrational antidote to a truly irrational policy of regulating crude-oil and gasoline prices. If Congress was not going to allow gasoline prices to rise to world marketclearing levels, thereby encouraging conservation, it would have to mandate conservation more directly by requiring that automobiles be produced to deliver more fuel economy than consumers would desire at artificially low prices.

Of course, we finally came to our senses and abandoned oil-price controls. After the Iranian debacle, oil prices made one last surge. By early 1981, crude-oil prices had risen to the range of $35 a barrel and gasoline prices had climbed to about $1.40 a gallon. Since that time, as we all know, oil and gasoline prices have declined dramatically. In fact, gasoline prices in February were less than 70% of their 1981 level in real terms despite an increase in the federal gasoline tax, and they will continue to drop. The cost of the crude oil in a gallon of gasoline has fallen from about 65 cents to 30 cents in the past three months. With real gasoline prices falling so rapidly, why do we want to require auto makers to direct their scarce capital and trained manpower to increasing fuel economy far beyond the level that consumers would willingly pay for? Obviously, if the price of gasoline is falling, you and I are likely to be less willing to pay more for each additional mile per gallon promised by Detroit's newest models.

Visionaries say we need CAFE to protect us against another round of OPEC price increases somewhere in the distant future. But are they better equipped to predict these price increases than today's market participants? And if they are, why do they focus only on the gasoline consumed by new cars, which are only about 8% of all cars on the road and account for less than 3% of oil consumption? Why don't they argue for conservation standards on industrial boilers, home furnaces, locomotives and plastics producers?

If the conservationists were truly interested in reducing oil consumption, they would advocate a tax on all petroleum products. If they were concerned about OPEC-led embargos or other supply disruptions, they would press for more rapid accumulation of oil in the Strategic Petroleum Reserve, which Congress has chosen to ignore just when the reserve could be filled at low prices.

In the past year, the debate over CAFE standards has taken a number of twists that suggest fuel economy is not really the issue. The United Auto Workers union has become an ardent supporter of CAFE even though the program raises Detroit's costs and thereby leads to fewer new-car sales. The reason for this anamalous behavior is to be found in the law's curious distinction between imported and domestic cars. Manufacturers must tote up their CAFE numbers for cars they produce in the U.S. separately from those they import. Given General Motors' and Ford's success with large cars, they have fallen short of the CAFE standard the past three years. As a result, they will have to increase their production of small cars in the U.S. or make heroic progress on their larger cars if they are to comply.

Recent studies suggest that the U.S. companies are not competitive with Japan or Korea in producing small cars. Therefore, without CAFE, it would make sense for Ford and General Motors to import their small cars. Unfortunately, CAFE makes this difficult because these companies are required to pay $50 a car for every mile per gallon they fall short of CAFE. In short, CAFE serves as a nontariff trade barrier for small-car imports.

Even more curious are the strategic battles among the domestic Big Three companies. Chrysler insists that the CAFE program not be weakened because the company has complied easily while Ford and GM will owe potentially hundreds of millions of dollars of fines a year for not meeting the standard. Last year, Chrysler argued strenuously but unsuccessfully against the secretary of transportation's decision to lower the standard to 26 mpg for the current (1986) model year, saying that since Chrysler had spent the capital resources to meet the standard, GM and Ford should be forced to do so as well. In fact, Chrysler has the worst fuel economy of the Big Three for given weight of car and engine power. It has succeeded in meeting CAFE because it was forced to end its production of large cars during its brush with bankruptcy in the late 1970s. Now it wants to penalize Ford and GM for having the foresight and financial wherewithal to keep their full line of cars.

Even Ford and General Motors are not arguing for an abolition of this misguided program. They simply want the 26-mile-per-gallon standard to be extended to the 1987 and 1988 model years. Why? Could the answer be that a 26 mpg standard severely constrains the major large-car competitors in the world—Mercedes, Volvo, BMW, Peugeot, and Saab—from exporting freely to the U.S.? These European companies are forced to offer diesels or simply lower-performing cars in order to comply with the standards. Incidentally, the first company to pay CAFE penalties was not an American company, but Jaguar.

The CAFE program has become an anomaly or even an absurdity in an era of declining oil prices. If the visionaries in Congress wish to protect us from unforeseen disasters, they should look to improving our ability to survive a shock, perhaps by enlarging the Strategic Petroleum Reserve. CAFE standards simply penalize U.S. consumers by offering them cars with too much fuel economy and too little performance, and a reduced choice between imported and domestically produced smaller models. Or Congress could enact an oil-consumption tax. Who knows, such a tax might even help to solve certain other pressing problems of the day.

Discussion

1. Is Crandall saying that auto mileage standards are *always* a bad idea or just a bad idea when gasoline prices are low? Explain your answer.

2. If the free-market system worked, wouldn't high gasoline prices lower the demand for gas guzzlers (and increase the demand for fuel-efficient cars) and make auto mileage standards redundant? Did this happen?

3. Crandall seems to find it "curious" that at least one of the same automobile makers who opposed the mileage standards when they were introduced is now arguing to have them retained. Would the special interest effect make this more understandable? How?

22

The Supply of and Demand for Productive Resources

TRUE OR FALSE

T F

☑ ☐   1. An increase in demand for wheat would cause the price of wheat-producing land to rise.

☑ ☐   2. Under pure competition, the marginal revenue product of a resource would be equal to the resource price.

☑ ☐   3. A profit-maximizing firm will continue to employ a resource as long as its marginal revenue product exceeds its marginal cost to the firm.

☐ ☑   4. The availability of good substitutes for a resource will tend to make the demand for it less elastic.

☑ ☐   5. In the short run, the supply of doctors is quite inelastic.

☐ ☑   6. In the short run, the supply of filling station attendants is quite inelastic.

☐ ☑   7. Physical capital and human capital cannot be substituted for each other.

☑ ☐   8. The marginal products—and therefore wage rates—of employees will be positively influenced by the amount of physical capital per worker in a firm.

☑ ☐   9. An increase in the price of a resource increases the incentive of producers to find a substitute for it.

☑ ☐ 10. The demand for a resource will be negatively related to its price partly because producers will substitute other factors of production for the resource as it increases in price.

☑ ☐ 11. A firm that purchases resources competitively must buy at the price that is determined in the market.

☐ ☑ 12. An employer will hire workers as long as their marginal revenue product is positive.

☑ ☐ 13. Because of the law of diminishing marginal returns, the value of a worker's marginal product eventually declines as more workers are hired in a given plant.

☑ ☐ 14. The demand for a resource is strongly dependent upon its contribution to the production of a good demanded by consumers.

☐ ☑ 15. A unique resource will command a high price, regardless of demand conditions.

PROBLEMS AND PROJECTS

Exhibit 1

Units of labor	Total output (per week)	Marginal physical product (per week)	Product price	Total revenue	Marginal revenue product (per week)
1	5	_____	100	_____	_____
2	9	_____	100	_____	_____
3	12	_____	100	_____	_____
4	14	_____	100	_____	_____
5	15	_____	100	_____	_____

1. Nick sells building materials in a competitive industry. His firm receives $100 for each unit of material. Given the firm's current fixed capital, Exhibit 1 shows how total output changes as additional units of labor are hired. Assume that Nick hires labor from a competitive market in which the market-determined wage is $200 per week.

   a. Fill in the marginal physical product, total revenue, and marginal revenue product columns.
   b. How many employees should Nick hire if he wants to maximize profits?
   c. How many units of labor should Nick hire if the wage rate goes up to $300?

Exhibit 2

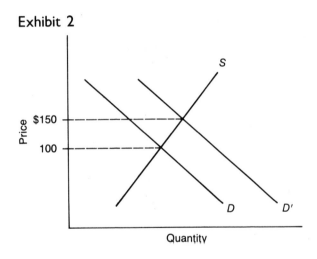

   d. The supply-and-demand conditions in the building market are represented in Exhibit 2. Suppose that the demand for building materials increases as indicated by D'. Given the new wage rate in part c, indicate the firm's new employment level, total revenue, and profits (refer to Exhibit 3).

Exhibit 3

Units of labor	Units of output	Product price	Total revenue	Variable cost	Profit
0	0	$150	_____	_____	_____
1	5	150	_____	_____	_____
2	9	150	_____	_____	_____
3	12	150	_____	_____	_____
4	14	150	_____	_____	_____
5	15	150	_____	_____	_____

   e. Nick has a weekly fixed charge of $800 in addition to his variable cost for labor. Given his *fixed costs,* would Nick stay in business if he operated at the level of output you determined in part d?

2. Magic Carpet, Inc., produces and sells handmade oriental rugs in a competitive industry. The firm receives $100 per square meter for each rug produced. Given the firm's current fixed capital, Exhibit 4 shows how total output (in square meters) changes as additional units of skilled labor are hired.

Exhibit 4

Units of skilled labor	Total output (square meters per week)	MPP	Price per square meter	TR	MRP
0	0	0	$100		0
1	5	5	100	500	500
2	12	7	100	1200	700
3	18	6	100	1800	600
4	21.5	3.5	100	2150	350
5	24	2.5	100	2400	250
6	25	1	100	2500	100

a. Complete the table.
b. What is the firm's demand schedule for labor?
c. Given the equilibrium wage rate as $200 per week, indicate how many workers the firm would hire if it wanted to maximize profits.
d. How many workers would Magic Carpet hire if the market wage increased to $300 per week?

3. Use the diagrams below to indicate the changes in demand (D), supply (S), equilibrium price (P) and equilibrium quantity (Q) in response to the events in the resource markets. First show in the diagrams how the described event or events affects demand and/or supply of the resource, and then fill in the table to the right of the diagrams using + to indicate increase, − to indicate decrease 0 to indicate no effect, and ? to indicate uncertain.

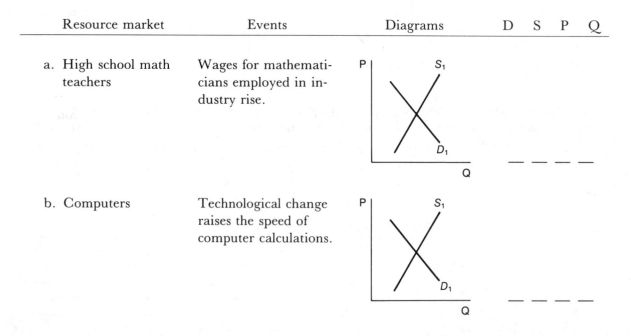

Resource market	Events	Diagrams	D	S	P	Q
a. High school math teachers	Wages for mathematicians employed in industry rise.		___	___	___	___
b. Computers	Technological change raises the speed of computer calculations.		___	___	___	___

c. Computer technicians

The cost of obtaining computer training falls.

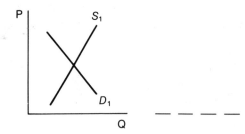

d. Welders

Technological change lowers the cost of robots used to weld auto parts on auto assembly lines.

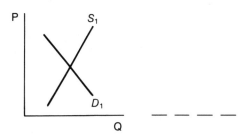

e. Agricultural land in Southern California

Population migration raises homesite values; a vitamin C fad raises the price of oranges.

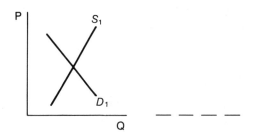

4. In the growing of corn a farmer uses two fertilizers, Vitacorn and Cornpower. The farmer has estimated that at his current rate of usage of the two fertilizers, the marginal (physical) product of one ton of Vitacorn is 200 bushels of corn per acre and the marginal product of one ton of Cornpower is 400 bushels per acre. The best price quotations the farmer has been able to get are $800/ton for Vitacorn and $1200/ton for Cornpower.

   a. From the above information, does the farmer's current usage of the two fertilizers meet the "condition for cost minimization when multiple resources are employed"?

   b. Suppose the farmer used one more ton of Cornpower and two less tons of Vitacorn. How would total output change? How would total cost change? Would this substitution be consistent with the goal of profit maximization?

   c. If the farmer continued to substitute Cornpower for Vitacorn, assume that the marginal product of Cornpower would fall. Would these changes lead toward fulfillment of the condition for cost minimization you discussed in part a? How?

5. Suppose that the world's long-run and short-run demands for crude petroleum can be represented by the diagram in Exhibit 5.

Exhibit 5

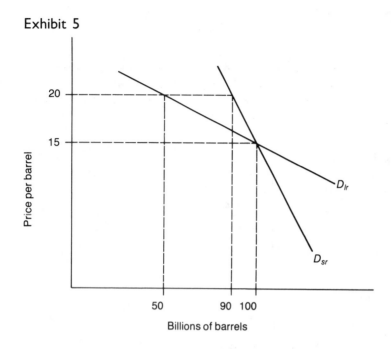

a. From the information in the diagram, calculate the arc-price elasticity of demand for crude petroleum in the short run and in the long run.

b. List several reasons why you think the demand for petroleum would be more elastic in the long run than in the short run. Be as specific as possible.

LEARNING THE MECHANICS—MULTIPLE CHOICE

1. The short-run supply of a human resource will be more elastic the
    a. more elastic the demand for the product to be produced. ✔
    b. more inelastic the demand for the product to be produced.
    c. lower the skill level necessary to perform the job.
    d. harder it is to acquire the skill and knowledge necessary to provide the resource.

2. A decrease in the demand for a product will cause
    a. the price of resources to decrease and, therefore, output to increase.
    b. output to decrease, and demand for (and prices of) resources used to produce the product to decrease also. ✔
    c. output to decrease, but the demand for resources to remain constant.
    d. output to decrease and resource prices to fall if, and only if, their supply is elastic.

3. Empirical evidence indicates a close relationship between quantity of schooling and income. A cost-minimizing firm would be willing to pay a highly educated person higher wages than those with less education if
    a. the marginal revenue product of the highly educated person was greater.
    b. the demand for the highly educated group was inelastic.
    c. the supply of the highly eduated group was smaller.
    d. the total cost of schooling was greater for the highly educated employee.

4. The more elastic the demand for a product
    a. the more inelastic the demand for the productive resources used.
    b. the less elastic the supply of factors used in producing the product.
    c. the more elastic the demand for the productive resources used. ✔
    d. the longer the time period before the product will be sold.

5. Which of the following expresses the correct decision-making rule for a profit-maximizing firm hiring units of labor?
   a. If the MRP were rising, less labor would be employed as time passed.
   b. The firm should continue to hire workers as long as their MRP is greater than the wage rate.
   c. The firm should continue to hire workers until the total costs of all workers equals the total revenue from the output of the workers.
   d. The firm should continue to hire workers until the wage rate equals the price of the product.

6. The demand for a productive resource
   a. is a derived demand.
   b. is independent of the selling price of the product.
   c. is dependent on the supply side of the resource at the time.
   d. shifts when the price of the resource changes.

7. Increasing the price of a natural resource will
   a. cause consumers to choose substitute goods that do not use the natural resource intensively.
   b. decrease the demand for the natural resource.
   c. increase the demand for the natural resource.
   d. increase the quantity of the resource demanded.

8. Compared to the short-run demand, the long-run demand for carpenters is
   a. less elastic.
   b. more elastic.
   c. equally elastic.
   d. either more or less elastic; we cannot predict which.

9. In a purely competitive industry, the marginal revenue derived from the sale of an additional unit of the product is equal to the market price of the product. In these circumstances, the additional revenue derived from the employment of an additional unit of a resource is referred to as the resource's
   a. marginal cost.
   b. value of marginal product.
   c. marginal physical product.
   d. marginal productivity.

10. If the cost of using skilled labor was twice the cost of using unskilled labor, and both were used by a profit-maximizing firm, the firm would adjust the quantity of each type of labor until
    a. the marginal physical product of each was the same.
    b. twice as much unskilled labor was used.
    c. half as much unskilled labor was used.
    d. the marginal physical product of unskilled labor was half that of skilled labor.

11. If a firm used only two factors of production, labor (L) and capital (K), which of the following conditions would be present if the firm were minimizing its costs of production?
    a. The $MPP_L/P_L = MPP_K/P_K$.
    b. MPP_L times the price of labor $= MPP_K$ times the price of capital.
    c. $MRP_L = MRP_K$.
    d. $MPP_L = MPP_K$.

12. A shift in the demand for a particular resource can be caused by all the following *except*
    a. a change in the demand for the product that uses the resource as a factor of production. √
    b. a change in the productivity of the resource.
    c. a change in the price of *other* resources that could be used as substitutes for the resource in question.
    d. a change in price of the resource.

THE ECONOMIC WAY OF THINKING—MULTIPLE CHOICE

1. Which of the following resources will have the most inelastic supply in the short run?
   a. Land in a suburb of Tallahassee, Florida
   b. Trucks used to transport a variety of products
   c. Elevator operators
   d. Secretaries in Eagle Rock, California

2. Suppose that the number of economists engaged in teaching positions in 1985 decreased 10 percent from the 1975 level, while the number of economists in all positions declined 5 percent. Furthermore, suppose that the median salary of those teaching declined relative to the average for economists as a group. The apparent paradox of a relative decrease in economists in teaching positions concurrent with their lower salaries relative to all economists can be explained by which of the following?
   a. The demand for teachers in economics is positively sloped, as evidenced by the smaller quantity employed at the lower salary rate.
   b. The demand elasticity for teachers in economics was smaller than that of the demand for all economists.
   c. The demand for economists decreased, and the demand for teachers in economics decreased relative to the demand for all economists.
   d. The larger decrease in the demand for research economists increased the relative median salaries of all economists.

3. Given the education required to become an engineer, which of the following best describes the expected market reaction to an increase in demand for the services of engineers?
   a. A large decrease in the wages of engineers in the short run, but a small increase in wages over time
   b. A substantial increase in the wages of engineers, followed (later) by an increase in the number of engineers, moderating the initial wage increase
   c. A substantial increase in the number of engineers and no increase in the wage level
   d. A substantial increase in the wages of engineers in the short run, and no change in the number of persons choosing to become engineers

4. In which of the following resource markets do you think supply would be most elastic in the short run?
   a. Pharmacists
   b. Physicians
   c. Unskilled labor
   d. Airplane pilots

5. Empirical evidence indicates a close relationship between schooling and income. A cost-minimizing firm would be willing to pay a better-educated secretary higher wages than those with less education if
    a. the total cost of schooling was greater for the better-educated secretary.
    b. the demand for highly educated secretaries was inelastic.
    c. the supply of highly educated secretaries was smaller.
    d. the marginal revenue product of the better-educated secretary was greater.

6. Suppose that a school board adopted a policy whereby all teachers were paid at the same wage rate. Furthermore, suppose that there was a vacancy in economics for which there were no applicants, and there was no vacancy in political science but there were 50 inquiries regarding any possible vacancy. Economic analysis implies that
    a. the nation needs to train more economists.
    b. the wage rate paid the teachers is below the market wage for economists.
    c. economists have fewer alternatives to teaching than do political scientists.
    d. the wage rate offered is below the market wage for political scientists.

7. Suppose that the United Auto Workers Union is successful in obtaining a 15 percent increase in the wages of auto workers and that the large wage increase necessitates an increase in automobile prices. Employment in the automobile manufacturing industry would be *least* likely to fall if
    a. the demand for American automobiles was relatively constant, but highly elastic.
    b. the supply of foreign-produced automobiles was highly elastic.
    c. American consumers felt that foreign automobiles were a good substitute for American automobiles.
    d. the demand for American automobiles was increasing and highly inelastic.

8. Human capital differs from physical capital in that
    a. only physical capital depreciates.
    b. the use of physical capital is affected by working conditions and monetary return; human capital is predominantly affected by monetary return.
    c. physical capital may be purchased and sold; human capital may not be sold in a nonslave society (only the services of human capital may be purchased and sold).
    d. only human capital depreciates.

9. According to marginal productivity theory, a law forcing firms to pay higher wages to HHLs (heads of households with large families) would tend to
    a. decrease the employment and marginal productivity of HHLs.
    b. decrease the employment of HHLs, but lead to a higher marginal productivity for those HHLs hired.
    c. reduce the wages of workers without families.
    d. have no impact on HHLs.

10. The cost of electricity is a large component of the cost of making aluminum. In the Pacific Northwest, federal agencies sell electricity to aluminum manufacturers at roughly one-fourth its market value. Among those eager to eliminate this implicit subsidy would be
    a. firms that make wooden bats and wooden canoes.
    b. firms that supply aluminum ore to aluminum makers, since ore would then be a smaller part of the total cost of producing aluminum.
    c. buyers of aluminum products (who gain when aluminum profits decline).
    d. employees of the aluminum makers (who would then be justified in asking for higher wages when aluminum prices go up).

11. Where human capital is concerned, nonpecuniary considerations are likely to be
     a.   irrelevant, since owners' decisions are based on money prices.
     b.   unimportant, since people are very mobile.
     c.   important, since workers have objectives other than money.
     d.   important, since human capital is not transferable.

12. If the demand for chemical engineers suddenly increased, salaries for them would be higher one year later if
     a.   several other kinds of engineers became chemical engineers by enrolling in a special one-semester training course.
     b.   the price of goods produced by the chemical engineers was highly sensitive to changes in price.
     c.   chemical engineering was so specialized that few persons in other areas could become chemical engineers without taking at least three additional years of training.
     d.   there were many unemployed chemical engineers before the increase in demand.

THE ECONOMIC WAY OF THINKING—DISCUSSION QUESTIONS

1. In recent years, the computer industry has grown quite rapidly as a result of technological advances. Show how economic theory suggests that the following would be affected by this growth.
    a.   The short-run earnings of computer technicians (for example, programmers, engineers, and computer scientists)
    b.   The supply of computer technicians
    c.   The long-run earnings of computer technicians
    d.   The demand for inputs (for example, bookkeepers and clerks) for which computers are substitutes

2. Is human labor really a "thing" that can be bought and sold like any other productive resource? What about the feelings of the human beings involved? While we can buy a person's time, we can't buy his or her enthusiasm or loyalty so easily. What sort of advantages and disadvantages does the "human element" in purchasing labor inputs have?

3. In your own words, explain why the amount demanded of a productive resource is negatively related to its price. Why would the demand curve of a resource (typically) be more elastic if it were assumed that buyers had more time in which to respond?

4. Why are individuals willing to supply resources? Do they seek to maximize their income? Do they seek to gain the highest possible rate of return on their ownership of resources? Does the rate of return to resource suppliers influence their investment decisions? Explain.

5. Suppose that the annual real earnings of aerospace engineers increases by 15 percent because of a sharp expansion in the demand for their services. Do you think that the number of aerospace engineers will increase very much after six months? After two years? After five years? Explain.

6. What impact would each of the following have on the demand for economists?
    a.   An increase in government research funds for the study of wage–price controls
    b.   Increased reliance on student tuition as a method of financing education
    c.   The establishment of a planning agency that must analyze and decide whether labor-management contracts are inflationary
    d.   Reduced emphasis on government planning and an increased reliance on the market mechanism

PERSPECTIVES IN ECONOMICS

Are Professional Athletes Worth the Price?
by Timothy Tregarthen

[Reprinted with permission from *The Margin,* November 1985, pp. 6–8, abridged.]

Is Reggie Jackson worth $975,000 per year? Or, for that matter, is Wayne Gretsky worth $825,000? Is John Elway, with his 1983 B.A. in economics from Stanford, worth $900,000 to the Denver Broncos?

In one sense, the answer is obviously "yes." Those salaries are, after all, agreed to voluntarily. But what determines how much someone is willing to pay for a player's services?

A firm will pay any factor of production—be it a ton of coal or a cornerback—up to the marginal revenue product of the factor. That marginal revenue product is simply the extra revenue attributable to hiring an additional unit of the factor.

George Steinbrenner, owner of the New York Yankees, puts the point somewhat more colorfully: "You measure the value of a ballplayer by how many fannies he puts in the seats."

Howard University economist John Leonard estimates that Reggie Jackson put as much as $1.5 million worth of fannies in the seats in 1982—his first year with the California Angels, and their second year in the playoffs.

The technique most commonly used to estimate the marginal revenue product of a player was developed by George Scully, an economist at Southern Methodist University. Writing in the December, 1974 American Economic Review, Mr. Scully estimated the factors that determined a baseball team's total revenue in the 1968 and 1969 seasons.

Mr. Scully found, not surprisingly, that a major determinant of team revenues was the percentage of games won. He estimated the relationship between winning and the batting and pitching skills of a team's roster. By measuring an individual player's contribution to the team averages that determined winning, and then translating that contribution to an increase in the percentage of games won, Mr. Scully was able to measure the career marginal revenue products of players.

The results were startling. Players did not earn their marginal revenue products. They earned far less.

Table 1 gives Mr. Scully's findings. He grouped hitters and pitchers into performance categories. His measure of net marginal revenue product subtracts costs such as training and transportation associated with a single player from the marginal revenue product estimate. Mr. Scully assumed career lengths of four, seven, and ten years for mediocre, average, and star players, respectively.

Star pitchers and hitters were handsomely paid; their annual salaries were about $50,000 per year (remember this was the '60's). But, in terms of their contributions to team revenues, they were grossly underpaid, receiving only about 15 percent of their net marginal revenue products.

Mr. Scully suggests the explanation of salaries so far below marginal revenue product lies in the theory of monopsony. Under the "reserve clause" in effect then, a player was owned by his team. The team could sell or trade him, but the player was not free to offer his services to other teams. A player who wanted a baseball career could deal with only one team; that team thus had monopsony power over the player's services.

A monopsony team faces an upward-sloping supply curve for players of a particular category. That means that each extra player of a given type requires more money. That, in turn, is likely to drive up the wages paid to the players of that category the team already has. The result is that the extra cost of an extra player is higher than that player's actual salary.

Figure 1 shows the result, using Mr. Scully's estimate of marginal revenue products and salaries of star hitters. The supply curve facing a team for these hitters has the usual shape; the marginal factor cost curve shows the increase in salary costs associated with hiring each additional player. The demand curve, with star hitters as the only variable factor, is the marginal revenue product curve for these players.

Players, understandably, were unhappy with this arrangement. The reserve clause was challenged successfully by Andy Messersmith in 1975. The first group of "free

Table 1
Career Marginal Revenue Products and Salaries

Hitters	Net MRP	Salary
Mediocre	$−124,300	$ 60,800
Average	906,700	196,200
Star	3,139,100	477,200
Pitchers		
Mediocre	−$53,600	$ 54,800
Average	1,119,200	222,500
Star	3,969,600	612,500

Figure 1. Monopsony Exploitation of Star Hitters

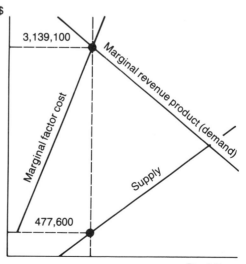

agents," players now able to negotiate with other teams, was available for the 1977 season.

With competitive bidding for their services, the monopsony power of teams was weakened. Salaries should have moved closer to marginal revenue products.

They did. Paul Sommers and Noel Quinton, of Middlebury College, reported their estimates of the marginal revenue products of 14 of these free agents in the Summer, 1982 issue of the Journal of Human Resources. Using Mr. Scully's approach, they found that the salaries of pitchers had increased to about half of marginal revenue products; pitcher salaries were about equal to estimated marginal contributions to team revenue.

Monopsony power still exists in baseball. Players are allowed to become free agents only after six years in the game. But the opportunity to be a free agent has clearly had a powerful effect on salaries.

In a study reported at the Western Economic Association meeting last summer, Mr. Leonard estimated the same relationships for the 1982 season. He calculates that the monopsony gap has been closed still further; hitters had salaries averaging 75 percent of estimated marginal revenue product.

According to Mr. Leonard, one of the most spectacular examples of monopsony exploitation of athletes is in college football. He argues that NCAA rules against paying players a salary can be viewed as a monopsony price-fixing scheme to keep player costs down.

If that is its goal, it certainly succeeds. Mr. Leonard estimates that a star college football player, defined as an athlete that leads the national rankings in a category such as yards rushing or is named to an All-American team, has a marginal revenue product to his school of $100,000 per year. He is paid scholarship revenues of only about $5,000 per year.

Estimates of marginal revenue products are, necessarily, somewhat arbitrary. There is more to a hitter's appeal than his slugging average, more to a quarterback than the number of touchdown passes relative to interceptions. But the work of economists studying sports salaries suggests quite clearly that the salaries paid professional athletes are not as outrageous as they may seem. To the extent that players are still subject to monopsony power, their salaries are still much lower than would prevail in a competitive market.

Discussion

1. The results cited in this article seem to be at odds with the general view that "professional athletes are overpaid, spoiled brats." What reasons can you think of that would explain this difference of opinion?

2. As Tregarthen admits, one of the weaknesses of this analysis is the manner in which marginal revenue product was measured. How would *you* go about measuring the marginal revenue product of an employee?

3. What about players who are hurt or who are in the minor leagues still improving their skills (human capital). If owners have to pay players whose marginal revenue products are zero, then shouldn't they be allowed to pay the other players less than their MRPs to even things out? Why or why not?

23

Earnings, Productivity, and the Job Market

TRUE OR FALSE

T F

☑ ☐ 1. Immobility of labor is a major source of wage differentials.

☑ ☐ 2. Higher productivity generally leads to higher wages.

☐ ☑ 3. Firms seeking to maximize monetary profit will tend to hire very few minority workers.

☐ ☑ 4. Owners of physical capital in the United States receive about 40 percent of national income.

☐ ☑ 5. Automation always reduces production costs and employment within a firm.

☐ ☑ 6. Automation almost always reduces the demand for labor in the economy.

☑ ☐ 7. An expansion in production per worker is the primary source of high living standards.

☑ ☑ 8. Minimum wage legislation helps low-wage workers, particularly teenagers, whereas the burden of the legislation is imposed almost exclusively on high-wage workers.

☑ ☐ 9. The average wage rate in the United States is high in comparison with that of other countries largely because of the large amounts of physical and human capital with which the average American works.

☑ ☐ 10. Other things constant, the more dangerous a job, the higher the wage rate it will command.

☐ ☑ 11. The wages of workers on jobs that require special skills or technical know-how will necessarily be high.

☑ ☐ 12. The job opportunities of a minority group would be reduced if consumers discriminated against firms that hired minorities.

☑ ☐ 13. The almost total exclusion of women from many high-paying professional occupations is consistent with the employment discrimination explanation of earnings differences according to sex.

PROBLEMS AND PROJECTS

Exhibit 1

Quantity demanded per month	Price	Quantity supplied per month
0	$600	6000
1000	500	5000
2000	400	4000
3000	300	3000
4000	200	2000
5000	100	1000
6000	0	0

1. Exhibit 1 is a hypothetical demand-and-supply schedule for sophisticated pocket calculators in a competitive industry.
    a. What will be the equilibrium quantity and price in this market?
    b. Suppose that a new labor-saving technology is developed, resulting in an increase of 2000 in quantity supplied at every price. What will happen to the equilibrium quantity and price?
    c. The new technology reduces the quantity of labor used *per calculator* by 20 percent. What will happen to total employment in the industry? (Original employment was 120 workers.)
    d. Owing to the new technology, the computer industry substituted more machines for labor. Using the elasticity-of-demand argument, refute or support the following statement: "If we continue to allow machines to replace men, we will run out of jobs. Automation is the major cause of unemployment."

2. The following statement was made by John Kendrick of George Washington University:

    > I might point out that investment is a smaller portion of gross national product in the United States than in most other industrialized countries. And I believe this is one reason that we have a slower rate of advance in productivity than most other advanced nations.

    Try to find data on the amount of investment, the gross national product, and the *rate* of increase in output for socialist countries such as the USSR and Yugoslavia. Compare these results to those of the United States, France, and West Germany. Do your findings agree with Kendrick's contention? Why or why not?

3.   Exhibit 2 illustrates a hypothetical market for teenage workers which is initially in competitive equilibrium at an hourly wage rate of $3.00. Suppose governmental authorities pass legislation setting minimum wages at $4.00 per hour.

Exhibit 2

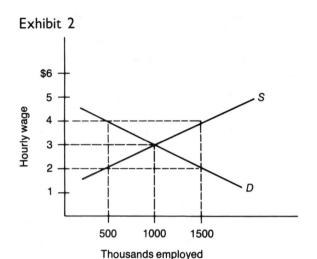

Thousands employed

a. Indicate the amount of unemployment at the minimum wage of $4.00.

b. Of the total amount of unemployment, part is comprised of individuals who were working before the minimum wage was imposed and part who were not. Can you identify these two groups in the diagram?

c.   As a result of the minimum wage, what has happened to the total earnings of teenagers? What does this tell you about the elasticity of demand for teenage workers?

d.   Suppose that, instead of the minimum wage, government decides to subsidize employment of teenagers by paying employers $2.00 per hour for every teenager employed. In the exhibit, illustrate the impact of this approach. [*Hint:* Along with the marginal revenue product of each teenager employed, employers receive an additional $2.00 per hour from the government. This affects employers' demand for teenage labor. How?]

LEARNING THE MECHANICS—MULTIPLE CHOICE

1.   If money wages increased by a factor of four, and the cost of living doubled, real wages would rise by
    a.   50 percent.
    b.   300 percent.
    c.   200 percent.
    d.   100 percent.

2.   Real wages would be most likely to decrease over a period of time if
    a.   the rate of inflation was higher than 3 percent.
    b.   the demand for consumer goods decreased relative to the demand for capital goods.
    c.   automation increased.
    d.   output or productivity per labor-hour decreased.

3.   If all persons were identical regarding preferences and productivity factors (ability, skill level, education, experience, etc.), the highest-paying jobs would be the most
    a.   prestigious.
    b.   convenient.
    c.   pleasant.
    d.   disagreeable.

4. If a minimum wage law was enacted and the demand for workers was inelastic
    a. employers would substitute machines for most of the present workers in the short run.
    b. the total income for workers would fall.
    c. the reduction in employment would be small.
    d. employers would hire more low-skill workers to keep the wage rate from rising even further.

5. Evidence suggests that education raises the earnings of the work force mainly by
    a. increasing the marginal productivity of labor.
    b. keeping young people out of the labor force, thereby reducing the supply of labor.
    c. teaching workers how to demand more pay.
    d. teaching people to read and write, although education beyond that point does not seem to increase worker productivity.

6. Increasing the minimum wage will probably result in
    a. lower profits and the same level of product prices.
    b. greater employment, since more people want to work at the new wage than at the previous equilibrium wage.
    c. reduced employment of the unskilled, as firms produce less output and substitute away from the more expensive unskilled labor.
    d. a decrease in the demand for workers in previously unionized high-wage firms.

7. Within an occupation, when a given job provides steadier work (fewer layoffs), the hourly wage tends to be
    a. lower than wage rates in jobs that are otherwise similar.
    b. higher than wage rates in jobs that are otherwise similar.
    c. no different from wage rates in jobs that are otherwise similar.
    d. determined by factors other than supply and demand.

8. Employment discrimination against members of a minority group invariably exists when the minority group members
    a. are paid less than other workers.
    b. are hired less frequently than other workers.
    c. are treated differently than other workers.
    d. are treated differently than other workers who are similarly qualified.

9. Indicate which of the following most accurately represents the capital formation rate of the United States relative to other countries.
    a. The United States invests a larger share of its GNP than most other industrial countries.
    b. The United States invests a smaller share of its GNP than most other industrial countries.
    c. The United States invests about the same share of its GNP as Japan and West Germany.
    d. The United States invests about the same share of its GNP as most other industrial countries.

10. Automated production methods are attractive to a producer when
    a. they reduce cost.
    b. they replace workers.
    c. output is increased.
    d. wages are low.

11. In 1984, the female–male earnings ratio indicated that the earnings of single women relative to the earnings of single men were
    a. much higher than the relative earnings of women in other marital status groupings.
    b. about the same as the relative earnings of women in other marital status groupings.
    c. much less than the relative earnings of women in other marital status groupings.
    d. not directly comparable to the relative earnings of women in other marital status groupings.

12. (**I**) Entry restrictions are an important form of job discrimination. (**II**) Entry restrictions tend to concentrate women and minorities in low-paying, unrestricted jobs.
    a. Both I and II are true.
    b. I is true, II is false.
    c. I is false, II is true.
    d. Both I and II are false.

THE ECONOMIC WAY OF THINKING—MULTIPLE CHOICE

1. Use statements I and II to answer this question. (**I**) Differences in worker productivity are one major reason why individual earnings differ. (**II**) Even if all workers were identical, differences in the desirability of jobs would still cause earnings differentials.
   a. Both I and II are true.
   b. I is true, II is false.
   c. I is false, II is true.
   d. Both I and II are false.

2. When wage rates for a group of workers (teenagers, for example) are far above the equilibrium level, discrimination by employers on noneconomic grounds becomes
   a. more costly.
   b. more costly, but necessary.
   c. necessary and less costly.
   d. more costly and unnecessary.

3. Economic theory suggests that, relative to low wages with a draft, voluntary procurement of military personnel via higher wages would
   a. be more efficient than the draft, because the volunteer army would take into account opportunity cost.
   b. be inefficient, because persons with little comparative advantage in military production would volunteer.
   c. lead to higher total incomes of military personnel only if the demand were inelastic.
   d. lead to lower total incomes of military personnel only if the demand were elastic.

4. Suppose that the government passed a law that required that all government employees be paid the average wage rate in the private sector. Which of the following would be true?
   a. Output would be maximized.
   b. Costs would be maximized.
   c. Those individuals with higher skills (and thus more options) could be expected to leave government employment for higher-paying alternatives.
   d. There would be no change in the allocation of resources.

5. Which one of the following would be *least* likely to occur if Congress passed legislation exempting teenagers from the minimum wage?
    a. The training opportunities available to teenagers would improve.
    b. The white–black unemployment differential would increase.
    c. The rate of unemployment for teenagers would decline.
    d. The rate of labor force participation for black teenagers would increase.

6. After correcting for differences in age, education, marital status, language, and regional characteristics, the earnings of women are only about two-thirds as great as those of men. This large differential is due in part to
    a. discrimination against women in employment.
    b. work specialization within the family following traditional male–female patterns.
    c. both a and b.
    d. neither a nor b.

7. Which of the following most correctly states the relationship between machinery and the earnings of labor?
    a. Machines tend to reduce the demand for labor, thereby reducing the earnings rate of labor.
    b. Production of machinery creates jobs, thereby increasing the demand for (and wages of) labor.
    c. High productivity per man-hour is a necessary ingredient for the attainment of high real earnings, and adoption of labor-saving machinery enhances the ability of labor to attain such high productivity.
    d. Output and real earnings can always be increased whenever a machine can be substituted for a function previously performed by labor.

8. A salesman for a firm selling equipment to automate car washes would probably be happy to see the minimum wage law
    a. abolished.
    b. changed to exempt teenagers from the law.
    c. extended to cover all car-wash establishments (including weekend operations run by service clubs).
    d. changed so that car-wash establishments would not be covered by the law (but other businesses would be).

9. Economic theory suggests that the standard of living for American workers would rise if
    a. the minimum wage was doubled.
    b. automation was outlawed.
    c. a new law required all wage rates to double.
    d. technological progress continued.

10. If large numbers of young American men thought the life of a cowboy was great (despite the hardships), we would expect
    a. an increase in the wages of cowboys, to fit the image.
    b. a decrease in the wages of cowboys, since supply would be enlarged.
    c. no impact on wages, which are determined by supply and demand, not romantic notions.
    d. a decrease in the wages of cowboys, since demand would be reduced.

11. "One way to get higher labor productivity is to set higher wages. If bricklayers had to be paid $30 per hour next year, we could trust that virtually every bricklayer *working at that time* would be worth (have a marginal revenue product of) at least $30 per hour." This statement is

    a. true, and everyone would gain because of the higher productivity.
    b. true, although many of the current bricklayers would be unable to find employment at the $30 wage rate.
    c. false, since the marginal productivity of bricklayers could not rise so fast in one year.
    d. false, unless very rapid technological change occurred.

12. The effects of job discrimination in a given time period are

    a. not likely to carry over into the future.
    b. likely to carry over into the future, since human capital formation is often influenced.
    c. measured without consideration of past experience or discrimination.
    d. strictly dependent on employer actions at the time, not on what came earlier in the worker's career.

THE ECONOMIC WAY OF THINKING—DISCUSSION QUESTIONS

1. Suppose that a new invention halved the cost of making automobiles. Would *total* employment fall if today's demand for automobiles were inelastic? If it were elastic? Explain your answer. Don't forget the secondary effects and the role of time.

2. What are the major determinants of the elasticity of demand for a specific category (for example, physicists, craftsmen) of labor? Explain. Be specific. How does time affect the elasticity of demand for labor?

3. Substantial differences, sometimes up to 150 percent, in wage rates for essentially the same kind of labor (for example, semiskilled labor) prevail between different industries even in the same locality. Cite what you believe to be the basic causes for these interindustry wage differentials; indicate which kinds of industries are likely to be at the top and bottom of the wage scale.

4. In recent years, there has been considerable discussion of quotas—either explicit or implicit—as a method of eliminating employment discrimination. Discuss the pros and cons of such a policy.

5. If a firm were relatively nondiscriminating, how would you expect the representation and relative wages of minorities (or women) in the firm to compare with those in high-discriminating firms? Explain.

6. A recent issue of importance has been that of illegal immigration from one country to another. Analyze the impact of such illegal immigration on (a) the immigrants, (b) the new employers of the immigrants, (c) workers who remained in the home country of the immigrants, and (d) workers in the country to which the immigrants came. Given this analysis, attempt to develop a solution for the problem of illegal immigration.

PERSPECTIVES IN ECONOMICS

Against "Comparable Worth"
by Morris B. Abram

[Reprinted with permission from the *New York Times,* November 4, 1985.]

Both houses of Congress and a number of courts are grappling with the question of whether wages should be fixed on the basis of equal pay for work of comparable value to the employer—a proposed remedy for lower pay received by women. One can already see developing many complications and dangers built into the concept of "comparable worth."

These proposals would tie us up in a tangle of definitions that would reduce options for women and ultimately be a detriment to all of society. Comparable worth proposals do not attempt to equalize the wages of men and women doing the same job but to arbitrarily equate jobs that have entirely different market values.

What is the actual situation with regard to women's wages in this country? During the last Presidential campaign, Geraldine A. Ferraro frequently repeated that women are "paid 59 cents on the dollar for the same work as a man," implying a wage gap of 41 percent. This misleading statistic has been the basis for much well-meaning support of the proposals now before us.

But the 59 percent wage scale, with a 41 percent gap, comes from statistics for 1977; by 1983, that 41 percent gap had narrowed to 36 percent. This figure declines to 28 percent when the number of hours worked by women and men is taken into account, and then to 14 percent when other factors, including schooling and work experience, are considered.

The 14 percent gap, the real starting point for discussions of comparable worth, has not been adequately explained. Of course, part of it may be attributable to discrimination, but the Equal Pay Act of 1963 and the Civil Rights Act of 1964 already prohibit such practices. An alternative explanation could be that women may be willing to accept lower paying jobs that permit them to spend more time with their families.

More meaningful insights can be drawn from statistics of particular groups of employees. Among men and women between the ages of 20 and 24, for instance, the wage gap is only 10 percent. And for single men and women who have never been married, the gap is almost nonexistent— 2.4 percent to 4 percent.

One of the dangers of comparable worth is that it would create a new claim by certain advocacy groups on the right to legislate economic equality. These groups would have us adopt a system of permanent wage and salary controls, first in Federal employment and inevitably in private business. Under their plan, wages and salaries would be decreed by "experts" and bureaucrats, and deviations from their edicts would generate lawsuits in which the employer would bear the burden of proof that discrimination did not exist.

What's more, gender-based legislation is only the start. A bill introduced last July in the House brought race and ethnic qualifications into the wage formula as well. The latest proposals are likely to become a mechanism to give leverage to any subgroup of employees seeking a raise.

How would women fare in the proposed brave new world of comparable worth? Women would suffer a decline in the standard of living as does everyone in society when wages are inflated artificially. To maintain their previous standard, more women than at present would find work a necessity rather than an option. Even women in occupations targeted for wage raises would not benefit. For example, if secretarial wages were mandated to rise to a certain level, one could expect more businesses to opt for automation. The result would be fewer jobs for women and further narrowing of their options.

The attempt to write comparable worth into Federal laws marks a reversal of the civil rights revolution. Comparable worth moves from the assertion of civil and political equality, which we all support, to economic and social equality, which many of us do not support.

Guaranteed economic and social equality have never been part of the heritage of a free country because they ultimately impinge on freedom, by making government the arbiter of the rewards of human effort. This raises the old question of whether government should be dependent on the people or people on government.

Discussion

1. What exactly *is* comparable worth? Pick two occupations you know fairly well and describe how a comparable worth program would work in those occupations.

2. Abram admits that there is an unexplained gap of at least 14% between the earnings of male and female workers. How then could he be against legislation that would get rid of this discriminatory difference?

3. One of the hardest problems to solve when implementing a comparable worth program is choosing the jobs which have equivalent "worth." In particular, some jobs which are similar in terms of skills required have differences in terms of working conditions (such as more flexible hours). Are such jobs comparable or not? Explain.

24

Capital, Interest, and Profit

TRUE OR FALSE

T F

☑ ☑ 1. We must divert resources from the production of current consumption in order to expand the availability of capital goods. T

☐ ☑ 2. The two general categories of productive factors are physical capital and land. F

☑ ☑ 3. Physical capital can increase the productivity of individuals. T

☑ ☑ 4. Agricultural price support programs don't always work perfectly, but they are un-questionably effective at increasing farmers' incomes. F

☑ ☐ 5. The net present value of a payment to be received a year in the future can be ex-pressed as the receipts one year from now divided by one plus the interest rate. T

☑ ☐ 6. A higher rate of time preference implies a higher interest rate. T

☑ ☐ 7. If a governmental price control and acreage allotment program increases the price of raw tobacco above the market equilibrium level, the price of land with an acreage allotment to grow tobacco will rise. T

☑ ☐ 8. The real rate of interest rises when the rate of inflation accelerates. F

☑ ☐ 9. Risk usually influences the interest rate agreed to by business decision-makers. T

☑ ☐ 10. The pure interest component of a money rate of interest includes an adjustment factor for risk. F

☑ ☐ 11. Investment projects are more attractive when the interest rate is high than when it is low. F

☑ ☑ 12. Entrepreneurial decision-making usually involves choosing under conditions of un-certainty. T

PROBLEMS AND PROJECTS

Use the net present values in Exhibit 3, Chapter 24 of the text to work on problems 1–4.

1. Suppose that you have $1000. Broker A offers an opportunity that should pay $2000 after six years. After considering the expected rate of inflation and the risk involved, you determine that a 12 percent discount rate is appropriate. Broker B offers a different opportunity that will pay $1000 in five years and another $1000 in ten years. Since it is safer, an 8 percent discount rate is appropriate.
   a. What is the value to you, today, of broker A's option? Broker B's option?
   b. Suppose you learn that broker B's option is a bit more risky, and it, too should be evaluated with a 12 percent discount rate. Now what is it worth today?
   c. Having evaluated both options at 12 percent, you are advised that an extra 2 percent should be allowed as an annual inflation factor. If 12 percent was the initial appropriate rate (and the money payoff and timing remain the same), what interest rate is appropriate now that the expected rate of inflation has risen by 2 percent?

2. The owner of a small forest in Florida is raising trees as a cash crop. A forester friend tells him that certain silvicultural practices, costing $334 now, will yield an extra 10,000 board feet of timber when the forest is harvested in 30 years. Harvesting and other costs will not change significantly. What price of timber per board foot would be required for the silvicultural practices to be worthwhile if the appropriate discount rate is 12 percent?

3. How stable has the real rate of interest been? From the *Federal Reserve Bulletin*, or the *Economic Report of the President* (available in your library), find the money rate of interest (the short-term AAA corporate bond rate, for example) and the rate of inflation for 1930, 1935, 1940, . . . 1980, and the most recent year. Calculate the real rate of interest for each year by subtracting the rate of inflation from the money rate of interest.

4. Reconstruct Exhibit 4 from Chapter 24 of the text by using $14,000 per year as the expected income, and 12 percent as the discount rate. What is the net present value? (*Hint:* Be sure to round the discounted value to three digits, as the text does, for your answers to check exactly.)

5. You have an opportunity to attend a six-month course in computer programming. The course meets every afternoon and would require that you work at your present job only half-time, in the mornings. Your employer has agreed to your half-time absence, but you must accept only half-time pay for the duration of the course, which would reduce your take-home pay by $1,250 per month. You have personal savings which would comfortably cover the $6,000 cost of the course itself. In discussions with your present employer, you have decided that if you acquire the skills offered by the course, it will raise your take-home pay by $2,000 per year for the next ten years until you retire. If the appropriate discount rate is 8 percent, should you make this investment in your "human capital"?

6. Refer to Chapter 19, "Problems and Projects," question 3e of this Coursebook. Again supposing that the university competitively auctions the food service rights to the highest bidder, what is the maximum amount a firm would pay for these property rights in perpetuity (that is, forever, or until the firm decides to sell the rights to another firm) if the appropriate interest rate (what the firm could earn on alternative investments) is 10 percent? [*Hint:* see the "Perspective on Agricultural Price Supports" and footnote 3 in Chapter 24 of your text.]

LEARNING THE MECHANICS—MULTIPLE CHOICE

1. The development and construction of machines that enhance our ability to produce goods and services in the future require
    a. the owners of these capital assets to borrow.
    b. the owners of these capital assets to reduce the growth rate of their consumption.
    c. that current consumption be sacrificed.
    d. that future consumption be sacrificed.

2. If the rate of time preference increased, we would expect
    a. the interest rate to fall.
    b. more capital investment.
    c. less capital investment.   *more borrowing*
    d. more *future* consumption.

3. A higher rate of inflation mainly tends to   *↑ Inflation*
    a. raise the real rate of interest.   *↑ money Rate of Interes*
    b. reduce the real rate of interest.
    c. raise the money rate of interest.
    d. lower the money rate of interest.

4. The net present value of $100, delivered one year from now, would
    a. rise, if inflation rose.
    b. fall, if the money rate of interest fell.
    c. rise, if the money rate of interest rose.
    d. fall, if the money rate of interest rose.

5. If the interest rate were 6 percent, the net present value of $100 to be received one year from now would be
    a. $94.34. $\dfrac{100}{1+.06}$
    b. $93.04.
    c. $100.00.
    d. $106.00

6. The pure interest yield, a component of the cost of an investment project
    a. is positively related to the risk of undertaking the project.
    b. is negatively related to the risk of undertaking the project.
    c. is unaffected by the riskiness of the project.
    d. is irrelevant to whether the project will be undertaken.

7. The net present value of $100 received one year from now will
    a. increase with the interest rate.
    b. be greater than $100 as long as the interest rate is positive.
    c. be greater than the net present value of $100 to be received two years from now.
    d. be unaffected by the money rate of interest.

8. Use statements I and II to answer this question. (**I**) Discounting procedures apply to decisions to invest in physical capital, but are not relevant to human capital investment decisions. (**II**) Nonmonetary considerations are usually more important in human capital investment decisions than in nonhuman capital investment decisions.
    a. I is true, II is false.
    b. I is false, II is true.
    c. Both I and II are true.
    d. Both I and II are false.

9.   Monopoly profit that stems from a patent
     a.   will quickly be eliminated by competitive imitators.
     b.   can never be reduced by close (but slightly different) imitations.
     c.   becomes capitalized into the value of the patent, which could then be sold.
     d.   has no impact on resource allocation, but only makes the patent owner wealthy, in a dynamic economy.

10. Pure interest is the payment to
     a.   an investor bearing little or no risk.
     b.   business entrepreneurs.
     c.   owners of capital items.
     d.   people who clip coupons, but contribute nothing to production.

11. According to Joseph Schumpeter, what is the major source of economic growth within the framework of a capitalist economy?
     a.   Pure competition
     b.   Innovative behavior by entrepreneurs
     c.   Financial capital provided by bond holders
     d.   Consumer expenditure

THE ECONOMIC WAY OF THINKING—MULTIPLE CHOICE

1.   If an era of new inventions began next year, with many and new promising investment opportunities suddenly appearing, we would expect
     a.   a lower interest rate as many people saved more.
     b.   a higher interest rate as the demand for loanable funds increased, along with investment.
     c.   more investment, but no change in the interest rate.
     d.   a higher interest rate with no change in investment.

2.   In an economy without money, an interest rate
     a.   would be meaningless.
     b.   could not exist.
     c.   would simply be the price of earlier availability.
     d.   would always be zero.

3.   For an individual, the rate of time preference
     a.   indicates irrational decisions.
     b.   is greater whenever inflation is greater.
     c.   is a subjective valuation.
     d.   could never be negative, whatever the circumstances.

4.   Economic analysis indicates that if usury laws held the interest rate below the equilibrium level
     a.   saving would increase.
     b.   borrowers would demand less from the loanable funds market.
     c.   anyone who wanted to borrow would be happy with the lower interest rates.
     d.   funds must be rationed to borrowers by some means other than price (the interest rate).

5.   If inflation increased during a year, the dollar price of existing corporate bonds would
     a.   rise because during times of inflation it takes more dollars to buy an asset.
     b.   rise because the bond is really a loan, and loans rise in value with inflation.
     c.   fall because each bond promises a fixed return, which falls in value as the price level rises.
     d.   fall because the risk element (the likelihood of not receiving payment) is roughly proportional to inflation.

6. In the West, a great many people want to be cattle ranchers. Relatively few seem to aspire to raise hogs or sheep. Thus, if we examined the financial records of ranchers raising cattle, we would expect to find that (relative to hog and sheep ranches)
   a. cattle ranches would show a higher rate of return.
   b. cattle ranches would show a lower rate of return.
   c. there would be no difference in the rates of return.
   d. the preference for cattle ranching would have no effect on the financial rate of return.

7. We would expect most risky investment ventures to be financed by owners rather than by bankers lending money because
   a. bankers are always cautious.
   b. bankers want interest payments, not profits.
   c. with a bank loan, the bank might lose all it puts in, but can never get more than the agreed-upon principal and interest.
   d. most entrepreneurs think bank interest rates are too high.

8. Theresa spends $1000 on General Motors stock and $1000 on General Motors bonds. However, inflation develops unexpectedly, and prices rise steadily at a rate 5 percent faster than what was previously anticipated. GM product prices rise with inflation, and its sales are unaffected. Theresa will probably find that the
   a. real value of her bonds rises, whereas the real value of her stocks falls.
   b. real values of her bonds and stocks fall equally.
   c. real values of her bonds and stocks rise equally.
   d. real value of her bonds falls *relative* to the value of her stocks.

9. A company that mines coal on federally owned land is about to be told by the federal government that, beginning in five years, it must abandon the mine it expected to operate for another 20 years. This will mean a reduction in accounting profits beginning in five years. If the announcement of this ruling was made tomorrow, the price of the firm's stock would
   a. fall in about five years, just before the reduction in accounting profit was to begin.
   b. fall gradually, as the reduction in the firm's accounting profit drew near.
   c. fall immediately by the full amount of the discounted value of the decrease in future profit.
   d. fall immediately, since some investors would panic irrationally, whereas smart investors would put the same value on the stock as before, up to the time of the decline in accounting profit.

10. Use statements I and II when answering this question. (**I**) When the government restricts the number of acres that farmers can utilize to raise a crop such as wheat, the supply of the product will decline, making it possible for farmers to receive a higher price for the product. (**II**) If a price support and acre restriction program increases the price of a farm product, persons purchasing farm land with an acreage allotment for that product will be able to make a higher rate of return on their investment than would be true in the absence of the government program.
    a. I is true, II is false.
    b. I is false, II is true.
    c. Both I and II are true.
    d. Both I and II are false.

11. Which of these are the major sources of economic profit?
    a. Uncertainty, entrepreneurial alertness, and barriers to entry
    b. Competition, perfect information, and elasticity of market demand
    c. Size of firm, economies to scale, and freedom from unionism
    d. Externalities, inflation, and size of firm

222   24/CAPITAL, INTEREST, AND PROFIT

THE ECONOMIC WAY OF THINKING—DISCUSSION QUESTIONS

1. Assume that Congress is debating two plans to increase the profitability of wildcat oil-drilling firms. Those in Congress agree that more profits in drilling would lead to more drilling. Plan A would give a tax break on current drilling activities, so that profits on current drilling operations would rise by $10 billion—providing that much extra capital for future investment. Plan B would give tax breaks on *future* discoveries. The tax breaks derived from plan B would be worth $3.3 billion per year for the next three years to the same wildcat drillers. Which plan is likely to generate more oil production? (*Hint:* Remember the effects of marginal price changes *and* the discount rate.)

2. What uncertainty is involved in the purchase of a U.S. government bond, assuming *no* risk or default in bond payments? It is possible to realize economic profit from the purchase and sale of these bonds? If so, how?

3. What are the two main reasons for a positive interest rate, even when neither risk nor inflation is present? From the self-interested viewpoint of a future generation, is *either* reason a good one to use in rationing loanable funds among existing investment opportunities? Explain.

4. Why would a group of investors be willing to pay a higher interest rate on borrowed funds when they believe that inflation will be higher during the course of their investment project? Would the same be true if the products from their project were bought on an already contracted basis at a price *not* influenced by the added inflation?

5. "When a firm's total costs are less than its sales, the firm has increased the value of the resources it has used. Such firms will be rewarded with profits. In contrast, losses indicate that the resources used to produce a good were more valuable than the good that was produced. Profits are evidence of the wise utilization of resources, whereas losses are indicative of waste and inefficiency." Use economic analysis to defend or criticize this view.

25

Labor Unions and Collective Bargaining

TRUE OR FALSE

T F

☐ ☐ 1. Union membership as a percentage of the labor force has steadily increased since 1960.

☐ ☐ 2. Approximately one-half of all workers in the United States belong to a labor union.

☐ ☐ 3. A union shop labor contract requires all workers to join a union after a specified length of employment.

☐ ☐ 4. Right-to-work laws require all union–management contracts to contain a union shop provision.

☐ ☐ 5. In recent years, approximately 97 percent of all collective bargaining contracts have been signed without a work stoppage.

☐ ☐ 6. Each year, approximately 4 percent of the total work time in the United States is lost because of strikes.

☐ ☐ 7. The amount of work time lost because of strikes has steadily increased since World War II.

☐ ☐ 8. Strikes involving public employees and community services often result in inconvenience and reductions in output in other sectors of the economy.

☐ ☐ 9. The greater the ability of management to substitute machines and nonunion labor for union labor, the weaker the bargaining power of a union.

☐ ☐ 10. A monopsony is to a monopoly as a seller is to a buyer.

☐ ☐ 11. The evidence from other countries indicates that unions raise the wages of workers, including nonunion workers.

☐ ☐ 12. Failure to organize all of the firms in an industry does not greatly limit the ability of a union to attain large wage gains from the individual firms of the industry that are unionized.

☐ ☐ 13. Most unions have been able to increase the wages of their members by at least 40 percent.

☐ ☐ 14. The share of national income going to labor has increased steadily as more and more workers have joined unions.

PROBLEMS AND PROJECTS

Exhibit I

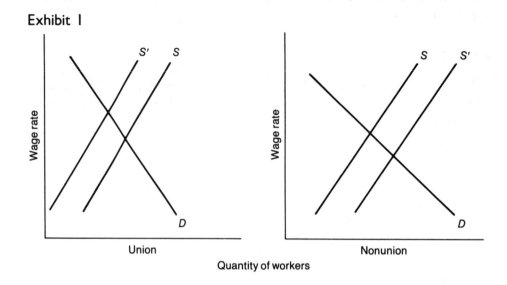

1. "The problem with unions is that they bring higher wage rates for workers and thus force all employers to raise wages in order to compete in the labor market." Refute this statement by explaining the phenomenon described by the supply-and-demand conditions in Exhibit 1.

Exhibit 2

Quantity of labor demanded	Wage rate	Quantity of labor supplied
100	$10	1000
300	9	900
500	8	800
700	7	700
900	6	600

2. Exhibit 2 is a demand-and-supply schedule for the competitive engineering labor market. Suppose that you are the president of the American Machines Corporation, and you must hire a group of engineers for your firm.
   a. What wage rate will you offer the hired engineers?
   b. Assume the UEU, the United Engineers Union, is formed, reducing the quantity supplied of engineers at every wage rate by 300 because of increased qualifications in this discipline. What will be the new wage rate?
   c. What effect will the union have on employment and total incomes of the unionized engineers?
   d. Calculate the elasticity of demand for engineers between these two equilibrium points.

3. International Manufacturing, Incorporated (IMI) is a monopsonistic employer of labor. Exhibit 3 shows the quantity of labor IMI demands at each wage and the supply curve that IMI faces in its hiring of labor.

Exhibit 3

Labor demanded (hundreds of hours)	Hourly wage (dollars)	Labor supplied (hundreds of hours)	Total labor cost (dollars)	Marginal labor cost (dollars)
450	$16	100	$1600	
				$20
400	18	200	3600	
				____
350	20	300	____	
				____
300	22	400	____	
				____
250	24	500	____	
				____
200	26	600	____	

a. Fill in the missing information in the table.
b. On a piece of graph paper plot IMI's labor demand curve, labor supply curve and marginal labor cost curve. (Be sure to plot values for marginal labor cost at the appropriate *midpoints* of the quantities.)
c. What quantity of labor will IMI hire? What wage will it pay?
d. Suppose that IMI workers form a union and establish a wage floor of $22 per hour. Will this new (and higher) wage result in more or less employment at IMI? Exactly how many hours of labor will IMI employ at this minimum wage?

LEARNING THE MECHANICS—MULTIPLE CHOICE

1. Which of the following factors will substantially *improve* the ability of a union to raise the wages of its workers?
   a. A tax increase on firms that employ the union labor
   b. An inelastic demand for the product produced by union labor
   c. A reduction in tariffs on the type of products the union workers produce
   d. Passage of a right-to-work law in the state where the union operates

2. Wages of unionized workers are usually estimated to be how much higher than they would have been under nonunion conditions?
   a. 90–110 percent
   b. 50–70 percent
   c. 10–25 percent
   d. 40–45 percent

3. A monopsony is
   a. another word for a monopoly.
   b. the existence of a single buyer in a market.
   c. the existence of several sellers in a market.
   d. the existence of a single seller in a market.

4. If a craft union was able to reduce the supply of workers into the craft, it would most likely
    not
    a.   increase wages.
    b.   reduce employment.
    c.   increase the wages of all workers in the economy.
    d.   increase wages without the need for hard bargaining.

5. Unions are not likely to obtain large wage increases for their workers when
    a.   the demand for the product is inelastic.
    b.   the supply of substitute inputs is highly inelastic.
    c.   the demand for the product the workers produce is elastic, and machines can readily be
         substituted for labor.
    d.   the demand for the product is rapidly increasing.

6. "Marginal factor cost is to a monopsonist as marginal revenue is to a monopolist." Which
    of the following is true?
    a.   The quotation is inherently incorrect.
    b.   The quotation is basically correct.
    c.   The quotation is partially correct, but the comparison should be to marginal revenue for
         a perfectly competitive firm.
    d.   The quotation is partially correct, but the comparison should be to average revenue for
         a monopolist.

7. The number of workers covered by collective bargaining contracts negotiated in any one year
    in the United States is
    a.   3-4 million.
    b.   6-9 million.
    c.   10-12 million.
    d.   22-24 million.

8. A union shop provision means that a worker
    a.   cannot be employed until he has joined the union.
    b.   must agree when he is hired never to join a union.
    c.   must join the union within a specified length of time after he is hired.
    d.   has the freedom to join the union at any time, should he wish to do so.

9. The major source of work stoppages has been
    a.   the strike.
    b.   the lockout.
    c.   monopsony power.
    d.   the injunction.

10. In winning concessions from employers, a labor union has as its most important tool
    a.   the strike.
    b.   the lockout.
    c.   monopsony power.
    d.   the injunction.

11. Use statements I and II to answer this question. (**I**) During the past 20 years, the number of man-hours of work time lost as a result of strikes has been less than three-tenths of 1 percent of the total—far less than the work time lost due to absenteeism. (**II**) A strike often imposes substantial costs on secondary parties (wholesalers, consumers, and other manufacturers, for example) who are not involved in the labor–management collective bargaining.
    a. I is true, II is false.
    b. I is false, II is true.
    c. Both I and II are true.
    d. Both I and II are false.

12. The data on the distribution of income among individuals and families in the United States
    a. indicate that the power of labor unions is the major determinant of income inequality.
    b. indicate that unions have no impact on the incomes of members.
    c. indicate that substantial inequality in annual income emanates from differences in education, age, hours worked, and family size.
    d. indicate that differences in annual income emanating from ownership of capital assets is the major source of economic inequality.

THE ECONOMIC WAY OF THINKING—MULTIPLE CHOICE

1. As the baseball season approaches, the likelihood of a player strike would
    a. give neither party much incentive to bargain seriously.
    b. give only management incentive to bargain seriously.
    c. give only players incentive to bargain seriously.
    d. give both players and management incentive to bargain seriously.

2. Suppose that during a ten-year period the number of coal miners declined from 400,000 to 300,000. The hourly wages of the mine workers doubled during this same period because of the strength of the United Mine Workers. Which of the following set of economic factors is most consistent with the wage and employment data of the mining industry?
    a. The supply of miners was highly inelastic, and therefore a small reduction in the demand for mining labor led to a small reduction in employment.
    b. Even though the demand for mining labor was inelastic, as wages increased, the number of miners employed declined significantly.
    c. While the supply of miners was increasing, the demand was increasing more rapidly, leading to higher wages.
    d. The demand for mining labor was elastic, and the supply of miners was reduced, leading to higher wages.

3. Over the last four decades, the share of national income going to labor, including self-employed workers, has
    a. remained nearly constant at slightly more than 80 percent of national income.
    b. fluctuated between 50 and 75 percent of total national income.
    c. increased, as union members became a larger percent of the total work force.
    d. decreased from nearly 75 percent to its current level, approximately 50 percent of national income.

4. The empirical evidence strongly suggests that unions have increased
   a. wages of industrial workers more than those of craft employees.
   b. the share of national income going to labor by 25 percent.
   c. the average wage of union members, but have had little impact on the share of income going to labor.
   d. the wages of most union members by at least 35 percent.

5. Regarding union strength, the "importance of being unimportant" refers to
   a. a lack of political clout on the part of the union.
   b. the union's having organized only a small share of workers in its trade.
   c. the union's wage bill being small, compared to the costs the management would incur if operations were shut down because of a strike.
   d. the union leadership's desire to avoid headlines.

6. As a result of union strength, nonunion workers might suffer if
   a. inflation were an indirect result of the attempts of macroplanners to offset union wage increases.
   b. supply restrictions in unionized areas increased the supply of workers in nonunion markets, causing nonunion wage rates to decline.
   c. union wage increases in competitive industries were passed on to consumers in the form of higher prices.
   d. All of the above are likely to harm nonunion workers.

7. (I) Unions have often used their political clout to effect legislation that increases the demand for their services. (II) A union and the employer with whom it bargains are frequently political enemies when tariffs are discussed in Congress.
   a. I and II are true.
   b. I is true, II is false.
   c. I is false, II is true.
   d. I and II are false.

8. Because the demand for a broadly defined product line (automobiles, for example) is less elastic than the demand for a more narrow product category (Fords, for example), a union will be better able to raise wages without large unemployment effects when
   a. it has organized an entire industry, rather than only one firm.
   b. it organizes only a few firms in each industry.
   c. it bargains with all firms in a narrow product line, but ignores the rest of the industry.
   d. only a small part of the industry that makes the broadly defined product is unionized.

9. By raising wages, unions typically have
   a. increased total productivity, which must rise proportionally with the wage rate.
   b. encouraged employers to find a substitute for the union labor.
   c. raised the wages of nonunion workers.
   d. caused much of the inflation experienced in the United States.

10. (I) "On the average, unions have been able to obtain a high level of pay for their members."
    (II) "Unions are widely recognized for their role in giving workers on-the-job 'civil rights,' a system of industrial jurisprudence which protects workers from arbitrary treatment by employers."
    a. I and II are true.
    b. I is true, II is false.
    c. I is false, II is true.
    d. I and II are false.

11. The addition of a player's union to the originally monopsonistic baseball industry is likely to
    a. decrease the number of players hired.
    b. increase the average wage of the players.
    c. decrease the average wage of the players but allow more players to be hired.
    d. have little impact on the average wage of the players but allow more players to be hired.

12. According to recent figures, the percentage of nonfarm-working time lost due to strikes is the lowest it has been in the last forty years. This decrease can be attributed in part to the fact that
    a. union membership as a proportion of nonfarm employment has been increasing at only approximately 1% a year.
    b. unions have increased the wages of all workers, both union and nonunion, higher than they would have been otherwise, so strikes are less necessary.
    c. both a and b.
    d. neither a nor b.

THE ECONOMIC WAY OF THINKING—DISCUSSION QUESTIONS

1. "The right to strike is a basic right of all workers. Without the strike unions would be powerless against the industrial interests in bargaining for the employee." Do you agree? Why or why not?

2. "The threat of a strike is a form of economic blackmail. The right to strike grants unions the power to collect bribes, for failing to halt a perfectly legitimate economic function—the productive process." Do you agree or disagree? Explain.

3. "The wages of union workers are higher than the wages of nonunion workers." Scientifically speaking, what conclusion do you draw from this statement about the ability of unions to
   a. raise the wage rates of union members?
   b. organize low-wage employees?
   c. raise the wages of all employees?
   Explain your answer in each case.

4. Business decision-makers can sometimes argue that they cannot make a profit because of the excessive wage demands of unions. Suppose that a strong union in a highly competitive industry obtains for its members a 15 percent increase in wages.
   a. Will the higher wage rates reduce the industry's rate of profit in the short run? In the long run?
   b. Who will actually shoulder the burden of the higher wage rates?

5. Henry Smith belongs to the textile workers' union. Approximately two-thirds of Henry's fellow workers at the plant belong to the union. Fewer than half of all textile mills are unionized. Evaluate the ability of Henry's union to raise his wages. Explain.

6. John Harrison is a unionized tool- and diemaker. All the employees at the plant where John works must belong to the union as a condition of permanent employment. In order to become a tool- and diemaker, one must be admitted to the union's apprenticeship program, and serve for three years. Evaluate the ability of John's union to raise wages. Explain.

7. ''Every union knows that an airline is more vulnerable to strikes than most other businesses. Airlines have high fixed costs regardless of whether their planes are flying. They can neither stockpile seats during a strike nor sell from inventory afterward. Strike losses cannot be recovered. The strong impulse is to avoid a strike, even if that means settling on an unsatisfactory basis.'' [From an airline newsletter.]

    a. Do you think the airline industry is particularly vulnerable to union demands? Why or why not?

    b. If the airlines are vulnerable, who would pay for an ''unsatisfactory'' labor settlement in the short run? In the long run? Explain.

26

Inequality, Income Mobility, and the Battle Against Poverty

TRUE OR FALSE

T F

☐ ☐ 1. Differences in hours worked are an important source of income inequality among households in the United States.

☐ ☐ 2. Official poverty figures indicate that more than 11 percent of U.S. families lived in poverty in 1984.

☐ ☐ 3. The wealthiest 5 percent of all income recipients in the United States receive approximately 40 percent of all income.

☐ ☐ 4. Income is distributed more unequally in the United States than in most other countries in the world.

☐ ☐ 5. In general, income is distributed more equally in Sweden and England than in the United States.

☐ ☐ 6. One way to help the social security system solve its future financial problems would be to decrease the normal eligibility age from 65 to 62.

☐ ☐ 7. Households headed by females are overrepresented among the poor.

☐ ☐ 8. Of all children born to parents in the top fifth of the income distribution, more than three-fourths maintain that high-income status.

☐ ☐ 9. U.S. income inequality has remained virtually unchanged during the last several decades.

☐ ☐ 10. Official poverty figures fail to recognize transfers in kind.

☐ ☐ 11. In most cases, societal choice that will maximize efficiency will also maximize equity.

PROBLEMS AND PROJECTS

1. Susan Smith is an orthodontist. Jane Jones is a part-time clerk in a small store, where she earns $3.50 per hour. Jane would like Dr. Smith to straighten the teeth of Brenda Jones, Jane's daughter. Jane is willing to work an extra part-time job (at the same pay) to meet this expense,

even though it is not a medical necessity. Dr. Smith would be willing to take on this extra work if she were paid $700.

a.   In the absence of taxes, how many hours does Jane have to work in order to pay for her daughter's treatment?

b.   If Dr. Smith was in the 50 percent tax bracket, and Jane received transfer payments (for example, food stamps, housing subsidies, AFDC) that put her in the 65 percent *implicit* tax bracket (see Exhibit 11 in Chapter 26 of the text), how many hours must Jane work to enable Dr. Smith to earn the same $700 in exchange for the treatment? (*Hint:* Hours $\times$ $3.50 $\times$ 0.35 $\times$ 0.5 = $700.)

c.   If Dr. Smith paid no taxes, but Jane was in the 65 percent implicit tax bracket, how many hours must Jane work to earn the $700?

d.   If Dr. Smith paid 70 percent of her income in taxes, and Jane paid none at all, how many hours would Jane have to work for Dr. Smith to take home $700?

e.   Considering your answer to part d, would you say that high taxes on productive, highly-paid people hurt low-income people?

f.   Considering your answer to part c, would you say that taxes on productive lower-paid people hurt high-income recipients?

g.   Would Jane (and Brenda) Jones be better off without the transfer program that puts Jane in the implicit 65 percent tax bracket? Why?

2.   Suppose that the government passed a negative income tax that involved a $4000 government subsidy to a family of four if zero income was earned. Assume a 50 percent marginal tax rate on earned income; that is, for every $1000 earned, the subsidy is reduced by 50 percent of the $1000. Using this NIT plan, fill in the columns labeled government subsidy and total income in Exhibit 1. Do you think this is a good plan for achieving a more equal income distribution? Why or why not?

Exhibit 1

Earned income	Government subsidy	Total income
$ 0	$4000	_____
2000	_____	_____
3000	_____	_____
4000	_____	_____
5000	_____	_____
6000	_____	_____
7000	_____	_____
8000	_____	_____

3.   Robert Reckman is currently unemployed and qualifies for unemployment compensation of $138.00 per week. He has been offered a new job paying $200.00 per week, subject to income taxes of 33 percent and social security taxes of 7 percent.

a.   From society's point of view, is it desirable that Reckman accept the job? Why?

b.   Is it to Reckman's financial advantage to accept the job? Why?

c.   Calculate Reckman's marginal tax rate (including both explicit and implicit taxes) if he accepted the job.

d.   If Reckman's unemployment benefits had been subject to an income tax of 20 percent, would it have been in his financial interest to accept the job? Why?

LEARNING THE MECHANICS—MULTIPLE CHOICE

1. As of 1983, the poorest 20 percent of all families received what percentage of the total income?
   a. Approximately 2 percent
   b. Approximately 5 percent
   c. Between 11 and 12 percent
   d. Between 18 and 20 percent

2. The distribution of income in which of the following countries is more equal than that of the United States?
   a. India
   b. Japan
   c. Brazil
   d. Australia

3. Under the negative income tax concept, an additional dollar of earnings would cause the disposable income of
   a. a high-income taxpayer to increase by an additional dollar.
   b. a low-income recipient to increase by more than a dollar.
   c. a low-income recipient to increase, but by less than a dollar.
   d. a high-income taxpayer to decrease by some positive tax, and that of a low-income recipient to remain unchanged.

4. From 1968 to 1984, the official poverty rate for *nonelderly* families
   a. has been falling steadily.
   b. has been rising steadily.
   c. has remained virtually unchanged.
   d. fell steadily until President Reagan took office.

5. In the last 30 years or so, it appears that family incomes have
   a. become less equal.
   b. become more equal.
   c. maintained the same level of inequality.
   d. declined substantially.

6. Compared to high-income families, low-income families tend to have
   a. fewer workers.
   b. more workers.
   c. fewer youthful or retired members.
   d. about the same level of education.

7. Which of the following is false about data on the inequality of annual family (or household) incomes?
   a. The degree of inequality is reduced when transfers and taxes are considered.
   b. The inequality in annual income data actually understates the degree of inequality in lifetime income.
   c. Differences in age and family characteristics contribute to the degree of inequality.
   d. The difference between the after-tax and transfer income per hour worked between high- and low-income recipients is much smaller than the difference in annual income.

8. The official definition of poverty in the United States does not account for
   a. social security income.
   b. cash income transfers.
   c. income earned by workers other than the head of the household.
   d. in-kind transfers.

9. The negative income tax, a scheme that would have the Internal Revenue Service pay money directly to individuals with low incomes, is closely identified with
   a. Milton Friedman.
   b. Adam Smith.
   c. Arthur Okun.
   d. Alan Blinder.

10. By the year 2025, when some of you may be retiring, it is estimated that the number of workers per social security beneficiary will be
    a. ten.
    b. five.
    c. four.
    d. two.

11. A detailed University of Michigan study followed families for seven years and attempted to measure income mobility by noting how the incomes of those families changed during that time period. The study found that the percentage of the lowest fifth in terms of income who moved to the highest fifth in seven years was
    a. 20%.
    b. 6%.
    c. 2%.
    d. 0%.

THE ECONOMIC WAY OF THINKING—MULTIPLE CHOICE

1. In a market system, each individual chooses how to employ his own resources. One who chooses not to employ his resources is held responsible by
   a. the high prices of goods.
   b. laws against vagrancy.
   c. welfare case workers.
   d. the opportunity cost of leisure.

2. (I) High implicit marginal tax rates reduce the incentive of the poor to earn. (II) The transfer program unwittingly encourages activities that lead to poverty.
   a. Both I and II are true.
   b. Both I and II are false.
   c. I is true, II is false.
   d. II is true, I is false.

3. With a few exceptions, it is generally true in most countries that the share of income going to the wealthiest people is greater in
    a. more developed countries.
    b. less developed countries.
    c. countries with a homogeneous population.
    d. industrialized countries.

4. Even if lifetime incomes were equal, there still might be substantial inequality in annual income data because
    a. wage rates might differ substantially.
    b. some might have inherited their wealth.
    c. some might have retired, while others are prime-age earners.
    d. educational levels might differ substantially.

5. The poverty threshold income level is calculated and adjusted in such a way that, for a given family, it would rise 10 percent in one year if
    a. the family's income rose 10 percent.
    b. the family's income fell 10 percent.
    c. the price of all consumer items rose 10 percent.
    d. national income rose 10 percent.

6. Of all poverty families, approximately one-half are headed by
    a. a female.
    b. a female who does not work.
    c. a male who does not work.
    d. a male working full time.

7. From 1960 to 1980, social welfare payments in the United States
    a. rose slightly as a percentage of personal income.
    b. fell slightly as a percentage of personal income.
    c. stayed remarkably constant as a percentage of personal income.
    d. more than doubled as a percentage of personal income.

8. The advantages of a negative income tax system include which of the following?
    a. Som of the degradation and despair associated with our current transfer system would be avoided.
    b. The costs of our redistribution system would almost surely fall.
    c. An individual would never have an implicit marginal tax rate greater than 100%.
    d. All of the above.

9. (I) In 1984, two-thirds of all poor people were white. (II) In 1984, blacks and persons of Hispanic origin were overrepresented in the poverty population.
    a. Both I and II are true.
    b. I is true, II is false.
    c. I is false, II is true.
    d. Both I and II are false.

10. **(I)** Our tax transfer system frequently adds thousands of dollars to the income of poor families, in the form of cash as well as in-kind transfers. **(II)** A poor family receiving welfare payments and in-kind benefits will generally be able to take home a larger share of a $1000-per-year increase in its earnings than would a family earning $20,000 per year and receiving no transfers.
    a. I and II are true.
    b. I is true, II is false.
    c. I is false, II is true.
    d. I and II are false.

11. Imagine two cities, Engelgrad and Legreeville, that have identical average annual incomes. In the city of Engelgrad, the poorest families one year almost always end up as the richest families the next year and become middle-income families the year after that. In the city of Legreeville, however, poor remain poor and rich remain rich. Which of the following is true about the two cities?
    a. The distribution of income in any given year is more equitable in Engelgrad than it is in Legreeville.
    b. The distribution of income in any given year is more equitable in Legreeville than it is in Engelgrad.
    c. The dynamic distribution of income over time is more equitable in Engelgrad than it is in Legreeville.
    d. The dynamic distribution of income over time is more equitable in Legreeville than it is in Engelgrad.

THE ECONOMIC WAY OF THINKING—DISCUSSION QUESTIONS

1. "Income inequality in the United States has been increasing over the last three or four decades." True, false, or uncertain? Explain.

2. Indicate why variations in the annual income of individuals may be a misleading indicator of inequality in their economic standard of living. What are some of the problems with annual income data at a given time as a measure of one's economic well-being? Explain.

3. Do you think the United States could eliminate poverty? What policy would you recommend to accomplish this objective? How much would your program cost? Would it have undesirable secondary effects? Explain.

4. Poverty is not a numbers game; however, what about the human side of an unequal income distribution? How long can we ignore the suffering poverty causes? What are the external costs to society of having about fifteen percent of the population living in poverty? What are the socially negative side-effects of poverty?

5. Many economists, including Marxists, suggest that people born into low-income families in market economies have little chance to escape their low-income positions, whereas those born to rich parents will remain wealthy. What empirical evidence can you cite to support, modify, or reject this view?

6. How does income distribution in the United States compare with that of other developed nations? Of less developed nations?

7. Do you think the official poverty statistics in the United States are misleading? Is so, in what ways? What impact on social welfare policy would you expect as a result?

8. "All this worry about marginal tax rates is silly. Anyone who thinks a poor person will remain poor just to collect welfare payments has never had to live on those meager payments." Comment.

9. What are the characteristics of a fair distribution of income? Left to itself, will a free-market economy result in a socially optimal distribution of income? Why or why not? If your answer is no, what can be done to make the income distribution of a free-market economy fairer?

PERSPECTIVES IN ECONOMICS

Why the "Income Distribution" is so Misleading
by Mark Lilla

[Reprinted with permission from *The Public Interest,* Fall 1984, pp. 62–67, abridged.]

Among social scientists, the yearly distribution of money income is one of the most frequently used measures of economic and social well-being. Whether expressed graphically (as a bell-shaped curve), in terms of averages (a certain percentage of the population receives less than half of median income), or in percentiles (people in the top X percent receive over Y percent of national income), this distribution is assumed to tell us a great deal about our social and economic reality.

But what is this reality? Frequently, the income distribution is taken to reflect something about the extent of "relative poverty." Even though, in the United States at least, we have rather complicated needs indices that are official poverty measures, many social scientists (and others) believe that one's relative position in the income distribution will make one feel and act poor, quite apart from objective needs. The income distribution is also taken to be our best indicator of the degree of economic inequality, which may be measured in a rough manner or with more sophisticated calculations such as the "Gini coefficient." Some go so far as to make this straightforward tautology: Economic inequality simply *is* an unequal distribution of income. Finally, underlying the concerns over both poverty and income inequality is the belief that income distribution is a matter of basic social justice, which may be measured, or at least approximated, with statistics. Even philosophy professors have come to address the original philosophical question—"What is justice?"—in terms of the social sciences, asking, "What is a just distribution of income?" and, "Is the distribution of income in the U.S.—or the West, or the world—becoming more or less just?"

Yet social scientists who make it their business to study the workings of the economy have understood for some time that the *idea* of "the income distribution" presupposed by these debates is somewhat problematic. To begin, all income that enhances economic well-being is not captured in the official income statistics. Net income, which would factor in government taxes and benefits (both money and in-kind), is undoubtedly a better measure, but is not always easy to calculate. Also missing is the implicit, "nonpecuniary" income produced within the family household; for example, a housewife's work in the home is not included, but if she works outside the home it is—even if she then must hire someone to fill her former "jobs" of housekeeper or babysitter. (In Third World counties much income is of this implicit kind, rendering official income statistics virtually worthless.) Studies that attempt to determine the value of this implicit income and then compute *real* net income are highly speculative, though they probably do give a "truer" measure of income.

A stickier problem is measuring life-cycle earnings. Since an individual's lifetime earnings typically follow an up-and-down pattern—low while a young adult, highest just before retirement, and then a leveling or reduction— there always will be a "natural level" of income inequality at any one time, if only because of the age distribution. Ideally, one would want to compute each individual's earnings in each year—discounted and adjusted for inflation— and then over an entire lifetime before comparing. Such a research project would be very expensive and difficult, so social scientists either have had to use special samples that make generalization difficult, or they have had to rely on the questionable econometric technique of "controlling" a cross-sectional income distribution for age and assuming that this corrected distribution represents the life-cycle distribution over a very long period. (In truth, no one knows.)

Researchers who specialize in the study of income and poverty fully understand these shortcomings of ordinary income distribution statistics, and usually compute "corrected" figures before studying these issues seriously. Ordinarily, however, these results can only be understood by the econometrically literate and bear an uncertain relation to ordinary conceptions of poverty, equality, and economic justice. The simple, official income distribution is easier to use than the "corrected" measures, so this is what nonspecialists—other social scientists, philosophy professors, public officials, political activists—generally do use. When social research enters the public realm, it is an axiom that, between a simple but misleading statistic and a complicated precise one, the simple one will always survive.

Income Dynamics: The Missing Link But even if we were able to produce a simple, problem-free, fully corrected measure of the distribution of American income, would it tell us what we think it should about the nature of poverty, equality, or justice? The simple answer is no, because the income *distribution* can never reflect anything about income *dynamics.* By dynamics I mean the processes by which individuals and families change their economic fortunes, processes that tell us something different from what their economic positions are at any one time.

To illustrate this distinction, imagine two economies with the same relative distributions of (net, fully corrected) income. Each year, economists studying the two economies take cross-sections of the populations and announce that the distributions are unchanged and identical. But in the first economy, let us say, everyone remains in the same position each year: If someone was in the ninetieth percentile last year, he will be there this year; if he was below the poverty level, there he will remain; and so on. In the second economy, however, everyone changes places each year. Indeed, every three years there is complete turnover in this economy, every family spending one year each in the upper, middle, or lower class; no one is rich for more than one year at a time, and no one is poor for more than one year at a time. Ordinary common sense tells us that our two hypothetical economies have very different poverty problems, have different levels or kinds of inequality, are not equally just. *But in terms of their annual income distributions they are indistinguishable.*

This seems very strange. But even a moment's reflection on such a simple example makes clear that dynamics of income can be as or more important than its distribution—yet the former is an economic phenomenon about which social scientists know surprisingly little. There are, of course, countless studies of economic and social mobility, most relying on limited or specialized samples—for example, twins reared apart—to understand this fundamental economic process. Together they do not give a clear picture of this process, nor can they offer an economic theory of income dynamics. Real income dynamics among real families are difficult and expensive to measure, and the standard statistical methods for testing the data do not seem to apply. Consequently, the complicated questions of poverty, equality, and economic justice have remained on the Procrustean bed of income distribution.

Dynamic Poverty Take poverty, for example. Even though poverty is clearly more than a question of income, every official or academic definition of poverty in current use depends (explicitly or implicitly) on a fixed notion of the income distribution. Those families of a certain size that fall below a certain income level for a whole year are said, by definition, to be in poverty. Long-term and short-term poverty are to be distinguished as different social problems, but in any particular year they are said to be the same condition. There are ongoing debates inside and outside government over the level at which poverty is to be defined, and different federal and state agencies compute different family budget standards using the local costs of food, housing, clothing, and the like. Defining poverty in this way has notorious problems, among them accounting at the federal level for local price differences, valuing work in the home, including the value of different welfare benefits, and allowing for differences in "lifestyle."

Still, there are good, practical reasons for using such a fixed poverty standard. It allows government to decide easily how many people deserve benefits and how many people have been served each year; for program advocates, it provides a comprehensible—and, more important, a relatively stable—measure of the job still to be done. But can a fixed standard really tell us what we want to know about what poverty is and how public policy might cope with it? Most research on poverty has clearly shown that the long-term poor and short-term poor face dissimilar problems and opportunities, and that different sorts of programs and incentives may be required for these two subgroups. A simple income distribution cannot tell us the relative sizes of these groups. If a significant proportion of the people poor in 1984 were not poor in 1983, and will not be poor in 1985, then the character of American poverty is radically different from what it would be if there was no turnover in this population. This is not to say that the problem would necessarily be more or less severe; it is simply to recognize that the problem and the programs meant to cope with it would have to be conceived in quite different terms.

Discussion

1. Do you agree with Lilla that an important measure of the fairness of the distribution of income in a society is income mobility as well as the income statistics at any given time? Why or why not?

2. Exhibit 5 in your textbook presents a measure of income mobility from a seven-year study of a group of families. Would you say that this group did or did not experience reasonable income mobility? Explain your answer.

3. Philosopher John Rawls makes the case that income inequalities are only justified if they make the worst-off the best off they can be. To best measure Rawls's version of economic justice, should we use a static income distribution or a dynamic income distribution? Do you think Rawls would agree with your opinion?

27

Energy and Natural Resources Economics

TRUE OR FALSE

T F

☐ ☐   1.   The economic way of thinking indicates that, for certain vital resources, such as energy, the demand curve will be vertical.

☐ ☐   2.   According to the economic way of thinking, consumers will adjust more completely to a rise in the price of energy products when more time is allowed for their adjustment.

☐ ☐   3.   From 1950 to 1973, the real price of energy products declined.

☐ ☐   4.   The real price of energy rose sharply during 1973–1974 and again during 1978–1980.

☐ ☐   5.   The low elasticity of demand for crude oil, particularly in the short run, enhanced the ability of OPEC to raise the world price of crude oil during the 1970s.

☐ ☐   6.   The energy crisis reflects the fact that the energy needs of consumers are greater than the absolute reserves of crude oil.

☐ ☐   7.   Proved reserves of petroleum are less than absolute reserves.

☐ ☐   8.   When the Reagan administration eliminated all price controls on crude oil and gasoline in early 1981 the price of gasoline in the United States rose by approximately 35 cents per gallon during the 12 months subsequent to decontrol.

☐ ☐   9.   Federal regulation of natural gas prices led to lower prices, higher consumption, and lower rates of discovery during the 1960s and into the 1970s.

☐ ☐   10.   Following the oil embargo of 1973–1974, the price of ''new'' oil was allowed to rise to the level of international markets.

☐ ☐   11.   The entitlement allocation program induced oil refiners in the United States to import more oil.

☐ ☐   12.   In 1914, the U.S. Bureau of Mines announced that the total supply of crude oil in the United States was about 6 billion barrels, although we now produce that much every 20 months.

☐ ☐   13.   On average, oil companies keep approximately 25 percent of every sales dollar as profit.

PROBLEMS AND PROJECTS

Exhibit 1: Hypothetical Condition
of U.S. Gasoline Market

Price (dollars/gallons)	Quantity demanded (millions of gallons/day)	Quantity supplied (millions of gallons/day)
1.57	85	112
1.47	90	110
1.38	95	105
1.30	100	100
1.22	105	95
1.15	110	90

1. Assume that Exhibit 1 accurately describes the conditions of the U.S. gasoline market.
   a. What is the market-clearing price?
   b. Considering your answers to the above question, what would be the impact of a 16-cent additional tax per gallon imposed on this market? What would be the new price? The new quantity sold per day?
   c. Is the demand schedule above more likely to be a short-run or a long-run demand schedule, given the demand elasticities for gasoline reported in the text?
   d. Using positive economics, how could you argue that a tax is the most efficient way to bring about a given reduction in quantity demanded? Explain also why such a tax introduces some inefficiency into the market, and show the gains from trade that are eliminated by the tax.

2. Suppose that an African nation unfriendly to the United States has a huge oil strike, and sells to anyone *except* the United States. How will this affect oil supplies reaching the United States? How much could the United States gain by making political concessions to the oil-rich country in order to buy the oil? Use a supply–demand diagram for the world oil market in writing an explanation of why the United States might gain nothing from such concessions, so long as a worldwide market for oil exists.

3. With some difficulty (and with decreasing success) OPEC has managed during the 1970s and early 1980s to coordinate and control the supply decisions of OPEC producers of crude oil. Controlling the supply decisions of its members allowed OPEC to significantly influence the world price of oil. One thing that OPEC could not control, however, was the long-run supply decisions of *non*-OPEC producers of crude petroleum whose products, of course, compete with OPEC's. Producers in countries like the United States, Mexico, and the Soviet Union (among others) were free to adjust their supplies in response to OPEC's pricing policies, and the long-run response of these countries was much greater than the short-run. Though hypothetical, Exhibit 2 is designed to represent these circumstances. It assumes that the quantity of crude oil supplied by non-OPEC producers is determined in the long and short run by the non-OPEC producers according to the supply schedules given in the exhibit. It further assumes that when OPEC sets the price of crude oil, it sells an amount of oil equal to the difference between the world quantity demanded at that price and the quantity supplied by non-OPEC producers. Finally, we will assume that OPEC can produce oil at a constant cost of $10 per barrel.

Exhibit 2

Price (dollars/barrel)	World quantity demanded	Non-OPEC quantity supplied		OPEC quantity supplied	
		Short-run	Long-run	Short-run	Long-run
		(billions of barrels)			
$40	60	60	120	0	0
35	70	55	105	15	0
30	80	50	90	30	0
25	90	45	75	_____	15
20	100	40	60	_____	_____
15	110	35	45	_____	_____
10	120	30	30	_____	_____
5	130	25	15	_____	_____

a. Fill in the missing information for OPEC's quantity supplied in the short run.

b. Suppose that initially the world price of oil is $10 per barrel. What will OPEC's total profits be at this price?

c. Now suppose that OPEC raises the price of oil from $10 to $25 per barrel. In the short run, what will happen to OPEC's profits? What is the short-run elasticity of supply of non-OPEC producers between these two prices? [Use the arc formula to calculate the short-run elasticity.]

d. Now fill in the missing information for OPEC's long-run quantity supplied.

e. In the long run, what will OPEC's profits be at a price of $25 per barrel? How does this compare to their short-run profits at this price? What is the long-run elasticity of supply of non-OPEC producers? Why might it be greater in the long run than in the short run?

LEARNING THE MECHANICS—MULTIPLE CHOICE

1. The mythical view that energy prices do not matter implies that
   a. both supply and demand are horizontal curves.
   b. both supply and demand are vertical curves.
   c. energy supplies will expand more with time.
   d. energy demands will adjust more thoroughly with time.

2. After gasoline prices skyrocketed in the middle 1970s, many people did not believe that the higher prices would induce Americans to change their energy consumption habits.
   a. Such critics were approximately correct in the short run but clearly incorrect in the long run.
   b. Such critics were approximately correct in the long run but clearly incorrect in the short run.
   c. Such critics were essentially correct.
   d. Such critics would have been correct had it not been for the discovery of oil in Alaska.

3. Which of the following approaches to values and costs should be used when dealing with natural resources?
   a. Opportunity costs
   b. Marginal values
   c. Both a and b
   d. Neither a nor b

4. Use statements I and II to answer this question. (**I**) The demand for energy products is considerably less elastic in the short run than is true for the long run. (**II**) As the result of the lengthy time period between exploratory activities and the refining of a petroleum product, the supply of petroleum is generally more elastic in the short run than in the long run.
   a. Both I and II are true.
   b. Both I and II are false.
   c. I is true, II is false.
   d. I is false, II is true.

5. Oil is sometimes a common-pool resource; therefore,
   a. a well owner may try to pump oil too slowly.
   b. a well owner may try to pump oil too quickly.
   c. no single owner wants to bear a full share of the pumping costs, leading to a slow pumping rate.
   d. too few owners have a claim on the pool and monopoly results.

6. Proved reserves of petroleum are
   a. the only reserves likely to be available in the future.
   b. refined products waiting to be shipped to market.
   c. the oil industry's equivalent to raw material inventories.
   d. the same thing as absolute reserves.

7. Which of the following was a side effect of the price control program that fixed the price of domestic crude oil below the world market level during the 1970s?
   a. Independent of taxes, the controls reduced the price of gasoline in the United States below the prices paid by gasoline consumers in other countries.
   b. The controls induced the owners of petroleum resources to channel their products to other countries until, independent of taxes, the price of refined gasoline in the United States rose to the world level.
   c. The controls encouraged domestic producers to expand output, reducing the dependence of the United States on imported oil.
   d. The controls induced foreigners to sell crude oil cheaper in the United States than in other contries because they had to cut their price in order to compete with the artificially low price received by domestic crude oil suppliers.

8. When the demand for whale oil increased sharply during the mid-1800s, the price of whale oil rose sharply. As a result
   a. many people were unable to afford to light their homes until electricity was developed.
   b. the supply of whale oil increased rapidly, as entrepreneurs developed a new technique for breeding whales.
   c. consumers turned to substitute energy sources, which eventually provided much cheaper heating and lighting than could be supplied with whale oil.
   d. the government imposed rigid price controls and rationed whale oil in order to mitigate the energy crisis.

9. The Federal Power Commission (FPC) regulated natural gas prices during the 1950s and 1960s. The FPC
   a. set the price of natural gas higher than the price of oil, in energy equivalents.
   b. set the price of natural gas slightly below oil prices, in energy equivalents.
   c. set the price of natural gas at about one-third the level of oil prices in energy equivalents throughout the 1960s (and into the 1970s).
   d. encouraged consumers to conserve energy by keeping natural gas prices high.

10. The classic study of Barnett and Morse found that
    a. resource costs have been rising at a rate that implies that within 50 years, we will have impossibly high prices for natural resources.
    b. the ever-increasing availability of substitutes has outrun our ability to use up scarce natural resources.
    c. resource costs have been rising for a long period, but predictions of a coming "doomsday" are unlikely to be correct.
    d. the currently proven reserves of most minerals are becoming perilously low.

11. The demand for energy products is
    a. perfectly inelastic, since energy is needed to produce everything we consume.
    b. quite inelastic in the short run, but considerably more elastic in the long run.
    c. quite elastic in the short run, but considerably more inelastic in the long run.
    d. highly elastic in both the short and long runs.

12. Proved reserves are
    a. the total reserve supply of a resource that will be available for future consumption.
    b. the total reserve supply of a resource that is recoverable, assuming that energy prices and technology continue to increase at current rates.
    c. the total amount of reserves in existence.
    d. the current holdings of verified reserves that we can expect to recover at current energy prices and technology.

THE ECONOMIC WAY OF THINKING—MULTIPLE CHOICE

1. Environmental regulations adopted in the 1960s had the effect of
    a. reducing an implicit subsidy to drivers of high-pollution, high-gas-mileage cars.
    b. increasing the number of oil refineries built in the United States during the 1970s.
    c. subsidizing automobile usage.
    d. increasing the gas mileage of U.S. cars.

2. When the 1973 oil embargo began, the capital assets of the United States were largely
    a. energy saving, because of previously high energy prices.
    b. energy intensive, because of low energy prices that were present previously.
    c. flexible as to energy usage, even in the very short run.
    d. inflexible as to energy usage, even in the very long run.

3. Opportunity cost is used in determining the most valued use of a resource like land or capital; when deciding how to use natural resources, opportunity cost is
    a. not applicable because natural resources are not replaceable.
    b. just as applicable.
    c. only as applicable in cases where wildlife is not involved.
    d. only applicable in cases where cost–benefit analysis is involved.

4. Cost–benefit analysis sometimes does a poor job of separating the efficient from the inefficient because
    a. assigning a dollar amount to the costs and benefits of a project can be difficult.
    b. an inappropriate rate of interest may be used when calculating the present value of the benefits and costs.
    c. political decision-makers often listen to special interest groups.
    d. all of the above.

5. Since the price controls on domestic crude oil kept the price of "old oil" below the market level, these controls
   a. reduced the production rate from "old oil" wells.
   b. reduced the demand for both "old" and "new" oil.
   c. reduced the demand for oil imports that were more expensive.
   d. reduced the price of gasoline in the United States below the world level because, at the margin, the production costs were less in the United States.

6. The entitlement allocation program of the 1970s
   a. taxed domestic-based oil producers in order to provide a subsidy to foreign producers.
   b. taxes foreign oil producers in order to provide a subsidy to domestic producers.
   c. taxed oil refineries that utilized domestically produced "old oil" intensively in order to provide a subsidy to refineries that utilized a high percentage of imported oil.
   d. taxed oil refineries that utilized a high percentage of imported oil in order to provide a subsidy to refineries that relied primarily on domestic sources of "old oil."

7. Recent experience indicates that regulating the price of domestic crude oil by non-market price controls
   a. is extremely difficult.
   b. did not work in the U.S. until the establishment of the entitlement allocation program.
   c. worked in the U.S. until the establishment of the entitlement allocation program.
   d. has its problems but is basically a good and workable idea.

8. The fact that most people believed that OPEC had and was using monopoly power in the crude oil market
   a. caused oil prices to be higher than they would have been otherwise.
   b. caused oil prices to be lower than they would have been otherwise.
   c. had no impact on oil prices.
   d. had an unknown impact on oil prices; the only known impact was on *expected* oil prices.

9. Which of the following is the most accurate description of what the energy crisis of the 1970s was all about?
   a. The need for energy was expanding, while the availability of energy was fixed; eventually our needs exceeded the fixed supply of energy.
   b. The major oil companies created an artificial shortage of petroleum in order to raise their profit rate from approximately 20 percent of sales to nearly 40 percent of sales.
   c. The OPEC cartel imposed higher taxes and decreed higher prices, which led to a sharp increase in the world price of petroleum; in the short run it was difficult (costly) for energy users to reduce consumption and substitute other energy sources for the more expensive crude oil supplied by the cartel.
   d. The proven reserves of petroleum resources relative to current consumption have, of course, been declining for several decades; the situation reached a crisis in the 1970s, causing the sharply higher prices.

10. Use statements I and II to answer this question. (**I**) The experience of the last decade clearly indicates that price makes a great deal of difference in energy markets. (**II**) The shortage of gasoline in the United States during the summer of 1974 and again during the summer of 1979 illustrates how perilously close the world is to running out of petroleum resources.
    a. I is true, II is false.
    b. I is false, II is true.
    c. Both I and II are true.
    d. Both I and II are false.

11. All but one of the following made the United States highly vulnerable to a substantial price hike by the OPEC cartel in 1973. Which did *not* contribute to the vulnerability of the United States?
    a. Falling energy prices during the period from 1950 to 1973 induced U.S. consumers to purchase assets that utilized large amounts of energy per unit of output.
    b. Environmental regulations increased energy consumption, while reducing our ability to expand the supply of energy.
    c. Price controls on natural gas caused shortages and induced consumers to switch to crude oil.
    d. The discovery of the Alaskan field increased the proved reserves of the United States, expanding the expected future domestic supply of crude oil.

12. The irreversibility effect makes decision-making about natural resource preservation especially difficult because
    a. a natural resource, once ruined, is ruined irreversibly.
    b. a delay in taking advantage of an economically sound use of a natural resource can postpone benefits in a way that loses them irreversibly.
    c. both of the above.
    d. neither of the above.

THE ECONOMIC WAY OF THINKING—DISCUSSION QUESTIONS

1. Are some of the instances of price responsiveness cited in the text surprising? Can you explain why they surprise many people? Why would students of microeconomics be any less surprised by them?

2. Diesel fuel can be rationed several different ways: by price, or by waiting in line, or by government allocation. If government allocation is used, how will trucking firms, farmers, and others divide their efforts among (a) conservation efforts, (b) lobbying for greater allocations, and (c) public demonstrations, strikes, and/or violence to get greater allocations? If price is used, how will the same decision-makers divide their time?

3. How did governmental policy to keep energy-company profits and prices down during the 1960s and 1970s influence our demand for energy and our vulnerability to political pressures from OPEC in 1980?

4. Do you think the whale oil crisis of the early 1800s really has any lessons for us now? Why or why not?

5. How could one go about measuring the scarcity of oil in 1955 relative to its scarcity now? Explain.

6. What are the social costs of massive substitution of nuclear power for fossil fuel power to alleviate future energy shortages? How can society go about deciding between economic costs and social costs in such a case?

PERSPECTIVES IN ECONOMICS

Lessons Of History For OPEC
by A. Gary Shilling

[From *The Wall Street Journal,* March 10, 1975. Reprinted with the permission of Wall Street Journal. © Dow Jones & Company, Inc. (1975). All rights reserved.]

The OPEC oil cartel is developing small cracks. Weakened demand for oil has led to price discounts, stretched out payment terms and barter deals that over-value the goods taken in exchange for oil. Moreover, the purchasing power of oil revenues is falling because of the declining value of the dollar. Yet most observers still feel that the oil cartel is so strong, so different from earlier cartels, that there is little chance of its breaking down any time soon.

To put things in perspective, it might be useful to take a stroll down the memory lane of cartels. They are nothing new. Adam Smith observed in 1776 that "people in the same trade seldom meet together, even for merriment or diversion, but the conversation ends in a conspiracy against the public, or in some contrivance to raise prices." History teaches us, also, that a cartel only works so long as demand is so insensitive to price that higher prices will increase the seller's total revenue.

The earliest known example of an international cartel is the salt cartel of 1301. Salt was an extremely important commodity in those days of primitive methods of preserving food—perhaps as important as oil is today. Its price had been dropping because of competition between the salt mines of King Philip the Fair of France and those belonging to Charles II, King of Naples. The Florentine bankers who leased these mines proposed that competition be eliminated by forming a joint company that would sell both mines' output at a uniform and higher price, thereby increasing the royal incomes as well as their own. The two royal courts needed money, so the kings readily agreed.

Remembering Alum The curent oil cartel is not the first to pit Moslems against the West. In the alum cartel of 1470, the sides were reversed. For many years, the Turks had controlled the world production of alum, a key ingredient in cloth dyeing and leather tanning. Marketing in Europe was controlled by wealthy Italian firms which paid high royalties to the Turkish Sultan—reminiscent of the relationship between the international oil companies and the sheikhs.

In 1461, however, rich alum beds were discovered in the Papal State, and Pope Pius II, in conjunction with the Medici, set up a monopoly company for their exploitation. In order to eliminate competition, the Pope officially condemned Turkish alum as heathen and prohibited Christians from trafficking in it. With the boycott of Turkish alum effective, the Pope's company rapidly expanded throughout Europe. However, there was still serious competition from an alum mine owned by Ferdinand, King of Naples. Both mines tried to increase their market share by expanding production and the result was the usual collapse in prices. An agreement was urgently needed.

On June 11, 1470, Pope Paul II, Pius' successor, and King Ferdinand made a written and highly detailed cartel agreement. The stated purpose was to keep the price of alum as high as possible. The cartel took over alum sales throughout Europe at fixed prices but left production in the hands of the members. Profits were split, and if sales were made below the cartel price, the seller had to make up the other partner's loss.

The document of the alum agreement survives to this day and indicates the pact was for a fixed term of 25 years. Whether this restraint of trade actually lasted that long is unknown as is the life-span of the earlier salt cartel. Post mortem of business failures were almost unknown in that era and the passing of the cartel was probably so painful to its participants that they were glad to sweep the debris under the rug. What was missing was the equivalent of to-day's business school prof or financial journalist who would have tackled the dissection job with great glee.

The purpose of cartels, of course, is to exercise monopolistic control—to raise prices and revenues by limiting production, restricting exports, setting prices and dividing up markets. The factors that initiate cartels, however, are varied. Cutthroat competition, often the result of new sources of supply, has been the most common instigator. The alum cartel falls in this category, as do the rubber and sugar cartels of the 1920s and many, many in between. Reducing the risk of losses due to volatile markets and new entrants is another important reason. This encouraged the formation of medieval craft guilds which set working hours and output quotas, prohibited members from soliciting each other's customers or finishing the work started by another and prevented non-members from practicing their trade.

Generalized business weakness and excess capacity have spawned many cartels, especially in the 1920s and 1930s. World War I had created tremendous excess capacity which came to light with the severe recession and price collapses of 1920–1921, and the economic slack and further price declines in the Depression also encouraged cartel formation. It is estimated that in the 1929–37 period, 42% of world trade was cartelized to one degree or another.

Providing urgently needed funds for the government has been a great stimulator of cartels over the years, as in the case of the old salt and alum cartels and today's oil cartel. Furthermore, the private members of the cartel were only too happy to provide the local potentate with his share of the profits since they needed his protection.

Since ancient times, cartels have been consistently outlawed (but not with consistent success). The Constitution issued by Emperor Zeno in 483, part of the Justinian Code, very clearly outlawed cartels and monopolies, even those granted by the Emperor himself! English Common Law opposed monopolies of any type. But in 1600, the Newcastle coal cartel was chartered as a guild by Queen Elizabeth, who collected a fat royalty, in order to avoid prosecution and take advantage of the guild image as an ideal of Christian economic ethics and human brotherhood. Church doctrine also opposed cartels and advocated the "just price."

These laws, of course, did not preclude official participation in cartels. After all, funds from the alum cartel were needed for crusades against the Turks and, in other cases, local industries needed to be protected against foreign competition. More recent examples include the German cartels after World War I which were designed, in part, to help pay war reparations. The rubber cartel of the 1920s was initiated by one Winston Churchill, then Secretary of

State for the Colonies, who said that the scheme was "one of the principal means of paying the (war) debt to America."

Just as excessive competition is usually the initiator of cartels, it, paradoxically, has often led to their demise. Falling demand in the Depression killed many of the cartels set up in the 1920s and early 1930s. The development of substitutes or alternative supplies often had the same effect. The power of the nitrate cartel of the 1920s and 1930s was largely offset by the rapid development of synthetic plants.

Aristotle's Example Smuggling and outright cheating have broken some cartels. The copper cartel of 1498 was broken when the Fuggers, the rich and famous German bankers who originally formed it, sold considerable amounts on the side. Pressure from the public and from foreign governments can also be important, and American protests were a factor in breaking the British-led rubber cartel of the 1920s. In one of Aristotle's examples, a Sicilian iron cartel, formed by a banker of Syracuse who used his customers' deposits to buy up all the iron mines on the island, was broken when the Greek government banished him.

As suggested by this brief review of history, in most ways the oil cartel is nothing new—just one more government-sponsored price-setting group which has some financially strong members, faces no immediate alternative sources of supply and, as is typical of extractive industry cartels has few inventory problems. Viewed in this light, the cartel seems unlikely to break up until late in the current decade when alternative supplies of crude oil from the North Slope and North Sea should be increasing.

There is, however, a big difference between this cartel and earlier examples. Normally, cartels are set up in periods of weak demand, cutthroat competition, and falling prices. In fact, cartels are often abandoned as unnecessary during wars and other periods of strong demand. The timing of the oil cartel was the reverse, however. It was imposed by the Arabs in a period of strong demand, not to quadruple the price, but as a weapon against Israel. The Arabs were probably as surprised as anyone with the cartel's success in raising prices.

Now, however, the world-wide recession has reduced overall oil demand by about 10%, and further declines are likely if, as we expect, the slump lasts until late this year.

History shows clearly that cartels do not do well in periods of weak demand. OPEC oil output is now running 30% below capacity, and allocating further cutbacks, which have been voluntary thus far, may be difficult.

Furthermore, the industrial importance of oil and the sizes of the postboycott price increases have created huge balance of trade problems. Diplomatic pressure and military threats have already been made against the Arabs and may increase as the recession deepens and Western governments look more and more for a scapegoat.

Further weakness in oil demand in the next 12 months and increasing outside pressure should make the Arabs more conciliatory, as could some sort of workable settlement of the Palestinian-Israeli question. But if this doesn't occur in roughly the next year, any substantial decline in oil prices might well be delayed until late in the decade; the reasons being that oil demand should increase if there is any sort of economic recovery in 1976. And the 1976 presidential election could complicate the negotiation of a Middle East settlement. Obviously war in that area would throw all predictions out the window.

Oil And Sugar A break in world oil prices would probably not be felt to any great degree by consumers in Europe or the U.S. Import tariffs would likely be imposed to protect North Sea and U.S. domestic oil as well as encourage the development of substitute forms of energy. In many ways, the world energy situation could then resemble that of sugar in the 1920s. After the World War I and postwar sugar famine in Europe, consuming countries were determined to protect their domestic industries and develop self-sufficiency at any cost, and proceeded to encourage domestic sugar beet production and erect tariff barriers and import quotas. The result was the widespread but uneconomic replacement of high cost beet for low cost cane sugar, and chronic excess capacity and very low prices in the cane industry.

An end of the oil cartel, however, would not necessarily mean that international cartels would be absent from the scene in future years. Few have been formed since World War II, but few new ones would be expected in a period of strong demand. If however, the current worldwide recession, like the 1920–21 correction, sets the stage for continuing weakness in commodity prices then renewed international cartel activity of all sorts would be expected.

Discussion

1. Shilling's article is impressive because he predicted, in 1975, the hard times that OPEC encountered a decade later. Do you think Shilling was lucky, or are cartels in general doomed? Do you think OPEC's power lasted longer than Shilling would have predicted back in 1975?

2. How desirable is a cartel? In the end, who benefits? Who loses? Is it really just a transfer of funds, or is economic efficiency helped or hurt?

3. If OPEC does not fail, what is the likelihood of similar cartels being started in, say, tin or coffee? What would these cartels be likely to do in the international trade market for those items?

28

Problem Areas for the Market

TRUE OR FALSE

T F

☐ ☐ 1. Voluntary exchange is proof of expected mutual gain.

☐ ☐ 2. Private interest and ideal economic efficiency sometimes conflict, even for a smoothly functioning, competitive price system.

☐ ☐ 3. Poor information on the part of buyers is very seldom a factor in real-world markets.

☐ ☐ 4. Spillover, or neighborhood, effects are the same things as externalities.

☐ ☐ 5. When externalities are present, some parties must be trying to harm others.

☐ ☐ 6. Social costs include those accruing to consenting *and* secondary parties.

☐ ☐ 7. Prohibition is often less desirable than acceptance by society of activities that generate externalities.

☐ ☐ 8. When external costs are low, markets are unlikely to handle externalities in a socially desirable manner.

☐ ☐ 9. When large numbers of people are involved, external costs are usually low.

☐ ☐ 10. Poorly defined property rights increase external costs.

☐ ☐ 11. Taxing polluters according to the damage they do is administratively simple, but makes no sense economically.

☐ ☐ 12. When externalities are present, secondary effects are always negative, not positive.

☐ ☐ 13. Public goods are a special case of spillover benefits to secondary parties.

☐ ☐ 14. The free-rider problem occurs when an activity benefits people who are not forced to pay for their benefits.

☐ ☐ 15. An advantage of the zero-price solution to the public goods problem is that extra information is made available about consumer valuation of the goods.

PROBLEMS AND PROJECTS

Exhibit 1

Output (per month)	Supply producer's marginal cost	Demand consumer's valuation	External cost (for alternative levels of supply)	Marginal social cost
70	65¢	110¢	0¢	65¢
80	70	95	5	75
90	75	85	10	85
100	80	80	15	95
110	90	75	20	_____
120	100	70	30	_____

1. Exhibit 1 presents data on the producer's cost and consumer's valuation of paper pulp, a competitively produced product. Since production of the pulp generates an undesirable odor, the market supply curve does not accurately reflect the marginal social cost. The estimated external costs at alternative output levels are also presented in Exhibit 1.
   a. At what price and output would the quantity supplied equal the quantity demanded?
   b. Fill in the marginal social cost data for alternative output levels. How does the marginal social cost compare with the consumer's valuation of paper pulp at the competitive equilibrium price?
   c. What would be the ideal output level, considering the costs that are external to the producer?

2. You have just been hired as a junior staff member by a congressman from a coastal state. An electric utility is trying to build a power plant near the mouth of a river in the state and wants the right to use water from the river in its cooling towers. Agricultural interests own the water rights, however, and law forbids their transfer to industrial users. The utility points out that water rights among farmers trade for about $10 per unit, whereas the utility would pay $80. You are told to spend the night writing a short paper briefing the congressman on (a) whether or not the private property rights system is working efficiently in this case, (b) the true value of the water in dispute, and (c) the distribution of benefits (who would thank the congressman) and costs (who would complain to the congressman) if Congress overruled state law and gave the utility the right to bid for the water in this specific case. As you write this short, clear paper, remember the basic principles of economics concerning marginal valuation and the opportunity cost. (Would your analysis differ if the power plant location were 200 miles inland, where much of each farm's irrigation water returned to the river and was reused?)

3. Exhibit 2 shows the actual estimated costs of pollution reduction (measured in percentages) for a beet sugar refining firm and a petroleum refining firm, both of which initially emit identical amounts of pollution.

Exhibit 2

Amount of pollution reduction (percent)	Marginal cost of reduction	
	Beet refining	Petroleum refining
	(cents/pound)	
10	0.5	3.0
20	0.5	3.0
30	0.5	3.5
40	0.5	4.0
50	1.0	5.0
60	2.0	6.0
70	3.0	14.0
80	4.5	15.0
90	6.0	21.0

Source: Based on data in Allen V. Kneese and Charles Schultze, *Pollution, Prices and Public Policy,* (Washington, D.C.: Brookings Institution, 1975).

a. Suppose the government instituted a maximum emission standard that required each firm to reduce its pollution by 60 percent. What would be the marginal cost of reduction for the beet refiner? For the petroleum refiner?

b. If instead government instituted a pollution tax of 4.5 cents per pound of pollution emitted, by what percent would the beet refiner reduce pollution? The petroleum refiner?

c. Explain briefly why the second approach is more economical (efficient) than the first.

4. Dan Vencill is a likable fellow who hates yardwork, partly because he dislikes the activity and partly because he doesn't mind a somewhat unkempt yard. However, his neighbors all love to work on their yards and are extremely fastidious about them. Exhibit 3 shows Vencill's estimate of his marginal cost of yardwork (per hour) along with his estimate of the marginal value (to him) of his yardwork (per hour). Also shown is Vencill's neighbors' estimate of the value to them of Vencill's work on his yard, a benefit which has nothing to do with Vencill's private decision about how much time to spend working on his yard.

Exhibit 3

Quantity of Vencill's yardwork (hours/week)	Vencill's marginal cost of yardwork (dollars/hour)	Vencill's marginal value of yardwork (dollars/hour)	Vencill's neighbors' marginal value of Vencill's yardwork (dollars/hour)	Social marginal value of Vencill's yardwork (dollars/hour)
1	1.00	3.00	18.00	21.00
2	2.00	2.00	16.00	18.00
3	3.00	1.00	13.00	_____
4	4.00	0	10.00	_____
5	5.00	0	8.00	_____
6	6.00	0	6.00	_____
7	7.00	0	4.00	_____

a. Fill in the missing information in the table.
b. Considering only Vencill's benefits and costs of yardwork, how many hours per week will he spend working on his yard?
c. Calculate the *total net* benefit (to Vencill alone) of this many hours per week. How much do Vencill's neighbors benefit from this amount of work?
d. Considering all costs and benefits of Vencill's yardwork, what is the socially ideal (efficient) number of hours for Vencill to work on his yard? How much would Vencill's neighbors benefit if he spent this much time working? What is the total *social* net benefit of this many hours?
e. Suppose that Vencill's neighbors told him that if he spent 6 hours per week working on his yard, they would pay him $30.00. Based solely on the information in the exhibit, would Vencill accept this offer? Is the offer an economically sensible one from the neighbors' points of view? Explain.
f. Suggest some reasons why the solution above would probably not work as a general solution to this sort of problem. [*Hint*: Remember the free-rider problem.]

5. Research and write a paper on the economics of pollution. Be sure to discuss
    a. why air and water pollution are problems.
    b. the ideal amount of pollution from society's point of view.
    c. who gains (and loses) from failure to force polluters to pay for the use of valuable resources, such as clean air and water.
    d. alternative strategies for pollution control.

LEARNING THE MECHANICS—MULTIPLE CHOICE

1. Production and distribution of which of the following is most likely to impose significant externalities in the absence of government intervention?
    a. Ice cream
    b. Household maid service
    c. Paper pulp
    d. Soap

2. If there are no spillover effects, voluntary exchange results in
    a. expected net gain for each participant.
    b. expected social benefits that exceed the expected social costs.
    c. both a and b.
    d. neither a nor b.

3. If important social benefits (externalities) are associated with consumption of a product, it can be said that
    a. the supply curve for the product lies too far to the right to provide an efficient allocation of resources.
    b. the demand curve understates the relative importance of the product; therefore, resources are underallocated to its production.
    c. special excise taxes should be levied on producers of the product.
    d. government should enact legislation to prohibit the production of the commodity.

4. Which of the following activities is most likely to result in substantial costs that are external to the decision-maker?
    a. Consumption of an ice cream cone
    b. Production of a handcrafted billfold
    c. Consumption of a supersonic air flight from New York to Los Angeles
    d. A firing of a high-powered rifle in the desert lands of Nevada

5. The major distinction between pure private and pure public goods is that
    a. private goods generate external effects, whereas public goods do not.
    b. the government can product public goods, but not private goods.
    c. public goods must be consumed jointly, since supplying the goods to one person simultaneously makes them available to others.
    d. public goods are free, whereas private goods have a cost.

6. When costs are incurred that are external to the decision-maker, a firm is likely to be producing more of a good than is socially desirable
    a. because it is not required to fully consider external costs when its price and output decisions are made.
    b. because the firm will not pay attention to buyers' wishes in such a case.
    c. because the firm is a free rider.
    d. because communal property rights are absent.

7. Producers are more likely to be concerned with customer satisfaction when
    a. they are largely dependent on repeat customers.
    b. it is difficult for the customer to evaluate product quality accurately.
    c. they are dependent on tourism for their sales.
    d. the demand for the products of the producer is inelastic.

8. Even if one assumes a purely competitive market, the pricing mechanism can be (and is) criticized because it
    a. encourages firms to seek profits by neglecting the preferences of consumers.
    b. fails to register fully the benefits and costs resulting from externalities.
    c. encourages workers to unionize because of the low wages that will prevail in a market economy.
    d. fails to provide an incentive for firms to minimize their per unit dollar costs of production.

9. Emission charges increase the cost of
    a. catering to the preferences of repeat customers more than to tourists.
    b. producing pollution-intensive goods.
    c. using production methods that result in less pollution.
    d. using pollution control devices.

10. The Montagnais Indians were
    a. not willing to use any type of private property rights.
    b. successful at using private property rights to preserve buffalo populations.
    c. successful at using private property rights to preserve beaver populations.
    d. a tribe that was nearly responsible for the extinction of the plains buffalo.

11. When property rights to a farm are held by an individual, the individual
    a. has an incentive to see that the resource is put to the use of its highest valuation.
    b. has no incentive to use the resource such that others can benefit.
    c. has no choice but to use the resource wisely.
    d. cannot benefit *personally* when the resource is used such that society benefits.

THE ECONOMIC WAY OF THINKING—MULTIPLE CHOICE

1. Fish in the sea are "owned" communally. No individual, group of individuals, or firm has the right to buy, sell, and/or trade the fish of the sea. A leading consequence of this lack of ownership is
   a. monopoly power in commercial fishing because of the ease of restricting entry.
   b. that individual fishermen have almost no incentive to practice conservation.
   c. full economies of scale cannot be attained with respect to the size of individual fishing boats.
   d. that fishermen inevitably earn lower wages than persons in other activities.

2. One major advantage of the market is that it allows consumers to select freely among commodities. Yet, buyers of automobiles in America are forced by law to pay for additional safety equipment that many (perhaps the majority) would not freely choose to buy under an optional marketing arrangement. This procedure may be justified on efficiency grounds for which of the following reasons?
   a. The per unit cost of the safety equipment will fall whenever all buyers are forced to purchase it.
   b. The private demand for safety is low.
   c. External costs are associated with automobile accidents.
   d. Buyers who would choose safety equipment under the optional arrangement are likely to be those drivers who need the equipment least.

3. Courts have consistently held that people ("receptors") have a right to clean air (a property right); therefore, if a polluter begins to foul the air and cause problems for receptors, the receptors can collect all damages proved caused by the polluter. Yet, the market system recognizably fails to handle the pollution problem adequately. This is because
   a. receptors have no property rights regarding pollution.
   b. no one knows whether damage truly results from air pollution ("proof" does not exist).
   c. polluters are monopolists.
   d. receptors have property rights, but since it is difficult to *prove* damages, causation, and a specific culprit, *enforcement* of the rights is often very costly.

4. A pure market economy is unlikely to provide a sufficient amount of a public good like national defense because
   a. the consumers are poorly informed as to the value of national defense.
   b. it is generally impossible to withhold national defense from a nonpaying customer.
   c. national defense does not yield a benefit to individuals.
   d. private firms will be less efficient than public firms when producing a public good such as national defense.

5. Control of air and water pollution is likely to be an important economic issue in the foreseeable future. Using economic efficiency as our criteria, which of the following general approaches to pollution control would be best?
   a. Reduce the role of economic growth, which is the major cause of pollution.
   b. Prohibit all economic activities that cause pollution.
   c. Use our existing resources to eliminate all damage to our environment that results from pollution.
   d. Eliminate a pollution-causing activity only when the marginal damage costs of the action exceed the marginal social benefits associated with the use of the resource in a manner that leads to pollution.

6. Which of the following activities is most likely to generate a positive externality—an external benefit—that will result in a free-market output level that is less than the socially desirable amount?
    a. The production of crude oil and its by-product, natural gas
    b. Research on a new diet and exercise program that will reduce the likelihood of cancer
    c. The delivery of orange juice by milkmen, reducing the net cost to the consumer
    d. The development and patent of a new automatic clutch designed to improve the efficiency of the automobile

7. Suppose that on the outskirts of Orlando, Florida, a city of about 100,000 people, an orange grove were bought by the city and turned into Orange Grove Park, where the care, upkeep, and orange consumption will be handled by all city individuals on a volunteer basis, "not for the benefit of one greedy individual." The result of this institutional change, the elimination of *private* property rights, would most likely include
    a. more resources devoted to the orchard's upkeep, since roughly 100,000 people would have a stake in the orchard's production.
    b. many oranges to be picked before optimal ripeness, since for any individual, waiting for those particular oranges to ripen completely might mean only one chance in 100,000 that he or she would be the one to benefit from waiting.
    c. less wasting of oranges from the grove, since every picker would realize the social value of oranges.
    d. more fertilizer being purchased by volunteer individuals and applied at appropriate times.

8. Ronald Ridker, in a 1967 study, estimated that in St. Louis, people paid an average of $245 more for a home when pollution from sulfur oxides was less by 0.25 miligram SO_3 per square centimeters per day (a measure of the sulfation rate). He controlled for other factors influencing property values. If Ridker was correct, his results show that
    a. there is a market for clean air, and the price system satisfactorily handles air pollution.
    b. only renters would benefit if air pollution were controlled effectively.
    c. people's willingness to pay for clean air is sometimes revealed despite a lack of a formal market for clean air.
    d. home buyers had evaluated pollution costs correctly, having full knowledge of the effects of pollution.

9. Compared to the maximum emission standard method of control, the emission charge method will produce a given reduction in pollution with
    a. a larger impact on the product's social cost, since the polluter pays money in addition to control costs.
    b. a higher social cost, since many firms will continue to pollute.
    c. a lower social cost, since the most economical reductions in pollution will be made first.
    d. a lower social cost, since virtually all pollution will cease if it really costs firms money to pollute.

10. New products provide a classic case of the consumer information problem. However, in some cases consumers partially solve the problem by trusting the "brand name" of the producer of the new product. Since firms spend millions of dollars advertising and maintaining their brand names, the likelihood of a "brand name" firm's intentionally selling a dangerous or shoddy new product is
    a. high, because big firms are always after a quick dollar.
    b. high, because their brand name is a communal property right.
    c. low, because big firms do not make mistakes.
    d. low, because the firm with a brand name has a lot to lose if word spreads about bad consumer experiences.

11. The Soviet experience with private rights to small "private" plots of agricultural land indicates that
    a. output tends to be greater when producers can gain directly from production.
    b. private producers think only of their own consumption, and not of greater output.
    c. output is greater without private property rights.
    d. privately controlled land is used less efficiently.

THE ECONOMIC WAY OF THINKING—DISCUSSION QUESTIONS

1. Many individuals might be willing to contribute $25 to the local community charity drive if they could be assured that others would do so. Explain how the free-rider problem complicates the issue of raising money for charitable purposes.

2. Jones gets a real bargain on 100 acres of land because it is near an airport. He decides to use the land to breed his prize-winning race horses. One year after buying the land, Jones sues the airport because his horses, disrupted by the noise of jet planes, are not breeding. If you were the judge, how would you decide Jones's case? Why?

3. One argument against emissions charges as a way of controlling pollution is that some polluters would find it cheaper to pay the charge than to stop polluting, even if the pollution is damaging to the public's health. Advocates of this view usually argue that public health is our prime concern. Do you agree? Why or why not? In 1975, 1560 people were killed in the operation of railroads. Another 54,300 were injured. Should we shut down the railroads? Are the two situations comparable?

4. What problems are involved in setting the proper tax on pollutant emissions? Could one set an antipollution tax so high that pollution would be too low, from a *social* point of view? Explain.

5. At a busy freeway exit, why does a large franchised hamburger stand have more reason to provide customer satisfaction regarding price, quality, and quantity, than a home-owned, non-chain stand *in the same location?* Would a brand name whiskey distiller have the same incentive for quality control relative to a small, unknown distiller not attempting to establish a brand name? Why?

6. What's wrong with this way of thinking? "The unregulated private economy will always provide the consumer with what he wants at the lowest possible cost to society. As long as the consumer is willing to pay the cost of producing an item, the free market will provide it for him."

7. In general, we have argued that individuals in a market economy will allocate fewer resources to a public good with positive externalities (like national defense) than is socially optimal. Is there any evidence that the public sector allocates *too many* resources to such activities? What is that evidence? Given these two extreme possibilities, how do we go about determining the socially optimal amount of such public goods?

PERSPECTIVES IN ECONOMICS

The Public Use Of Private Interest
by Charles L. Schultze

[Reprinted from *Regulation,* September/October 1977. © 1977 The Brookings Institution. Adapted from Charles L. Schultze. *The Public Use of Private Interest* (Washington, D.C.: Brookings Institution, 1977).]

In 1929, some 9 percent of the gross national income was spent by federal, state, and local government for purposes other than national defense and foreign affairs. Between 1929 and 1960, however, the proportion of gross national income spent for domestic programs rose to 17.5 percent. Today, only sixteen years later, that figure is 28 percent.

The growth of federal regulatory activities has been even more striking. There is no good way to quantify regulatory growth, but a few figures will illustrate its speed. Even as late as the middle 1950s, the federal government had a major regulatory responsibility in only four areas: antitrust, financial institutions, transportation, and communications. In 1976 eighty-three federal agencies were engaged in regulating some aspect of private activity.

Even more relevant to my theme is the changing nature of government intervention. Addressed to much more intricate and difficult objectives, the newer programs are different; and the older ones have taken on more ambitious goals. In the field of energy and the environment the generally accepted objectives of national policy imply a staggeringly complex and interlocking set of actions, directly affecting the production and consumption decisions of every citizen and every business firm.

In a society that relies on private enterprise and market incentives to carry out most productive activity, the problem of intervention is a real one. After the decision to intervene has been taken, there remains a critical choice to be made: should intervention be carried out by grafting a specific command-and-control module—a regulatory apparatus—onto the system of private enterprise, or by modifying the informational flow, institutional structure, or incentive pattern of that private system? Neither approach is appropriate to every situation. But our political system almost always chooses the command-and-control response, regardless of whether that response fits the problem.

Once a political battle to intervene has been won in some broad area—environmental control, reduction of industrial accidents, or standards for nursing homes and day-care centers—the extent and scope of the resulting social controls are seldom grounded in an analysis of where and to what extent the private market has failed to meet acceptable standards. Similarly, there is seldom any attempt to design techniques of intervention that preserve some of the virtues of the free market.

Virtues Of The Market We acknowledge the power of economic incentives to foster steadily improving efficiency, and we employ it to bring us whitewall tires, cosmetics, and television sets. But for something really important like education, we eschew incentives. We would laugh if someone suggested that the best way to reduce labor input per unit of production was to set up a government agency to specify labor input in detail for each industry. But that is precisely how we go about trying to reduce environmental damage and industrial accidents.

The buyer-seller relationships of the market-place has substantial advantages as a form of social organization. In the first place, relationships in the market are a form of unanimous-consent arrangement. When dealing with each other in a buy-sell transaction, individuals can act voluntarily on the basis of mutual advantage. Organizing large-scale social activity through the alternative open to a free society—democratic majoritarian politics—necessarily implies some minority that disapproves of each particular decision. To urge that the principle of voluntary decision should be given weight is not to make it the sole criterion. But precisely because the legitimate occasions for social intervention will increase as time goes on, preserving and expanding the role of choice take on added importance.

A second advantage of the market as an organizing principle for social activity is that it reduces the need for hard-to-get information. The more complicated and extensive the social intervention, and the more it seeks to alter individual behavior, the more difficult it becomes to accumulate the necessary information at a central level. Obviously, one does not rush out, on the basis of information economies alone, and recommend, for example, that simple effluent charges displace all pollution-control regulations. But, where feasible, building some freedom of choice into social programs does offer advantages, either in generating explicit information for policy-makers about the desirability of alternative outcomes or in bypassing the need for certain types of information altogether.

A third advantage of the market is its "devil take the hindmost" approach to questions of individual equity. At first blush this is an outrageous statement and, obviously, I have stated the point in a way designed more to catch the eye than to be precise. To elaborate, in any except a completely stagnant society, an efficient use of resources means constant change. From the standpoint of static efficiency, the more completely and rapidly the economy shifts to meet changes in consumer tastes, production technologies, resource availability, and locational advantages, the greater the advances in technology and the faster they are adopted, the greater the efficiency. While these changes on balance generate greater gains from society in the form of higher living standards, almost every one of them deprives some firms and individuals of income. Under the social arrangements of the private market, those who may suffer losses are not usually able to stand in the way of change.

Dealing with the problem of losses is one of the stickiest social issues. There is absolutely nothing in either economic or political theory to argue that efficiency considerations should always take precedence. And sometimes there is no way to avoid unconscionably large losses to some group except by avoiding or at least moderating changes otherwise called for by efficiency considerations. Nevertheless, in designing instruments for collective intervention that will avoid loss, we place far too much stress on eschewing efficient solutions, and far too little on compensation and general income-redistribution measures. Over time, the cumulative consequences are likely to be a much smaller pie for everyone.

The final virtue of market-like arrangements that I wish to stress is their potential ability to direct innovation into socially desirable directions. While the formal economic theory of the market emphasizes its ability to get the most out of existing resources and technology, what is far more important is its apparent capacity to stimulate and take advantage of advancing technology. Living standards in modern Western countries are, by orders of magnitude, superior to those of the early seventeenth century. Had the triumph of the market meant only a more efficient use of the technologies and resources then available, the gains in living standards would have been minuscule by comparison. What made the difference was the stimulation and harnessing of new technologies and resources.

From a long-range standpoint, the effectiveness of social intervention in a number of important areas depends critically on heeding this lesson. Much of the economic literature on pollution control, for example, stresses the role of economic incentives to achieve static efficiency in control measures—that is, the use of existing technology in a way that reaches environmental goals at least cost. In the long run, however, the future of society is going to hinge on the discovery and adoption of ever-improving technologies to reduce the environmental consequences of expanding production. If, for example, we assume that per capita living standards in the United States improve from now on at only one-half the rate of the past century, the gross national product a hundred years from now will still have risen more than threefold. Median family income, now about $14,000, will equal about $55,000. Only if the amount of pollution per unit of output is cut by two-thirds can we maintain current environmental performance, let alone improve it—even on the assumption that the rate of economic growth is halved. There is simply no way such reductions can be achieved unless the direction of technological change is shifted to minimize pollution.

The point is not that the unfettered market can deal with the problem of environmental quality—or other problems for which some form of regulation already exists. Indeed, the problems arise precisely because the market as it is now structured does not work well. But the historically demonstrated power of marketlike incentives warrants every effort to install such incentives in our programs of social intervention.

The Causes Of Market Failure Within the sphere of activities not excluded from the market by considerations of liberty and dignity, there remain many situations in which private enterprise operating in a free market as we now know it does not produce efficient results. Where the deviations are serious, a prima facie case arises for collective intervention on grounds of efficiency alone.

Every modern society is based upon a set of property and contract laws that specify a highly complex set of dos and don'ts with respect to owning, using, buying, and selling property. The structure of the private enterprise system and the efficiency with which it operates depend on the content of this system of laws. How efficiently that system works at any point in time is strongly conditioned by how well it matches the underlying technological and economic realities.

A second basic proposition underlies an identification and analysis of market failure: to be an efficient instrument for society a private market must be so organized that buyers and sellers realize *all* the benefits and pay *all* the costs of each transaction. In other words, the price paid by the buyer and the costs incurred by the seller in each private transaction must reflect the full value and the full cost of that transaction not only to them, but to society as a whole.

As a rough-and-ready generalization, the body of laws governing property rights and liabilities is likely to yield inefficient results principally when dealing with the side effects of private market transactions. The problem is not

that side effects exist, but that the benefits they confer or the costs they impose are often not reflected in the prices and costs that guide private decisions.

Where side effects are confined to the parties to a transaction, proper specification of the laws governing private property can sometimes ensure that they are properly reflected in the private accounting of costs and benefits. Under these circumstances, establishing some continuing mechanism of social intervention is unnecessary. Individual buy-and-sell arrangements can efficiently reflect social values. In many cases, however, the very nature of the situation is such that merely redefining property rights will not resolve the problem; markets can be organized by purely private efforts only at great cost, if at all.

There are essentially four sets of factors that lead to market failure: high transaction costs, large uncertainty, high information costs, and, finally, what economists call the "free rider" problem.

Transaction costs. Markets are not costless. There are expenses of money, time, and effort in setting and collecting prices. Sometimes transaction costs are virtually infinite: there is no conceivable way that a market can be formed to deal with side effects. Sometimes transaction costs, while not infinite, exceed the benefits that a market could otherwise confer, and so it does not pay to set one up. Very often the scope and nature of the transaction costs strongly limit the range of effective social intervention and force society to organize markets in less than an ideal way.

Uncertainty and information costs. It is easier to treat the problems of uncertainty and information costs together since it is through information that we can, at least sometimes, reduce uncertainty. Market transactions cannot be an efficient method of organizing human activity unless both the buyer and the seller understand the full costs and benefits to them of the transactions they undertake, including any side effects that impinge on their own welfare.

However, in the case of hazards that are highly complicated, the provision of technically complete but neutral information may not be very helpful. Evaluating the significance of such hazards may itself require more technical ability and judgment and more time than it is reasonable to expect from most consumers. Where the potential harms from a product feature are serious and where the technical difficulty of evaluating information is very great, regulation may be the best alternative despite its inefficiencies—and in some cases a ban on certain types of products may be required. But in all cases the comparison should be between an imperfect market and an imperfect regulatory scheme, not some ideal abstraction.

The "free rider" problem. Where the side effects of private transactions have a common impact on many people—for example, in the discharge of sulfur into the atmosphere from coal-burning utilities—the possibility of purely private action is severely limited. In theory, if the rights to the use of the clean air were assigned by law to the polluter, those affected might band together and pay the polluter to reduce the emissions. But any one individual would enjoy the benefits of the improvement whether he paid his share of the cost or not. He could be a "free rider" on the efforts of everyone else. How could cost shares be decided and enforced? Without the coercive power of government, purely voluntary arrangements could not be successful.

Changing Attitudes Relying on regulations rather than economic incentives to deal with highly complex areas of behavior, as we do for control of air and water pollution and industrial health and safety, has a built-in dynamic that inevitably broadens the scope of the regulations. Under an incentive-oriented approach—effluent charges, injury-rate taxes, or improved workmen's compensation—the administering agency does not itself have to keep abreast of every new development. The incentives provide a general penalty against unwanted actions. But if specific regulations are the only bar to prevent social damages, the regulating agency must provide a regulation for every possible occasion and circumstance. First it will take twenty-one pages to deal with ladders and then even more as time goes on. Social intervention becomes a race between the ingenuity of the regulatee and the loophole closing of the regulator, with a continuing expansion in the volume of regulations as the outcome.

Relying on regulations rather than economic incentives to deal with highly complex areas of behavior . . . has a built-in dynamic that inevitably broadens the scope of the regulations. . . . Social intervention becomes a race between the ingenuity of the regulatee and the loophole closing of the regulator, with a continuing expansion in the volume of regulations as the outcome.

We try to specify in minute detail the particular actions that generate social efficiency and then command their performance. But in certain complex areas of human behavior, neither our imagination nor our commands are up to the task. Consistently, where social problems arise because of distorted private incentives, we try to impose a solution without remedying the incentive structure. And equally consistently, the power of that structure defeats us.

Market-like instruments can supplant current command-and-control techniques only gradually. But not much thought has been devoted to dynamic strategies that, step by step, mesh a dwindling reliance on regulations with a cautiously expanding use of market instruments.

When social intervention into new areas is considered, we start with a more or less clean blackboard. We do not have to erase an existing maze of command-and-control laws. But a different problem then confronts us—impatience. Major political initiatives come only after the public has been persuaded that an important problem exists. A sense of urgency has developed. How can politicians then put before the public a ten-year plan for gradually developing a new market structure? Instead, the inevitable strategy is to enact ambitious legislation stipulating share and immediate results, and then to erode the regulations piecemeal with postponements and loopholes as problems develop. The very rhetoric and political process that moves us finally to get something done often puts us in a position where that something is done poorly.

The American political system has been a marvelously effective tool for providing both freedom and governance. Its institutions have been well suited for generating the compromises and accommodations about national issues needed in a large and heterogeneous society. But those institutions were especially designed to settle conflicts of value. As society has intervened in ever more complicated areas, however, and particularly as it aims to influence the decisions of millions of individuals and business firms, the critical choices have a much lower ideological and ethical content. For economic or social reasons, we may still want to move some area of decision-making completely out of the market and into the sphere of specified rights and du-

ties. And the necessity will remain to form political battle lines around the very real question of whether to intervene at all. We cannot abandon the standard techniques and institutions for forming consensus and negotiating compromises among groups with widely different values.

But how does an ingrained political process which stresses value adjustments come to grips with the critical choices among technically complicated alternatives when some of the very political techniques that move society toward a decision themselves make it difficult to pursue workable methods of intervention? Identifying heroes and villains, imputing values to technical choices, stressing the urgency of every problem, promising speedy results, and offering easily understandable solutions which specify outputs and rights—these are the common techniques of the political process whereby consensus is formed and action taken.

There is no obvious resolution to this dilemma. The suggestions that the political debate be confined to ends, while technicians and experts design the means once the ends have been decided, is facile and naive. Ends and means cannot and should not be separated. In the real world they are inextricably joined: we formulate our ends only as we debate the means of satisfying them. No electorate or politician can afford to turn over the crucial question of how social intervention is to be designed to supposedly apolitical experts.

The only available course is a steady maturing of both the electorate and political leaders. How to intervene, when we choose to do so, is ultimately a political issue. I am convinced that the economic and social forces that flow from growth and affluence will continue to throw up problems and attitudes that call for intervention of a very complex order. How we handle those questions not only will determine our success in meeting particular problems, but cumulatively will strongly influence the political and social fabric of our society. Even if it were politically possible—which it is not—we cannot handle the dilemma by abjuring any further extension of interventionist policies. But, equally, we cannot afford to go on imposing command-and-control solutions over an ever-widening sphere of social and economic activity.

I believe—I have no choice but to believe—that the American people can deal intelligently with issues painted in hues more subtle than black and white. Indeed, the political winds of the last few years can be read as a sign that the electorate is somewhat ahead of many of its political leaders. Voters are not disillusioned with government per se. But they are fed up with simple answers to complicated problems. They are ready, I think for a more realistic political dialogue. Almost two centuries ago the arguments for the ratification of the Constitution were laid out in *The Federalist* papers—perhaps the most sophisticated effort at political pamphleteering in history. I have good reason to hope—and to believe—that voters can accept the same high level of political arguments as the farmers, mechanics, and politicians of the eighteenth-century colonies.

Ends and means cannot and should not be separated. In the real world they are inextricably joined: we formulate our ends only as we debate the means of satisfying them. No electorate or politician can afford to turn over the crucial question of how social intervention is to be designed to supposedly apolitical experts.

Discussion

1. Why do you think that Americans tend to view many public issues as "black and white" (as Schultze puts it) instead of in a deeper, more sophisticated fashion? Are people not intelligent enough?

2. How does Schultze assess the ability of a market with private rights to adjust to change in a dynamic fashion? Is this becoming less important or more important with time?

29

Public Choice: Understanding Government and Government Failure

TRUE OR FALSE

T   F

1. Market failure enhances the argument for, and likelihood of, government intervention and its success in overcoming particular shortcomings of the market.

2. A politician can be viewed as a political entrepreneur or supplier.

3. Voting, like other decisions, is carried out with imperfect information.

4. Most voters are chiefly concerned with just a few of the many issues decided legislatively.

5. With collective action, an individual can usually be sure that he will not pay for something he does not want.

6. Individual preferences will influence the outcome of democratic political decisions.

7. The "public good" quality of antipoverty efforts will, according to economic analysis encourage collective action for redistribution of income.

8. Government failure strengthens the case for use of the market system.

9. The individual voter has a strong economic incentive to fight special interest legislation with his time and money, because such legislation is very costly to society.

10. Passage of special interest legislation is not always inefficient.

11. Voters are more likely to be short sighted on a complex issue than a simple one.

12. Public sector decision-makers have a strong incentive to be efficient, since most of the people they deal with are their employers.

13. When exercising his options, the voter usually must choose among complex bundles of goods, services, and costs.

PROBLEMS AND PROJECTS

Exhibit 1

Voter	Actual net dollar benefits (+) or costs (−) for the voter			Political entrepreneur's estimate of the voter's perceived net dollar benefits (+) or costs (−)		
	Proposal A	Proposal B	Proposal C	Proposal A	Proposal B	Proposal C
1	$ 5	$ 10	$ 10	$ 5	$ 10	$ 10
2	5	4	−4	5	4	−4
3	5	3	−2	5	3	−2
4	3	1	−1	3	0	0
5	3	1	−1	3	0	0
6	3	1	−1	3	0	0
7	1	−8	−1	1	−8	0
8	1	−4	−1	1	−4	0
9	−2	−3	−1	−2	−3	0
10	−2	−3	−1	−2	−3	0

1. Exhibit 1 presents data on the actual and perceived benefits of voters resulting from the passage of three different legislative proposals.
   a. Calculate the actual benefit/cost ratio for each of the three proposals.
   b. Which of the three proposals do you think will be favored (opposed) by the political entrepreneur? Why?
   c. Given that proposal B exerts only a small impact on voters 4, 5, and 6, why might it be sensible for them to ignore proposal B?

2. Assume that price supports for dairy products are in the interests of U.S. dairy product producers but not in the interests of U.S. dairy product consumers.
   a. Use the concepts and analysis of this chapter to indicate why dairy farmers might be successful in organizing to persuade Congress to adopt price supports.
   b. Conduct a similar analysis to show why consumers might be unsuccessful in attempting to organize to persuade Congress not to adopt price supports.

3. Match the letters on the right with the numbers on the left.

   _____ (1) Special interest groups
   _____ (2) Externalities
   _____ (3) The free-rider problem
   _____ (4) The rational ignorance effect
   _____ (5) The short-sightedness effect
   _____ (6) Referendum decision-makers

   a. It explains why the market has trouble allocating public goods efficiently.
   b. It results because information is costly, and voters do not expect their vote to be decisive.
   c. They are a good potential source of campaign contributions for political entrepreneurs.
   d. It would reduce the power of special interest groups.
   e. They strengthen the case for government intervention.
   f. It explains why macropolicy is likely to be excessively expansionary 12–18 months before a major election.

4. Write a short essay either criticizing or supporting the economic analysis of public choice as outlined in the text. Be sure to consider factors that are important determinants of the behavior of voters, political entrepreneurs, and lobbyists. Do not ignore the importance of information.

LEARNING THE MECHANICS—MULTIPLE CHOICE

1. Ideal public sector action can potentially improve economic efficiency
   a. because goods can be provided free by the public sector.
   b. when market inefficiency results because of spillover effects.
   c. if prices can be fixed below the equilibrium level, thereby limiting the power of greedy businessmen.
   d. because political decision-makers generally place the public interest above the pursuit of personal gain.

2. With economic efficiency as the criterion, which of the following is the best justification for the government's providing some economic goods and services, rather than relying on the market?
   a. Government provision of goods eliminates misallocation that results from the power of special interest groups.
   b. It is important that political goods and services be provided free of charge.
   c. There is often no way to sell public goods in a private market, because the benefits cannot be limited to persons who pay for them.
   d. It would be unethical and unreasonable to allow private individuals to make a profit by providing education, police protection, and similar services.

3. The political roles of legislators and voters
   a. are analogous to those of producers and consumers in the market.
   b. have no relation to the actions of market participants.
   c. can serve to express collective preferences, but not individual preferences.
   d. are effective for expressing preferences only by voting.

4. In explaining public sector choices, economic theory
   a. is perfectly appropriate, since money prices are used in the public sector in the same way as in the private sector.
   b. is inappropriate, since individuals act in the public interest, not out of self-interest, when doing the public's business.
   c. is useful because individuals, including those who participate in the political process, will respond in a predictable way to changes in personal costs and benefits.
   d. is useful only if political entrepreneurs are highly selfish.

5. In general, voters are concerned
   a. with most issues, since information on most issues is cost free.
   b. with most issues, since each issue will have some impact, however slight, on each citizen.
   c. with the views of a particular political candidate on all issues.
   d. with a few specific issues—those that directly affect them in a substantial way.

6. According to the special interest effect, which of the following groups is likely to have the greatest influence on legislative collective decision-making?
   a. Nonunion employees
   b. Consumers
   c. Taxpayers
   d. Business interests and labor unions

7. A characteristic of the public sector is that individuals, in selecting their legislative representatives
    a. have no influence over political decision-makers.
    b. can normally use their voting power on an issue-by-issue basis.
    c. cannot effectively vote for politicians on an issue-by-issue basis, but must accept all the views of the candidate as a package.
    d. can usually find a representative who reflects the individual's views on all significant issues.

8. Governmental allocation will more likely be preferred to market allocation when
    a. consumers are well informed.
    b. the shortsightedness effect dominates.
    c. the rational ignorance effect dominates.
    d. high external costs are associated with market decision-making.

9. Economic theory suggests that it is often rational for a vote-maximizing politician to support special interest groups at the expense of other unorganized, widely dispersed groups (for example, taxpayers or consumers)
    a. when the gains that accrue to the special interest groups are much smaller than the costs imposed on others.
    b. when the non-special interest voter is unconcerned or uninformed, and campaign funds are readily available from the special interest.
    c. if, and only if, government action is socially efficient.
    d. if the government action would reduce the monopoly power of business or labor.

10. The special interest effect will be stronger if the issue is
    a. simple and easily understood by the voter.
    b. complex and difficult for the average voter to comprehend.
    c. decided by a referendum vote.
    d. one that promotes economic inefficiency.

11. Operational efficiency in the public sector tends to be low because the individual government employee
    a. is usually able, in a dishonest manner, to take home the money that would be called profit in the private sector.
    b. is unable to profit directly from the extra care and effort that efficiency requires.
    c. is usually not as competent as the private sector employee.
    d. usually is a victim of the bundle-purchase effect.

THE ECONOMIC WAY OF THINKING—MULTIPLE CHOICE

1. (**I**) In the public sector, unlike the private sector, personal gain is usually not the stated goal of entrepreneurial decision-makers. (**II**) In the public sector, as in the private sector, we can expect individuals, including political entrepreneurs, to be motivated by self-interest most of the time.
    a. Both I and II are true.
    b. I is true, II is false.
    c. I is false, II is true.
    d. Both I and II are false.

2. Economic theory leads us to expect that the typical voter will be uninformed on many issues because
   a. most issues are so complex that voters will be unable to understand them.
   b. even though information is free, most voters do not care what politicians are doing.
   c. information is costly, and the individual voter casting a well-informed vote can expect negligible personal benefit.
   d. citizen apathy about political matters is inevitable, except when decisions are made by referendum.

3. In a market system, individuals normally pay for what they get. With public sector operation
   a. the individual consumer often does not pay, although someone else must.
   b. the individual often does not pay, nor does anyone else, since production is not for profit.
   c. an individual's tax bill will approximate the value to him of government's service.
   d. payment is avoided since costs are irrelevant in the public sector.

4. Economic theory suggests that laws against crimes such as murder, arson, and robbery are
   a. the result of our moral code, even though they promote economic inefficiency.
   b. examples of government actions that improve resource allocation by discouraging activities that generate external costs and violate our moral code.
   c. impossible to understand from a strictly economic viewpoint.
   d. examples of government action that stem from the power of special interest groups.

5. Public choice theory suggests that political entrepreneurs will be most likely to favor redistribution of income from
   a. the rich to the poor.
   b. disorganized individuals to well-organized special interest groups.
   c. middle-income taxpayers to both the rich and the poor.
   d. well-organized business and labor groups to consumers.

6. According to economic theory, each voter supports the candidate
   a. who offers the greatest number of programs.
   b. who offers to make the greatest aggregate decrease in taxes, other things constant.
   c. who offers him the greatest personal gain, with no consideration of effects on others.
   d. who offers the greatest *net* benefits, including utility that might be derived as the result of improvement in the economic welfare of others.

7. "The ideal public policy, from the viewpoint of a political entrepreneur, is one that provides widespread benefits to the voting populace, even if it means that a small number of voters will *individually* bear substantial cost." This statement is probably
   a. correct, because voters will be well informed when they are the beneficiaries of a political action.
   b. incorrect, because most of the beneficiaries are likely to be rationally uninformed, whereas the special interest group that bears the cost will tend to oppose strenuously politicians who follow such a course.
   c. correct, since the political process dilutes the influence of special interest because each has only one vote.
   d. incorrect, because the well-informed voter will oppose policies that conflict with the views of small groups of people.

8. "Special interests will no longer have special influence, once we throw the rascals out of office and elect people who are basically honest." The facts of life bias representative government against this view because
   a. special interest group members are richer and can buy more votes than other people.
   b. all politicians are basically honest.
   c. even perfect and costless information for voters could not reduce special interest groups' influence by much.
   d. even honest politicians have a strong incentive to support special interest positions.

9. Suppose that macroeconomic policy increases output and employment between 6 and 18 months before it causes an acceleration in the rate of inflation. According to the shortsightedness effect, expansionary macroeconomic policy would be
   a. highly attractive to political entrepreneurs before each election.
   b. highly attractive to political entrepreneurs after an election.
   c. attractive to political entrepreneurs only if such a policy would help to stabilize the economy.
   d. unattractive to political entrepreneurs because of the future inflation it might cause.

10. Which of the following political positions does the special interest effect make more attractive to a vote-maximizing political entrepreneur?
    a. Abolition of the present tax credit for industry X
    b. Abolition of tenure for college professors
    c. 15 percent increase in social security benefits
    d. 50 percent reduction in import taxes on foreign-produced automobiles

11. Garbage-removal services are provided in different cities by different kinds of organizations. If a newly developed truck has just come on the market, and managers in all garbage-removal organizations are analyzing the net benefits of buying the new type of truck, which of the following should expect to undertake the most serious, painstaking examinations?
    a. Managers of city-owned garbage agencies
    b. Managers of large, profitable corporations in little danger of sinking below the normal level of profits
    c. Owner-managers of medium-sized private firms
    d. Big-city mayors

12. When a federal agency requests funds to build a dam to subsidize irrigation of farmland used to grow potatoes near a river in Idaho, we would expect the *least* active support from
    a. farmers with land near the proposed dam.
    b. the construction unions whose members would work on the project.
    c. the chamber of commerce in a city located near the project.
    d. consumers of potatoes nationally.

THE ECONOMIC WAY OF THINKING—DISCUSSION QUESTIONS

1. Do you think that real-world politicians consider how their positions on issues will affect their election prospects? In the last 20 years, how many congressmen
   a. from Michigan have opposed tariffs on foreign-produced automobiles?
   b. from the St. Petersburg, Florida, district (populated mostly by people over 65) have voted against a rise in social security benefits?
   c. from anywhere have supported the closing of a military installation in their home district?
   d. from Texas have voted against oil industry tax benefits?
   e. from the state of Washington have voted against an appropriations bill awarding a defense or space contract to the Boeing Company of Seattle?

2. "When public sector action fails, a government agency typically responds by doubling its budget and staff."
    a. Should government ever discontinue a current function? If so, when?
    b. Is the loss of the bankruptcy criterion a strength or weakness of the public sector?

3. Which of the following do you think are special interest issues?
    a. Tariffs on imports of television sets
    b. Tax-free interest income from municipal bonds
    c. Tenure for college professors
    d. Below-cost tuition for college students
    e. Rent controls for your local community.
    f. Interest-free educational loans for college students
    Are you in favor of some special interest issues? Which ones?

4. It is often charged that the tax structure of the United States is rife with loopholes. In light of the political influence of special interest groups, do you think this is surprising? Can you think of specific tax loopholes that reflect the special interest effect? Explain.

5. When is the case for market allocation strongest? What are the major factors that weaken the case for market allocation? Under what conditions is public sector intervention most likely to improve the situation?

6. Anthony Downs, Gordon Tullock, and others have argued that voters have very little incentive to acquire information relevant to decisions that are made collectively.
    a. Why is this so?
    b. Why may this factor enhance the strength of special interest groups? Explain.
    c. Why may it cause voters to be short sighted? Explain.
    d. Can you think of any institutional change that would give voters (consumers) more incentive to acquire information on "political goods" and their costs? Explain.

7. How would the power of special interest groups be reduced if legislators were to set a budget first, before appropriating expenditures? Do you favor such a plan? Would it create problems?

PERSPECTIVES IN ECONOMICS

The Limited Case For Government Intervention

[Reprinted from the *Economic Report of the President 1982*, pp. 29–36.]

Under certain assumptions discussed below, a competitive economy can be shown to lead to general economic efficiency. In standard economics, an economy is said to be "efficient" if it is impossible to make anyone better off without making someone else worse off. That is, there is no possible rearrangement of resources, in either production or consumption, which could improve anyone's position without simultaneously harming some other person. If there is a possibility of such a rearrangement occurring, then this means that someone could be made better off without harming anyone else. If such a possibility does exist, then the economy is not efficient.

Each person in such an economy is considered to be concerned primarily with his or her own welfare. Since there is no central authority directing the course of this economy, whatever results occur are the unintended consequences of millions of individual actions. Nonetheless, the outcome of this undirected but self-interested behavior is efficient in the sense mentioned above. Despite the absence of any central direction, it can be shown that an economic order is generated which has the desirable characteristic of being economically efficient. Moreover, an efficient economic system is responsive to individual wants: that is, efficiency is defined in terms of each person achieving his or her own goals.

Such a system relies on the ability of people to trade freely with each other, for a bargain entered into voluntarily by two individuals is expected by both of them to make both of them better off. Two conditions must be fulfilled for such trades to occur. First, individuals must have the right to enter freely into whatever bargains they wish: that is, there must be freedom of contract. Second, property rights must be well defined in all cases except those where the cost of enforcing the right would be greater than the value of the right.

Certain additional characteristics must be present if the economy is to be efficient. The most important of these characteristics are: the absence of externalities, the absence of significant monopolies, and the appropriate provision of public goods. Though such an economy is efficient, "efficiency" says nothing about the distribution of income which results from the process. By some criteria the market-generated distribution of income in an efficient economy may be unacceptable. Thus, government intervention may be justified to correct market failures or to change the resulting distribution of income. It is also possible that an efficient economy may be less stable than is generally considered desirable.

Externalities An externality is said to exist where an economic agent (be it producer or consumer) either does not bear the full marginal costs of an economic action or does not gain its full marginal benefits. Therefore, these agents may not undertake the activity at its optimal economic level. If there are external costs, the agent may undertake too high a level of the activity. If there are external benefits, the agent may not undertake enough of the activity.

An example of an activity with external benefits is education. Because some of the benefits of living in a nation of people with a common language and culture are external, individuals considering only their own benefit from education will most likely buy too little. The standard example of an activity that imposes external costs is manufacturing that results in pollution. Consider a factory which pollutes the air. Those who live near the factory will suffer the costs of the pollution, but the factory owner will probably not consider these costs in deciding how much to produce. Since the factory owner does not bear these costs, the product made in the factory will be underpriced in relation to its true economic cost. Hence, too much of the good, and too much pollution, will probably be produced. Government intervention may therefore be justified where either marginal costs or benefits are external.

Private transactions between parties may sometimes be adequate to solve externality problems, but this requires that transaction costs be low. This requirement will not in general be satisfied when many parties are involved.

Since externality problems occur because decision-makers either do not pay all the costs of their actions or do not reap all of the benefits, the most efficient way to correct the problem is to change the marginal costs and benefits. With respect to education the conventional solution has been to establish systems of public education paid for by taxes and offered below cost to students. This solution itself creates problems, since the creation of a tax-subsidized producer of education may lead to the producer having a monopoly over education. But monopoly is inefficient whether it is public or private. An alternative would be to grant a "voucher," with the amount of this voucher equal to the difference between private benefit (the benefit to the student) and total benefit (the benefit which accrues to other members of society as well as to the student). This would avoid the problem of monopoly and might generate pressures for more efficient schools.

To deal with the external costs of pollution, the conventional solution has been regulation of pollution control technology by government agencies. Since this form of regulation often does not take account of differences in abatement costs for different polluters, it is often inefficient in that the public pays more than is necessary for a given amount of pollution reduction (or a smaller reduction in pollution is achieved for a given expenditure than would be possible with a more efficient scheme).

Two ways of reducing pollution more efficiently have

been identified. One is to charge those who pollute a fee based on the cost imposed on others by the pollution. This method has been used in West German waterways and has been quite effective. Another alternative is for the government to create property rights in air or water. These rights would then be purchased by those who value them most— that is, by those who would pay the highest cost to reduce their pollution. These two methods, if implemented correctly, would probably lead to the same outcome.

Monopoly One of the conditions of market efficiency is that there must be enough buyers and sellers of a good so that each of them has little influence on its price. This condition is not always satisfied, however. Sometimes technical and cost conditions in an industry are such that there will be room for only one or a few firms. Two approaches have been taken in the United States to this problem. In cases of natural monopoly, direct government regulation of ownership is common. In industries where only a few firms exist, the antitrust laws are more commonly used to avoid the costs of monopoly.

Most of the natural monopolies arise from the need to provide public utility services, such as electricity and water. Regulation of most of these natural monopolies occurs primarily at the State and local level and is not covered in this *Report,* but there are some monopolies regulated at the Federal level. In some cases of natural monopoly, however, newer technology may so change technical and cost considerations that additional firms would enter the market if permitted to do so by regulatory authorities.

In an industry with few firms it may be possible for the firms to act in collusion and thus behave as a monopoly. When this occurs, the profits of the firms are increased, but efficiency losses are imposed on the economy. Even though such collusions are unstable, losses of efficiency occur during their existence. The antitrust laws make such behavior illegal.

The effects of mergers on economic efficiency are more difficult to discern than the effects of illegal monopoly. Two firms in the same industry may merge for any of at least three reasons. First, a merger may be an attempt to obtain monopoly power. When this occurs the merger will be inefficient and should be stopped. But, firms may also decide to merge to take advantage of economies of scale or because one is better managed and can therefore increase efficiency in resource use. In these latter two cases a merger is likely to improve efficiency and should be allowed. The difficulty, of course, is that it is not always obvious whether monopoly or an increase in efficiency will be the dominant effect of any given merger.

Though there are difficult cases, this Administration has already made some changes in policy in the administration of Federal antitrust laws, changes based on economic analysis. First, a merger between two firms which have a relatively small share of the market should be allowed, for there is little danger of monopoly. Second, no significant economic problems are likely to arise from a merger of firms in unrelated industries (a conglomerate merger); such a merger will not create any significant monopoly power. Third, there is little danger of monopoly and therefore no reason for Federal intervention when a firm merges with another firm that is a customer of a supplier of the first (a vertical merger). Finally, a firm that obtains a large share of a market by being a more efficient competitor is acting in a desirable fashion and should not be punished by antitrust action on the part of the Federal Government. In recent years, those in charge of administering Federal antitrust laws sometimes have behaved as if they viewed their function as protecting existing firms from competition. From an economic viewpoint the purpose of the antitrust laws is to maintain competition, even if competition leads to the decline of firms which are less efficient.

Public Goods A public good has two distinctive characteristics. The first is that consumption of the good by one party does not reduce consumption of the good by others, and the second is that there is no effective way to restrict the benefits of such goods to those who directly pay for them. The standard example of a public good is national defense. If national defense deters a foreign aggressor, everyone in the country benefits. This means that no individual will have sufficient incentive to spend his own resources on national defense, since he will benefit from his neighbor's spending. Hence, such public goods as national defense are usually provided by some action of the national government. Government action is usually necessary for the optimal provision of many public goods, and this point does not arouse controversy among economists. Sometimes there are debates, however, about whether a particular good is sufficiently public in nature to justify its being provided by the government.

Another public good is information. If one person learns some valuable fact and tells someone else, the use of the information by one does not reduce the use of the same information by the other. If a consumer organization spends resources to find out which products are best and sells a publication that provides this information to subscribers, these subscribers may then pass the information on to others who did not pay for it. This can be shown as a market failure, in the sense that the private market did not generate enough information; if the organization could capture all of the returns, it would provide additional information. Patents and copyrights are designed to reduce this problem by giving inventors and writers property rights in their product, thus providing incentives for production, but there are still cases where the private market does not generate sufficient information. This provides the rationale for government financing of certain kinds of research.

Income Redistribution In a market economy, individual income depends upon what one has to sell and on the amount which others are willing to pay for it. What most people sell on the market is their labor. About 75 percent of national income is in the form of wages and salaries and other forms of labor remuneration. Others have capital or land to rent, and their return is interest and dividends, or rent income. Most people can earn income from both capital and labor over their lifetimes. But some persons may have few or no valuable things to sell, and these persons will have low incomes. A decision may then be made to transfer income to such people directly through government. Two justifications can be presented for such transfers of income, one based on the social value of providing certain forms of income insurance, the other based on benevolence. We consider each.

Anyone may lose his ability to earn income. A worker may become physically disabled or find that technological progress has made his or her skills obsolete. Or an investor may find that changing market conditions have eroded the return on capital. Since individuals generally do not like the risk of losing their ability to earn income, they often seek to insure themselves against such a possibility.

But there are difficulties in providing insurance against falling incomes by way of private-market mechanisms. A major difficulty is what is called "adverse selection." Assume that some insurance company offered actuarially fair insurance against this risk and charged all persons the same premium. (That is, the amount of the premium equals the expected cost of having a low income.) Since most persons are averse to risk, they might buy this insurance even though the premium would be somewhat greater than the expected cost because of the expense of writing the insurance. Some persons would be better risks than average, and new insurance companies would compete with the first company for these better risks. This would leave the original company insuring only the bad risks, which the company would then find financially intolerable. Ultimately, one class of persons would be unable to obtain any insurance.

This would be an example of market failure and an argument for government provision of insurance, since the government can force everyone to join the same insurance pool. The appropriate form of insurance to those who experience a temporary loss of income is a cash grant. Welfare payments and unemployment compensation may be viewed as just this sort of insurance.

The second argument for government transfers to the poor is an argument based on benevolence. Many people prefer not to live in a society where there is poverty and thus have an incentive to transfer some of their resources to the poor voluntarily. When one individual performs such a transfer, all individuals who dislike poverty benefit. Thus, most people will have an incentive to reduce their contributions to the poor and rely on the contributions of others. In all likelihood, such voluntary transfers would be too low to keep people out of poverty; it may become necessary for the government to do it.

In cases where transfers of income are desirable, economic theory can indicate the most efficient form of transfer. One goal should be to minimize interference in private markets. Price controls on gasoline and laws decreeing minimum wages, for example, are considered by many economists to be inefficient ways of helping the poor.

The way in which resources should be transferred to the poor depends on the goal of the donors. If the goal is simply to improve the welfare of the poor, the most efficient solution probably would be a system of cash transfers, since it can be assumed that recipients are best able to determine the pattern of spending that maximizes their welfare. But if the donor is more concerned with the specific goods which the recipient consumes, a direct transfer of goods may be preferable. In this case the argument can be made for using some form of voucher. A voucher is essentially a coupon usable only for the purchase of a specific type of good. Food stamps are one example. Use of vouchers instead of a direct transfer of goods allows recipients to determine their own consumption but restricts the type of goods which the recipient may purchase.

Regardless of the form of transfer, there is still an efficiency cost. Transfers reduce the incentive of recipients to work, and the taxes imposed on the rest of society to finance these transfers also cause losses in efficiency. There are also costs of administering the program. Economists are able to give advice on ways of transferring income which may serve to minimize these effects, but the decision as to the amount of the transfers is a political decision, not an economic one.

Macroeconomic Stability A market system may sometimes be subject to unacceptably large fluctuations in income. When this occurs, it has implications for the general welfare. First, average income levels may be smaller with fluctuations than if the level of activity is more stable. Second, even if the average level of incomes is unaffected by such fluctuations, people are generally risk-averse. That is, most people prefer a steady stream of income to a fluctuating stream, even if their total income is the same over a period of time. For these reasons, government may have a role in helping to provide stability.

An alternative view is that a market economy is inherently quite stable. According to this view, government actions are the primary destabilizing factors in the economy. That is, many fluctuations in income which seem to be caused by private sector actions are actually caused by attempts to outguess the government.

Macroeconomic stability also involves the question of what to do about money. Money performs several functions in an economy. Its use economizes on transaction costs and on information costs, since all persons accept the same money and are aware of its value. However, the government must be careful in its money creating function not to exacerbate cyclical fluctuations. Excess creation of money leads to inflation, which reduces money's value.

Although the Federal Government is the appropriate agent for stabilizing the economy, the limits of such action must be understood. This Administration believes that "fine tuning" of the economy—attempting to offset every fluctuation—is not possible. The information needed to do so is often simply not available, and when it becomes available it is quite likely that underlying conditions will already have changed. As a result, a policy of fine tuning the economy is as likely to be counterproductive as it is to be helpful. Though it is necessary for the government to have macroeconomic policies, including both monetary and fiscal policies designed to achieve some desired growth of income, such policies are not suitable for correcting small fluctuations in economic activity.

Discussion

1. This reading is longer than most, but it is especially fascinating because it constitutes our government's statement about what kinds of activities it should and should not be undertaking. Do you see evidence that the federal government is going beyond its own guidelines for government intervention? In what areas?

2. Reread each of the subsections carefully and attempt to *rank* the reasons in order of importance. Which rationale is the most convincing? Which could you do without?

3. What would it be like if there *were* no government? Who would undertake the activities it now does for us? Would we be better or worse off?

30

Gaining from International Trade

TRUE OR FALSE

T F

☐ ☐ 1. Economic theory suggests that *both* partners gain from free trade. Voluntary exchange does *not* generate gain for one nation at the expense of the other.

☐ ☐ 2. Our analysis shows that every individual consumer gains from international free trade whenever it takes place.

☐ ☐ 3. The joint output of countries would be maximized if each country specialized in production of those commodities for which it is the low opportunity-cost producer, exchanging them for other commodities for which it is a high opportunity-cost producer.

☐ ☐ 4. In a sense, tariffs are like transportation costs—they are obstacles that prevent trading partners from fully realizing the potential gains from trade.

☐ ☐ 5. A secondary effect of policies that restrict imports is the additional demand generated for the nation's export products.

☐ ☐ 6. An import quota places a ceiling on the amount of a product that can be imported during a specified time period.

☐ ☐ 7. A country that is rich in resources and an efficient producer will gain if it refuses to trade, although this action hurts the rest of the world.

☐ ☐ 8. One problem with the removal of all tariffs would probably be increased unemployment in domestic import-competing industries in the short run.

☐ ☐ 9. If all tariffs were removed in the United States, fewer jobs would clearly be available to U.S. workers, since wage rates are high in the United States.

☐ ☐ 10. Regarding the removal of an import quota on automobiles: We would expect the chairman of the board of General Motors and the president of the United Auto Workers' union to disagree on the merit of quota removal.

☐ ☐ 11. The primary economic motive behind exports is the accumulation of foreign currency; imports are best regarded as a necessary evil, required at some level to keep the goodwill of the selling nations.

☐ ☐ 12. U.S. tariffs, in general, are much lower now than they were in 1930.

☐ ☐ 13. Foreign trade in most nations is less than 5 percent of GNP.

270

PROBLEMS AND PROJECTS

1. Use Exhibit 1 when answering the following.

Exhibit 1   The Production Possibilities of Rhineland and Nepal

	Rhineland			Nepal	
	Food	Clothing		Food	Clothing
A	0	900	A	0	500
B	100	750	B	100	450
C	200	600	C	200	400
D	300	400	D	300	300
E	400	200	E	400	150
F	500	0	F	500	0

a. What is the per unit opportunity cost of expanding food production from 200 to 300 in Rhineland? In Nepal?

b. In the absence of trade, the people of Rhineland will choose to produce at point D. The people of Nepal will choose point B. Given their preferences for food and clothing, could the nations gain from trade? How can you tell? How would trade flow between the two countries?

c. Suppose that both countries produced at point C and that Rhineland traded 100 units of its domestically produced clothing for 100 units of food produced in Nepal. Compared to the no-trade point B alternative, how would this transaction affect the goods available to the people of Nepal? What would happen to the joint output of the two countries?

d. Suppose that Rhineland produced at point B and Nepal at point D. If Rhineland traded 225 units of clothing for 200 units of Nepal's food, how much would each country gain, relative to the no-trade chosen combination of part *b*? What would happen to their joint output, relative to their mutual production at point C?

e. If Rhineland expanded its clothing production still farther, to 900, what would be its per unit opportunity cost of producing clothing in this range? What would be Nepal's per unit opportunity cost of producing the first 300 units of clothing domestically? Once Rhineland is producing at point B and Nepal at point D, can joint output be expanded by additional specialization? Are *additional* mutual gains from trade possible? Explain.

2. The country of Arcadia produces and consumes unique computers. Exhibit 2 shows Arcadia's demand and supply curves for their computers along with the demand for Arcadian computers from the rest of the world (ROW).

Exhibit 2

Price (dollars/unit)	Arcadia's quantity supplied	Arcadia's quantity demanded	ROW's quantity demanded	Total quantity demanded
$2400	1200	750	280	1030
2200	1100	800	300	_____
2000	1000	850	320	_____
1800	900	900	340	_____
1600	800	950	360	_____
1400	700	1000	380	_____
1200	600	1050	400	_____
1000	500	1100	420	_____

a. Fill in the missing information in the table.
b. If Arcadia has no trade with the rest of the world, what will be the equilibrium price of computers in Arcadia? What will be the equilibrium quantity demanded and supplied?
c. What will be the equilibrium price of computers if Arcadia trades with the ROW? Compare this price to the equilibrium price of part b. Why is it higher?
d. With trade, what is Arcadia's equilibrium quantity of computers supplied? Compare this with the quantity supplied without trade. What must have happened to Arcadia's production of other goods and services as a result of international trade?
e. With trade, what is Arcadia's quantity of computers demanded? Compare the quantity of computers demanded in Arcadia without trade. In what way can this difference be of benefit generally to Arcadia consumers?
f. What quantity of computers is exported by Arcadia? Do Arcadia's computer producers clearly benefit by unrestricted international trade in computers?
g. As a result of Arcadia's exports, what do you suppose has happened to the price of computers in the ROW? How would you feel about this if you were an ROW computer "producer," either worker or entrepreneur? And if you were an ROW computer buyer, how would you react?

3. Suppose that the United States can purchase motorcycles from abroad for $3,000 each, and that this price does not vary with the quantity the U.S. purchases. Alternatively, the U.S. can produce its own motorcycles according to the supply schedule given in Exhibit 3, which also shows the U.S.'s demand for motorcycles.

Exhibit 3

Price (dollars/unit)	Domestic quantity supplied	Domestic quantity demanded
	(thousands/year)	
$4500	1000	700
4000	900	900
3500	800	1100
3000	700	1300
2500	600	1500
2000	500	1700

a. In the absence of international trade what would be the price of motorcycles in the U.S.? What quantities would be demanded and supplied?

b. Suppose that motorcycles can be imported into the U.S. without restriction. What will be the price of motorcycles in the U.S.? What will be the quantities demanded and produced domestically? What will be the quantity of imports? By how much will domestic production decline relative to the no-trade amount?

c. Suppose that workers and management lobby Congress for a tariff on imports on the grounds that they need temporary protection from imports in order to maintain domestic markets while they "retool" to incorporate the latest and most efficient techniques of motorcycle production (a version of the "infant" industry argument). If government grants domestic producers a tariff on imports of $500 per cycle, what will be the domestic price of motorcycles? By how much will domestic production increase? (This is called the "protective effect" of the tariff.) By how much will U.S. purchases of motorcycles fall? By how much will imports fall?

d. Suppose that *instead of* the tariff of part c, government imposed a quota on imports of 300 motorcycles per year. In this case, what would happen to the price of motorcycles as compared to the unrestricted ("free") trade price? [*Hint:* locate a price at which the domestic quantity supplied plus 300 equals the domestic quantity demanded at that price.] What will be the protective effect (increase in domestic quantity produced) of the quota?

e. Judging from your answers to c and d above, what is the basic difference between a tariff and a quota?

LEARNING THE MECHANICS—MULTIPLE CHOICE

1. Which of the following best describes the implications of the law of comparative advantage? Each trading nation can gain by
    a. selling services for which it is a high opportunity-cost producer and buying goods that it produces at a low cost.
    b. selling those services that it enjoys, while buying goods for which it is a low opportunity-cost producer.
    c. selling services for which it is a low opportunity-cost producer and buying those things for which it is a high opportunity-cost producer.
    d. selling those services that it dislikes, while buying those that it finds most enjoyable to produce.

2. A trade policy that limits the entry of foreign goods to the U.S. market will
    a. benefit consumers at the expense of producers.
    b. increase the nation's real income by protecting domestic jobs from foreign competition.
    c. reduce the demand for U.S. export goods, since foreigners will be unable to purchase our goods unless they can sell to us.
    d. enhance economic efficiency by permitting domestic resources to be fully utilized.

3. A country can gain from international trade if
    a. it is unusually efficient in producing all goods.
    b. it is very inefficient in producing all goods.
    c. it always operates at full employment.
    d. the relative prices of the nation's products differ from those of other countries.

4. A higher tariff on foreign-produced steel would be most likely to benefit
    a. domestic consumers of products that contain steel.
    b. producers in export industries.
    c. producers and workers in the steel industry.
    d. producers and workers in all industries except steel.

5. The national defense argument for high tariffs on a commodity
   a. is stronger if large supplies of the commodity can be stored cheaply.
   b. is stronger if storage of the commodity is costly.
   c. is based on the economic principle of comparative advantage.
   d. is based on the economic principle of absolute advantage.

Use the following information to answer the next *three* questions. Exhibit 4 outlines the production possibilities of Italia and Slavia for food and clothing.

Exhibit 4

Italia		Slavia	
Food	*Clothing*	*Food*	*Clothing*
0	8	0	20
4	6	2	15
8	4	4	10
12	2	6	5
16	0	8	0

6. What is the opportunity cost of producing one unit of food in Italia?
   a. One-quarter of a unit of clothing
   b. One-half of a unit of clothing
   c. Two units of clothing
   d. Five units of clothing

7. Which of the following is true?
   a. Slavia has a comparative advantage in the production of both goods.
   b. Italia has a comparative advantage in the production of food.
   c. Slavia is the low opportunity-cost producer of food.
   d. None of the above

8. The law of comparative advantage suggests that
   a. neither country would gain from trade even if the transportation costs for the products were zero.
   b. Slavia would not gain from trade because it has an absolute advantage in the production of both goods.
   c. both countries could gain if Italia traded food for Slavia clothing.
   d. both countries could gain if Slavia traded food for Italia clothing.

9. A nation will benefit from international trade when it
   a. imports more that it exports.
   b. exports more than it imports.
   c. imports goods for which it is a high opportunity-cost producer, while exporting goods for which it is a low opportunity-cost producer.
   d. exports goods for which it is a high opportunity-cost producer, while importing those goods for which it is a low opportunity-cost producer.

10. The percentage of the U.S. GNP devoted to international trade is
    a. more than 30 percent.
    b. between 25 and 30 percent.
    c. between 15 and 20 percent.
    d. less than 12 percent.

11. The major trading partner of the United States in 1984 was
    a. the United Kingdom.
    c. Mexico
    c. Canada.
    d. Japan.

12. Exhibit 5 compares the production possibilities of the country of Brenton for wine and bread before specialization and trade (point O) with a number of post-trade consumption possibilities. International trade (based on comparative advantage) which resulted in the export of wine and the import of bread will move Brenton from point O to point

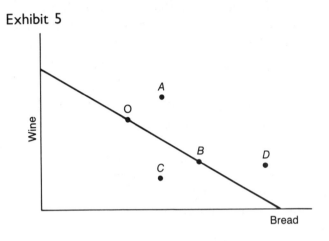

Exhibit 5

    a. *A.*
    b. *B.*
    c. *C.*
    d. *D.*

THE ECONOMIC WAY OF THINKING—MULTIPLE CHOICE

1. Suppose that the United States eliminated its tariff on automobiles, granting foreign-produced automobiles free entry into the U.S. market. Which of the following would be most likely to occur?
    a. The price of automobiles to U.S. consumers would decline, and the demand for U.S. export products would increase.
    b. The price of automobiles to U.S. consumers would increase, and the demand for U.S. export products would decline.
    c. The price of automobiles to U.S. consumers would decline, and the demand for U.S. export products would decline.
    d. The price of automobiles to U.S. consumers would increase, and the demand for U.S. export products would decline.

2. Economic incentives suggest that the union leaders of workers in a protected "infant industry" will support tariff protection for the industry
    a. if, and only if, they believe that the industry is still immature.
    b. unless they believe that the tariff is harming the consumers of the industry's product.
    c. if management is opposed to the protection.
    d. regardless of how mature the industry may be at the time.

3. If a country had a comparative disadvantage in the production of watches, a tariff on imported watches set just high enough to offset this disadvantage in the retail market
   a. would help the entire economy by increasing employment.
   b. would help watch consumers as a group, by giving them a real choice between foreign and domestic brands.
   c. would help workers in the watch industry by increasing the demand for their services.
   d. would help watch producers at the expense of the workers in the domestic watch industry.

The following quotation from a U.S. textile industry executive applies to the next *two* questions.

   "What bothers our manufacturers is that it is not really a matter of Japanese competitiveness, but a maze of impenetrable supports and subsidies. Our people feel that whatever they do, the Japanese will just lower their prices."

Assume that the Japanese government does, in fact, continually subsidize their textile industry so that they can undersell other textile exporters.

4. A textile-importing nation would best take advantage of the Japanese subsidization policy by
   a. setting a tariff high enough to keep cheap foreign competitors out of its own potential textile industry.
   b. setting a declining quota on the import of Japanese textiles such that its own textile industry could continue growing at the same rate as the rest of the economy.
   c. gladly accepting the subsidy of the Japanese government to textile users, making whatever adjustment assistance seems appropriate to the temporarily displaced resources in the domestic textile industry.
   d. setting a tariff just to equalize Japanese and domestic textile prices to the consumer.

5. We would expect that domestic textile industry executives and textile union leaders would
   a. gladly accept the reduced burden of having to produce ever-increasing amounts of textile goods domestically.
   b. fight for tariffs and quotas on imported Japenses textiles "to protect the American economy."
   c. argue that comparative advantage should prevail, so that domestic producers would be forced to meet the price of textiles that prevails in the world market if they were to survive.
   d. disagree among themselves, with the industry executives demanding protection, whereas union leaders would favor a tariff reduction that would benefit the worker-consumers.

6. Relative to a no-trade situation, what effect will importing a good from foreign nations have on the domestic market for the good?
   a. Equilibrium price will rise and total domestic output will fall.
   b. Equilibrium price will rise and total domestic output will rise.
   c. Equilibrium price will fall and total domestic output will fall.
   d. Equilibrium price will fall and total domestic output will rise.

7. Economic theory suggests that the popularity of tariffs among politicians is
   a. surprising, since tariffs generally lower a nation's level of real income.
   b. not surprising, since tariff protection for an industry is generally a special interest issue.
   c. surprising, since numerous consumers are generally harmed in order to help a few industrial and labor interests.
   d. not surprising, since tariffs generally help domestic investors, workers, and consumers at the expense of foreigners who cannot vote.

8. Economics suggests that some of the political popularity of tariffs stems from the fact that "jobs lost" due to an expansion of imports are easily identifed
   a. whereas "jobs created" by an increase in foreign spending on domestic exports can seldom be traced back to the reduction in tariffs.
   b. whereas the gains associated with holding larger amounts of foreign currencies are elusive, even though they are real gains.
   c. and they cannot be replaced by an expansion in other industries.
   d. and they cannot be replaced without a trade policy to restrict competition with cheap foreign labor.

9. If all tariffs (and quotas) between countries on the North American continent were eliminated
   a. small Central American countries would be hurt, since they would be unable to compete with larger nations.
   b. the United States would gain at the expense of the less-developed North American countries.
   c. the combined wealth of the countries would increase, since the elimination of trade restrictions would permit greater gains from specialization.
   d. wage rates in the United States would decline to the average for the North American continent.

10. Relative to a no-trade situation, what effect will exporting a good to foreign nations have on the domestic market for the product?
    a. Equilibrium price will rise and total domestic output will fall.
    b. Equilibrium price will rise and total domestic output will rise.
    c. Equilibrium price will fall and total domestic output will fall.
    d. Equilibrium price will fall and total domestic output will rise.

11. The law of comparative advantage
    a. is applicable to both domestic and international production and trade.
    b. applies only in domestic situations, such as occur when doctors who are good typists hire secretaries to do medical typing.
    c. applies only when one nation is absolutely more efficient in the production of the first good and another nation is absolutely more efficient at the production of the second.
    d. is only theoretical; it does not work in the real world.

12. The infant-industry argument about tariffs states that
    a. it is unfair to place tariffs on items intended for use by infants.
    b. tariffs should be placed on items produced by new domestic industries only in the short run.
    c. tariffs should be placed on items intended for infants in order to protect domestic infant industries.
    d. tariffs should be placed on items produced by new domestic industries in the short or long run.

THE ECONOMIC WAY OF THINKING—DISCUSSION QUESTIONS

1. "We are not opposed to competition when it does not destroy jobs. But last year, while many American auto workers were idle, we exported a million jobs to foreigners by importing automobiles that could have been produced by domestic workers. An increase in the tariff on automobiles would strengthen our economy, provide jobs, and improve our standard of living." [Auto Workers' Union official]
   a. Would a higher tariff on automobiles create jobs in the automble industry?
   b. Would a higher auto tariff destroy jobs in other industries—particularly export industries? Explain.
   c. Does unemployment indicate a lack of jobs? Why or why not?

2. Why would you expect the management of U.S. Steel and the president of the United Steel Workers' Union to fight strongly together for tariffs on imported steel "for the good of the nation," when they disagree on so many other matters of public concern? Would you expect both to oppose lower tariffs on copper, aluminum, or other steel substitutes? Why or why not?

3. What arguments could you make for self-sufficiency within a nation? A state? A locality? How much should we sacrifice to attain this?

4. Is the creation of a new industry a good thing? The state of Connecticut could create a banana industry, complete with hothouses, if it found a way to ban imports of bananas to the state. Should it do so? The state of Montana currently encourages a small liquor-bottling industry by taxing bulk imports to the state at lower rates than bottled liquors. Does this make more sense? Why?

5. Wages in the United States are among the highest in the world. Yet most U.S. trade is with other industrial high-wage nations, rather than with low-wage developing countries. Is this consistent with the law of comparative advantage? Explain.

6. Suppose that Brazil, the world's largest coffee producer, levied an export tax on coffee. Use supply-and-demand analysis to examine the impact of the tax on
   a. the price of coffee in the United States.
   b. U.S. expenditures on coffee.
   c. the revenue of Brazilian coffee growers.
   Do you think the Brazilian coffee growers would favor or oppose the tax? Explain.

PERSPECTIVES IN ECONOMICS

Unfair Competition With The Sun
by Frédéric Bastiat

[From Frédéric Bastiat, "Petition of the Manufacturers of Candles, Wax-Lights, Lamps, Candlesticks, Street Lamps, Snuffers, Extinguishers, and of the Producers of Oil, Tallow, Resin, Alcohol, and, Generally, of Everything Connected with Lighting." To messieurs the members of the Chamber of Deputies.]

Gentlemen,—You are on the right road. You reject abstract theories, and have little consideration for cheapness and plenty. Your chief care is the interest of the producer. You desire to protect him from foreign competition, and reserve the *national market* for *national industry*.

We are suffering from the intolerable competition of a foreign rival, placed, it would seem, in a condition so far superior to ours for the production of light that he absolutely *inundates* our *national market* with it at a price fabulously reduced. The moment he shows himself our trade leaves us—all consumers apply to him; and a branch of native industry, having countless ramifications, is all at once rendered completely stagnant. This rival, who is no other than the sun, wages war to the knife against us, and we suspect that he has been raised up by *perfidious Albion* (a good policy as times go); inasmuch as he displays towards that haughty island a circumspection with which he dispenses in our case.

What we pray for is, that it may please you to pass a law ordering the shutting up of all windows, skylights, dormer-windows, outside and inside shutters, curtains, blinds, bull's-eyes, in a word, of all openings, holes, chinks, clefts, and fissures, by or through which the light of the sun has been in use to enter houses, to the prejudice of the meritorious manufactures with which we flatter ourselves we have accommodated our country—a country which, in gratitude, ought not abandon us now to a strife so unequal.

We trust, Gentlemen, that you will not regard this our request as a satire, or refuse it without at least previously hearing the reasons which we have to urge in its support.

And, first, if you shut up as much as possible all access to natural light, and create a demand for artificial light, which of our French manufacturers will not be encouraged by it?

We foresee your objections, Gentlemen, but we know that you can oppose to us none but such as you have picked up from the effete works of the partisans of Free Trade. We defy you to utter a single word against us which will not instantly rebound against yourselves and your entire policy.

You will tell us that, if we gain by the protection which we seek, the country will lose by it, because the consumer must bear the loss.

We answer:

You have ceased to have any right to invoke the interest of the consumer for, whenever his interest is found opposed to that of the producer, you sacrifice the latter. You have done so for the purpose of encouraging workers and those who seek employment. For the same reason you should do so again.

You have yourselves obviated this objection. When you are told that the consumer is interested in the free importation of iron, coal, corn, textile fabrics—yes, you reply, but the producer is interested in their exclusion. Well, be it so; if consumers are interested in the free admission of natural light, the producers of artificial light are equally interested in its prohibition.

If you urge that the light of the sun is a gratuitous gift of nature, and that to reject such gifts is to reject wealth itself under pretense of encouraging the means of acquiring it, we would caution you against giving a death-blow to your own policy. Remember that hitherto you have always repelled foreign products, *because* they approximate more nearly than home products to the character of gratuitous gifts.

Nature and human labour co-operate in various pro-portions (depending on countries and climates) in the production of commodities. The part which nature executes is very gratuitous; it is the part executed by human labour which constitutes value, and is paid for.

If a Lisbon orange sells for half the price of a Paris orange, it is because natural, and consequently gratuitous, heat does for the one what artificial, and therefore expensive, heat must do for the other.

When an orange comes to us from Portugal, we may conclude that it is furnished in part gratuitously, in part for an onerous consideration; in other words, it comes to us at *half-price* as compared with those of Paris.

Now, it is precisely the *gratuitous half* (pardon the word) which we contend should be excluded. You say, How can national labour sustain competition with foreign labour, when the former has all the work to do, and the latter only does one-half, the sun supplying the remainder? But if this *half*, being *gratuitous*, determines you to exclude competition, how should the *whole*, being *gratuitous*, induce you to admit competition? If you were consistent, you would, while excluding as hurtful to native industry what is half gratuitous, exclude a *fortiori* and with double zeal, that which is altogether gratuitous.

One more, when products such as coal, iron, corn, or textile fabrics are sent us from abroad, and we can acquire them with less labour than if we made them ourselves, the difference is a free gift conferred upon us. The gift is more or less considerable in proportion as the difference is more or less great. It amounts to a quarter, a half, or three-quarters of the value of the product, when the foreigner only asks us for three-fourths, a half or a quarter of the price we should otherwise pay. It is as perfect and complete as it can be, when the donor (like the sun is furnishing us with light) asks us for nothing. The question, and we ask it formally, is this: Do you desire for our country the benefit of gratuitous consumption, or the pretended advantages of onerous production?

Make your choice, but be logical; for as long as you exclude as you do, coal, iron, corn, foreign fabrics, in proportion as their price approximates to zero what inconsistency it would be to admit the light of the sun, the price of which is already at zero during the entire day!

Discussion

1. What does this reading have to do with our chapter? Can you see any evidence of a vested interest here? Do you think a successful politician would pay attention to such a petition? Why?

2. What arguments would you, as an economist, use before a congressional hearing on a bill to accomplish what Bastiat suggests? How would you deal with the political problems involved?

3. As explained in this chapter, both nations can expect to gain from international trade. In addition, for most products, there are far more voting consumers than voting producers. How can the ideas in the chapter on Public Choice explain laws being passed to reduce trade and its net gains? (*Hint:* Special interest effect.)

31

International Finance and the Foreign Exchange Market

TRUE OR FALSE

T F

☐ ☐   1. Foreign exchange markets enable an individual to exchange the currency of one nation for units of currency of another nation.

☐ ☐   2. A nation's exports generate a demand for the currency of the exporting nation on the foreign exchange market.

☐ ☐   3. Under a system of fixed exchange rates, a balance-of-trade equilibrium is automatic.

☐ ☐   4. Under a system of flexible exchange rates, the government must use monetary policy to ensure balance-of-payments equilibrium.

☐ ☐   5. The economic analysis of foreign trade is unique in that supply-and-demand relationships do not usually determine equilibrium.

☐ ☐   6. One problem with a system of flexible exchange rates is that black markets in foreign currencies are more likely to develop than with controlled rates of exchange.

☐ ☐   7. A country's balance of trade has no bearing on its balance of payments on current account.

☐ ☐   8. The United States would invariably import more than it exports if foreigners were willing to accumulate ever larger amounts of dollars.

☐ ☐   9. If imports consistently exceeded exports, U.S. consumers would be hurt as a result of the unfavorable balance of trade implied by such a situation.

☐ ☐ 10. If Israel sold U.S. dollars to France, the U.S. balance of payments would be unaffected.

☐ ☐ 11. A rapid U.S. monetary expansion would tend to make the price of German marks rise, in dollar terms, other things constant.

☐ ☐ 12. Domestic macropolicy-makers can effectively disregard the foreign-exchange markets when making a choice between alternative policies.

PROBLEMS AND PROJECTS

1. Match the letters on the right with the numbers on the left.

    _____ (1) balance-of-payments deficit–
    fixed exchange rates

    _____ (2) will cause the domestic
    currency to appreciate

    _____ (3) will cause the domestic
    currency to depreciate

    _____ (4) flexible exchange rates

    _____ (5) fixed exchange rates

    _____ (6) gold standard

    a. an increase in the nation's exports
    b. will cause a depreciation of the nation's
    currency when it is experiencing a balance-
    of-payments deficit
    c. international monetary system in effect
    before World War I
    d. excess supply of the nation's currency on
    the exchange market
    e. higher interest rates abroad
    f. reduce the flexibility of macropolicy

2. Each of the diagrams below represents the U.S. demand for and supply of foreign exchange
    (English pounds). For each of the events described below, diagram how the demand and/or
    supply of pounds changes (use a +, −, or 0 to show no change); and then fill in the blanks
    to the right of the diagram, indicating in the last blank whether the dollar has appreciated,
    depreciated, or undergone an indeterminant change as a result of the event(s). (The first ques-
    tion has been answered as an example.) (Hint: P = dollars per pound.)

Events	Diagrams	D	S	Change

a. As a result of recovering
    from a depression, U.S.
    incomes rise signifi-
    cantly.

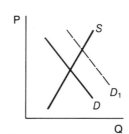

$\underline{+}$ $\underline{0}$ $\underline{depreciated}$

b. The United Kingdom
    experiences a serious
    recession causing a de-
    cline in income.

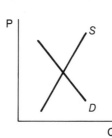

___ ___ _____

c. Restrictive monetary pol-
    icy in the U.S. causes
    U.S. interest rates to rise
    relative to United Kingdom
    rates.

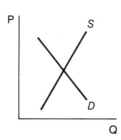

___ ___ _____

(*continued*)

Events	Diagrams	D	S	Change

d. The Chairman of the Fed is quoted as saying, "If the high value of the dollar is not soon corrected by market forces, the Fed will take corrective action."

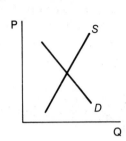

___   ___   _____

e. While the U.S. experiences stable prices, prices in the United Kingdom rise by 15 percent.

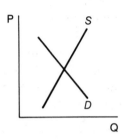

___   ___   _____

f. In an effort to stimulate the economy, the U.S. embarks on an expansionary fiscal policy.

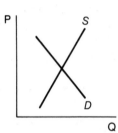

___   ___   _____

g. Both the U.S. and the U.K. experience inflation rates of 20 percent.

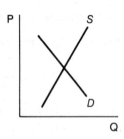

___   ___   _____

3. Exhibit 1 presents balance-of-payments data for the United States for 1980.

Exhibit I

	Debit		Credit	
		(billions of dollars)		
Current account				
Merchandise imports	249.3	Merchandise exports	224.0
Service imports	84.6	Service exports	120.7
Net unilateral transfers	7.1		
Capital account				
U.S. investment abroad	18.5	Foreign investment in the U.S.	10.9
Loans to foreigners	58.1	Loans from foreigners	70.2

a. Use the data of Exhibit 1 to calculate the balance on (1) merchandise trade account, (2) services account, (3) current account, (4) capital account, and (5) current-and-capital account.

b. Compare these balances to the ones for 1984 in exhibit 5 of the text. What happened to U.S. international balances between those years? Why do you think this occurred?

LEARNING THE MECHANICS—MULTIPLE CHOICE

1. Since each nation has its own currency
    a. transactions across national borders normally require the conversion of one currency into another.
    b. gold must be used as the international medium of exchange.
    c. direct exchange of goods, through brokers, is the normal means of exchange.
    d. one dominant currency (currently the English pound) is used in more than 95 percent of all international transactions.

2. An appreciation in the value of the U.S. dollar would
    a. encourage foreigners to make more investments in the United States.
    b. encourage U.S. consumers to purchase more foreign-produced goods.
    c. increase the number of dollars that could be purchased with a Mexican peso.
    d. discourage U.S. consumers from traveling abroad.

3. The balance of payments is an annual accounting statement of a nation's
    a. exports and imports.
    b. balance due on imports and exports.
    c. holdings of gold and foreign currencies.
    d. international trade and financial transactions.

4. A nation that has a balance-of-payments surplus is
    a. importing more goods and services than it is exporting.
    b. selling more goods, services, and financial assets abroad than it is purchasing from foreigners.
    c. exporting more tangible goods than it is importing from foreigners.
    d. exporting more tangible goods than intangible services and financial assets.

5. Which of the following would *not* be likely to cause a nation's currency to depreciate?
    a. An increase in the nation's exports
    b. More rapid domestic rate of inflation than that of the nation's trading partners
    c. Lower domestic interest rates
    d. Higher foreign interest rates

6. Under a system of flexible exchange rates, transactions that supply the nation's currency to the foreign-exchange market will cause the nation's
    a. currency to depreciate in value.
    b. balance-of-payments surplus to increase.
    c. balance-of-payments deficit to fall.
    d. products to increase in price in terms of foreign currencies.

7. A system of fixed, rather than floating, exchange rates
    a. eliminates problems that arise from changing prices or comparative advantage in international trade.
    b. forces traders to bear the risk involved in making manufacturing or farming commitments well in advance of retail market sales.
    c. ensures that those who benefit most by buying or selling in international markets bear the cost of any uncertainty associated with such trade.
    d. grants international traders some protection from uncertainty at the expense of a reduction in the nation's freedom to follow an independent course in other areas of economic policy.

8. If, to correct a balance-of-payments deficit, U.S. authorities increased import tariffs in order to cut imports, we should also expect
    a. foreign demand for U.S. exports to increase.
    b. U.S. consumers to benefit.
    c. decreased exports as well as decreased imports.
    d. strong opposition from U.S. industries now forced to supply goods formerly imported.

9. With fixed exchange rates, a balance-of-payments surplus would probably be lessened by
    a. restrictive monetary policy, keeping prices down and real interest rates up.
    b. expansionary monetary policy, pushing prices up and real interest rates down.
    c. a decrease in foreign-aid grants.
    d. an increase in income from investments abroad.

10. Which of the following is *not* a debit item in the U.S. balance of trade?
    a. A U.S. import of a German car
    b. A U.S. purchase of insurance from Lloyds of London
    c. A trip to Japan by an American student
    d. A short-term loan to a U.S. resident from a South American

11. With time, a depreciation in the value of the nation's currency in the foreign market will cause the nation's
    a. imports to increase and exports to decline.
    b. exports to increase and imports to decline.
    c. both imports and exports to decline.
    d. both imports and exports to rise.

THE ECONOMIC WAY OF THINKING—MULTIPLE CHOICE

1. ''Wine experts are discovering that California wines of several varieties and vintages are comparable to many of the best French wines. The result is an increased demand, here and abroad, for California wines.'' With regard to the U.S. balance on current account, this trend will
    a. increase the U.S. deficit, because of the rise in the price of California wine.
    b. decrease the U.S. deficit, because of increased shipments of California wines abroad.
    c. decrease the demand for U.S. dollars.
    d. increase the U.S. demand for Franch francs.

2. In a world of fixed exchange rates, if a country cut its foreign-aid grants by 50 percent, and if the aid had been "tied" so that 75 percent of the grant had to be spent in the granting country for exports to the recipient, we would expect the change to
   a. increase any existing balance-of-payments deficit existing in the granting nation, since its exports would fall.
   b. decrease any existing balance-of-payments deficit existing in the granting nation by the amount of the cut in foreign aid.
   c. decrease any existing balance-of-payments deficit by less than the cut in foreign aid.
   d. have no impact on the granting nation's balance-of-payments.

3. If the United States could, with fixed exchange rates, run a perpetual balance-of-trade deficit so that other countries held ever increasing stocks of dollars, Americans would, compared to a no-trade deficit situation, be
   a. better off, since consumption could be perpetually higher.
   b. worse off, since the balance of payments would always be unfavorable.
   c. better off, since exports would have to be higher.
   d. worse off, since imports would have to be lower.

4. A fad that made a particular brand of cross-country skis, imported from Norway, extremely popular in the United States would tend to
   a. increase any existing balance-of-trade surplus for the United States.
   b. decrease any existing balance-of-trade deficit in the United States.
   c. decrease any existing U.S. balance-of-trade surplus.
   d. affect the U.S. balance of payments, but not the balance of trade.

5. The major impact of a restrictive monetrary policy on the domestic exchange rate would be (assuming that domestic real interest rates rise in the short run)
   a. an increase in the foreign-exchange value of the domestic currency.
   b. a decrease in the foreign-exchange value of the domestic currency.
   c. no change in the foreign-exchange value of the domestic currency.
   d. It is impossible to predict the impact of the foreign-exchange value of the domestic currency.

6. Which one of the following transactions would increase the supply of dollars on the foreign-exchange market?
   a. Sale of wheat to the Russians
   b. The spending of a French trade delegation touring the United States
   c. The purchase of a Mexican copper mine by U.S. businessmen
   d. The earnings of a California businessman on a Canadian investment

7. Under a system of flexible exchange rates, which of the following will cause the nation's currency to depreciate in the exchange market?
   a. An increase in foreign incomes
   b. A domestic inflation rate of 10 percent while the nation's trading partners are experiencing stable prices
   c. An increase in domestic interest rates
   d. A reduction in interest rates abroad

8. A major advantage of flexible exchange rates is that
   a. they cost less to administer than fixed rates.
   b. they automatically equilibrate the balance of trade.
   c. they do not require as much government intervention as fixed exchange rates do.
   d. they allow easier business planning for trade.

9. A major difference between devaluation and depreciation is that
    a. a depreciation does not involve a change in the price of gold, in domestic terms.
    b. a devaluation can be a depreciation, but a depreciation can never be a devaluation.
    c. a devaluation is an official governmental act under fixed exchange rates.
    d. All of the above are correct.

10. The dollar is said to have depreciated if
    a. it once was exchanged for 10 pesos, but now it is exchanged for 12.
    b. foreign goods are now more expensive to Americans even though the prices of the goods
        in the foreign country remained constant.
    c. under fixed exchange rates the number of dollars supplied exceeds the number of dollars
        demanded.
    d. the U.S. has a balance-of-trade deficit under flexible exchange rates.

11. If a nation imports more goods and services than it exports to foreigners, then it must be
    a. borrowing more from foreigners or loaning less to foreigners.
    b. borrowing less from foreigners or loaning more to foreigners.
    c. experiencing a deficit on its current account transactions.
    d. trading under a system of fixed exchange rates, because it would be impossible for imports
        to exceed exports under a system of flexible exchange rates.

12. A depreciation in the value of a nation's currency on the foreign-exchange market will *not*
    immediately induce additional exports relative to imports if
    a. the short-run demand of foreigners for the nation's imports is inelastic, whereas the de-
        mand of the nation's consumers for foreign goods is also inelastic.
    b. the short-run demand of foreigners for the nation's imports is elastic, whereas the demand
        of the nation's consumers for foreign goods is also elastic.
    c. the long-run demand of foreigners for the nation's imports is elastic, whereas the long-
        run demand of the nation's consumers for foreign goods is inelastic.
    d. the long-run demand of foreigners for the nation's imports is inelastic, whereas the long-
        run demand of the nation's consumers for foreign goods is elastic.

THE ECONOMIC WAY OF THINKING—DISCUSSION QUESTIONS

1. ''A nation must pay for its imports with exports. Without exporting goods, services, and fi-
    nancial assets to foreigners, a nation would be unable to import goods from abroad.'' Do you
    agree? Explain.

2. ''No patriotic Americans want the value of the dollar to continue falling on the exchange mar-
    ket.'' Do you think that a depreciation in the value of the dollar is bad? A depreciation comes
    about because we have been receiving more goods, services, and financial assets from foreigners
    than we have been sending to them. Is this bad? Explain.

3. Most economists now pay a significant amount of attention to international capital flows and
    interest rates when determining the likely impacts of specific domestic fiscal and monetary
    policies. Given that domestic macroeconomic policy is becoming more interrelated with inter-
    national trade and finance policy, should the United States move to take account of that in-
    terdependence in its macropolicy, or should it attempt to protect its domestic economy from
    international financial affairs having an impact? Explain your reasoning.

4. ''A nation's balance of payments must always be in balance.'' In what sense is this true? What
    is a ''balance-of-payments deficit''? Under a flexible exchange system, will a balance-of-pay-
    ments deficit automatically be corrected? Explain.

5. If the foreign demand for a nation's major export commodities is highly inelastic, will flexible exchange rates equalize the value of a nation's exports and the value of its imports? Why or why not?

6. ''A system of flexible exchange rates is advantageous because it enables a nation to stablize domestic employment and prices without regard to the foreign sector.'' True, false, or uncertain? Explain.

7. Discuss the role of time in balance-of-payments adjustments. Why will short- and long-run effects of a depreciation probably differ?

8. Briefly review the advantages and disadvantages of a gold standard. Why do you think that most economists oppose a return to such a standard?

32

Economic Development and the Growth of Income

TRUE OR FALSE

T F

☐ ☐ 1. The most obvious characteristic of a less-developed nation is low per capita income.

☐ ☐ 2. Almost half of the world's population lives in countries with per capita incomes of less than $400 a year.

☐ ☐ 3. The exchange-rate conversion method of comparing GNPs is a good indicator of differences in the purchasing power of currencies for goods and services that are not exchanged on international markets.

☐ ☐ 4. A nation may experience extensive economic growth, even though output per person is not rising.

☐ ☐ 5. Small differences in rates of economic growth can, over a span of 20 or more years, cause large differences in income levels.

☐ ☐ 6. The vicious circle of underdevelopment arises when low living standards cause low savings rates which stifle capital formation and economic growth.

☐ ☐ 7. Technological advance, defined as the invention of—but not adoption of—new techniques, enables workers to produce additional output with the same amount of resources.

☐ ☐ 8. The concept of the vicious circle of underdevelopment states that living standards barely above the subsistence level make it difficult for a nation to generate the investment and human capital necessary to foster future economic development.

☐ ☐ 9. For approximately one-quarter of the world's population, the gap between the developed and less-developed nations appear to be getting worse instead of better.

☐ ☐ 10. The dependency ratio is typically greater for developed than for less-developed countries.

☐ ☐ 11. The annual per capita growth rate of real GNP for Taiwan, Hong Kong, and South Korea exceeds the growth rate of most industrial nations, including the United States.

PROBLEMS AND PROJECTS

1. Almost half of the world's population lives in countries where average annual per capita income is less than $400. Plan a budget and try to figure out how you might get through a year with only $400. How much is that per month? Suppose that you could live for free (on the floor) with some relatives. Would you then have enough to pay for food, clothes, or school?

2. Exhibit 1 is a compound interest table in which each entry shows the amount to which $1.00 will accumulate at various rates of interest after *n* years. For example, if $10.00 were to grow at 2% interest for 5 years, it would grow to a value of $11.04 = $10.00 × 1.104.

Exhibit I

| Years | | | Rate of interest or growth | | | |
	2%	3%	4%	5%	6%	7%
5	1.104	1.159	1.217	1.276	1.338	1.403
10	1.219	1.344	1.480	1.629	1.791	1.967
15	1.346	1.558	1.801	2.079	2.397	2.759
20	1.486	1.806	2.191	2.653	3.207	3.870
25	1.641	2.094	2.666	3.386	4.292	5.427
30	1.811	2.427	3.243	4.330	5.743	7.612
35	2.000	2.814	3.946	5.516	7.686	10.677
40	2.208	3.262	4.801	7.040	10.286	14.974
45	2.438	3.781	5.841	8.985	13.765	21.002

   a. Suppose the mythical economy of Gromangro has in 1950 a real GNP of &20 billion and a population of 100 million. (& is the symbol for "mango," the national currency of Gromangro). What is the real GNP per capita of Gromangro in 1950?

   b. In 1950, the U.S.'s real GNP per capita was $6,330. If in 1950 the exchange rate between the dollar and the mango was &1 = $2, what was Gromangro's 1950 GNP per capita in dollars? What was the difference in dollars between the per capita GNPs of the two?

   c. Suppose that Gromangro's GNP grows at 7% from 1950 to 1985 while her population grows at 3%. Use Exhibit 1 to calculate the value (in mangos) of Gromangro's GNP and her population in 1985. What is Gromangro's per capita GNP in 1985?

   d. Suppose the U.S.'s per capita GNP grows at 2% from 1950 to 1985. What is its value in 1985?

   e. If the dollar/mango exchange rate remains the same as in part b, what is Gromangro's 1985 per capita GNP in dollars? What is the dollar difference between two countries' GNPs in 1985?

3. One way of analyzing economic growth is through simple equilibrium GNP models. Consider a hypothetical economy in which

$$Y = C + I + G$$
$$C = 200 + 0.9Y_D$$
$$Y_D = Y - T$$

investment is constant at 50, government expenditure is 300, and taxation is 250. Verify that equilibrium GNP is 3250. One problem with this economic model is that it is for a closed economy. How could you change it to incorporate international trade? (*Hint:* Remember that our definition of GNP also includes net exports.) How could an economy incapable of borrowing from abroad or from the public increase equilibrium GNP? Try a few alternatives to see what could be done; as you will quickly realize, without capital of some sort, it is very difficult to generate sustained economic growth.

LEARNING THE MECHANICS—MULTIPLE CHOICE

1. Which of the following is *not* a typical characteristic of most less-developed countries?
   a. Low per capita income
   b. Rapid population growth
   c. A large agricultural sector
   d. Fairly equal (but low) income distribution

2. Which of the following is a true statement about the percentages of the world's population and the level of per capita income in the countries in which they lived in 1983?
   a. Over 85 percent of the world's population lives in nations with annual per capita incomes under $500.
   b. Over 45 percent of the world's population lives in nations with annual per capita incomes under $400.
   c. Over 25 percent of the world's population lives in nations with annual per capita incomes over $7000.
   d. Over 40 percent of the world's population lives in nations with annual per capita incomes over $3000.

3. The poorest countries in the world today contain about two-thirds of the world's population and produce approximately what portion of the world's output?
   a. 50%
   b. 35%
   c. 25%
   d. 15%

4. In the United States, 2 percent of the work force is employed in the agricultural sector. In the less-developed countries of South America, Africa, and Asia, what percentage of the work force is generally employed in agriculture?
   a. Less than 5 percent
   b. 10–15 percent
   c. 25–30 percent
   d. More than 50 percent

5. The exchange-rate conversion method is
   a. a method of converting per capita income from one nation into another nation's currency through exchange rates.
   b. a method of converting exchange rates between countries to allow for differences between levels of per capita income.
   c. a method of converting exchange rates to allow for purchasing-power parity.
   d. a method of converting per capita income from one nation into another nation's currency through purchasing-power parity.

6. Although it has become increasingly popular to define economic growth in terms of the rate of change in real GNP, economic development is now widely perceived
   a. as a normative concept that ignores growth and concentrates on distribution and structural changes in the economy.
   b. as a normative concept encompassing not only growth, but a general improvement in the standard of living of the masses of the population.
   c. as a positive concept that quantifies the net economic welfare of the masses of the population.
   d. as a normative concept concentrating on the distribution of income, since economic welfare is only marginally related to income level.

7. When real GNP is expanding
    a. economic growth is extensive, but not necessarily intensive.
    b. economic growth is intensive, but not necessarily extensive.
    c. economic growth is both extensive and intensive.
    d. economic growth is neither extensive nor intensive.

8. The trickle-down theory
    a. states that hydroelectric generating stations are the most efficient sources of power for developing nations.
    b. was suggested by Keynes when he noted that an increase in investment trickles down to the rest of the economy and brings about an increase in GNP greater than the original change.
    c. states that an increase in per capita income will eventually increase the well-being of all segments of society as it trickles down to these groups.
    d. is best understood by analyzing the economy of Brazil.

9. A 3 percent growth rate in GNP will bring about a doubling of GNP in about how many years?
    a. 3
    b. 12
    c. 24
    d. 48

10. If the results of a recent study are to be believed, a high level of marginal tax rates appears to be associated with low growth rates of per capita income in developing countries. One possible reason for this observation is that
    a. countries that are growing slowly have greater fiscal needs than countries that are growing quickly, and so tax rates are higher.
    b. high tax rates can potentially discourage productive activity.
    c. both a and b.
    d. neither a nor b.

11. The *simplest* method for comparing income levels between nations is the
    a. exchange-rate conversion method.
    b. dependency ratio method.
    c. purchasing-power parity method.
    d. trickle-down method.

12. The most *accurate* method for comparing income levels between nations is the
    a. exchange-rate conversion method.
    b. dependency ratio method.
    c. purchasing-power parity method.
    d. trickle-down method.

THE ECONOMIC WAY OF THINKING—MULTIPLE CHOICE

When answering the next *two* questions use the information (from 1976) in Exhibit 2.

Exhibit 2

	Per capita GNP (dollars)	GNP growth rate (percent)	Rate of population growth (percent)
India	140	3.5	2.3
Mexico	1060	6.5	3.5
United States	7880	3.5	1.1

1. In which country is the level of economic development (not growth) the highest?
   a. India
   b. Mexico
   c. United States
   d. It is impossible to tell because of the problems of comparing GNP's from different countries and the lack of information about items other than per capita GNP.

2. In which country is the *growth rate* of per capita GNP the highest?
   a. India
   b. Mexico
   c. United States
   d. It is impossible to tell because adequate information is not given.

3. Which of the following best characterizes the relationship between the developed nations and the less-developed nations?
   a. The developed nations are growing and the less-developed nations are stagnating.
   b. The less-developed nations are growing, but the developed nations are growing even faster.
   c. Population is growing faster in developed nations.
   d. It is an oversimplification to divide the world into the growing, developed nations and the stagnating, less-developed nations.

4. Which of the following is *not* a good reason for using indices other than per capita GNP to measure economic development?
   a. Per capita GNP does not take income distribution into account.
   b. Per capita GNP is overly influenced by changes in population.
   c. Per capita GNP does not take nonmarket transactions into account.
   d. Per capita GNP does not take externalities, such as pollution, into account.

5. Which of the following is most likely to meet our definition of a less-developed nation?
   a. A country with a small agricultural sector, low rate of population growth, and low per capita GNP
   b. A country with a high population growth rate, a high per capita GNP growth rate, and an unequal distribution of income
   c. A country with inadequate health care, poor educational facilities, and low per capita GNP
   d. A country with low per capita GNP, a large population, and a small agricultural sector

6. If annual per capita GNP in the United States is $7880 and in Great Britain is £3000, then under which of the following exchange rates would Great Britain have a larger GNP than the United States?
   a. £1 = $2
   b. £1 = $3
   c. £3 = $1
   d. £2 = $1

7. The difference between extensive and intensive economic growth is about the same as the difference between the growth rate of
   a. total GNP and per capita GNP.
   b. total GNP and total net economic welfare.
   c. per capita GNP and per capita net economic welfare.
   d. real per capita GNP and per capita net economic welfare.

8. What is the difference between economic growth and economic development?
   a. Growth has to do with the area of a country, while development has to do with the maturity of a country.
   b. Growth has to do with the rate of change of GNP, while development has to do with the improvement of the overall standard of living.
   c. Growth can be extensive or intensive, while development can only be extensive.
   d. When you come right down to it, both growth and development can only be measured with per capita GNP, so there is *no* difference.

9. Which of the following would be most likely to impove the rate of growth of a less-developed nation?
   a. Development of strong labor unions
   b. An increase in foreign investment attracted by the expectation of economic and political stability
   c. An increase in the dependency ratio
   d. Foreign aid to construct a steel plant

10. The vicious circle of underdevelopment is exemplified by
    a. low incomes, leading to high rates of consumption, leading to low rates of saving, leading to low levels of investment.
    b. low incomes, leading to high population, leading to low levels of per capita investment.
    c. low incomes, leading to poor nutrition, leading to increased imports of food, leading to low rates of investment.
    d. low incomes, leading to low consumption, leading to high rates of saving, leading to capital leaving the country as a result of the low level of investment.

11. The interrelationship between population and economic development has been debated since the time of Malthus. Today's development economists feel that
    a. the worry about population growth is unfounded, since technology will always offset any population gains.
    b. all other things equal, it does indeed appear that a high rate of population growth does slow development.
    c. whereas a high population lowers per capita income, it increases total income, and so population has a positive impact on development.
    d. a high dependency ratio will encourage development, even if the per capita income of a nation is low.

12. According to Michael Todaro, development
    a. is a purely economic phenomenon.
    b. is essentially a material process.
    c. involves the reorientation of the entire social system.
    d. involves mainly technological innovation.

THE ECONOMIC WAY OF THINKING—DISCUSSION QUESTIONS

1. What are the major sources of economic growth? What are the major obstacles to economic growth? Can economic growth occur without a high rate of investment? Without a strong natural resource base? Without a slowing in the rate of population growth? Without substantial education expenditure to upgrade the literacy rate of a nation? Discuss.

2. What are the two major methods used to compare incomes between nations, and what are the strengths and weaknesses of each?

3. Economists know very little about the best way to try to help a less-developed country to attain a rapid growth rate. What are the major points on which most development economists might agree? What do you think the developed nations could do to promote the economic growth of the less-developed countries? Discuss.

4. What do you think of the vicious circle of underdevelopment? Is it a valid theory? If it is valid, how can the vicious circle possibly be broken? How did the developed nations break it? Discuss.

5. In this chapter, it is implicitly assumed that most countries *want* to become developed. What arguments can you think of that might lead a country to want to stall its development?

6. The descriptions of life in a less-developed nation graphically illustrate the meaning of poverty. If per capita GNP in the United States is so much higher than it is in less-developed countries, why do we have so much poverty in the United States?

PERSPECTIVES IN ECONOMICS

Third World Facts and Fictions
by Charles Wolf Jr.

[Reprinted with the permission of Charles Wolf Jr. from the *Los Angeles Times*, January 27, 1981.]

Secretary of State Alexander Haig Jr. has observed that the Third World ("A misleading term if ever there was one") is a myth.

"Recent American foreign policy," Haig said, "has suffered from the misperception which lumps together nations as diverse as Brazil and Libya, Indonesia and South Yemen, Cuba and Kuwait . . . (The) failure to tailor policy to the individual circumstances of developing nations has frequently aggravated the very internal stresses which Western policy should seek instead to diminish."

Following Haig's lead, it may be timely to try to separate myths from realities, because the conventional wisdom about the so-called Third World is more conventional than wise.

Myth: The "Third World," consisting of some 130 less-developed nations, is a reasonably cohesive entity, unified by similar interests and ideologies that enable its members to act effectively and in concert.

Reality: The nations of the Third World are, in fact, divided in many more ways and by many more conflicting interests than those that unify them.

Of course, it is a fact that certain attitudes—intense nationalism, hypersensitivity to foreign condescension, a liking, perhaps waning, for socialist ideology, to name only a few—are shared by many developing nations. But more objective circumstances tend to divide them.

For example, the Third World includes oil importers (Brazil, India, Pakistan) and oil exporters (Saudi Arabia, Libya, Iraq, Mexico, Venezuela); rapidly growing economies (Korea, Brazil, Singapore) and slowly growing or stagnating ones (most of the remaining nations); centrally planned economies as well as market economies; major international debtors (Brazil, Mexico, Turkey) and major international creditors (Saudi Arabia, Libya, Kuwait); communist nations, procommunist nations and vigorously anticommunist nations (as well as many in between), and nations ruled by military governments and nations that profess the primacy of civil over military control.

The rhetoric of Third World unity is more spurious than real. The reality of the Third World is cultural; political and economic diversity.

Thus, almost any action by the Reagan administration

is likely to evoke support from some Third World nations, opposition from others and indifference from many. Our policy-makers would be well advised to think about the "Third World" as a plural, not a singular, entity.

Myth: Achieving significant and sustained economic development in the Third World is an overwhelming and intractable problem, made even more difficult by the rigidity and discrimination of the present international economic order.

Reality: Achieving rapid and sustained development, with the present international economic order, is a much less formidable problem than is usually supposed. The means and methods for realizing economic development are well known, have been widely demonstrated and are generally acknowledged even if they are not widely adopted. By and large, these recipes have been amply demonstrated by the impressive development of the small number of Third World nations (Brazil, Korea, Taiwan and Singapore) that have maintained average rates of real economic growth of 9 percent annually during the 1970s.

These nations have made economic progress possible by achieving political stability, including infrequent changes of government. In addition, such nations have provided a hospitable economic climate for market forces and market prices, have encouraged infusions of foreign capital and the selective import of foreign technology, and have avoided hyperinflation.

Orientation toward the market, while typical of these relatively successful Third World nations, does not necessarily imply private ownership, or an inactive role for government. Where government interventions occur, they usually are selective and limited in number.

As to the rigidity and adverse effects of the present economic international order, and the sometimes shrill call for a "new international economic order," again the reality departs sharply from the myth. In fact, the "old" order has been remarkably flexible, rather than rigid, and hospitable rather than resistant to development in the Third World.

For example, the drastic shift from a regime of fixed exchange rates to fluctuating ones, the recycling of several hundred billion petrodollars over the last half dozen years, and the transfer of technology are all indications of the adaptability of the present international economic setup to changing needs and forces.

Myth: Economic development is essential for political stability and democratization in the Third World.

Reality: There is no significant relationship between economic development and either political stability or democratization. Nations such as South Korea have developed dramatically without significant progress toward democracy. Nations such as India have maintained relatively democratic and stable institutions without notable success in economic development. In some nations—for example, Iran—rapid economic development has brought with it political instability. And in other nations, such as Turkey, adverse economic conditions have provided an environment in which terrorism has flourished and emerging democratic institutions have been set back.

Perhaps there is a weak relationship between economic progress and political stability. If an economy stagnates and if unemployment is high, it is probably easier for opposition to be kindled, simply because idle hands are more likely to be mischievous ones.

Myth: The primary objective of Third World nations is to modernize their economies as rapidly as they can.

Reality: On the contrary, most Third World leaders have other goals and objectives. These include achieving greater national recognition and prestige in the international community; acquiring modern and advanced military equipment; pursuing ideological preferences; and agitating for international redistribution of income, rather than domestic economic growth.

If one looks at behavior rather than rhetoric, development is among the goals and priorities of most of the nations of the Third World, but not at the top of the list.

There is a paradox in all this: If development is accorded primary emphasis among national objectives, success seems to depend on imposing limits on the scope and character of government intervention. Few Third World leaders are willing to let go of the reins of control and unleash the market forces that can help their economies grow.

Discussion

1. Do you agree with Wolf's perceptions of reality in all four cases? About which are you skeptical? Why?

2. What sort of changes in policies toward Third World nations do these new "realities" imply? How easy would it be to bring these policy changes about?

3. Can you think of other "Third World facts and fictions"? If so, what are they?

33

Comparative Economic Systems

TRUE OR FALSE

T F

☐ ☐   1. More has been written about Karl Marx than about any other economist.

☐ ☐   2. Ownership of physical capital differs between socialist and market systems, but the mechanism for allocating resources is the same.

☐ ☐   3. Under socialism, investment decisions normally are decentralized.

☐ ☐   4. In a market system, the price mechanism determines the distribution of income as well as the allocation of resources.

☐ ☐   5. In reality, all modern economies are a combination of capitalist and socialist economic organization.

☐ ☐   6. The concept of opportunity cost does not apply in a socialist system.

☐ ☐   7. Private garden plots in the Soviet Union account for a significant share of the total agricultural output.

☐ ☐   8. The centralized Soviet economy invests a substantially smaller share of its product annually than does the U.S. economy.

☐ ☐   9. The state sector of the Soviet economy is the largest economic unit in the world.

☐ ☐ 10. Under Soviet planning, resources are centrally rationed in physical terms.

☐ ☐ 11. Well-organized industry-wide unions have played a major role in promoting the rapid growth of the Japanese economy since World War II.

☐ ☐ 12. Workers' Councils (business managers) in Yugoslavia can choose the methods of production and the price to be charged for their products.

PROBLEMS AND PROJECTS

1. Match the letters on the right with the numbers on the left.

_____	(1) A characteristic of a Socialist economy	a. They are market determined under capitalism, but made by central planners under socialism.
_____	(2) Gosplan	
_____	(3) Yugoslav economy	b. Nonhuman resources are owned by individuals.
_____	(4) Investment decisions	
_____	(5) A characteristic of a capitalist economy	c. Central planning agency in the Soviet Union.
_____	(6) Investment as a share of GNP	d. Physical resources are owned by the state.
_____	(7) Per capita gross national product	e. Nearly twice as great in the Soviet Union as in the United States
		f. Market socialism
		g. More than twice as great in the United States as in the Soviet Union

2. Use the list of distinguishing economic characteristics of economies as presented in column 1 of Exhibit 1 in the text to devise a similar exhibit describing these characteristics as they apply to the specific economies of Japan and Yugoslavia rather than to the general categories of "capitalism" and "socialism."

3. Write a short paper outlining the dominant economic characteristics of socialist and capitalist economies. Indicate the features of both systems that you find most attractive (or unattractive).

LEARNING THE MECHANICS—MULTIPLE CHOICE

1. The business firms in a socialist economy
    a. are guided by boards of directors that perform functions similar to those of boards of directors of U.S. corporations.
    b. typically confront a strong labor union.
    c. are guided by central planners who use a reward-penalty system to affect the decisions of plant managers and workers.
    d. operate outside of the central planning apparatus.

2. Which of the following would *not* be included in a central economic plan of a socialist economy such as the Soviet Union?
    a. A list of target outputs for each industry
    b. An input–output plan linking the availability of productive resources to the production of each product
    c. An input–output plan for each industry
    d. An input–output production function for each enterprise

3. The gross national product in the Soviet Union is
    a. less than one-third the size of the U.S. GNP.
    b. approximately one-half the size of the U.S. GNP.
    c. approximately three-fourths the size of the U.S. GNP.
    d. approximately nine-tenths the size of the U.S. GNP.

4. Which of the following is not a characteristic of a socialist economy?
   a. Detailed central planning
   b. Government ownership of physical capital
   c. Government ownership of human capital
   d. Wages and prices that are fixed by government edict

5. The choice between production of capital goods and consumer goods in the Soviet Union
   a. is made by consumers and business enterprises.
   b. results in a rate of investment that is similar to the rate of investment in the United States.
   c. is made by the central planners, who apparently have assigned a low priority to consumption goods.
   d. is made by planners who, in the past, have assigned a high priority to consumer goods.

6. Which of the following nations would best be described as a centrally planned socialist economy?
   a. Yugoslavia
   b. Sweden
   c. United Kingdom
   d. Soviet Union

7. Private plots constitute approximately 1.5 percent of the agricultural land in the Soviet Union. In 1980, what percentage of the total agricultural output was produced on these private plots?
   a. Less than .5 percent
   b. Approximately 1 percent
   c. Approximately 10 percent
   d. Approximately 25 percent

8. Which of the following is the most accurate description of the Yugoslavian economy?
   a. A detailed, centrally planned, socialist economy
   b. A free-enterprise market economy
   c. A decentralized, market-socialist economy
   d. A true communist economy characterized by the communal ownership of property

9. All but one of the following have contributed to the rapid rate of growth of the Japanese economy. Which has *not* been a significant source of economic growth in Japan?
   a. High rate of capital formation
   b. Persistent tax cuts
   c. Adoption of modern technology borrowed from other industrial Western nations
   d. A strong national federation of unions that has established a uniform national wage scale in most major industries

10. Which of the following was an important part of Karl Marx's economic philosophy?
    a. History is a dynamic process characterized by the struggle between social classes.
    b. Workers must directly control not only the means of production but also the political process.
    c. Capitalistic economic activity oppresses the people.
    d. All of the above.

11. From 1950 to 1980, the real GNP of Japan grew at an annual rate of approximately
    a. 3 percent.
    b. 5 percent.
    c. 7 percent.
    d. 9 percent.

12. Labor unions in Japan are
    a. strongly centralized national unions.
    b. influential in setting wage differentials.
    c. seldom company unions.
    d. important primarily for blue-collar workers.

13. (**I**) The Japanese tax structure is progressive. (**II**) In Japan, individuals can partially avoid paying taxes by saving or investing in specified industries.
    a. Both I and II are true.
    b. I is true, II is false.
    c. I is false, II is true.
    d. Both I and II are false.

THE ECONOMIC WAY OF THINKING—MULTIPLE CHOICE

1. Which of the following is *not* a characteristic of socialist economic organization?
    a. Centralized economic planning
    b. Workers are employed by government or by government-controlled cooperatives.
    c. The rate of return of human capital is determined by market forces.
    d. Investment in nonhuman capital is determined by political factors.

2. If socialist planners wanted to allocate resources efficiently, they would
    a. attempt to have each product produced by the low opportunity-cost producer.
    b. expand the use of a resource as long as its marginal product were positive.
    c. expand the production of a good as long as consumers received some positive marginal utility from it.
    d. not need to utilize such capitalist concepts as opportunity cost and comparative advantage.

3. Suppose that producers of cut-glass jewelry were rewarded according to the weight of the glass used in producing the jewelry. As a result, necklaces made with very thick glass would be produced. If the rules were changed to piecemeal production—that is, the managers were rewarded by the number of necklaces made—and the quantity of output increased, it could be concluded that
    a. the cost of production of the latter method is lower.
    b. the latter method implies increased production, higher rates of growth, and thus good management on the part of the central planning authority.
    c. the jewelry makers' behavior implies that incentives count in any economy.
    d. the enterprises increased output only for the purpose of amplifying their level of achievement.

4. Which of the following is *not* an accurate statement about economic incentives and production methods in a Yugoslav-type system (where employees of each firm elect a Workers' Council to purchase raw materials and to determine the level of employment, the quantity of goods produced, and the price of the finished product)?
    a. Since the employees are the residual wage earners, they strive for efficient operation and high levels of profits.
    b. Profits tend to move toward distribution among workers, rather than investment or future benefits.
    c. There are increased incentives to invest funds in new enterprises, since investors would be able to draw interest and claim dividends on new ventures.
    d. In this type of system, firms would tend to substitute capital for labor if this approach keeps the profit share per individual worker high.

5. The material balance method
   a. uses a planning agency to keep track of and allocate resources.
   b. uses a planning agency to keep a balance between keeping track of and allocating resources.
   c. uses a hypothetical market to keep a balance between the supply of and the demand for material resources.
   d. uses a hypothetical market to keep a balance between the needs of various state enterprises which are in need of material resources.

6. A comparison of the rates of economic growth among primarily capitalist nations and primarily socialist countries suggests that
   a. capitalist countries grow more rapidly.
   b. socialist countries grow more rapidly.
   c. both capitalist and socialist economies are among those experiencing rapid rates of economic growth.
   d. socialist countries have been unable to increase the standard of living of their citizens.

7. In socialist economies, there is a problem of providing managers of productive resources with incentives to follow the rules designed by the government to achieve its goals. One remedy for this would be to base the manager's salary directly on the returns from his productive resource. The problem with this remedy is that
   a. the returns from productive resources in socialist economies are too small to be an effective incentive.
   b. this would essentially give the property rights to capital back to private individuals, and this is one of the things that socialists want to avoid.
   c. all socialist societies object to the use of monetary incentives.
   d. there is an abundance of evidence that the managers and workers of socialist societies fail to respond to economic incentives.

8. (**I**) "Japanese workers have been more likely to accept a reduction in wages during a business slump than workers in most Western nations." (**II**) "The rate of unemployment in Japan has generally been higher than that in the United States."
   a. I is true, II is false.
   b. II is true, I is false.
   c. Both I and II are true.
   d. Both I and II are false.

9. Use statements I and II to answer this question. (**I**) Taxes generally consume a larger share of the gross national product in Japan than in other major industrial nations. (**II**) The incomes of Japanese workers have risen rapidly as a result of the bargaining strength of a powerful national federation of unions, which has successfully redistributed income from the capitalist business sector to wage earners.
   a. I is true, II is false.
   b. II is true, I is false.
   c. Both I and II are essentially true.
   d. Both I and II are false.

10. **(I)** Whereas Adam Smith viewed the market mechanism as a vehicle that would free individuals from the oppression of government, Karl Marx believed that the socialist economic system would free individuals from the oppression of capitalist economic activity. **(II)** Both the manner and location in which modern communist societies developed were largely consistent with the prediction of Karl Marx.
    a. Both I and II are true.
    b. Both I and II are false.
    c. I is true, II is false.
    d. I is false, II is true.

11. Karl Marx believed that
    a. the market brings individual self-interest and economic progress into harmony.
    b. history is a dynamic process perpetuated by conflict and class struggle.
    c. through socialist intervention, the government will eventually get large enough and strong enough to prevent worker alienation.
    d. the only way to truly help the proletariat is to abolish democracy.

THE ECONOMIC WAY OF THINKING—DISCUSSION QUESTIONS

1. How do you think capitalist and socialist economies compare with regard to
    a. the diversity of products available?
    b. innovative behavior?
    c. equality of the income distribution?
    d. share of income allocated to investment?
    Explain.

2. Compare and contrast the socialist systems of the Soviet Union and Yugoslavia. Which do you prefer? Why?

3. How do the economies of the United States and the Soviet Union compare with regard to
    a. size of GNP?
    b. composition of GNP?
    c. per capita income?

4. How large is the market sector in the Soviet Union? What types of goods and services are traded in the market? Given its socialist objectives, why does the Soviet Union permit a market sector?

5. How efficient is Soviet planning? What problems arise from detailed planning? How has the Soviet Union attempted to reduce planning inefficiencies? Do the planners consider the importance of economic incentives? Explain.

6. Compare the Japanese economy with that of the United States. Which aspects of the Japanese economy do you find attractive? Which are unattractive? Explain. Do you think that the United States would be better served by labor unions organized on a company-by-company basis, rather than by the industry-wide structure that currently characterizes the U.S. economy?

PERSPECTIVES IN ECONOMICS

The Art of Queuing
by Hedrick Smith

Shopping generally resembles a grand lottery. I had
heard about consumer shortages before going to Moscow
but at first it seemed to me that the stores were pretty well
stocked. Only as we began to shop in earnest as a family
did the Russian consumer's predicament really come
through to me. First, we needed textbooks for our children
(who went to Russian schools) and found that the sixth-
grade textbooks had run out. A bit later, we tried to find
ballet shoes for our 11-year-old daughter, Laurie, only to
discover that in this land of ballerinas, ballet shoes size 8
were unavailable in Moscow. At G.U.M., the celebrated
emporium on Red Square with a water fountain and the
baroque atmosphere of a rambling, indoor, 1890's bazaar,
I tried to find shoes for myself. They were out of anything
in my size but sandals or flimsy, light-weight shoes that the
clerk, with one look at me, recommended against buying.
"They won't last," he admitted. Ann went out to buy some
enamelware pans (Russians advised against getting the
standard zinc-aluminum because it leaves a taste in the
food; stainless steel, copperware and teflon do not exist).
She scoured four major Moscow department stores and
several smaller shops without any success. In other words,
the stocks that had impressed me at first turned out mostly
to be racks of suits and coats that were poorly made or had
gone out of style, or the shelves of pots and pans and other
unwanted items that Russian housewives refused to buy.

In spite of the various tinkering reforms, the Soviet
economy still operates by Plan from above rather than in
response to consumer demand from below and this produces a lopsided assortment of goods. Goods are produced
to fill the Plan, not to sell. Sometimes the anomalies are
baffling. Leningrad can be overstocked with cross-country
skis and yet go several months without soap for washing
dishes. In the Armenian capital of Yerevan, I found an ample supply of accordions but local people complained they
had gone for weeks without ordinary kitchen spoons or tea
samovars. I knew a Moscow family that spent a frantic
month hunting for a child's potty while radios were a glut
on the market. In Rostov, on a sweltering mid-90s day in
June, the ice-cream stands were all closed by 2 P.M. and a
tourist guide told me that it was because the whole area
had run out of ice cream, a daily occurrence. A visiting
American journalist friend hunting flints for his cigarette
lighter was advised by Russian smokers to forget it because
Moscow had been without flints for a couple of months.

The list of scarce items is practically endless. They are
not permanently out of stock, but their appearance is unpredictable—toothpaste, towels, axes, locks, vacuum
cleaners, kitchen china, hand irons, rugs, spare parts for
any gadget from a toaster or a camera to a car, stylish
clothes or decent footwear, to mention only a few listed in
the Soviet press. Traveling in the provinces I have also no-
ticed the lack of such basic food items as meat. In cities like
Nizhnevartovsk and Bratsk during winter, people had become so accustomed to the fact that the meat departments
of food stores had simply shut down. I knew one young
man whose family lived near Kalinin, a city of about
380,000 located 150 miles northwest of Moscow. He told
me he never went to see his parents without taking meat
because they were unable to buy anything in Kalinin but
bologna and sausages.

* * *

But this is an old story. What is new and revolutionary
in the Soviet Seventies is that Russian consumers are becoming fussier shoppers. The country folk may still buy
practically anything, but urbanites are more discriminating
and fashion-conscious. They may have more cash in their
pockets than ever before, but they are less willing to part
with it. Yet because the supplies of consumer goods are
about as unpredictable as the weather (and there is little
effective advertising to help shoppers), Russians have developed a series of defense mechanisms to cope with the
situation. They know that some Soviet factories, especially
those in the Baltic Republics, produce nice items—women's
clothing with a bit of style, brighter men's shirts, good
sleeping bags, radios, or outboard motors—and that these
items sell out in a flash whenever they appear. So they prowl
the stores incessantly, hoping to be in the right place at the
right time when, as the slang expression has it, *oni vybra-
syvayut chtoto khoroshoye,* "they throw out something good,"
meaning put choice items on sale. For just that lucky break,
women all carry a string bag, an *avoska,* which comes from
the Russian word for maybe, perchance. In other words,
a string bag for the odd chance that you might find something unexpected, because stores do not provide paper bags.
Likewise, almost any man carries a briefcase wherever he
goes. I remember thinking at first how studious and busi-
nesslike all these Russian men looked with their briefcases.
Then one day, I was talking with a well-established scientist
in a park and suddenly he reached into his briefcase. I
thought he was going to pull out some paper to illustrate a
point he was making. But as my gaze followed his hand
into the briefcase, I spotted a bloody hunk of meat wrapped
loosely in newspaper. The scientist, who lived outside of
Moscow, had bought the meat to take home and was just
checking to make sure it was not leaking badly. As time
went on, I discovered that briefcases were far more likely
to be loaded with oranges, hoards of toothpaste or pairs of
shoes than with books or papers.

Another precaution is to carry plenty of cash at all
times, for the Soviet system is devoid of credit cards, charge
accounts, checkbooks, or easy loans. Installment credit is
available only on items like the less desirable models of radios and television sets which are grossly overstocked and
not moving well. So to be ready for the happy chance of
finding something rare, one sturdy blonde women told me,
"you have to carry a lot of cash. Suppose you suddenly
discover they are selling good kneeboots for 70 rubles. You
have to get in line right away. You don't have time to go
back to your apartment and get money. The boots will be
gone by the time you get back."

One of the attractive qualities among Russians that
this situation has fostered is an almost frontier readiness to
share cash with friends and co-workers, to help them make

the big purchases. Paradoxically, Russians have less money than most Americans but are more instinctively generous with it to friends. People think nothing of borrowing—or loaning—25, 50 or 100 rubles until the next pay day, if they can spare it—and sometimes even if they can't. For most people, money is less important than a good opportunity to use it.

Another cardinal rule of Russian consumer life is shopping for others. It is an unforgivable sin, for example, to run across something as rare as pineapples, Polish-made bras, East German wall lamps or Yugoslav toothpaste without buying some extras for your best friend at work, your mother, sister, daughter, husband, brother-in-law, or some other kin or neighbor. As a result, I was amazed to discover, people know by heart the shoe, bra, pant and dress sizes, waist and length measurements, color preferences and other vital particulars for a whole stable of their nearest and dearest to be ready for that moment when lightning strikes a store they happen to be in. Then they spend until the money runs out.

One middle-aged Moscow woman also told me how office-workers organize shopping pools, the way American housewives operate car pools, and rotate the daily chore of shopping for food. In their little office "collectives," she said, someone goes out to buy basic food items for all during the lunch hour to help everyone escape the terrible crush in stores after work. Often the women also take turns sneaking out during regular working hours to scout the main downtown stores for something special and return to sound the alert if reinforcements are needed for bulk-buying. In such cases, a bit of petty profiteering on the resale is perfectly normal. A young man told me how he had seen one woman get on a bus with 20 tubes of popular Yugoslav "Signal" brand toothpaste in her *avoska*. She was immediately inundated with questions about where she found it and a few whispered offers to buy some at a premium.

* * *

The urge for a touch of class, for something better than others have, has put the new pressure on that classic Russian institution—the queue. Customers the world-over wait in lines, but Soviet queues have a dimension all their own, like the Egyptian pyramids. They reveal a lot about the Russian predicament and the Russian psyche. And their operation is far more intricate than first meets the eye. To the passerby they look like nearly motionless files of mortals doomed to some commercial purgatory for their humble purchases. But what the outsider misses is the hidden magnetism of lines for Russians, their inner dynamics, their special etiquette.

The only real taste of stoical shopping vigils in recent American history were the pre-dawn lines at service stations during the gasoline crisis in the winter of 1973–74. That produced a wave of national self-pity in America. But it ws temporary and only for one item. Imagine it across the board, all the time, and you realize that Soviet shopping is like a year-round Christmas rush. The accepted norm is that the Soviet woman daily spends two hours in line, seven days a week, daily going through double the gauntlet that the American housewife undergoes at her supermarket once, maybe twice a week. I noted in the Soviet press that Russians spend 30 billion man-hours in line annually just to make purchases. That does not count several billion more man-hours expended waiting in tailor shops, barbershops, post offices, savings banks, dry cleaners and various receiving points, for turning in empty bottles and so on. But 30 billion man-hours alone is enough to keep 15 million workers busy year-round on a 40-hour week.

Personally, I have known of people who stood in line 90 minutes to buy four pineapples, three hours for a two-minute roller coaster ride, 3 and a half hours to buy three large heads of cabbage only to find the cabbages were gone as they approached the front of the line, 18 hours to sign up to purchase a rug at some later date, all through a freezing December night to register on a list for buying a car, and then waiting 18 more months for actual delivery, and terribly lucky at that. Lines can run from a few yards long to half a block to nearly a mile, and usually they move at an excruciating creep. Some friends of ours, living in the southwest part of Moscow, watched and photographed a line that lasted two solid days and nights, four abreast and running all through an apartment development. They guessed there were 10,000–15,000 people, signing up to buy rugs, an opportunity that came only once a year in that entire section of Moscow. Some burned bonfires to keep warm out of the snow and the crackling wood and din of constant conversation kept our friends awake at night.

Yet despite such ordeals the instinctive reaction of a Russian woman when she sees a queue forming is to get in line immediately—even before she knows what is being sold. Queue-psychology has a magnetism of its own. Again and again, I have been told by Russians that anyone's normal assumption on seeing people up front hurrying to get in line is that there must be something up there worth lining up for. Never mind what it is. Get in line first and ask questions later. You'll find out when you get to the front of the line, or perhaps they'll pass back word before then. A lady lawyer told me she once came upon an enormous line stretching all through the Moskva Department Store, and when she asked those at the end of the line what was on sale, "they said they didn't know or else snarled at me and told me not to interfere. I walked up 20 or 30 yards asking people and no one knew. Finally, I gave up asking."

Nina Voronel, a translator of children's literature, said she happened to be at an appliance counter one day buying an ordinary hand mixer for 30 rubles ($40), when a clerk carried in a box of East German wall-lamps. "I told the salesgirl, 'I'll take one and I'll go pay the cashier.' And while I went to the cashier, a line of 50 people formed. How they found out about it, I don't know, word spreads—that is the way we always learn here. Practically everyone in the store was there. It didn't matter whether they needed the lamps or not. People here don't just buy what they need, but whatever they see that is worth having. Some may sell those lamps. Some may give them to friends. But mostly they keep them on the shelf. A lamp is always needed, fur coats, fur hats, good winter boots, bright summer dresses, floor rugs, dishes, enamel pots and pans, kettles, good woolen cardigan sweaters, umbrellas, a decent purse, a nice writing table, a typewriter, a good woman's bra—not a floppy, ugly Soviet one with no support and no adjustments, made for big-bosomed country girls. But a Czech bra or a Polish one, white and pretty instead of blue and baggy with rose buds. That is why people are so quick to join a line. It might be any of those things."

* * *

The cheapness of medicines—often under a dollar for prescriptions—is one of the great pluses of the system, but it is frequently canceled out by shortages. This is one problem that Russians complain about quite openly. Even the press periodically chides the drug industry for shortages of standard medicines or medical ingredients like nitroglycerine for heart patients, tincture of iodine, ammonium hydroxide, novacaine, even first-aid kits and tourniquets, let alone sophisticated antibiotics. One doctor told me that there were standing instructions for doctors not to prescribe medicines they knew were out of stock. Like many other foreign residents in Moscow, I was frequently approached by Russian friends with urgent pleas for help in obtaining critically needed medicines, unavailable at any price in Moscow. Nonetheless, for most Russians such problems are outweighed by the improvements over the past. They regard the system of free health care as one of the most positive features of Soviet socialism.

Discussion

1. Many prices in the Soviet economy are set administratively, rather than through market response to supply and demand. How does this help explain the surpluses and shortages that Smith describes?

2. How are goods rationed among consumers if prices are not doing this?

3. Pretend you live in Russia. Would you get into a line without knowing what the line was for? Why? What assumptions are you making if you do so?

Answer Key

CHAPTER 1

True or False

The following are true: 1, 3, 5, 7, 8, 11, 13.

Problems and Projects

1. See the discussion, pp. 7–13.
2. b. Positively related.
   c. 15 miles; 1/15
3. b. 8/1; 4/1
4. b. Positively related.
   c. $124 billion; 124/168 = 0.74
   d. 0.83; no.
5. See the discussion, pp. 7–13.
6. c. Negatively related.
   d. Increase by 160 thousand tons.

Learning the Mechanics—Multiple Choice

1. d. It alone involves what ought to be done. (p. 14)
2. c. The statement concerns what the U.S. ''ought'' to do. (p. 14)
3. c. See the definition, p. 4.
4. c. It alone involves what ''will'' as opposed to ''ought'' to be. (p. 13)
5. a. The statement concerns what the government ''ought'' to do. (p. 14)
6. d. The first three are listed as guideposts, but the last confuses scarcity with poverty. (pp. 6–13)
7. c. It involves prediction—a testable hypothesis; the others involve prescription. (pp. 13–14)
8. d. See item 3, p. 8 and item 6, p. 11.
9. a. It stresses the interdependence of economic effects. (p. 11)
10. d. Each can be used to produce economic goods. (p. 5)
11. c. Statement (erroneously) says what is true for one must be true for all; this is the fallacy of composition. (p. 15)
12. b. Humans may *provide* freely but cannot *acquire* or produce freely. (p. 7)

The Economic Way of Thinking—Multiple Choice

1. c. All other answers are characteristics of *both* micro and macro. (p. 16)
2. b. All other answers involve costs with no gains. (p. 8)
3. d. In the other answers, individuals act contrary to their self-interest. (pp. 8–9)

4. c. "Should" implies normative economic reasoning. (p. 14)
5. b. Both positive and normative economics deal with costs, benefits, and theory. (pp. 13–14)
6. d. In each answer benefits and costs of action must be weighed. (pp. 7–8)
7. a. Incentives matter, even for "non-economic" behavior. (pp. 8–9)
8. b. Both high food prices and inflation may be caused by some other factor. (p. 15)
9. d. Neither good is freely available in amounts consumers desire. (pp. 4–5)
10. b. Other answers are tests, but this is usually accepted as *best*. (pp. 12–13)
11. d. Persons often desire nonmaterial items and sometimes their actions are ill-informed or appear to be irrational to others. (p. 8)
12. a. Smith opposed *b* but had some sympathy for *c* and *d;* see pp. 18–19.

CHAPTER 2

True or False

The following are true: 3, 4, 7, 8, 9, 11.

Problems and Projects

1. a. 2; 1
    b. no; Sam makes 10 chairs, Larry makes 4 tables.
2. a. yes
    b. yes; yes; increased (orange production up by 100 bushels).
3. United States

4. a. yes; yes; no.
    b. 900 million bushels; 200 million bushels.
    c. 100 million bushels; 1 bushel of wheat.
    d. 2 bushels of wheat.
5. a. $13,000
    b. $19,600
    c. The U.S. birthrate would fall.

Learning the Mechanics—Multiple Choice

1. c. See the definition, p. 30.
2. c. The opportunity cost of time spent not working is the wage forgone. (p. 31)
3. c. Opportunity cost always refers to values of *alternatives*. (p. 30)
4. a. Comparative advantage ensures efficiency which raises available output. (p. 42)
5. a. Since *each* trader can gain, exchange will arise voluntarily. (p. 43)
6. c. See the discussion, pp. 46–47.
7. d. It represents output combinations available using factors of production. (p. 36)
8. d. Two units of food must be sacrificed for eight units clothing; 2/8 = 1/4. (pp. 30 and 41–42)
9. d. Italia's opportunity cost of food = 1; Slavia's = 4. (pp. 41–42)
10. c. Gains arise when countries export their low opportunity cost goods. (p. 42)
11. c. Curve represents output possibilities when resources are fully utilized. (p. 37)
12. d. See the definition, p. 36.
13. c. See the definition, p. 33.
14. b. "Middlemen" specialize in providing information and arranging trades so you will not have to. (p. 33)
15. c. See the definition on p. 34.

The Economic Way of Thinking—Multiple Choice

1. b. Failure to realize specialization gains means inefficient resource use. (pp. 37 and 39–40)
2. c. Crusoe's opportunity cost of good $y = 1/2$; Friday's $= 1$. (pp. 30 and 41–42)
3. b. See Exhibit 2, p. 37.
4. b. Going to school means sacrificing the alternative of working and earning income. (pp. 31–32)
5. a. Specialization raises efficiency and reduces costs (time) of production. (pp. 39–41)
6. b. The alternative to the date is to have $10 and play tennis. (p. 30)
7. b. Higher investment means greater production possibilities in the future. (pp. 37–38)
8. d. The extra money cost of driving is $(3 \times \$80) - \$50 = \$190$. (p. 31)
9. b. Because production according to comparative advantage concentrates on minimizing opportunity cost. (p. 42)
10. a. Most (not all) wealth was built through voluntary (non-exploitive) trade. (p. 45)
11. c. He developed the theory of comparative advantage. (p. 42)
12. c. This is a part of the ''worker alienation'' that can accompany specialization. (p. 44)
13. b. If misuse of property is not enforced, there is no incentive to consider the wishes of others. (p. 35)

CHAPTER 3

True or False

The following are true: 1, 2, 3, 5, 7, 8, 9, 10.

Problems and Projects

1. b. $12
    d. $15
2. a. $4; 10
    b. $7; 12
    c. raise both

4. b. 0, −, +, −
    c. −, 0, −, −
    d. +, +, ?, +
    e. −, +, −, ?
5. b. increase
    e. no

Learning the Mechanics—Multiple Choice

1. d. A below-equilibrium price results in an excess of quantity demanded relative to quantity supplied. (p. 59)
2. b. If soybean prices rise, demand for wheat rises (demand curve shifts right). (pp. 54, 61)
3. c. The demand curve shows how quantity responds to *changes* in price. (p. 60)
4. a. When cigar prices rise, smokers will substitute cigarettes for cigars. (p. 54)
5. d. Sellers will want to supply more and buyers will demand less, resulting in a surplus. (p. 59)
6. a. Assuming Bud is a substitute for Miller. (pp. 54–55)
7. a. This reflects the law of demand; see the definition, p. 54.
8. a. Travelers will substitute bus, train and air travel for auto travel. (pp. 54–55)
9. a. The price mechanism rations goods to their most highly valued use. (pp. 55–56)
10. b. This is necessary to eliminate excess supply; see Exhibit 4, p. 59.
11. b. See the last paragraph of the discussion on pp. 62–63.
12. b. This is ''abstract'' as opposed to ''historical'' time. (pp. 58–60)

The Economic Way of Thinking—Multiple Choice

1. b. Increased price raises quantity supplied and reduces quantity demanded. (pp. 59, 67)
2. c. The tax raises price causing *quantity demanded* (not demand) to fall. (pp. 60–61)
3. a. Driving smaller cars is one way of economizing on higher priced gas. (p. 66)
4. b. With lower prices, landlords attempt to maintain profits by cutting costs. (pp. 67–68; 69)
5. b. A lower price increases quantity demanded and reduces quantity supplied. (pp. 59 and 67–68)
6. d. The drought reduced supply; the millers' expectations of higher future prices raised current demand. (p. 61)
7. a. Florida's demand is not affected; if California's supply rises, price falls. (pp. 61 and 64–65)
8. c. All other answers involve "interferences" with the price mechanism. (p. 71)
9. b. This lowers auto *demand,* which changes *quantity supplied,* not supply. (pp. 63–64)
10. c. Response *a* would lower price; *b* lowers quantity; *c* sharply raises quantity. (pp. 60–65)
11. a. "Shortages developed" during control and prices rose afterwards. (p. 67)
12. a. All other answers suppose a higher-than-equilibrium price. (pp. 67–68)

CHAPTER 4

True or False

The following are true: 1, 2, 4, 5, 6, 7, 8, 11.

Problems and Projects

3. a. $10, 100 billion
   b. $1000 billion
   c. $15; $1200 billion
   d. Consumer valuation of the last barrel is $15, which is greater than the producer valuation of $5, so this is inefficient.
4. a. P = $120, Q = 4,000 tons/year
   b. P = $130, Q = 3,000 tons/year (Hint: Add $20 to each price and graph new supply curve with the old quantity supplied and the new prices. Find the new equilibrium point.)

Learning the Mechanics—Multiple Choice

1. d. Lower quantity supplied leaves some mutual gains unrealized; see Exhibit 1, p. 81.
2. a. Answers *c* and *d* assume no "spillover effects" (externalities). (pp. 82–85)
3. c. The other responses may lead government to *reduce* efficiency. (pp. 91–93)
4. c. Such exchange reduces efficiency and may or may not lead to political action. (pp. 84–85 and 88)
5. b. Public goods are characterized by non-rivalry in consumption. (pp. 86)
6. c. External costs are not included in private production decisions; see Exhibit 3. (pp. 84–85)
7. b. Inefficiency may result from the special interest or shortsightedness effects. (pp. 94–96)
8. b. Element of compulsion may prevent public use of price mechanism. (p. 90)
9. a. Defining the ideal income distribution is a perplexing matter. (p. 92)

10. d. The personal benefits of casting an informed vote may be less than the costs of being informed. (p. 93)
11. d. This reflects the "no free lunch" guide to economic thinking. (p. 89)
12. d. Response *a* confers external benefits; *b* external costs; *c* external benefits. (p. 84)

Economic Way of Thinking—Multiple Choice

1. a. Spillover effects are unconsidered impacts of your actions on others. (p. 84)
2. c. Public goods break the individual consumption-payment link. (p. 85)
3. d. With no individual consumption-payment link, there may be insufficient private demand. (p. 89)
4. a. If either is violated, some mutual gains will be unrealized; see Exhibit 1. (pp. 80–81)
5. c. The *individual* consumption-payment link may be absent. (p. 89)
6. d. If individual costs are small it is rational for others to be ignorant. (p. 93)
7. c. Costs of organizing "influence" are justified by large potential gains. (p. 94)
8. b. Each of the others has *some* public good aspect, but clean air has more. (pp. 85–86)
9. c. One may *favor* an action (altruistically) without personally gaining. (p. 80)
10. a. Those who do not gain from voluntary exchange do not participate. (pp. 80–82)
11. d. Gains to special interest groups justify the costs to them of influencing politicians. (p. 94)
12. a. This appears to be an effective way of getting votes. (p. 96)

CHAPTER 5

True or False

The following are true: 1, 2, 3, 6.

Problems and Projects

3. a. $0.10(\$20,000) + 0.20(\$10,000) =$ $4,000
   b. $11,000
   c. progressive
   d. Add 10% to each income level, keeping tax rates the same.

4. a. 14.7%, 29.6%; progressive
   b. 19.6%, 44.0%; greater than
   c. no; yes; bracket creep
5. a. $150, $180, $200, $210, $210, $200
   b. Laffer curve

Learning the Mechanics—Multiple Choice

1. c. See Exhibit 11, p. 122.
2. a. See Exhibit 11, p. 122.
3. b. See the definition, p. 112.
4. b. See Exhibit 7, p. 111.
5. b. See the definition, p. 106.
6. d. Divide the increase in taxes ($200) by the increase in income ($1000). (p. 107)
7. c. The underground economy is used to avoid or reduce taxes. (pp. 113–14)
8. a. See Exhibit 6, p. 106.
9. d. See Exhibit 2, p. 101.

10. b. See Exhibit 12, p. 122.
11. d. By taking the same *number* of dollars, a low-income individual will pay a larger percentage of her income than will a high-income recipient. (p. 108)

The Economic Way of Thinking—Multiple Choice

1. a. The average tax rate would be greater for high-income families. (p. 106)
2. d. See Exhibit 8, p. 113.
3. c. The revenues that businesses use to pay taxes come from consumers, stockholders, or employees. (p. 120)
4. d. Such a special-interest group would oppose tax revision most of all.
5. d. Price would rise by 2 cents only if demand were completely vertical. (p. 112)
6. c. An increase in rates will tend to shrink the tax base, thus the tax revenues increase less than proportionally. (p. 115)
7. d. See the definition, p. 110.
8. d. One's *constant purchasing power* tax liability would remain the same. (p. 107)
9. a. The marginal rate determines after-tax value of *additional* income. (p. 107)
10. b. *Money* incomes rise with inflation placing people in higher brackets. (p. 107)
11. c. Laffer popularized, but did not discover, the principle involved. (p. 115)

CHAPTER 6

True or False

The following are true: 1, 2, 5, 6, 11.

Problems and Projects

1. a. 3993; 3555   b. 3993; 3555
2. 1064; 1481
3. 230; 190. The expenditure approach must be used because not enough information is given to use the resource allocation approach (Profits and Proprietor's Income must equal 10).
4. +, +, 0, +, +, −, 0   5. +, −, −, 0, +, −

Learning the Mechanics—Multiple Choice

1. c. Real GNP is what GNP is "really" worth, that is, adjusted for price changes. (pp. 137–38)
2. b. $RealGNP80 = MoneyGNP80 \times (GNPdeflator70/GNPdeflator80) = 2500 \times 1/2$. (p. 138)
3. c. Producers pay resource costs (incomes) which sum to GNP; see Exhibit 5, p. 137.
4. b. See the definition, p. 138.
5. a. If prices rise, moneyGNP80 must be adjusted downward; see answer 2 above. (p. 138)
6. c. The others represent current production of a final good. (pp. 128–30)
7. a. See Exhibit 5, p. 137.
8. d. Answer *a* is Net National Product (NNP); see the discussion, pp. 133–36.
9. c. NNP = Emp.Comp. + Prop.Inc. + Rents + Corp.Prof. + Interest + Ind.Bus.Tax&Tran. (p. 136)

10. c.   See Exhibit 11, p. 147; Personal Income = NNP − Ind.Bus.Tax&Tran. − Corp.Prof.
          + Soc.Sec.Contr. + Div. + Govt.Tran.Pay.,NetInt.Paid.&Bus.Tran.
11. b.   Disposable Income = Personal Income − Personal Taxes. (p. 147)
12. d.   GNP = NNP + Depreciation. (pp. 136 and 147)

The Economic Way of Thinking—Multiple Choice

1. b.   "Cleaning up" represents currently produced final goods and/or services. (p. 144)
2. c.   It is often difficult to obtain dollar prices for these transactions. (pp. 139 and 143)
3. d.   Measurements of the "production of the economy" should not reflect price changes. (p. 139)
4. b.   This would involve double counting of intermediate production stages. (pp. 128–29)
5. b.   See the definition, p. 138.
6. d.   If real GNP had not changed, prices would have risen by 3 percent. (pp. 137–38)
7. c.   GNP overstates net output since some of the capital stock depreciates. (p. 136)
8. b.   See the definition, p. 138.
9. d.   Real GNP is adjusted for price level changes but not for the other changes. (pp. 139 and 144)
10. a.   See the definition, p. 145.

CHAPTER 7

True or False

The following are true: 1, 3, 4, 6.

Problems and Projects

2. (1) a; (2) a; (3) b; (4) a; (5) c; (6) b; (7) c.
4. For 1964: 5.1; 5.2; 59.4; 58.7
5. a) N; b) E; c) N; d) U; e) N.

Learning the Mechanics—Multiple Choice

1. d.   See the definition, p. 158.
2. d.   See the definition, p. 154.
3. c.   Allowance must be made for "normal" unemployment. (p. 162)
4. b.   Inflation refers to a *process* of *general* rising prices. (pp. 166–67)
5. c.   See Exhibit 9, p. 167.
6. a.   Inflation = i = [(CPI82 − CPI81) / CPI81] × 100 = [15/300] × 100 = 5. (p. 167)
7. b.   See the definition and Exhibit 3, p. 155.
8. c.   Lenders would not have included price changes in terms of loan contracts. (pp. 168–69)
9. b.   Other answers do not result in an increase in the *general* price level. (pp. 166–67)
10. c.   Other answers refer to cyclical conditions; see the definition, p. 159.
11. c.   See Exhibit 1 and the discussion, pp. 152–153.
12. b.   See the definition and Exhibit 8, pp. 165–166.

The Economic Way of Thinking—Multiple Choice

1. a. This is an example of "search" unemployment; the other answers are incorrect. (p. 158)
2. a. If only one of the two is unemployed there is still *some* family income. (pp. 157-58)
3. c. The principal cause of frictional unemployment is imperfect information. (p. 158)
4. a. Idle plants and manpower allow increased output (supply) as demand grows. (pp. 153-54)
5. c. The Myopian lender and the Pessimismian borrower will both be worse off. (pp. 168-69)
6. a. There are other economic goals, all of which must be balanced against noneconomic ones, such as environmental goals. (p. 152)
7. b. Public policy must often anticipate changes in economic conditions. (p. 159)
8. a. Lenders would not have included price changes in terms of loan contracts. (pp. 168-69)
9. b. See the definition, p. 171; male deer weight gain is called stagobesity.
10. b. Money value of the loan would fall faster than interest accumulated. (pp. 168-70)
11. c. Economists think both caused an increase in the natural rate for the 1970's. (p. 162)
12. b. This is a part of frictional unemployment. (pp. 158 and 162)

CHAPTER 8

True or False

The following are true: 1, 5, 6, 7, 9, 12

Problems and Projects

1. b. 1933
   c. 1969
   d. 1979
2. a. 5%; real interest rate = nominal interest rate − rate of inflation.
   b. In the short run, the real rate of interest will be negative.
   c. In the long run, when inflation is anticipated, the real interest rate will move back up to 5% (nominal interest rate = 11%).
3. a. 1.4%; 8.8%; 5.6%; rising and then falling

Learning the Mechanics—Multiple Choice

1. b. Choice *a* represents part of the aggregate demand curve, *c* represents part of the resource market, and *d*, the price variable in the aggregate goods and services market. (p. 178)
2. c. A constant money supply and lower prices will increase the purchasing power of those holding money balances. (p. 180)
3. a. See the definition, p. 189, and the discussion, p. 190.
4. c. It represents an economy that is operating at its maximum sustainable rate of output. (pp. 183-84)
5. b. Any point on LRAS is at the natural rate of unemployment. (pp. 183-84)
6. d. The house is included in "goods and services." (pp. 187-88)
7. a. See the discussion, p. 189.
8. d. Money interest rate (10) − infla. premium (6) = real interest rate (4). (p. 190)
9. c. The inflationary premium reflects the expected rate of inflation. (p. 190)
10. d. People will buy now at the lower prices before their purchasing power declines. (p. 180)
11. d. The price of loanable funds is the interest rate. (pp. 178 and 189)

Economic Way of Thinking—Multiple Choice

1. a. This is the real balances effect. (p. 180)
2. b. A backward shift of aggregate demand will cause lower prices; choices *c* and *d* will shift aggregate demand forward. (pp. 179–81)
3. b. Producers will increase output only at a higher price level. (p. 186)
4. a. See the discussion, pp. 182–85.
5. d. The aggregate supply curve will become vertical. (p. 183)
6. d. Producers will increase output; the increase may lead to above- or below-capacity output level. (p. 182)
7. c. See the discussion, pp. 192–93.
8. a. AD must equal AS for short and long run equilibrium, but also in the long run, the current level of prices must equal the expected price level. (pp. 182–85)
9. a. Resources are being underutilized.
10. a. This is the definition of long-run equilibrium. (p. 186)
11. a. See the discussion, pp. 182–83.
12. a. The other three will decrease aggregate supply in the short run. (pp. 182–85)

CHAPTER 9

True or False

The following are true: 2, 4, 5, 8, 9, 10.

Problems and Projects

1. a. +, 0, 0, +, +
    b. 0, +, +, −, +
    c. −, 0, 0, −, −
    d. +, −, 0, +, ?
    e. 0, +, 0, −, +

3. a. 0, +, +
    b. −, −, +
    c. 0, 0, 0; without a strike, no change.
    d. −, −, +
    e. −, −, +

Learning the Mechanics—Multiple Choice

1. c. See Exhibit 2, p. 201.
2. c. An increase in the LRAS means a *higher* rate of sustainable output. (p. 202)
3. d. People will wait to buy goods and services when prices are lower. (p. 200)
4. a. Increased labor increases the economy's short and long term production possibilities. (Exhibit 4, p. 204)
5. b. See the definition, p. 203.
6. b. The SRAS will shift to the right. (pp. 209–10)
7. c. The market will adjust wages and prices to either stimulate or slow the economy to where unemployment equals the natural rate. (pp. 211–13)
8. d. People will wait to make purchases, shifting AD back. (p. 207)
9. c. A favorable supply shock will shift SRAS to the right. (pp. 204 and 209)
10. d. The aggregate demand curve shifts back. (pp. 207–208)
11. c. The SRAS curve shifts back. (pp. 210–11)
12. a. See the discussion, pp. 211–13.

Economic Way of Thinking—Multiple Choice

1. c. This is a favorable supply shock. (p. 209)
2. b. People will save more, shifting AD back. (pp. 199–200)
3. a. Optimism stimulates current investment and goods and services purchases. (pp. 206–207)
4. c. Increased productivity increases short- and long-term production possibilities. (p. 203)
5. b. A shortage of resources will cause costs and prices to rise, shifting SRAS back. (pp. 211–12)
6. b. People will use their savings to maintain their consumption level and decrease the supply of loanable funds. (pp. 210–11)
7. a. See the discussion, pp. 198–99.
8. a. See the discussion, pp. 207–208.
9. d. A favorable supply shock—the SRAS shifts to the right. (pp. 204 and 209)

CHAPTER 10

True or False

The following are true: 3, 4, 5, 6, 9, 11, 13.

Problems and Projects

1. a. 2/3
   b. $1/1.5 = 2/3$
   c. 1
   d. $(4-1)/4 = 3/4$
3. a. 3
   b. 3
   c. infinity
   d. 4
5. a. $600 + 3(50) = \$750$ billion
   b. $800 - 4(100) = \$400$ billion
   c. $Y = 3/4(Y - 300) + 100 + 300 = \$700$ billion

d. $Y = 200 + 4/5(Y - 500) + 150 + 600 = \$2750$ billion

6. a.

	Savit		Spendit	
Round 2:	12.5	6.25	22.5	20.25
Round 3:	6.25	3.13	20.25	18.23
Round 4:	3.13	1.56	18.23	16.40
Round 5:	1.56	0.78	16.40	14.76
All Others:	1.56	0.78	147.6	132.9
Total:	50.0	25.0	250.0	225.0

   b. Spendit
   c. 1/2; 9/10
7. increase by $20 trillion

Learning the Mechanics—Multiple Choice

1. c. See the definition, p. 231
2. b. Keynes rejected Say's Law. (p. 219)
3. b. The multiplier effect of the investment increase raises incomes and, hence, sales. (p. 232)
4. d. This is the basic Keynesian equilibrium condition. (p. 223)
5. c. See the definition, p. 223.
6. b. Remember (from Ch. 8) that the resource costs of production are also incomes. (p. 218)
7. a. The multiplier $= 1/(1 - MPC) = 1/(1 - 3/4) = 4$. (p. 233)
8. b. The notion "supply creates its own demand" is Say's law which Keynes attacked. (pp. 218–19)
9. b. The others do affect consumption, but this is the *primary* determinant. (p. 220)
10. c. It raises expected profits; others (including *b*) might *lower* investment. (pp. 220–21)
11. d. The higher the MPC, the more income there is to spend in the next round. (p. 233)

12. c. See the definition, p. 220.
13. b. The aggregate supply curve slopes up gradually *before* potential output is reached. (Exhibit 9b, p. 230)

The Economic Way of Thinking—Multiple Choice

1. c. MPC = additional consumption/additional income = 200/300. (p. 232)
2. c. This was one of Keynes' major challenges to classical thinking. (p. 219)
3. b. It may lead to increased borrowing or less saving currently. (p. 220)
4. b. This was one of Keynes' major objections to Say's Law.
5. d. The quote is a description of the multiplier process. (p. 232)
6. d. This is a major conclusion of Keynesian economics. (p. 219)
7. b. The multiplier applies: $(1/(1 - 0.75))(\$12 \text{ mil.}) = \$48$ million. (p. 233)
8. c. A greater MPC raises the multiplier, which equals $1/(1 - MPC)$. (p. 233)
9. d. See the discussion, pp. 218–20.
10. b. Part of increased income is spent, the remainder is saved, i.e., MPC < 1. (pp. 220 and 232)
11. c. See the discussion, pp. 228–29.
12. b. Aggregate demand (900) > aggregate supply (800), hence supply (GNP) increases. (pp. 223–25)
13. c. The Keynesian model, not the AD/AS model, has been the center of macroeconomics for four decades. (p. 218)

CHAPTER 11

True or False

The following are true: 2, 4, 8, 10, 11, 13, 14.

Problems and Projects

1. balanced reduction in G and T
2. a. AS;   b. AS;   c. both;   d. AD;   e. AS;   f. both;   g. AD;   h. both.

Learning the Mechanics—Multiple Choice

1. c. Government expenditure and taxation policy constitute fiscal policy. (p. 244)
2. a. Increase in government spending = $300 billion/multiplier(3) = $100 billion. (p. 232)
3. d. See the definition, p. 244.
4. d. See "Applications in Economics," p. 255.
5. b. A shortage of resources and labor cause higher prices and wages. (Ch. 10 and p. 246)
6. c. See the definition, p. 249.
7. c. See the discussion, pp. 261 and 263–65.
8. a. The public will have to pay higher taxes later to pay for current government expenditures. (p. 251)
9. d. Investment expenditures are not automatic and actually add to the unstable, cyclical nature of the economy. (p. 257)

10. b. Countercyclical policy to ensure general economic conditions replaced the concept of the annual balanced budget. (pp. 246–47)
11. b. See the definition, p. 249.
12. a. Taxpayers expect higher future taxes. (pp. 252–53)

Economic Way of Thinking—Multiple Choice

1. b. This is a result of the multiplier effect. (Ch. 10)
2. a. As long as the government can raise huge tax revenues, lenders can be sure money, plus interest, will be repaid when due. (p. 263)
3. a. The multiplier effect increases aggregate demand even more. (p. 246 and Exhibit 5)
4. b. Choices a and d will offset inflation, choice c combines expansionary and contractionary policy. (Ch. 10 and pp. 245–47, 254–57)
5. d. Increased disposable income will increase consumption. (p. 220 and Exhibit 5)
6. d. Refer to the introduction and first section of Chapter 10. (pp. 218–19)
7. a. The higher the marginal tax rates, the greater the benefits from tax-exempt income and tax-deductions. (pp. 254–55)
8. b. An adverse supply shock will cause AS to shift back; the effect of the others is disputed. (pp. 204, 254, 265)
9. c. Fiscal policy lags can cause more problems than remedies. (p. 207)
10. c. It calls for deficits during recessions and surpluses during "peaks." (p. 247)
11. b. See Exhibit 5, p. 254.
12. c. See the discussion, pp. 259–60.
13. b. See the discussion, pp. 263–65.
14. a. Imperfect information and a "world of dynamic change" cause fiscal policy often to become a source of economic instability. (p. 257 and Exhibit 7, p. 258)

CHAPTER 12

True or False

The following are true: 3, 6, 8, 11.

Problems and Projects

1. 4
2. $575 billion
3. purchase $5 billion worth
4. a. 25%

   b.

First stage:	2000	500	1500	1500	1500
Second stage:	1500	375	1125	1125	1125
Third stage:	1125	281	844	844	844
Fourth stage:	844	211	633	633	633
Fifth stage:	633	158	475	475	475
All others:	1898	475	1423	1423	1423
Total:	8000	2000	6000	6000	6000

   c. $(1500)(1/(0.25 + 0.15)) = \$3750$

Learning the Mechanics—Multiple Choice

1. d. It lowers banks' cost of funds, raising expected profits on loans. (pp. 287–88)
2. d. *Wealth* may be an end in itself, but money (a form of wealth) usually is not. (p. 270)
3. c. Usually it will perform its three basic functions no matter how much circulates. (p. 271)
4. c. Legislative bodies such as Congress levy taxes, not the Fed. (Exhibit 11, p. 288)
5. d. To pay for the bonds the public gives up $5 million in money (demand deposits). (pp. 286–87)
6. b. The contraction multiplier = 1/.10 = 10; 10 × $5 mill. = $50 mill. (pp. 279–80)
7. a. The Fed has substantial autonomy in carrying out this responsibility. (pp. 281–83)
8. c. Potential money deposit multiplier = 1/reserve ratio = 1/.10 = 10. (pp. 279–80)
9. a. Required reserves = reserve ratio × demand deposits; 1000 = reserve ratio × 5000. (pp. 283–84)
10. c. See the definition, p. 271.
11. a. See the discussion, pp. 288–90.
12. b. They are the most flexible hence the most often used. (p. 285)
13. a. The act lifted many of the restrictions from the latter that distinguished them from commercial banks. (p. 276)

The Economic Way of Thinking—Multiple Choice

1. b. Fiscal policy is *budget policy:* higher spending, lower taxes in this case. (Ch. 11 and p. 290)
2. a. Choices *c* and *d* reduce the money supply; the Treasury is a budgetary agency. (p. 290 and Exhibit 11, p. 288)
3. c. Open market operations affect the *volume* of bank reserves, not reserve *ratio*. (p. 285)
4. b. Early goldsmiths practiced fractional reserve banking. (p. 277)
5. c. Public writes checks for securities; Fed collects from banks, lowering reserves. (pp. 286–87)
6. b. Potential deposit multiplier = 1/reserve ratio. (p. 279)
7. d. See the discussion, p. 276.
8. b. See the discussion, p. 276.
9. a. Idle excess reserves do not enter the deposit expansion process. (pp. 280–81)
10. d. This is *fiscal* policy. (Exhibit 11, p. 288)
11. c. Open market policy is the responsibility of the Open Market Committee. (p. 282)
12. d. Checking accounts become more attractive relative to *all* alternatives. (p. 274)
13. b. They now account for one-third of the money supply. (p. 274)

CHAPTER 13

True or False

The following are true: 2, 3, 6, 7, 8, 10, 11, 12.

Learning the Mechanics—Multiple Choice

1. b. See the discussion, pp. 294–95.
2. d. Both types of policy can affect unemployment, inflation and the volume of government bonds bought or sold. (pp. 294–96)
3. b. The economy needs an expansionary policy. (pp. 299–302)

4.   d.   See Exhibit 3, p. 301
5.   a.   If people continually underestimate inflation, higher employment results. (p. 335)
6.   b.   Decision-makers expect a slower growth rate of money and will react accordingly. (p. 307)
7.   a.   See the definition, p. 297.
8.   c.   See the definition, p. 294 and Exhibit 1, p. 296.
9.   d.   See the discussion, pp. 300–302.
10.   d.   Inflation will be anticipated and money interest rates will rise. (pp. 307–308)
11.   c.   It can affect both through two different channels. (Exhibits 2, 3, pp. 300–301)
12.   c.   Open market operations are one of the ways to increase the money supply. (Ch. 12)
13.   d. M_1 increased and M_2 stayed the same; velocity decreased. (pp. 313–14)

Economic Way of Thinking—Multiple Choice

1.   b.   Excess money supply causes lower interest rates and increased spending. (pp. 300–301)
2.   d.   The government spending is expansionary; restrictive tax and monetary policies will offset it. (Exhibit 8, p. 308)
3.   a.   See the discussion, pp. 296–98.
4.   c.   Nominal interest rates and wages could adjust so real interest rates and income remain unchanged.
5.   c.   This is the primary belief of monetarists. (pp. 298–99)
6.   b.   Higher interest rates will affect interest-sensitive sectors more than others. (pp. 302–303)
7.   d.   See the discussion, pp. 315–17.
8.   d.   Below the full employment output, producers will increase output, not prices, until convinced increased demand is permanent. (p. 302)
9.   a.   Choices *b, c,* and *d* list the ways the Fed can implement expansionary policy. (Ch. 12 and pp. 295–96)
10.   b.   Higher income will raise the transactions demand for money. (p. 294).
11.   d.   Government spending recirculates the money received from security sales. (Ch. 12, p. 290)
12.   b.   See Exhibit 8, p. 308.
13.   c.   Real interest rate, (4) + inflationary premium (6) = nominal interest rate (10). (Ch. 7 and pp. 307–308)

CHAPTER 14

True or False

The following are true: 3, 4, 5, 13.

Problems and Projects

3.   a. 10%;   b. 3%;   c. 9%;   d. unhappy

Learning the Mechanics—Multiple Choice

1.   a.   Adjustments for anticipated inflation result in higher prices and no change in unemployment. (pp. 335–36)

2. b. Reduced aggregate demand initially lowers production and employment. (Ch. 13 and pp. 335–36)
3. c. Decision-makers began to expect higher rates of inflation. (pp. 335–37)
4. a. Older workers are more stable (less likely to change jobs). (pp. 341–42)
5. b. Temporarily higher anticipated profits will stimulate the economy. (Exhibit 7, p. 335)
6. c. See the discussion, p. 325.
7. b. The macroacceleration will catch decision-makers by surprise. (pp. 324 and 332)
8. c. Monetary acceleration may be unanticipated in the short term, but in the long term (if it is persistent) it will be expected. (pp. 323–27)
9. c. See the discussion, p. 324.
10. b. The result will be the same as an unanticipated expansionary policy. (pp. 335–36)
11. a. Prices will adjust to a higher level without an increase in output. (pp. 330–33)
12. b. See Exhibit 9, p. 341.

Economic Way of Thinking—Multiple Choice

1. c. An expansionary fiscal and/or monetary policy is wanted. (pp. 327–28)
2. c. See the discussion, p. 335; the Phillips curve shifts out.
3. a. On the new Phillips curve, a lower rate of inflation initially means higher unemployment than before. (Exhibit 5, p. 331)
4. a. Expected inflation will exceed actual inflation. (p. 336 and Exhibit 7, p. 335)
5. c. See the definition, p. 325.
6. c. Choices a and b increase unemployment; d increases inflation.
7. a. It lowers the opportunity cost of being unemployed. (p. 339)
8. b. The opportunity cost of job search is less. (p. 339)
9. b. The rate of return on saving would rise.
10. c. Younger people and retirees are more likely to dissave.
11. b. The cost of hiring youthful workers is reduced. (p. 340)
12. a. Expectations help us understand the past but make prediction difficult. (pp. 336–38)

CHAPTER 15

True or False

The following are true: 2, 3, 5, 7, 9, 10, 11.

Problems and Projects

1. a. Trash Pickup Plan
    b. Pork Barrel, Big Dam, Acid Rain Remover, Trash Pickup Plan

Learning the Mechanics—Multiple Choice

1. c. See the definition, p. 346.
2. a. See the definition, p. 346.
3. d. All three are discretionary expansionary policy actions. (p. 348)
4. d. Nonactivists emphasize that discretionary actions do more harm than good. (p. 349)
5. b. See the discussion, pp. 351 and 353.

6. b. It takes time for macropolicy to work, so policy-makers must anticipate economic changes. (p. 351)
7. b. See the discussion, pp. 355–56.
8. b. This is the rational expectations view. (p. 358)
9. c. He proposed the most widely advocated nonactivist monetary policy, the constant money growth rule. (p. 359)
10. d. The nonactivists only have a ''general strategy,'' not a practical, workable policy solution. (p. 361)
11. b. This is the policy ineffectiveness theorem. (p. 358)

Economic Way of Thinking—Multiple Choice

1. d. Lags, political objectives, and the policy ineffectiveness theorem are problems with discretionary action. (p. 349)
2. c. See the discussion, pp. 347–48.
3. c. Choices *a* and *b* are restrictive activist stabilization policies. (pp. 347–48)
4. c. This means the Fed conducts an open market purchase. (Ch. 12 and pp. 347–48)
5. c. A primary argument for nonactivist policies is uncertainty about the future. (pp. 355–56)
6. b. This is the policy ineffectiveness theorem. (p. 358)
7. a. Nonactivists' fiscal goal of a balanced budget requires actions inconsistent with their pursuit of stable policies. (p. 361)
8. a. These tools serve as an early warning system, allowing time for the lags before the impact of the policy change needs to be felt. (p. 355)
9. c. Time lags and political versus stabilization objectives are two of the problems nonactivists find with activists' policies. (pp. 355–57)
10. a. See the discussion, p. 351.
11. a. See the discussion, pp. 355–56.
12. c. Monetary rule does not allow any discretionary actions for severe changes in the economy. (pp. 360–61)

CHAPTER 16

True or False

The following are true: 1, 3, 4, 8, 9, 12, 14, 15.

Problems and Projects

1. Gasoline and air travel are substitutes; gasoline and auto tires and gasoline and Yellowstone tourism are complements.
2. a. 1500, 1400, 1650; elastic, inelastic
    b. Price elasticity between \$1 and \$2 = (800/1100) / (1/1.5) = (−)1.09
        Price elasticity between \$2 and \$3 = (150/625) / (1/2.5) = (−)0.60
3. a. Food: 30, 25, 20, 15, 10, 5
        Clothing: 10, 7,   5,   4,   2,   1
        Housing: 35, 30, 20, 15, 10, 8
    b. 3/2; 1; 35/30; food

c.   3 food, 1 clothing, 2 housing

d.   2 units of food are purchased when P = $30; 4 units of food are purchased when P = $15.

e.   Food consumption would increase from 3 to 5 units, clothing would increase from 1 to 3 units, and housing from 2 to 4 units.

4. a.   4 cups

b. $1.75 + 0.75 + 0.25 = $2.75

c. $2.75 + (−0.15) + (−0.20) + (−0.25) = $2.15; it is less.

5.   down; up; none; up; 1.0; up

Learning the Mechanics—Multiple Choice

1. b.   Demand is *elastic* (elasticity = 30%/15% = 2); when P rises, spending falls. (p. 379)
2. c.   This causes a *movement along* the demand curve for green peas. (p. 378)
3. c.   This reflects the basic postulate of economizing behavior. (Ch. 3 and pp. 370–72)
4. b.   See the definition, p. 376.
5. d.   When income rises, purchases fall (negative change); see the definition, p. 385.
6. a.   Consumers substitute oranges for grapefruit at any given price of oranges. (p. 377)
7. d.   "Demand" refers to the entire demand curve which shifts to the right. (Ch. 3 and p. 378)
8. a.   For inferior goods, changes in income and demand are inversely related. (p. 385)
9. c.   Each alternative answer suggests a change in the *quantity* of milk *demanded*. (p. 377)
10. d.   The large quantity of rock music caused a low *marginal* utility. (p. 372)
11. c.   If beef is normal; also, other answers suggest a decrease in demand for beef. (p. 377)
12. a.   A change in price of pork chops results in a movement along the demand curve. (pp. 376–78)
13. d.   Demand is inelastic (elasticity = 10%/50% = .2); when P rises, spending rises. (p. 384)

The Economic Way of Thinking—Multiple Choice

1. d.   The new information shifted (decreased) the demand for cigarettes. (pp. 377–78)
2. c.   A decrease in quantity sold is expected to raise both price and spending. (p. 384)
3. b.   Butter price went up, quantity down; margarine price went down, quantity up. (pp. 373 and 377)
4. c.   If demand increases (shifts) more than supply, both price and quantity rise. (pp. 376–78)
5. d.   Choice *a* and *b* increase demand; *c* decreases *quantity demanded*. (pp. 376–78)
6. c.   "Snob" goods do not conform to the usual law of demand. (p. 386)
7. c.   Reduced quantity and spending with an increased price implies elastic demand. (p. 384)
8. c.   Elastic implies that lower price increases revenues; costs are constant. (p. 384)
9. c.   Color set demand will decrease; elasticity of demand for b&w sets is unknown (pp. 377 and 384)
10. a.   Both (I) and (II) are basic assumptions of consumer choice theory. (pp. 370 and 372)
11. a.   See Exhibit 7, p. 381.
12. d.   The owners expect an increase in price to lower quantity but raise revenues. (p. 384)
13. b.   The opportunity cost of listening is the (increasing) pay sacrificed. (pp. 374–75)
14. c.   Income and purchases are positively related for normal goods. (pp. 373 and 377)
15. a.   He receives trust earnings whether he listens or not. (pp. 373 and 397–98)

CHAPTER 17

True or False

The following are true: 1, 2, 3, 4, 5, 7, 8, 9, 10, 12.

Problems and Projects

1. a. $9,000
    b. Owner's labor services and interest income foregone on Joe's equity capital.
    c. $48,000 + 0.10(30,000) + 10,000 = $61,000
    d. $4,000 loss
2. b. 5
    c. beyond 3
3. a. Auto A = 32 cents per mile; Auto B = 31 cents per mile; Auto B is cheaper.
    b. Auto A = 25 cents per mile; Auto B = 25.5 cents per mile; Auto A is cheaper.
    c. They decline primarily because average fixed cost is falling as the miles driven increases from 10,000 to 20,000.
4. a. Marginal product: 20, 15, 10, 5
        Marginal cost: 2.50, 3.33, 5.00, 10.00
        Total cost: 250, 300, 350, 400, 450

Learning the Mechanics—Multiple Choice

1. c. See Exhibit 2, panel (c), pp. 406 and 410–12.
2. d. Use of variable inputs expands relative to fixed inputs so productivity falls. (pp. 408 and 410–11)
3. a. It involves no actual money payments; it is income sacrificed. (p. 404)
4. c. Demand informs firms; resources are scarce because they have alternative uses. (p. 403)
5. c. Usually the case since labor is normally variable in the short run. (p. 405)
6. b. See the definition, p. 417.
7. b. One of the major reasons for the popularity of this legal structure. (p. 402)
8. c. This is simply not the case. (pp. 413–14)
9. a. A shift in demand will not cause the cost curves to shift. (p. 416)
10. d. When MC > ATC, ATC must rise and vice-versa; see Exhibit 6, p. 411.
11. d. Implicit costs are included in economic, but not in accounting, profits. (p. 405)
12. a. Carefully study the definition, p. 408.
13. d. This indicates that an increase in supply has no effect on price. (pp. 426–27)

The Economic Way of Thinking—Multiple Choice

1. a. Answer d would mean higher price; answers b and c are nonsense. (p. 416)
2. d. Usually plant is fixed in the short run; the other inputs are variable. (pp. 406 and 412)
3. d. Relaxing these physical constraints offsets short-run diminishing returns. (Ch. 18, p. 439)
4. a. Efficient (ideal) plant size is an output where long-run unit cost is minimized. (p. 415 and Exhibit 9, panel b)
5. d. The car will last more than one year; implicit interest is an opportunity cost. (pp. 404–405 and 417)

6. b. The $300 mortgage payment is a sunk cost; local service charges are avoidable. (pp. 417–19)
7. c. All marginal concepts relate to *changes* such as additions. (p. 409)
8. c. Sacrificed rental value is an implicit cost included in economic profit. (p. 409)
9. c. Both product spoilage and change in market conditions are valid reasons. (p. 418)
10. c. Increased output would significantly reduce *average* fixed cost and ATC. (pp. 406–408)
11. d. Higher demand for orange-growing inputs raises their prices and hence, the price of grapefruit. (p. 416)
12. c. Harvester productivity is raised, lowering harvester cost per unit produced. (p. 416)

CHAPTER 18

True or False

The following are true: 1, 3, 4, 5, 6, 9, 10, 11.

Problems and Projects

1. b. 6; $1 per month
   c. 7; $35 per month
2. b. 6; $9,000 per month
   c. 7; $26,000 per month
   d. 5; $17,000 per month loss; 4; $36,000 per month loss; yes, in the short run, but not in the long run.
3. b. $29,000
   c. Each firm is making profits of $6,000 per month; yes.
   d. It will fall as new profit-seeking firms enter the market.
4. a. 1000; 8,000; 8; 0
   b. yes
   c. no change
   d. go out of business—but the firm's expectation that market conditions will remain the same is probably incorrect because the market price will rise as some of the firms in the industry go out of business.

Learning the Mechanics—Multiple Choice

1. c. All of the firm's inputs are variable in the long run, hence all costs are, too, (Ch. 17 and p. 439)
2. d. They will seek better profit opportunities in alternative industries. (p. 435)
3. b. If P > ATC, firms earn economic (excess) profits which attract new entrants. (pp. 433–35)
4. a. *b* should read "average *total* cost"; *c* "total *variable* cost"; *d*, "average *variable* cost." (pp. 428–32)
5. c. Costs (hence prices) would be lower; other answers raise demand (hence price) (Ch. 17 and p. 433)
6. d. Firms exit alternative industries where profit opportunities are less attractive (pp. 433–35)
7. b. Entry and expansion require that all resources be variable (the long run). (p. 439)
8. c. The *market* refers to the aggregate supply decisions of all suppliers. (p. 433)
9. c. See the discussion, p. 441.

10. c.   AFC = (Fixed Cost/Output) must decline as output rises. (Ch. 17)
11. b.   Some inputs are fixed, hence output responds less to changes in price. (p. 439)

The Economic Way of Thinking—Multiple Choice

1.   d.   During long-run adjustment some firms would exit and price would rise. (pp. 432–33)
2.   a.   Price nearly tripled suggesting increased demand and inelastic supply. (pp. 434, 439)
3.   d.   The cost of the inputs, grains, rose for each of these outputs. (p. 432)
4.   a.   Price will initially exceed ATC causing entry and expansion in the wheat market. (p. 432)
5.   c.   Both supply and demand would increase (curves shift to right). (Ch. 16)
6.   b.   Firms want more than zero profits, but free entry prevents this outcome. (p. 426)
7.   b.   Short run supply is less elastic than long run supply. (p. 439)
8.   d.   Peak-period quantity demanded would be reduced. (p. 435)
9.   b.   At prices below average variable cost, the firm would shut down. (pp. 431–32)
10. a.   The producer should sell out since she expects only losses in the long run. (p. 431)
11. c.   Knowing ''how to do well'' (maximizing profit) implies the ability to compete. (pp. 428–29)
12. b.   One more unit would *add* more to cost (MC) than it would to revenue (MR). (pp. 428–29)

CHAPTER 19

True or False

The following are true: 1, 2, 5, 7, 9, 10, 11, 12, 14.

Problems and Projects

3.   b. $1.20
     c.   yes; $1,100 per month
     d. $1.00
     e.   approximately $13,200 or the present value of the expected economic profit; the university would then reap the monopoly benefits.

4.   a. P_4
     b. P_2
     c. P_3

5.   a.   1
     b.   1
     c.   2
     d.   2

Learning the Mechanics—Multiple Choice

1.   a.   See the definition, p. 484.
2.   a.   Usually in monopoly P > MC leading to allocative inefficiency. (pp. 457–58)
3.   a.   The profit-maximizing behavior is restriction of output to raise price. (Exhibit 7, p. 458, and pp. 457–58)
4.   a.   MR should = MC for maximum profit which may not occur if (II) is achieved. (pp. 452–53)
5.   b.   Each firm would operate at an inefficient small level of output. (p. 460)
6.   d.   Output should always be raised if MR > MC and lowered if MR < MC. (pp. 452–53)

7. d. This may be a *result* of monopoly, but it is not a source of monopoly. (p. 449)
8. d. A competitive firm produces an output at which P = MC. (p. 453)
9. b. A monopolized firm produces an output at which P > MC. (pp. 457–58)
10. d. Each serves to restrain price increases by the monopolist. (pp. 467–68)
11. a. These barriers are probably as old as government itself. (p. 449)
12. c. Product development may depend on statically inefficient monopoly profits. (pp. 449 and 470)

The Economic Way of Thinking—Multiple Choice

1. d. This is a potential outcome of the special interest effect. (p. 465)
2. d. Each of these potential solutions has limitations: there's no general ideal one. (pp. 461–67)
3. a. The profit-maximizing behavior is to raise profits at the expense of consumers. (p. 449)
4. a. Special interest effects may lead potentially socially efficient policy astray. (p. 465)
5. d. See the discussion, pp. 463–65.
6. c. The benefits of efficiency are widely dispersed over the consumers of the product. (pp. 449 and 463–64)
7. c. The others compete with producers of several (if not many) close substitutes. (pp. 467–68)
8. c. Voters' difficulty in detecting efficiency impedes rewarding efficient managers. (p. 466)
9. d. DuPont's control over price depends on how closely other wraps can be substituted. (pp. 449 and 467–68)
10. b. Return trips must be made whether price is artifically high or somewhat lower. (pp. 452–53 and Ch. 21, p. 518)
11. a. For inelastic demand, higher prices reduce sales, raise total revenues, and lower total costs. (p. 452)

CHAPTER 20

True or False

The following are true: 1, 2, 5, 6, 10, 12, 13.

Problems and Projects

1. b. $150; 24,000; 6,000   d. $250
    c. $400; $300; $250

2. b. by 5000 units to a total of 25,000 tricycles
        [TR − TC = profits → $9(Q) − (120,000 + $4(Q)) = 5000 → Q = 25,000]
    c. Price elasticity = [(5000/22500)/(1/9.5)] = 2.11
3. b. $70; $240   d. no
    c. 5; $60; $250; profit has increased

Learning the Mechanics—Multiple Choice

1. a. Entry increases competition which drives down market price and eliminates profits. (p. 486)
2. c. Better products at the same price from competitors limits price increases. (pp. 483 and 485)

3. a. P > MC due to product differentiation; P = AC due to low entry barriers. (pp. 476–78)
4. d. Stable, fairly certain information makes agreement easier to reach and enforce. (pp. 484–86)
5. a. Oligopolies control competition to some extent, but less than monopolists can. (pp. 483–84)
6. d. See Exhibit 7, p. 488 and pp. 487–88.
7. c. See Exhibit 8, p. 490.
8. b. Firms would pay Amy premium wages up to the value of her extra efficiency. (p. 478)
9. a. The more producers, the more difficult it is to collude. (p. 485)
10. b. The ratio gives us an indication of industry structure but not firm behavior. (pp. 489–90)
11. c. Long-run normal profits are a result of low entry barriers. (pp. 477–78)
12. c. Since entry barriers are low, economic profits will attract new entrants. (p. 477)

The Economic Way of Thinking—Multiple Choice

1. d. A better product at the same price is equivalent to a price cut (competition). (pp. 485–86)
2. b. This increases supply of medical services; other answers increase demand (pp. 482 and 486)
3. d. Buyers are willing to pay a premium for such stocks; the "early bird . . ." (pp. 492 and 494)
4. a. This is a basic similarity between pure and monopolistic competition. (p. 478)
5. a. Evidence shows no strong relation between concentration and profit. (p. 492)
6. c. This would limit entry allowing higher prices and some economic profit. (p. 486)
7. d. The innovative spirit might be dulled but certainly not eliminated. (pp. 485–86)
8. c. Return to zero-profit equilibrium causes price to rise as much as costs. (pp. 476–78)
9. d. Successful collusion + little entry = successful price control. (pp. 485–86)
10. b. Price competition might be used in an attempt to restore sales. (p. 486)
11. b. Reduction in supply as some firms exit raises price and restores normal profits. (p. 477)
12. a. Since profits are higher, it would pay more to protect them.
13. d. This also helps to explain the success of McDonald's. (p. 475)

CHAPTER 21

True or False

The following are true: 1, 3, 8, 11.

Problems and Projects

1. a.

Q	AFC	ATC
50	.20	.26
60	.17	.23
70	.14	.20

   b. At each output level, there is a $10 million loss (the total fixed cost)
   c. At each output level, there is no profit and no loss; total revenue = total cost

Learning the Mechanics—Multiple Choice

1. c. See Exhibit 3, p. 504.
2. c. See the definition, p. 516.
3. c. Sure it's strange, but they are both true. (pp. 508 and 516-19)
4. c. See Exhibit 1, p. 502.
5. d. See the Thumbnail Sketch, p. 508.
6. c. See the evidence presented, pp. 514-15.
7. c. (I) political machines work slowly; (II) a result of special interest effects. (p. 513)
8. c. Apparently the income elasticity of demand for these services is high. (pp. 500-501)
9. c. This tends to promote rather than restrict competition. (p. 507)
10. c. If there are hundreds of small competitors, at least 60%; if only 1-4, 100%. (Ch. 20, pp. 489-90)
11. b. Rivalry to promote divisional interests; cooperation to promote GM's interest. (p. 502)
12. c. Social regulations can be seen as taxes on productive activity; see Exhibit 5. (p. 520)

The Economic Way of Thinking—Multiple Choice

1. a. As it is a license to earn excess profits, it is worth some effort to acquire. (p. 513)
2. a. Cost minimization is an aspect of profit maximization. (p. 509)
3. b. Efficiency requires reliance on lowest (opportunity) cost sources of output.
4. b. Other proposals promote entry which tends to defeat the aim of the proposal. (p. 513)
5. c. The political mechanism does not always yield consistent public policies. (pp. 514-21)
6. c. The guaranteed support price causes increased production of Grade A milk. (p. 515)
7. d. Government and service sectors have been growing more rapidly than manufacturing (pp. 500-501)
8. b. This increases the number of relevant competitors for the industry in question. (Ch. 20)
9. b. Such regulation has much the same impact as a production tax; see Exhibit 5. (p. 520)
10. d. It is tough to stay on top in a competitive struggle; see discussion, (pp. 504-505)
11. d. The ICC tended to be dominated by those whom it was intended to regulate. (pp. 516-18)
12. d. Each of the others inhibits competition by raising the cost of entry. (Thumbnail Sketch, pp. 508 and 516)

CHAPTER 22

True or False

The following are true: 1, 2, 3, 5, 8, 9, 10, 11, 13, 14.

Problems and Projects

1. b. 3 or 4
   c. 2 or 3
2. c. 5
   d. 4

    d. 3 or 4; $1800 or $2100; $900 less capital costs.
    e. yes

3. a. 0, −, +, −   d. −, 0, −, −
    b. +, 0, +, +   e. +, −, +, ?
    c. 0, +, −, +
4. a. No, MP of Vitacorn/P of Vitacorn = 200/800 < 400/1200 = MP of Cornpower/P of Cornpower
    b. The farmer could produce the same output for $400 less.
    c. Yes, the decrease in the MP of Cornpower as its usage increases will cause the ratio of the MP of Cornpower to its price to decrease, eventually fulfilling the condition for cost minimization: MP of Vitacorn/P of Vitacorn = MP of Cornpower/P of Cornpower
5. a. short-run: (10/190)/(5/35) = 0.37; long-run: (50/150)/(5/35) = 2.33

Learning the Mechanics—Multiple Choice

1. c. There will be many workers with these skills (many close substitutes). (pp. 540-41)
2. b. The demand for resources is *derived from* the demand for the product. (p. 530)
3. a. The "marginal revenue product" is the value of the labor services to the firm. (p. 533)
4. c. A small change in resource price raises product cost and reduces sales greatly. (p. 531)
5. b. Additional employment would *add* more to revenue than it would *add* to cost. (p. 533)
6. a. The greater the demand for the product, the greater the demand for the resources (p. 530)
7. a. Products which use the resource intensively will become more expensive. (p. 530)
8. b. It takes time to develop substitutes for the skills of carpenters. (pp. 538-41)
9. b. Since P = MR, marginal revenue product = value of marginal product. (p. 533)
10. d. It would use the cheaper resource intensively, driving down its marginal product. (p. 536)
11. a. If, e.g., $MPP_l/P_l > MPP_k/P_k$, diverting $1 from buying K to buying L raises output. (p. 536)
12. d. This causes a *movement along* the demand curve (change in quantity demanded). (pp. 531-32)

The Economic Way of Thinking—Multiple Choice

1. a. The other three have more easily available substitutes. (pp. 538-39)
2. c. Price and quantity usually decrease when demand decreases. (pp. 529-30)
3. b. The large short run wage increase will encourage acquisition of engineering skills. (pp. 540-41)
4. c. This requires few acquired skills, hence there are many substitutes. (p. 538)
5. d. It is sensible to be willing to pay more for something that is worth more. (p. 533)
6. b. Economists are choosing alternative employments. (pp. 538-41)
7. d. Both would tend to offset the decrease in quantity demanded caused by higher prices. (pp. 530-31)
8. c. In most "capitalist" countries, but trading physical capital is illegal in some countries. (p. 529)
9. b. Lower cost resources would be substituted; less intensive use raises marginal product. (pp. 535-36)
10. a. Aluminum bats and canoes are artificially under-priced. (pp. 530 and 533)
11. c. If machines have human sensibilities we are unaware of them. (p. 529)
12. c. This would make supply very inelastic in the (one year) short run. (p. 539)

CHAPTER 23

True or False

The following are true: 1, 2, 7, 9, 10, 12, 13.

Problems and Projects

1. a. Q = 3,000; P = $300
    b. Q = 4,000; P = $200
    c. Employment rises from 120 to 128.
3. a. 1000 thousand (one million) unemployed.
    b. 500 to 1000 (500 thousand total) were employed previously.
        1000 to 1500 (500 thousand total) are new to the labor market.
    c. Earnings before: $3(1000) = $3,000; earnings now: $4(500) = $2,000; total earnings are $1,000 dollars less; the demand for teenage workers is elastic.
    d. It increases their demand because their cost is now only $2.00 per hour instead of $4.00.

Learning the Mechanics—Multiple Choice

1. d. Real wages would double, i.e., rise by 100 percent.
2. d. Real wages are principally determined by productivity; see Exhibit 4, p. 555.
3. d. By assumption the question eliminates other reasons for earnings differentials. (Thumbnail Sketch, p. 554)
4. c. Elasticity measures responsiveness between wage changes and employment changes. (pp. 559–60)
5. a. Believe it or not, your marginal productivity is rising as you read these words. (p. 549)
6. c. When required to pay more, firms will reduce employment of the least skilled. (pp. 560–61)
7. a. Security of income attracts more workers (increases supply) and lowers wages. (p. 552)
8. d. See the definition, p. 550.
9. b. See Problems and Projects, question 2.
10. a. Profit-minded producers are usually interested in keeping costs low. (pp. 556–57)
11. a. A result of traditional work specialization patterns within the family. (pp. 564–66)
12. a. See the discussion, pp. 550–52.

The Economic Way of Thinking—Multiple Choice

1. a. Services of more productive workers are worth more; undesirable jobs would pay more. (pp. 548–49 and 552)
2. c. There would be excess supply of these workers' services. (pp. 560–62)
3. a. Artificially low wages make the military appear erroneously cheap. (pp. 549–50)
4. c. They could earn more than the average wage by working in the private sector. (pp. 548–49)
5. b. The exemption would increase employment of black teenagers. (pp. 561–63)
6. c. See the discussion, pp. 564–66.
7. c. True, although automation can harm *specific* individuals or groups. (pp. 556–57)

8. c. The extension would encourage automation in the car wash industry. (pp. 556–57 and 559–60)
9. d. Technological progress raises labor productivity which raises real wages. (pp. 555–58)
10. b. Is that a "discouraging word?" (p. 552)
11. b. Only the most productive bricklayers would find employment at that high wage. (pp. 559–61)
12. b. Training (human capital formation) is often acquired on the job. (p. 551)

CHAPTER 24

True or False

The following are true: 1, 3, 5, 6, 7, 9, 12.

Problems and Projects

1. a. $2000(0.5066) = $1013.20 = value of broker A option
        $1000(0.6806) + $1000(0.4632) = $1143.80 = value of broker B option
    b. $1000(0.5674) + $1000(0.3220) = $889.40
    c. 14% = 12% + 2% inflationary premium
2. $334/0.0334 = $10,000, so $334 now = $10,000 in 30 years = $1 per board foot for 10,000 board feet (price would have to exceed $1)
4. $12,502 + $11,158 + $9,968 + $8,904 = $42,532
5. The present value of the cost of the course is $6,000 + 6($1,250) = $13,500. The present value of the income stream of $2,000 a year at an interest rate of 8% is $13,420 (from Exhibit 3 in the text), so you should *not* make this investment in your "human capital" for income reasons alone. If the course (or the skills it provides you with) is worth $81 or more in personal enjoyment, then you should take it.
6. $R/i = $13,200/0.10 = $132,000

Learning the Mechanics—Multiple Choice

1. c. Constructing capital equipment uses resources that could produce consumption goods. (p. 570)
2. c. More resources would be used for present consumption leaving less for investment. (p. 571)
3. c. To offset the decline in the real value of a given nominal amount invested. (p. 573)
4. d. Net Present Value = $100 / (1 + i). (p. 575)
5. a. Net Present Value = $100 / (1.06) = $94.34 (p. 575)
6. c. "Pure" interest is yielded regardless of the risk premium. (p. 574)
7. c. NPV after 1 year = $100 / (1 + i); NPV after two years = $100 / (1 + i)^2. (p. 575)
8. b. Discounting applies to *any* investment decision; do machines have feelings? (pp. 575–79)
9. c. As the legal right to monopoly profit, the patent itself is valuable.
10. a. See the definition, p. 576
11. b. He perceived entrepreneurs as the major dynamic force of capitalism. (p. 581)

The Economic Way of Thinking—Multiple Choice

1. b. A change in profit expectations will *shift* the demand for loanable funds out. (pp. 570–71, 581)
2. c. Interest could be paid in corn or fish or any other item of value. (p. 571)
3. c. Grasshoppers have high time preference, ants have low (remember the fable?). (p. 571)
4. d. A below-equilibrium interest rate means excess demand for loanable funds. (p. 572)
5. c. Dollar price falls so fixed dollar return yields a higher nominal *rate* of return. (p. 573)
6. b. Heavy investment raises supply of cattle, reducing return to cattle ranching. (p. 572)
7. c. The owner could benefit from high risk premiums. (p. 574)
8. d. Bond prices fall so their fixed returns may yield higher nominal rates of return. (pp. 575–78)
9. c. Current value of investments reflects current expectations of future profits. (pp. 580–83)
10. a. See the discussion, pp. 584–86.
11. a. Luck, efficiency and protection from competition can yield economic profit. (pp. 579–82)

CHAPTER 25

True or False

The following are true: 3, 5, 8, 9.

Problems and Projects

2. a. $7
   b. $8
   c. employment will decrease by 200 and total income will fall by $900 from $4,900 to $4,000 per hour
3. a. 6000, 8800, 12000, 15600; 24, 28, 32, 36
   c. 250; $19
   d. more, 300

Learning the Mechanics—Multiple Choice

1. b. Making the demand for union labor relatively inelastic increasing union strength. (pp. 601–602)
2. c. See the data, pp. 603–604.
3. b. See the definition, p. 598.
4. c. To the contrary, increased supplies in other areas might reduce other wages. (pp. 607–608)
5. c. Higher product prices would cause layoffs; machines would replace lost jobs. (pp. 601–603)
6. b. Just as MFC > resource price, so MR < product price. (pp. 598–600)
7. b. See the data, p. 591.
8. c. See the definition, p. 592.
9. a. See the discussion, p. 592.
10. a. Strikes can be extremely costly to employers. (pp. 593–94)
11. c. See Exhibit 2 and pp. 593–94.
12. c. These factors largely determine income. (a preview from Ch. 26!)

The Economic Way of Thinking—Multiple Choice

1. d. A strike would be extremely costly to both. (p. 593)
2. b. Arc elasticity of demand = (100,000/700,000) / 1.00 = 0.14 < 1. (p. 601)
3. a. See the "Myth," pp. 607–608.
4. c. See the data, pp. 603–604.
5. c. Management would be more likely to grant wage increases. (pp. 602–603)
6. d. All would reduce the real wages of nonunion workers. (pp. 596, 601 and 604–605)
7. b. Political clout is a source of union power; tariffs limit foreign competition. (p. 597)
8. a. The more inelastic is product demand, the more powerful is the union. (pp. 601–602)
9. b. A specific result of the general phenomenon of "economizing behavior". (pp. 601 and 603)
10. a. See the discussion, pp. 603–606.
11. b. Monopoly power may successfully bargain with monopsony power. (pp. 598–600)
12. d. Union membership has been declining; there is no evidence that unions raise the wages of all workers. (Exhibit 1, p. 591 and pp. 607–608)

CHAPTER 26

True of False

The following are true: 1, 2, 5, 7, 9, 10.

Problems and Projects

1. a. 200 hours
   b. 1143 hours
   c. 571 hours
   d. 667 hours
   g. Probably not; presumably, Jane could drop out of the transfer program if she wished.
3. b. No, he will lose $18 a week by taking the job.
   c. Marginal tax rate = 109%
   d. Yes, his net income from the job would be greater than his net unemployment compensation.

Learning the Mechanics—Multiple Choice

1. b. See Exhibit, p. 612
2. b. See Exhibit 4, p. 616.
3. c. Some of the recipient's transfer income would be reduced.
4. b. See Exhibit, p. 624.
5. c. See Exhibit, p. 612.
6. a. See Exhibit, p. 614.
7. b. Lifetime income inequality is overstated by annual income data. (pp. 613–14)
8. d. See the discussion, pp. 620–22.
9. a. That's right, a "conservative." (p. 627)
10. d. See Exhibit, p. 631.
11. b. See Exhibit, p. 618

The Economic Way of Thinking—Multiple Choice

1. d. Which equals the return the individual would have earned on employed resources. (p. 612)
2. a. We have created a system that actually makes it more difficult to escape poverty.
3. b. See Exhibit, p. 616.
4. c. Annual incomes for the retired are less than their lifetime average; vice versa for prime-age earners. (pp. 613–14)
5. c. The threshold income level is measured in "real" (inflation adjusted) terms. (p. 621)
6. a. See the discussion, p. 621.
7. d. See Exhibit, p. 623.
8. d. All three have been suggested as reasons for a negative income tax system. (pp. 627–28)
9. a. See Exhibit, p. 623.
10. b. Increased earnings usually mean decreased welfare benefits, often equally. (pp. 626–27)
11. c. Income mobility and time are important in determining income inequality. (p. 617)

CHAPTER 27

True or False

The following are true: 2, 3, 4, 5, 7, 9, 10, 11, 12.

Problems and Projects

1. a. $1.30
    b. $1.38; 95 million gallons per day
    c. long run
3. a. 45, 60, 75, 90, 105

    b. zero
    c. profits will increase to $675; 0.47
    d. 40, 65, 90, 115
    e. $225; profits are lower in the long run; 1.00

Learning the Mechanics—Multiple Choice

1. b. Changes in energy prices would not affect either quantity demanded or supplied (pp. 650–51)
2. a. Long run response is greater than short run; see, e.g., Exhibit 2, pp. 639–41.
3. a. Marginal values are used, but opportunity costs *should* be used. (pp. 642–44)
4. c. It takes time to adjust consumption; lengthy time period means inelastic short run. (pp. 639–42)
5. b. Before other pumpers do . . . "the early pumper gets the oil." (p. 647)
6. c. See the definition and discussion, p. 642.
7. b. A predictable response based on the principle of economizing behavior. (pp. 649–50)
8. c. An economic response based on the principle of economizing behavior. (pp. 655–56)
9. c. The unintended side effect was to make OPEC more powerful. (pp. 648–49)
10. b. See "Myths of Economics," pp. 655–56.
11. b. The development of substitutes (energy saving technology) requires time. (pp. 639–40)
12. d. See the definition, p. 642.

The Economic Way of Thinking—Multiple Choice

1. a. Without the regulations, drivers could pollute freely. (p. 649)
2. b. This made economic sense, of course, in a "cheap energy" world. (pp. 649–50)

3. b. Natural resources should be used in their most valued use. (p. 644)
4. d. See the discussion, pp. 644–46.
5. a. The quantity supplied is, of course, positively related to price. (p. 652)
6. c. See the definition, p. 652.
7. a. Such regulation is complex and generates unintended consequences. (pp. 652–53)
8. a. People expected higher future prices so they increased their current demand. (p. 654)
9. c. The "sharp" price increases were the embodiment of the "crisis". (p. 650)
10. a. See Exhibit 3, p. 641; shortages were a result of price controls.
11. d. To the contrary; increased domestic supplies make us less import-dependent. (pp. 647–49)
12. c. See the discussion, p. 645.

CHAPTER 28

True or False

The following are true: 1, 2, 4, 6, 7, 10, 13, 14.

Problems and Projects

1. a. 80 cents, 100 per month
    b. 110, 130 (marginal social cost = producer's marginal cost + external cost)
    c. 90 per month
3. a. 2.0 cents per pound for the beet refiner and 6.0 cents per pound for the petroleum refiner
    b. beet refiner: 80%; petroleum refiner: 45%
4. a. 14.00, 10.00, 8.00, 6.00, 4.00
    b. 2
    c. $5.00 − $3.00 = $2.00; $34.00
    d. 6; $71.00; $56.00
    e. yes; yes

Learning the Mechanics—Multiple Choice

1. c. There are significant external costs of production: both air and water pollution. (pp. 664–65)
2. c. No net gains means no participation; sum of individual net gains = net social gain. (p. 664)
3. b. Demand curve includes only private benefits, not the external social benefits. (p. 671)
4. c. This generates both noise and air pollution, which are external costs. (pp. 664–65)
5. c. See the discussion, pp. 678–79.
6. a. External costs are external to (not included in) private price and output decisions. (pp. 666–67)
7. a. Unsatisfied customers may not return. (p. 681)
8. b. Externalities are not part of the decisions of competitive decision makers. (p. 664)
9. b. Since they add significantly to the costs of producing pollution-intensive goods. (pp. 672–74)
10. c. See the discussion, pp. 669–70.
11. a. The socially highest-valued use is also of the highest value to the individual. (p. 667)

The Economic Way of Thinking—Multiple Choice

1. b. What one individual does not catch (conserve), another most likely will. (pp. 668–70)
2. c. One individual's misuse of an automobile causes injury to other individuals. (p. 665)
3. d. Courts have given receptors property rights, but enforcement costs can be high. (pp. 668 and 677–78)
4. b. This is an instance of the "free rider" problem. (p. 679)
5. d. Economizing behavior means acting only when benefits exceed costs at the margin. (p. 672)
6. b. Such information is easily available and subject to the free rider problem. (p. 679)
7. b. Overutilization is one of the problems associated with common property rights. (pp. 668–70)
8. c. People "buy" clean air by paying more for homes in cleaner air districts. (p. 667)
9. c. Only reductions costing less than the emission charge will be undertaken. (pp. 672–76)
10. d. The firm may lose sales of *all* its various products, not just the new one. (pp. 682–83)
11. a. Evidently, these plots are much more productive than state property. (p. 670)

CHAPTER 29

True or False

The following are true: 1, 2, 3, 4, 6, 7, 8, 10, 11, 13.

Problems and Projects

1. a. 26/4, 20/18, 10/13.
   b. Proposal A will be attractive to the political entreprenuer. B will be unattractive. Proposal C will be attractive since the perceived benefit/cost ratio is 10/6 = 1.67, and the voters would favor it.
3. (1) c; (2) e; (3) a; (4) b; (5) f; (6) d.

Learning the Mechanics—Multiple Choice

1. b. Public sector action may correct the inefficiency of the market. (p. 691)
2. c. If some persons benefit without paying, private demand is inefficiently low. (p. 691)
3. a. Legislators and voters are self-interested as well as socially-interested. (p. 690)
4. c. These persons are guided by self-interest as well as the public interest. (p. 689)
5. d. Information costs may be worthwhile only if there are direct personal benefits. (pp. 694–97)
6. d. These groups are less costly to organize and gain substantially from lobbying. (pp. 696–97)
7. c. The collective process only imprecisely reflects individual preferences. (p. 700)
8. d. Government allocation can efficiently correct this market failure. (pp. 691–92)
9. b. This minimizes vote loss and maximizes vote gain for the politician. (pp. 696–99)
10. b. Information costs are high and personal benefits low. (pp. 696–97)
11. b. In fact, savings due to extra efficiency may *reduce* the agency's budget. (pp. 701–702)

Economic Way of Thinking—Multiple Choice

1. a. Pursuit of gain is a strong motivator in both sectors, regardless of whether decision-makers admit it. (pp. 689–90)
2. c. This is the rational ignorance effect. (pp. 694–95)
3. a. There's no free lunch for society, but individuals may take a "free ride". (pp. 692–93)
4. b. Private market demand for this enforcement is low due to free rider effects. (pp. 691–94)
5. b. This is likely to maximize political entrepreneurs' votes. (pp. 696–97)
6. d. This is consistent with maximum self-interest for the voter. (p. 689)
7. b. This is consistent with maximum self-interest for the voters. (pp. 694–99)
8. d. This is consistent with vote maximization for the politician. (pp. 690–91)
9. a. Voters perceive only benefits before election, maximizing politicans' chances. (p. 701)
10. c. Low organization costs would produce strong opposition from the other groups. (pp. 696–700)
11. c. They stand to benefit directly from cost reductions; the others do not. (pp. 701–703)
12. d. Each consumer benefits little while the others reap substantial individual benefits. (pp. 696–99)

CHAPTER 30

True or False

The following are true: 1, 3, 4, 6, 8, 12.

Problems and Projects

1. a. 2 units of clothing; 1 unit of clothing
   b. Mutual gain would result if Rhineland traded clothing for Nepal's food.
   c. 100 *additional* units of clothing are available to Rhineland; 50 *additional* units of clothing are available to Nepal; joint output has increased.
   d. 125 *additional* units of clothing are available to Rhineland; 75 *additional* units of clothing are available to Nepal; joint ouput has increased.
   e. 2/3 of a unit of food; 2/3 of a unit of food; no; no; additional gains are not possible because the opportunity costs of production have been equalized in the two countries.
2. a. 1100, 1170, 1240, 1310, 1380, 1450, 1520.   d. 1100
   b. $1800; 900   e. 800
   c. $2200   f. 300
3. a. $4000; 900
   b. $3000; 1300; 700; 600; 200
   c. $3500; 100; 200; 300
   d. rise to $3500; 100
   e. The only difference is that with a tariff the government gets the $500 per motorcycle, and with the quota the motorcycle importers receive the $500 difference (per imported motorcycle) between the import price of $3000 and the domestic motorcycle price of $3500.

Learning the Mechanics—Multiple Choice

1. c. Having a comparative advantage means being a low-opportunity-cost producer. (pp. 719–21)

2. c. Foreign exports (our imports) provide foreign buying power for our exports. (p. 721)
3. d. Relative price differences mean different opportunity costs, the basis of trade. (pp. 719–21)
4. c. Such a tariff protects them from foreign competition. (p. 726)
5. b. Otherwise we should buy and store cheap imports. (p. 727)
6. b. 2 units of clothing must be sacrificed to obtain 4 units of food; 2/4 = 1/2. (pp. 717–19)
7. b. Slavia's opportunity cost of food = 5/3 clothing > 1/2 = Italia's opportunity cost. (pp. 719–21)
8. c. Each country should export its low-opportunity-cost product. (pp. 719–21)
9. c. Buy goods abroad when they are cheaper than alternative domestic production. (p. 717)
10. d. See Exhibit 1, p. 714.
11. c. See Exhibit 3, p. 716.
12. d. Total consumption increases and less wine is consumed in order to trade it for more bread. (pp. 719–21)

The Economic Way of Thinking—Multiple Choice

1. a. Increased competition lowers price; increased foreign sales raise their incomes. (pp. 724–25)
2. d. Reduced foreign competition from tariff benefits workers in the industry. (p. 728)
3. c. Increased price of foreign watches causes increased demand for domestic watches. (pp. 725–27)
4. c. Consumers gain through low prices; producers at worst do not lose. (pp. 724–25)
5. b. Arguments for restrictions usually appeal (wrongly?) to the "national interest." (pp. 725–27)
6. c. Foreign competition lowers price which lowers domestic quantity supplied. (pp. 724–25)
7. b. Special interest groups have a disproportionate influence on politicians. (p. 730)
8. a. Try, for example, to trace increased farm employment to reduced auto tariffs. (pp. 729–30)
9. c. This is the *basic* lesson of comparative advantage. (pp. 717–19)
10. b. Foreign demand raises price which increases domestic quantity supplied. (pp. 722–23)
11. a. Iowa exports corn both to the other states and to the rest of the world. (pp. 717–18)
12. b. To help them "mature" (become efficient) in the long run. (p. 728)

CHAPTER 31

True or False

The following are true: 1, 2, 8, 10, 11.

Problems and Projects

1. (1) d; (2) a; (3) e; (4) b; (5) f; (6) c.
2. b. 0, −, depreciate   e. −, +, appreciate
    c. −, +, appreciate   f. +, 0, depreciate
    d. +, −, depreciate   g. 0, 0, no change
3. a. (1) −25.3; (2) 36.1; (3) 3.7; (4) 4.5; (5) 8.2

Learning the Mechanics—Multiple Choice

1. a. Residents usually want payment in their own national currency. (p. 736)
2. b. Cheaper foreign currency means cheaper foreign goods and services. (p. 738)
3. d. The statement includes *all* the international economic transactions. (p. 747)
4. b. Excess sales mean excess receipts (a surplus) of payments. (p. 748)
5. a. More exports mean greater demand for nation's currency causing *appreciation*. (pp. 740–43)
6. a. An increase in supply (of *anything*) tends to decrease price (depreciate). (p. 738)
7. d. Exchange rates do not fluctuate but monetary policy is commited to fixing them. (pp. 752–53)
8. c. Foreign ability to buy from us depends (partly) on the amount we buy from them. (Ch. 30 and p. 748)
9. b. High prices promote imports; low interest rates promote financial asset exports. (pp. 746–47)
10. d. This creates a foreign (South American) demand for U.S. currency (to be loaned). (pp. 747–50)
11. b. Depreciation makes foreign goods more expensive and domestic goods cheaper. (p. 738)

The Economic Way of Thinking—Multiple Choice

1. b. Increased sales increase U.S. receipts and reduce the deficit. (pp. 747–49)
2. c. Unilateral transfers abroad decrease; exports decrease but by a lesser amount. (p. 749)
3. a. U.S. receives more goods to consume and gives up only pieces of paper. (pp. 746 and 748)
4. c. Increased imports mean increased payments to foreigners. (pp. 747–48)
5. a. Higher real interest rates promote financial asset exports. (pp. 746–47)
6. c. Dollars are spent to acquire the pesos to buy the mine. (pp. 747–50)
7. b. Higher prices raise demand for foreign exchange (imports) and lower supply (exports). (p. 744)
8. c. Monetary policy is freed to pursue other goals such as price stability. (pp. 752–53)
9. c. See the definition, pp. 738 and 746.
10. b. It raises dollar price of foreign currency, raising dollar price of foreign goods. (p. 738)
11. c. It is making excess payments on current account transactions. (pp. 747–49)
12. a. Inelastic means *quantities* imported and exported respond little to price changes. (pp. 738–40)

CHAPTER 32

True or False

The following are true: 1, 2, 4, 5, 6, 8, 9, 11.

Problems and Projects

2. a. $200
    b. $400; $5930 = difference
    c. $20 billion(10.677) = $213.3 billion = GNP in 1985;
        100 million(2.814) = 281.4 million; $213.3 billion/281.4 million = $758.0

d. $6330(2.000) = $12660
e. $1516; the difference has grown to $11144 despite Gromango's superior economic performance.

Learning the Mechanics—Multiple Choice

1. d. Poor countries usually have more unequally distributed incomes than rich ones. (p. 762)
2. b. See Exhibit 1 and p. 761.
3. b. See Exhibit 2, p. 762.
4. d. See the discussion, p. 761.
5. a. See the definition, p. 763.
6. b. This definition is economically meaningful to the wide body of the population. (p. 765)
7. a. Population may be growing more rapidly than real GNP. (p. 765)
8. c. See the definition, p. 765.
9. c. See Problems and Projects, Exhibit 1.
10. c. See the discussion, pp. 773–74.
11. a. It uses readily available data. (p. 763)
12. c. It attempts to measure the actual consumption bundles available. (pp. 763–64)

The Economic Way of Thinking—Multiple Choice

1. c. U.S. per capita GNP is seven times the per capita GNP of Mexico. (p. 765)
2. b. % per capita GNP growth = % GNP growth − % population growth. (p. 765)
3. d. There is a wide variety of growth experiences *within* each of these groups. (pp. 760–62)
4. b. The influence of population change is precisely what is meant by *per capita*. (p. 765)
5. c. Find in the other answers the characteristic unrelated to poverty. (pp. 760–62)
6. b. 3000 pounds × $3 per pound = $9000. (Ch. 31)
7. a. See the definitions, p. 765.
8. b. A rapidly growing country is not necessarily also improving the general standard of living. (p. 765)
9. b. Low investment caused by such instability is a main obstacle to growth. (pp. 769–73)
10. a. This leads to low productivity, and therefore to low incomes. (pp. 769–70)
11. b. See the discussion, pp. 770–71.
12. c. See the opening quote to this chapter, p. 759.

CHAPTER 33

True or False

The following are true: 1, 4, 5, 7, 9, 10, 12.

Problems and Projects

1. (1) d; (2) c; (3) f; (4) a; (5) b; (6) e; (7) g.

Learning the Mechanics—Multiple Choice

1. c. Significant guidance by central planners is a common characteristic of socialism. (p. 786)
2. d. Individual enterprise managers are principally responsible for these. (p. 790)

3. b.   See Exhibit 7, p. 796.
4. c.   This would imply some form of human slavery, certainly not an aspect of socialism. (pp. 785–86)
5. c.   In an attempt to generate rapid growth and industrialization. (p. 791)
6. d.   The others rely much more on markets for resource allocation than the U.S.S.R. does. (p. 787)
7. d.   Startling, but true, perhaps because of greater motivation on private plots. (pp. 793–94)
8. c.   Yugoslavia relies significantly on decentralized planning and market mechanisms. (p. 798)
9. d.   See the discussion, pp. 803–804.
10. d.   All were important parts of Marx's philosophy. (pp. 784–85)
11. d.   See the data, p. 802.
12. b.   See the discussion, pp. 802–803
13. a.   See the discussion, p. 804.

The Economic Way of Thinking—Multiple Choice

1. c.   Wage structures and training costs are strongly influenced by central planners. (pp. 785–86)
2. a.   An appropriate principle of efficiency in *any* economic system. (pp. 782–83)
3. c.   Apparently the change in reward structure caused the change in behavior. (p. 783)
4. c.   Such incentives are reduced because of state ownership of means of production. (p. 799)
5. a.   See the definition, p. 789.
6. c.   See Exhibit 8, p. 797.
7. b.   It would probably exacerbate the inequality of income distribution. (pp. 785–86 and 790–91)
8. a.   This is perhaps because of little conflict between labor and management. (pp. 802–803)
9. d.   See the discussion, pp. 803–804.
10. c.   See the "Outstanding Economist" discussion, pp. 784–85.
11. b.   See the "Outstanding Economist" discussion, pp. 784–85.

7
8
9
C 0
D 1
E 2
F 3
G 4
H 5
I 6
J

LINDA

JENNY RAY
PURCHASING.